The Vermont Brigade
in the Seven Days

ALSO BY PAUL G. ZELLER

*The Ninth Vermont Infantry:
A History and Roster* (McFarland, 2008)

*The Second Vermont Volunteer Infantry Regiment,
1861–1865* (McFarland 2002; softcover 2009)

The Vermont Brigade in the Seven Days

The Battles and Their Personal Aftermath

Paul G. Zeller

McFarland & Company, Inc., Publishers
Jefferson, North Carolina

LIBRARY OF CONGRESS CATALOGUING-IN-PUBLICATION DATA

Names: Zeller, Paul G., 1946– author.
Title: The Vermont Brigade in the Seven Days : The Battles and their Personal Aftermath / Paul G. Zeller.
Description: Jefferson, North Carolina : McFarland & Company, Inc., Publishers, 2019 | Includes bibliographical references and index.
Identifiers: LCCN 2018054292 | ISBN 9781476676616 (softcover : acid free paper) ∞
Subjects: LCSH: United States. Army. Vermont Brigade, 1st (1861–1865) | Seven Days' Battles, Va., 1862. | Vermont—History—Civil War, 1861–1865—Regimental histories. | United States—History—Civil War, 1861–1865—Regimental histories. | Soldiers—Vermont—Biography.
Classification: LCC E533.4 .Z45 2019 | DDC 973.7/443—dc23
LC record available at https://lccn.loc.gov/2018054292

BRITISH LIBRARY CATALOGUING DATA ARE AVAILABLE

ISBN (print) 978-1-4766-7661-6
ISBN (ebook) 978-1-4766-3537-8

© 2019 Paul G. Zeller. All rights reserved

No part of this book may be reproduced or transmitted in any form or by any means, electronic or mechanical, including photocopying or recording, or by any information storage and retrieval system, without permission in writing from the publisher.

Front cover artwork *Rear Guard at White Oak Swamp*, artist Julian Scott (member of 3rd Vermont Infantry Regiment in the Vermont Brigade), 1869 (courtesy of the Vermont State Curator's Office)

Printed in the United States of America

*McFarland & Company, Inc., Publishers
Box 611, Jefferson, North Carolina 28640
www.mcfarlandpub.com*

Table of Contents

Acknowledgments   vii

Preface   1

1. The Formation of the Vermont Brigade   3
2. The Peninsula Campaign   23
3. The Battles of Garnett's Hill and Gouldin's Farm   46
4. The Battle of Savage's Station   78
5. The Ambush at White Oak Swamp   114
6. The Aftermath   133

Chapter Notes   167

Bibliography   182

Index   187

Acknowledgments

I wish that I could say that I researched and wrote this book all by myself, but that would not be true. There was a host of people that helped me and it is here that I would like to thank them.

First, I would like to thank my good friend Euclid D. Farnham, president of the Tunbridge, Vt., Historical Society. As with my other books, he read every word of the draft of this book and gave me sound feedback.

Tom Ledoux, webmaster of Vermont in the Civil War, the best state Civil War site on the internet which I use almost daily. He has put his heart and soul into this site for the past twenty-some years.

A special thanks to the following descendants of men of the Vermont Brigade who provided copies of letters, diaries, photographs and encouragement: Doris King, Ron Foster, Robin Van Mechelen, Karen Meyers-Yakjmi, Brad Winne, Charles and Marion Walter, Joseph Broom, Mark Hersey, and Carleton Young, author of *Voices from the Attic: The Williamstown Boys in the Civil War*.

The following historical societies, libraries and institutions provided me with research assistance, copies of letters and diaries, photographs and other materials: Paul Carnahan, librarian, Marjorie Strong, assistant librarian, and Fred Pond, volunteer, Vermont Historical Society, Barre, Vt.; staff of the Vermont Department of Libraries, Montpelier, Vt.; staff of the University of Vermont Bailey/Howe Library, Burlington, Vt.; staff of the University of Vermont Special Collections, Burlington, Vt., especially Prudence Doherty; staff of the National Archives and Records Administration, Washington, D.C.; staff of the Library of Virginia, Richmond, Va.; staff of the Virginia Historical Society, Richmond, Va.; staff of the Vermont State Archives and Records Administration, Middlesex, Vt.; Eva Garcelon-Hart, Stewart-Swift Research Center, Henry Sheldon Museum, Middlebury, Vt.; Margo Caulfield, Cavendish Historical Society, Cavendish, Vt.; and staff of the U.S. Army Heritage & Education Center, U.S. Army War College, Carlisle, Penn., especially Marlea Leljedal for her photographic support.

A very big thanks to Robert E.L. Krick, historian at the Chimbarazo Medical Museum, Richmond Battlefield Park, Richmond, Va., for research assistance and reviewing the final draft of this book and being brutally honest. His effort has made this a much better book.

I am deeply indebted to the following Civil War photograph collectors that graciously allowed me to use copies of their Vermont soldier photographs: Francis C. Guber and Tim Cooper.

I also owe a debt of gratitude to George Skoch who created the maps for this book.

As with my other books, George's beautifully detailed maps greatly enhance the narrative.

Thanks to my friend, Maureen O'Donnell, for reviewing and commenting on the section concerning the reconnaissance to Lewinsville, Va.

Finally, I would like to thank my wife, Sally, who puts up with my spending more time with my computer than with her. In spite of that she still reads and edits every page I write. I could not make it without her.

I sincerely hope I have not left anyone out of this acknowledgment. If I have, I apologize.

Preface

There has been very little written about the Vermont Brigade's participation in the Seven Days' battles, June 25 to July 1, 1862, during Major General George B. McClellan's Peninsula Campaign. The best account was written by George G. Benedict in 1886. While Benedict's history is an excellent account of the role played by the Vermont Brigade it does not get down to the level of what the men themselves saw, heard or felt. This book makes an attempt to correct that shortcoming. Research for this book became somewhat frustrating when trying to obtain personal accounts of the battles in the soldiers' own words since the Vermont Brigade was fighting and marching almost continuously from June 27 to July 2, 1862, leaving the men little to no time to write home and the diaries that were kept had only one or two short sentences per day, if that. Finally, persistence paid off and I was able to find enough first-hand accounts to flesh out what the Green Mountain Boys had experienced. This is the story of those ordinary men in extraordinary times.

While this book tells the story of the Vermont Brigade in the Seven Days it goes one step further and tells what happened to 29 of the men that were wounded, and/or captured, and killed and discusses the effects on the families. Sometimes we tend to forget that there are very serious consequences to wounds beyond the initial pain and destruction. Men's civilian careers and lives can be ruined, such as a man who was a farmer who lost both of his legs in battle. He had little to go back home to. Blood is not spilled without cost. The men's government disability pension files and compiled military service files at the National Archives in Washington, D.C., give vivid accounts of how the men were wounded, the damage that was done to their bodies and the medical attention they received, but more importantly they provide a window through which we can see the effects their wounds had on their lives as they grew older. It usually was not pretty.

While this book concentrates on the Seven Days' battles, the first two chapters cover the formation of the Vermont Brigade and formulation and execution of the Peninsula Campaign of which the Seven Days was a part. I felt this was necessary to tell the story of how farmers, factory workers, students and lawyers were turned into one of the best fighting brigades of their time.

This book does not glorify war. In fact, it does just the opposite. It shows the realities of war, not just the death and wounds, but the stories of heroes as well as the stories of men who were anything but heroes. From the Vermonters' own writings one can feel the fear and exhilaration of combat, as well as the agony of the extreme southern heat, the thirst and hunger, and the sheer exhaustion of marching and fighting for days with little or no sleep, food or water.

Preface

I have let the men of the brigade tell their own stories through their letters and diaries. I have left the spelling and punctuation in the passages as they appeared, except where they had run-on sentences, in which cases I added periods for ease of reading.

I have made every effort to ensure this book's historical accuracy, and I accept full responsibility for any inaccuracies that may be found.

1

The Formation of the Vermont Brigade

During the Civil War the state of Vermont supplied 17 infantry regiments, one cavalry regiment, three light artillery batteries, one company of heavy artillery and three companies of sharpshooters. Of these units the most famous was the Vermont Brigade, sometimes referred to as the "First Vermont Brigade" or the "Old Brigade," that consisted of the 2nd through the 6th Vermont Infantry Regiments.

To illustrate the type of unit the Vermont Brigade would become during the war the following excerpt from an article that first appeared in the *New York Citizen* and was reprinted in the St. Johnsbury, Vt., *Caledonian* on February 16, 1866, is provided. It was written by Martin T. McMahon, who served as adjutant general and chief of staff in the VI Corps for Major Generals William B. Franklin, John Sedgwick and Horatio G. Wright and had four years of experience with the Vermont Brigade. Apparently trying to appear impartial about the brigade Gen. McMahon did not use his name as the author of the article, but instead indicated that it was written by "one who did not belong to it, and who never was in Vermont."

They were honest farmers turned vagabonds. They were simple countrymen changed into heroes. They were quiet townsmen that had become rovers. They stole ancient horses and bony cows on the march. They pillaged moderately in other things. They swept the dairies and after long marches stripped the orchards for miles where they traveled. They chased rabbits when they went into camp, and they yelled like wild Indians when neighboring camps were silent through fatigue. They were ill disciplined and familiar with their officers. They swaggered in a cool, impudent way, and looked down with a patronizing Yankee coolness upon all regiments that were better drilled, and upon that part of the army generally that did not belong to the Vermont brigade. They were strangely proud, not of themselves individually, but of the brigade collectively, for they knew perfectly well they were the best fighters in the known world. They were long of limb and could out march the army. They were individually self-reliant and skillful in the use of arms, and they honestly believed that the Vermont brigade could not be beaten by the combined armies of the rebellion.

They were veterans in fighting qualities almost from their first skirmish. This was at Lee's Mill. They crossed a narrow dam under a hot fire, made the attack they were instructed to make and came back, wading deep in the water with a steadiness that surprised the army. They were an incorrigible, irregular, noisy set of rascals. They were much sworn at during their four years; yet they were at all times a pet brigade.—There were but two things they could do—march and fight; and this they did in a manner peculiarly their own. They had a long, slow, swinging stride on the march which distanced everything that followed them. They had a quiet, earnest, attentive, individual way of fighting that made them terrible in battle. Each man knew that his neighbor in the ranks was not going to run away, and he also knew that he himself intended to remain where he was. Accordingly none of the attention of the line was directed from the important duty of loading and firing, rapidly and carefully. When moving into action and while hotly engaged they made queer, quaint jokes, and enjoyed them greatly. They crowed like cocks, they ba-a-ed like sheep, they neighed like horses, they bellowed like bulls, they barked like dogs; and they counterfeited with excellent effect the indescribable music of the mule. When, perchance, they held a picket line in a forest it seemed as if Noah's ark had gone to pieces there.

In every engagement in which this brigade took part, it was complimented for gallant conduct. One of the most remarkable of its performances, however, has never appeared in print, nor has it been noticed in the reports. After the battle of Gettysburg, when Lee's army was in the vicinity of Hagerstown and the Antietam, the Vermont brigade was deployed as a skirmishing line, covering a point of nearly three miles. The enemy were in force in front near Beaver Creek. The Sixth corps was held in readiness in the rear of the skirmish line, anticipating a general engagement. The enemy had evidently determined to attack. At last his line of battle came forward. The batteries opened at once and the skirmishers delivered their fire. Our troops were on the alert and stood watching for the skirmishers to come in and waiting to receive the coming assault. But the skirmishers would not come in, and when the firing died away it appeared that the Vermonters thus deployed as a skirmish line had actually repulsed a full line-of-battle attack. Twice afterwards the enemy advanced to carry the position and were each time again driven back by this perverse skirmish line. The Vermonters it is true were strongly posted in a wood, and each man fired from behind a tree. But then everybody knows that the etiquette in such matters is for a skirmish line to come in as soon as they are satisfied that the enemy means business. These simple-minded patriots from the Green Mountains, however, adopted a rule of their own on this occasion and the enemy, disgusted with such stupidity, retired across the Beaver creek.

When the Vermonters led a column on a march; their quick movements had to be regulated from corps or division headquarters, to avoid gaps in the column as it followed them. If a rapid or forced march were required, it was common thing for Sedgwick to say with a quiet smile—"Put the Vermonters at the head of the column to-day and keep everything well closed up."[1]

Three days after the Confederate batteries surrounding Charleston Harbor opened fire on Fort Sumter, President Lincoln issued a proclamation to 25 states and the District of Columbia for 75,000 volunteers to serve for three months. As a result of this levy Virginia seceded from the Union on April 17 with Arkansas, Tennessee, and North Carolina following soon afterward. With the succession of these four states the formation of the Confederate States of America was complete.[2]

The quota of troops from Vermont was 780 and Governor Erastus Fairbanks acted immediately by issuing orders necessary to raise troops, called a special session of the legislature to organize, arm, and equip the militia. In a firm commitment to support President Lincoln, the Vermont legislature passed a bill appropriating the staggering sum of one million dollars for the war effort.[3]

By order of the Vermont Adjutant General several senior militia officers met in Burlington on April 19 to review and select 10 companies for the 1st Vermont Infantry Regiment. Eight companies from the Vermont Militia were found to be in suitable condition and were immediately selected. Of the others surveyed, two companies who would need only a small recruitment effort to round them out were also selected. With that, the 1st Vermont Infantry Regiment was formed under the command of Col. John W. Phelps.

The 1st Vermont Infantry was mustered into service in Rutland, Vt., on May 8, 1861, and left for duty at Fort Monroe in Hampton, Va., the next day. While in Virginia, the 1st Vermont mainly performed picket and scouting duty, with the exception of three of its companies that were involved in the battle of Big Bethel on June 10. The regiment returned home after its three months of duty and was mustered out of service on August 25.[4]

Realizing the magnitude of the effort to put down the rebellion, President Lincoln made another call for troops this time to serve for three years. In response to this call Vermont raised two infantry regiments. The 10 companies for the 2nd Vermont Infantry Regiment were picked from about 60 militia companies which tendered their services to the state for the war.[5]

Governor Fairbanks wanted a commanding officer for the 2nd Vermont with a military education and combat experience. He offered the command to Israel B. Richardson of Michigan, a native Vermonter who had won fame and rank in the regular army in the Mexican war, but Richardson had recently accepted command of the 1st Michigan Infantry Regiment. In declining Fairbank's offer; however, Richardson recommended Henry Whiting who had been one of his classmates at the U.S. Military Academy and was at that time living in St. Clair, Mich.[6]

Henry Whiting was born in Bath, N.Y., on February 17, 1818. At the age of 13 he left school and went to work for Whiting & Boardman as a clerk. He remained in this position for four years. In the summer of 1836 he entered the U.S. Military Academy graduating in 1840 ranking 17th in a class of 41 cadets. He was commissioned a second lieutenant in the 5th U.S. Infantry on July 1, 1840. In the fall of 1845, with war about to break out with Mexico, Whiting was ordered to the southern frontier. He resigned his commission on March 25, 1846, just before the U.S. Army crossed the Rio Grande. There are any number of reasons why Whiting may have resigned, but there are two that are the most plausible. The first is that Whiting disagreed with President Buchannan's decision to invade Mexico. Ulysses S. Grant wrote in his memoirs, "Generally the officers of the army were indifferent whether the annexation was consummated or not; but not all. For myself I was bitterly opposed to the measure, and to this day regard the war, which resulted, as one of the most unjust ever waged by a stronger against a weaker nation." Because of the unpopular invasion a number of officers resigned in protest and Whiting may have been one of them. The second possibility is that Whiting was afraid of combat. Henry Whiting was commissioned colonel of the 2nd Vermont Infantry Regiment on June 6, 1861.[7]

Governor Holbrook chose 41-year-old George Jerrison Stannard of St. Albans, Vt., as the 2nd Vermont's lieutenant colonel. Stannard, the son of Samuel and Rebecca (Pattee) Stannard, was born in Georgia, Vt., on October 20, 1820. After completing public school at age 15 he worked on the family farm and taught school for five years. In 1845 Stannard went to work as a clerk at the St. Albans Foundry Company and by 1860 was a joint owner of the company where he remained until the outbreak of the war. Stannard joined the Vermont militia as a private at the age of 16 and rose through the ranks. He was commissioned as colonel of the 4th Regiment in 1858. When President Lincoln called for troops after the fall of Fort Sumter, Stannard wired the governor offering his services. Thus it is believed, he was the first man in Vermont to volunteer for the war.[8]

The 2nd Vermont's companies rendezvoused at Burlington, Vt., and were mustered into service on June 20, 1861. The regiment left for Washington, D.C., on June 24 and by July 10 was in camp in Alexandria, Va. In Alexandria the 2nd Vermont was brigaded with the 3rd, 4th and 5th Maine Regiments under the command of Colonel Oliver O. Howard.[9]

On July 16 the 2nd Vermont moved out with the rest of Maj. Gen. Irwin McDowell's army for a confrontation with the rebels at Bull Run, near Manassas, Va., on July 21. Howard's brigade was one of the last Union units to engage the Confederate forces. From their position on Chinn Ridge the 2nd Vermont was engaged with the 2nd and 8th South

Left: Colonel Henry Whiting, commander of the 2nd Vermont Infantry Regiment. After being bypassed for promotion to brigadier general several times, he resigned from the army on February 2, 1863. *Right:* George J. Stannard, the first lieutenant colonel of the 2nd Vermont Infantry Regiment. Stannard was promoted to brigadier general for his gallantry at the Battle of Ft. Harrison in 1864 although it cost him an arm. By the war's end he was a brevet major general (both photographs U.S. Army History and Education Center).

Carolina. Not long after the Vermonters' confrontation with the South Carolinians the Union army started to retreat and the Green Mountain Boys were obliged to follow suit. The 2nd Vermont's loss during the battle and on the retreat were six enlisted men killed, one officer and 21 enlisted men wounded, and one officer and 91 enlisted men captured.[10]

After hours of constant marching the Vermonters finally reached the safety of Alexandria and the next day returned to their original camp. Not long after reaching camp talk began about Colonel Whiting hiding behind a tree during the battle. True or not, the men disliked Whiting as long as he served with the regiment. The fact that he was not a Vermonter did not help the situation.[11]

The 3rd Vermont Infantry Regiment was recruited at the same time as the 2nd Vermont but, was not filled as quickly. The 10 companies of the 3rd Vermont rendezvoused at Camp Baxter in St. Johnsbury starting on June 7, 1861, with the last company arriving on July 3. Breed Noyes Hyde, the son of Major Russell B. and Caroline (Noyes) Hyde, the regiment's lieutenant colonel, was in temporary command until a commander could be found. Lieutenant Colonel Hyde was born in Hyde Park, Vt., on August 14, 1831, and entered the U.S. Military Academy in 1855, but for some unknown reason did not graduate. He returned to Vermont and became a merchant. At the time he was chosen as lieutenant colonel he was serving on Governor Fairbank's staff. Governor Fairbanks initially wanted Colonel John W. Phelps, who's term of service as commander of the 1st Vermont Infantry Regiment was about to expire, but the War Department wanted him to stay in

Virginia. Fairbanks finally decided on 37-year-old William "Baldy" Farrar Smith who was currently a captain in the regular army. Smith was born in St. Albans, Vt., on February 17, 1824. He graduated from the U.S. Military Academy in 1845 and was appointed as a lieutenant in the Topographical Engineers. He served as a topographical engineer in mapping the northern states and the Mexican border in Texas. For a while he was an instructor at West Point and in 1859 he was the superintendent of harbor improvements in Chicago where he became friends with ex-army Captain George B. McClellan, then the vice president of the Illinois Central Railroad. Smith was a short, portly man, with a light brown shaggy mustache. Fond of controversy, Smith spent much of his time criticizing the plans of other generals, particularly those of his superiors. Although he had more hair than most men his age, Smith retained his U.S. Military Academy cadet nickname "Baldy," given because at that stage of his life, his hair was thinner than normal.[12]

Smith's commission was backdated to April 27, 1861, so he would out-rank Colonel Whiting. Although nothing official remains to explain why Smith's commission was backdated, it may have been a way to punish Colonel Whiting for his performance at Bull Run. Smith would thus be eligible for promotion to brigadier general before Whiting.[13]

The 3rd Vermont was mustered into service on July 16. At that time the regiment numbered 882 officers and men.[14]

Left: William F. "Baldy" Smith, first commander of the 3rd Vermont Infantry Regiment, pictured here as a brigadier general. He was relieved of command of the XVIII Corps in July 1864 for his poor performance in the assault on Petersburg, but would finish the war as a brevet major general (Library of Congress). *Right:* Colonel Breed N. Hyde, the first lieutenant colonel of the 3rd Vermont Infantry. Hyde was promoted to colonel and selected for command of the 3rd Vermont on August 13, 1861. He resigned from the army for health reasons on January 15, 1863 (Vermont Historical Society).

While every Vermont regiment had difficulty in turning strong-headed, independent farmers into order-following soldiers, the 3rd Vermont seemed to have more than its share. Before it even arrived in St. Johnsbury Company F had problems as reported by the company's wagoner Pvt. Jesse Adams, a 20-year-old farmer from Cavendish, Vt.:

> We had not gone more than five miles before there was a row started by a fellow by the name of [Chauncey] Miles, a member of our company. It began in fun in the first place. Miles and Jim Welch got to sparing and Jim gave him the worst of it and he quit and pitched on to Dick Abbott and they were clipping away smartly when the Capt. stepped between them and Miles pitched on to Capt. Tom [Seaver] and there was some smart work for about a minute when the Capt. caught him by the throat and brought him into a seat in a great hurry.... When Ayers our drill master came up and tried to quiet him, it could not be done. He [Miles] told Ayers to kiss his damned ass, but instead he hit him in the eye and it stilled him for a minute. When we got here he was put in the guard house. He has got the worst looking eye that I ever saw.[15]

There also appears to have been an apparent major lack of discipline in the 3rd Vermont's camp of instruction. On July 20 at approximately 8:30 p.m. a group of soldiers tried to break into Pike's refreshment saloon. The men were upset with the high prices that Pike was charging them and were determined to wreak vengeance. Several days earlier there had been trouble between some of the men and Pike and Lt. Col. Hyde had placed a guard in the saloon. As the men were trying to batter down the door the guard inside fired four shots from his pistol into the floor trying to scare off the hot heads, but to no avail. He then fired several shots into the crowd. One shot hit a soldier in the shoulder, but only tore his uniform. Another shot slightly wounded a soldier in the foot. A third shot was fired and Sgt. John Terrill of Co. I from Pittsburgh, N.H., went down with a pistol ball in his chest. The guards escaped and the rioters tore the saloon to pieces. Terrill was rushed to the regimental hospital where he died within 15 minutes.[16]

The 3rd Vermont left for Washington on July 24. On a stop in Hartford, Conn., the regiment was joined by Colonel Smith who accompanied it south. The Vermonters arrived in Washington, D.C., on July 26. The next day the regiment marched to Camp Lyon on Georgetown Heights overlooking Chain Bridge some six miles above the capitol. Here the 3rd Vermont shared its camp with the 6th Maine and an artillery company and was soon joined by the 2nd Vermont and the 33rd New York. Second Lieutenant Erastus Buck, from Charleston, Vt., in Co. D, wrote of the 3rd Vermont's mission at Camp Lyon, "Our regiment [and] the Maine 6th Regiment are guarding the Chain Bridge across the Potomac. It is ¾ of a mile long. It is the principle [bridge] from Virginia. We have got 12 pieces of artillery that commands the bridge. It [is] a good position and strongly fortifyed."[17]

On August 30, as was done every morning and evening, pickets were put out to guard the Chain Bridge and the Georgetown Heights reservoir, which provided most of Washington's drinking water. Sometime between 3 and 4 a.m., on the 31st, Captain Thomas F. House of Co. H, 3rd Vermont, while checking on the pickets near the north end of Chain Bridge he found three pickets asleep. House awakened the pickets and found out that Pvt. William Scott was the one that should have been awake. Scott, a member of the 3rd Vermont's Co. K, had pulled picket duty the night before. This night he was standing for a friend and was exhausted. Scott, a 22-year-old, five-foot, six-inch tall farmer from Groton, Vt., was relieved from duty and was arrested.[18]

On September 4, 1861, Pvt. Scott was brought before a general court martial. He was charged with sleeping on his post which was in violation of the 46th Article of War. To this Scott pleaded not guilty. The officers of the court thought otherwise and found him guilty. He was sentenced to be shot to death. Scott's case made it all the way up the chain of command to Major General McClellan who confirmed the sentence and Scott was to be executed on September 9. In the meantime, at the request of many members of the regiment, the 3rd Vermont's chaplain, Moses P. Parmalee, drew up a petition for a pardon for Scott. Within days 191 officers and men had signed the petition. The petition for leniency was approved by McClellan and sent to President Lincoln who made the final decision to pardon Scott.[19]

Apparently, to impress upon the men of the Army of the Potomac the seriousness of the charge, the arrangements for the execution of Scott went on. There are various versions of this story. Some say Scott was told about the pardon and others say he was not. Regardless, on the morning of September 9 the brigade was drawn up in a hollow three-sided square, a firing squad was marched out and positioned. Pvt. William Scott was brought out and posted in front of the firing squad. Then the following order was read:

GENERAL ORDERS HEADQUARTERS OF THE ARMY OF THE POTOMAC
No. 8 Washington, September 8, 1861

Private William Scott, of Company "K," 3d Vermont Volunteers, having been found guilty by Court Martial of sleeping on his post while a sentinel on picket guard, has been sentenced to be shot, and the sentence has been approved and ordered to be executed.

The commanding officers of the Brigade, the Regiment and the Company of the condemned, together with many other officers and privates of his regiment, have earnestly appealed to the Major General Commanding to spare the life of the offender: and the President of the United States has expressed a wish, that, as this is the first condemnation to death in this Army for this crime, mercy may be extended to the criminal. This fact viewed in connection with the inexperience of the condemned as a soldier, his previous good conduct and general good character, and the urgent entreaties made in his behalf, have determined the Major General Commanding to grant the pardon so earnestly prayed for.

This act of clemency must not be understood as affording a precedent for any future case. The duty of a sentinel is of such a nature that its neglect, by sleeping upon or deserting his post, may endanger the safety of a command, or even of a whole army, and all nations affix to the offence the penalty of death.

Private *William Scott* of company "K," 3d regiment Vermont Volunteers, will be released from confinement and returned to duty.

By command of Major General McClellan,
S. Williams,
Assistant Adjutant General

According to a number of witnesses Scott remained emotionless. The men in the ranks broke out into cheer after cheer for Scott, General Smith, General McClellan and President Lincoln. In Vermont history William Scott will forever be known as the "Sleeping Sentinel."[20]

Sensing that another call for troops would be issued by Washington after the disaster at Bull Run, Governor Fairbanks issued a call on July 30 for two more three-year regiments to be raised. Within 30 days of the governor's call for troops enough men had been recruited to fill the two regiments. Edwin Henry Stoughton was selected as the colonel of the 4th Vermont. Stoughton, the son of Henry E. and Laura Elmira (Clark) Stoughton, was born in Chester, Vt., on June 23, 1838. He graduated from the U.S. Military Academy in 1859 and was assigned to the 4th U.S. Infantry from July of 1859 until the following September when he was transferred to the 6th U.S. Infantry. Stoughton resigned his commissioned in December of 1860, when many other regular army officers resigned, with their resignations to take effect on March 4, 1861, the day when President Lincoln was sworn in. However, before his resignation took effect, Stoughton withdrew it in hopes of entering the volunteer service. On August 1, 1861, he was commissioned as colonel of the 4th Vermont at the age of 23. At the time he was the youngest colonel in the army. Edwin Stoughton was a handsome, intelligent young man, but had an inflated ego that would be his downfall. He commanded the 4th Vermont until December 7, 1863, when he was selected for promotion to brigadier general.[21]

For the lieutenant colonel position in the 4th Vermont the governor selected Henry Niles Worthen. Worthen, the son of Thomas and Betsey Worthen, was born in Thetford, Vt., on December 10, 1833. He graduated from Norwich University in 1857 and after graduation he studied law in Chelsea, Vt., from 1857 to 1860. He was admitted to the bar in January 1861 and formed a partnership with

Colonel Edwin H. Stoughton, the first commander of the 4th Vermont Infantry Regiment. Stoughton was promoted to brigadier general on November 5, 1862, and selected for command of the Second Vermont Brigade (Library of Congress).

A.W. Dickey in Bradford, Vt., where he practiced law until he was commissioned as major of the 1st Vermont Infantry Regiment on April 26, 1861. He served with the 1st Vermont until its term of service was up on August 15, 1861. On that same day he was commissioned as the lieutenant colonel of the 4th Vermont.[22]

Henry A. Smalley, a native of Burlington, was selected as the commander of the 5th Vermont. Smalley, the son of David A. and Laura (Barlow) Smalley, was born in Jericho, Vt., on February 28, 1834. Smalley graduated from the U.S. Military Academy in 1854 and was commissioned a second lieutenant in the 1st U.S. Artillery. In April 1861 he was promoted to first lieutenant in the 2nd U.S. Artillery. He was commissioned as colonel of the 5th Vermont on July 30, 1861.[23]

Lewis Addison Grant of Bellows Falls, Vt., was selected to be Colonel Smalley's second in command. Grant, the son of James and Elizabeth (Wyman) Grant, was born in Winhall, Vt., on January 17, 1829, the last of 10 children. After finishing his schooling in Townshend, Vt., at age 16, he taught in that same school the next year. Later Grant taught school in New Jersey and Massachusetts. While teaching in Massachusetts he started reading the law. In 1852 he began working in the law office of Edwin H. Stoughton in Chester, Vt., and was admitted to the bar in 1857. The firm moved to Bellows Falls, Vt., and Grant became a partner.[24]

Four days after the Union defeat at Bull Run President Lincoln replaced Gen. McDowell with Maj. Gen. George B. McClellan. McClellan, born in Philadelphia in 1826, graduated from the U.S. Military Academy in 1846, ranking second in a class of 59 and was commissioned as a second lieutenant in the Corp of Engineers. He served admirably

Left: Colonel Henry A. Smalley, first commander of the 5th Vermont Infantry Regiment. Smalley's leave of absence from the regular Army was revoked on September 10, 1862, and he reverted to captain of the 2nd U.S. Artillery (Vermont Historical Society). *Above:* Lewis A. Grant, the first lieutenant colonel of the 5th Vermont Infantry Regiment. Grant was promoted to brigadier general on April 27, 1864, and selected for command of the Vermont Brigade (U.S. Army History and Education Center).

in the Mexican War and won brevets for first lieutenant and captain. Over the next decade he served as an instructor at West Point for three years, as an engineer in the west and finally as a military observer in the Crimean War. He resigned his commission in 1857 to become chief engineer of the Illinois Central Railroad. At the beginning of the Civil War he was living in Cincinnati, Ohio, and was president of the Ohio & Mississippi Railroad. On April 23, 1861, he became major general of the Ohio Volunteers, with command of all the forces in the state. Three weeks later he was promoted to major general in the regular army where he was outranked only by the aged and infirm General-in-Chief Winfield Scott. McClellan was responsible for maintaining Federal control of Kentucky and western Virginia (now West Virginia). He was personally in command during the Union success in the battle of Rich Mountain in western Virginia in 1861 and maintained control of the Baltimore & Ohio Railroad that was so vital to the North. Because of these successes McClellan was given command of the Army of Northeastern Virginia that was protecting Washington, D.C. He arrived in Washington on July 26 to assume his new command whose named he changed to the Army of the Potomac.[25]

In early September McClellan began to occupy those portions of Virginia within sight of the Capitol dome. Smith's brigade got orders to move across the Chain Bridge into Arlington on September 3. As the units moved out the men thought they were going to attack the rebels at Fall's Church. Their excitement was further heightened, when after crossing the bridge, they were put into line of battle; however, after moving several miles down the Leesburg Pike they were ordered to make camp for the night. The next morning, they quickly discovered they were not on a combat operation, but were, instead, to clear land and build fortifications. Because they had pushed out so far from Washington's defenses, their new camp was christened Camp Advance. Meanwhile, McClellan spent most of the first week of September planning and directly overseeing preparations for a reconnaissance by Smith's brigade north of Munson's hill to Lewinsville.[26]

The village of Lewinsville, five miles northwest of Camp Advance, was strategically important because five major roads converged there. One came in from Langley, a second came from the north and connected with the Leesburg Turnpike. A third road came from Falls Church to the south and a fourth, the Vienna Road, came in from the west. A fifth road ran parallel to and south of the Vienna Road and was known as the New Vienna Road. Smith was more than happy for the mission knowing that it was of strategic importance and it would probably provide a much better area to camp a division.[27]

On Wednesday, September 11, Baldy Smith was ordered to take a force to Lewinsville. Additionally, he was instructed not to bring on an engagement. Lieutenant Orlando M. Poe of the U.S. Topographical Engineers and Mr. Preston C.F. West of the U.S. Coast Survey were attached to Smith to map the area.[28]

Colonel Isaac I. Stevens of the 79th New York was selected to command the troops during the operation. The command consisted of Stevens' own 79th New York under the command of Captain David Ireland; four companies of the 65th New York (also known as the 1st Regiment U.S. Chasseurs) commanded by Lieutenant Colonel Alexander Shaler; companies A and F of the 2nd Vermont under the command of Lieutenant Colonel George J. Stannard; the 3rd Vermont under the command of Colonel Breed N. Hyde; companies A, D, F, H, and I of the 19th Indiana under the command of Colonel Solomon Meredith (nicknamed "Long Sol" because of his six-foot, five-inch frame); Captain Charles Griffin's battery of the 5th U.S Artillery; 50 men of the 5th U.S. Cavalry under the command of Lieutenant William McLean and 40 U.S. volunteer cavalrymen. In all, a little over 2,000 men.[29]

Smith's men left Camp Advance at 7:30 a.m. and headed up the Leesburg Turnpike. When the column reached Langley, Stevens sent Lieutenant McLean's cavalrymen ahead to clear any enemy pickets from the Lewinsville area. McLean reached Lewinsville and spread his men out to scout and secure the area. He sent 10 men down the road toward Falls Church, four on the road to Vienna and two on the road toward Alexandria. Then, McLean and his party drove off about 50 Confederate cavalrymen.[30]

Company M of the 1st Virginia Cavalry had been assigned the picket line from the Potomac River to Lewinsville. Company M was composed of men from Howard County, Maryland, known as the Howard Dragoons. They had crossed the Potomac and had been mustered into Confederate service at Leesburg, Va., in May of 1861. They had served with Colonel Turner Ashby's cavalry before being reassigned to the 1st Virginia Cavalry (also known as the "Black Horse Cavalry"). The Marylanders pulled back as McLean's

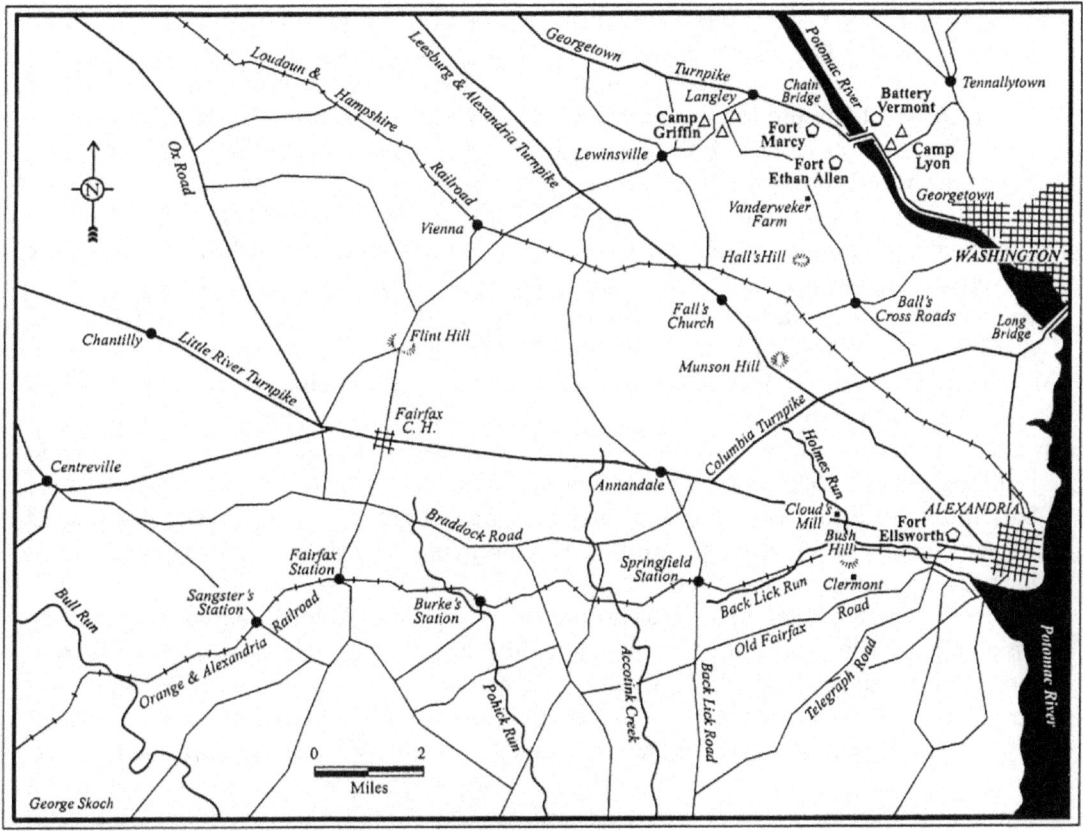

Map of Northern Virginia.

troopers and Stevens' overwhelming force approached Lewinsville. Several of the Confederate pickets were sent back to headquarters on Munson's Hill to report the Union advance to the 1st Virginia Cavalry's commander, Colonel James Ewell Brown "Jeb" Stuart.[31]

Stuart quickly cobbled together a force consisting of Company E of the 1st Virginia Cavalry, one battalion (305 men) of the 13th Virginia Infantry under Major James B. Terrill and a section of Captain Thomas L. Rosser's battery of the Washington Artillery of New Orleans, La., and moved out to drive the Federals back.[32]

Stevens' command arrived at Lewinsville at 10 a.m. Infantry and artillery were sent out to secure the area. One gun was placed on a commanding point west of the road leading north to the Leesburg pike and was supported by three companies of the 19th Indiana. A second gun was placed on the same road leading south to Falls Church. A third gun, supported by the 3rd Vermont, was placed on high ground beside the road leading directly from the crossroads of Lewinsville to Vienna to control the approaches on the new road to Vienna and the intervening country. A fourth gun, supported by the detachment of the 2nd Vermont, was held in reserve. Skirmishers from the 3rd Vermont and one company of the 19th Indiana covered the approaches on the two roads from Vienna and the road from Falls Church. A heavy body of Federal skirmishers was placed in the woods between the road to Falls Church and the New Road to Vienna. The entire area for more than a mile was thoroughly enveloped and watched by skirmishers, numbering some 500 men. The 65th and 79th New York, halted about one-third of a mile from the Lewinsville, deployed skirmishers to cover the country toward Falls Church.[33]

Lieutenant Poe and Mr. West were able to perform their reconnaissance and mapping mission without any enemy interference, although small groups of rebels were seen lurking in the woods observing the Union force. The engineers were finished by 2:15 p.m. that afternoon. At that time recall was sounded to bring in the pickets.[34]

Nearly 40 minutes elapsed between recall being sounded and the majority of the pickets getting back in. In the meantime, infantrymen from the 13th Virginia got in close enough to open up on the 19th Indiana pickets. In this initial volley one Indiana man was wounded in the foot.[35]

One small group of the Hoosiers disobeyed orders and charged out half a mile to chase after some rebels and was all of a sudden cut off. Private Hiram Antibus of Co. A eluded capture, but came running back so fast that he literally ran out of his shoes and lost his cartridge box. The chagrined 25-year-old sawyer from Owen County, Ind., came back into friendly lines panting heavily, but still had a tight grip on his musket. Lieutenant Benjamin F. Hancock, Sergeant Samuel M. Goodwin, and Private Oliver Hubble, not as lucky as Antibus, were captured.[36]

After Lieutenant Hancock and his men were captured, Colonel Meredith formed up his command while he awaited orders. Here the Hoosiers suffered heavy fire coming from a strip of woods. During this fusillade a soldier in Company D was killed when he was struck in the head by a rebel minie ball. A man in Co. I received a horrible face wound.[37]

Skirmishers from the 13th Virginia brushed up against the 3rd Vermont and sporadic firing broke out. Second Lieutenant Edwin M. Noyes and a platoon of Co. C were on the skirmish line facing a thick pine woods and could not see what was going on ahead of them. Twenty-seven-year-old Sergeant Evelyn H. Farnham, Jr., a cabinet maker from Newbury, Vt., in Co. C, along with Private George Stebbins from Groton, Vt., told Noyes they would volunteer to go forward as scouts. Noyes agreed and the two Vermonters had made their way about a quarter of a mile through the pines when Farnham spotted a rebel scout coming toward them. Farnham raised his musket to shoot the rebel when, for some reason, Stebbins grabbed Farnham's arm and said "don't shoot." The rebel disappeared behind some brush before Farnham could get him in his sights. Farnham waited about 10 minutes for the man to reappear, but to no avail. Then he decided he was in an exposed position and thought he had better get behind a pine tree a few feet away. As he moved a musket shot rang out, followed immediately by a pistol shot, but both missed him. Farnham wrote later that he then "sent him my compliments." He turned to tell Stebbins to cover him while he reloaded and discovered "all I could see of him was his coat tail pointing towards me some way off on the road toward camp." Farnham quickly jumped behind a tree and reloaded. As soon as he turned to go back the pistol cracked again and Farnham felt something hit his left ankle. He stopped long enough to check for damages and found a pistol ball embedded just under the skin above his ankle joint, but he was able to make it back to Lieutenant Noyes and the other men. After rejoining his comrades Noyes was able to cut the ball out with his pocket knife. When the 3rd Vermont returned to camp Farnham was evacuated to the Fairfax Seminary Hospital in Alexandria, carrying the pistol ball in his wallet.[38]

The 79th New York also came under heavy enemy rifle fire and within minutes three Highlanders were down.[39]

1. The Formation of the Vermont Brigade

Simultaneously with the commencement of the Confederate musket fire, Rosser's artillery opened up. The 3rd Vermont soon felt the effects of the rebel artillery as Pvt. Moses A. Parker of Co. C recalled:

> ... stood directly under their guns for ten or fifteen minutes and all we could do was take it. The balls and shells flying one after another over our heads thicker and faster but we succeeded in dodging them for some time. At length a well directed shell told dreadfully uppon some of our pour boys. It burst be hind me killing one ... behind me and my left hand man in rank wounding the other at my right also myself besides knocking down two or three more. A piece of shell passed between my arm and side inflicting a severe wound on the latter; another piece struck on my back but did not [hurt] me much. I was stunned so for a minute I did not know where I was or how I came there. I was supported from the field by two comrades; took an ambulance and went to Geo. Town hospital.[40]

The two men Parker mentions were privates Amos Meserve and William H. Colburn, both in Co. C. Twenty-four-old Meserve was horribly mangled by a shell fragment that hit him in the right side just above the hip and tore through his body exiting out his left side breaking his left arm. He died instantly. His body was brought back to camp when the 3rd Vermont returned from the reconnaissance. A fragment from the same shell that killed Meserve, ripped open Colburn's abdomen. He was so severely wounded the 3rd Vermont's surgeon, Henry Janes of Waterbury, Vt., said he could not be carried back to camp and Colburn was left in a deserted house by the road to die, attended by privates Amos H. Robinson and Jacob C. Goodell. The next morning Co. C's Second Lt. Edwin M. Noyes and 20 of his men went through Confederate lines and retrieved Colburn's body, as well as the body of a man from the 19th Indiana. Both Robinson and Goodell were missing having been captured by the Confederates.[41]

William H. Colburn, son of Zerah and Mary (Hoyt) Colburn, was born in Cabot, Vt., on December 21, 1838. He enlisted in Co. C, 3rd Vermont Infantry Regiment, on June 1, 1861, in Norwich, Vt. After William's body was brought back from Lewinsville he was buried at the National Military Asylum in Washington, D.C. Interestingly, William Colburn had inherited a family trait of six fingers on each hand and six toes on each foot. His father had the same defect, plus he was a mathematical prodigy. At an early age, even before he could recognize written numbers, Zerah Colburn could perform mathematical calculations in his head. He could for example tell how many minutes were in a given number of days. After becoming a sensation in Cabot Zerah's father took him on tour in New England. Not long afterward they went to Europe where Zerah became a star. While in England Zerah had the sixth finger on each of his hands amputated. At the age of 21 Zerah became a Methodist minister and in 1835 he was employed as a professor of mathematics at Norwich University in Norwich, Vt.[42]

Several other men in the 3rd Vermont's Co. C were less severely wounded in the action at Lewinsville. Oscar D. Eastman, a 23-year-old farmer from Bradford, Vt., received a slight contusion from a spent shell fragment. Co. C's first sergeant, Alonzo C. Armington, was slightly wounded in the hip, but the wound was serious enough that he was later admitted to the hospital. Pvt. Newell A. Kingsbury, of Littleton, N.H., was hit in the left hip by a rebel minie ball which was cut out several days later. Because of his wound, and other aliments, he would not return to his unit for almost a year. Corp. John G. Fowler, of Norwich, Vt., and Private Charles C. Meader II, of Newbury, Vt., were slightly wounded.[43]

The two companies of the 2nd Vermont supporting the Federal artillery took a direct hit from one of Rosser's guns, but the shell fragments only shredded a few of the men's uniforms and caused no serious wounds.[44]

When the Confederate artillery opened up, Captain Griffin had two of his rifled guns moved forward 1,800 yards toward the rebels. Within a few minutes these guns were belching counter-battery fire toward the enemy. Shortly afterward, Griffin's other four guns were brought forward and entered the fray. By the end of the encounter Griffin's guns had fired 58 rounds.[45]

General Smith started toward Lewinsville soon after he heard the artillery open up. Enroute he came upon Capt. Thaddeus P. Mott, with a section of 32-pounders from his 3rd New York Artillery on the road training his horses and ordered him to Lewinsville. About a mile from Lewinsville Mott pulled his guns over to the right of the road on the top of a wooded hill and put them into action directing their fire toward the smoke of the enemy's cannons.[46]

As the Union and Confederate artillery continued to pound away at each other, Colonel Stevens got his infantry into formation and headed back toward Camp Advance. He then had the artillery slowly fall back protecting the rear of the column. Within a half hour after Rosser's artillery opened up it fell silent as the Union troops marched out of range.

By the time Smith got his command half way back to Camp Advance, General McClellan, with a large entourage, came tearing up the road to see what was going on. After hearing Smith's report, McClellan congratulated him and his officers for a job well done and then took a few minutes to visit with the wounded.[47]

With the assignment of Colonel Smith's old friend McClellan as the head of the army, Smith's fortunes quickly started to rise. On August 13 Smith was promoted to brigadier general and given command of a division. Shortly after taking command, and anticipating the arrival of the 4th, 5th and 6th Vermont Infantry Regiments in a month or two, Baldy Smith asked McClellan if he would allow him to put the all the Vermont regiments into one brigade. This was a rather unusual request as army policy was against brigading regiments from the same state together because serious combat losses might be bad for the morale of the soldiers and the citizens of the home state; however, McClellan consented.[48]

William Thomas Harbaugh Brooks of McClellan's staff, who had just been promoted to brigadier general of volunteers on September 28, was chosen to lead the Vermont Brigade. Brooks was not a Vermonter, but was of Vermont linage with his father having been born in Montpelier. Brooks was born in Lisbon, Ohio, on January 28, 1821, and graduated from the U.S. Military Academy in 1841. He took part in the Seminole War in Florida in 1842–1843 and served in garrison duty in other parts of the United States. He fought in the Mexican War where he was awarded brevets of captain and major for gallantry. Prior to the outbreak of the Civil War he was promoted to captain in the regular army and was serving on the frontier fighting Indians.[49]

The brigades making up Smith's division were the 1st Brigade commanded by Brig. Gen. Winfield S. Hancock, the 2nd Brigade commanded by Brig. Gen. William T.H. Brooks and the third brigade commanded by Brig. Gen. Isaac I. Stevens. Although officially designated as the second brigade, Brooks' brigade was always known as the Vermont Brigade.[50]

Baldy Smith's rise to brigadier general left open the top command position in the 3rd Vermont. Lieutenant Colonel Breed Hyde was selected for the job. His position was filled by Wheelock Graves Veazey. Wheelock G. Veazey, the son of Jonathan and Annie (Stevens) Veazey, was born in Brentwood, N.H., on December 5, 1835. He attended

Left: Brigadier General William T.H. Brooks, first commander of the Vermont Brigade. Brooks resigned from the army due to illness on July 14, 1864, as a brigadier general. *Right:* Wheelock G. Veazey, the second lieutenant colonel of the 3rd Vermont Infantry Regiment. Veazey was promoted to colonel on September 27, 1862, and selected for command of the 16th Vermont Infantry Regiment. He was mustered out of service on August 10, 1863 (both photographs Vermont Historical Society).

Phillips Exeter Academy and then Dartmouth College, graduating in 1859. He graduated from the law school in Albany, N.Y., in 1860. He had just started his law career in Springfield, Vt., when the Civil War broke out. At age 26 he enlisted as a private in Co. A of the 3rd Vermont and was selected as its captain with a commissioning date of May 21, 1861. After the resignation of the 3rd Vermont's major he was selected for that position and with the promotion of Hyde he was promoted to lieutenant colonel of the regiment on August 13, 1861.[51]

General Smith soon made another short advance deeper into Virginia on October 9. The division moved four miles up the Potomac, where Smith established a camp which was named Camp Griffin, after the gallant commander of Griffin's Light Artillery Battery. The Vermont regiments stayed at Camp Griffin for five months, longer than they stayed in one spot during the war. The site was in fine rolling country, with open fields and sprawling woodlands. The knolls around the area had been dotted with mansions, most of which by this time were in ruins. Camp Griffin was located on the road from Chain Bridge to Lewinsville on and around Smoot's Hill. From the top of Smoot's Hill most of the camps of Smith's division could be seen. The Confederate outposts were five or six miles away and the mass of the Confederate army lay at Centreville and Manassas, 15 miles to the southwest. The location of Camp Griffin was near what is now Langley, Va., where the headquarters of the Central Intelligence Agency is located.[52]

The companies of the 4th and 5th Vermont rendezvoused at Brattleboro, Vt., starting

Top: The camp of the 2nd Vermont Infantry Regiment at Camp Griffin in Fairfax County, Virginia. The frame of a building at the left is the regimental hospital under construction. *Bottom:* The camp of the 3rd Vermont Infantry Regiment at Camp Griffin in Fairfax County, Virginia (both photographs Vermont Historical Society).

Top: The camp of the 4th Vermont Infantry Regiment at Camp Griffin in Fairfax County, Virginia. *Bottom:* The camp of the 5th Vermont Infantry at Camp Griffin. The mounted officers are Lieutenant Colonel Lewis A. Grant on the left and Major Redfield Proctor on the right (both photographs Vermont Historical Society).

The camp of the 6th Vermont Infantry Regiment at Camp Griffin in Fairfax County, Virginia (Vermont Historical Society).

on September 11 with the last company arriving on September 14. No sooner had the last company arrived than the War Department directed the regiments be sent immediately to Washington. Any necessary arms or equipment would be supplied upon their arrival in the nation's capital. The governor ordered the regiments south, but the officers resisted on the grounds that going south without being fully prepared would undermine the morale of the men. The governor agreed and the movement was delayed. The two regiments were quickly armed and equipped and the 5th Vermont was mustered into service on September 16 with the 4th Vermont following suit on September 21. The 4th Vermont left Brattleboro for Washington in the evening after they had been mustered in and arrived on September 23. The 5th Vermont departed Vermont on September 25. Upon arrival in Washington both regiments marched to Camp Lyon where they were they joined the 2nd and 3rd Vermont regiments.[53]

The same day that the 5th Vermont was mustered into service, Governor Fairbanks received a telegram from the War Department requesting him to raise yet another three-year regiment. Fairbanks quickly appointed recruiting officers and by October 2 the first company arrived in camp of instruction in Montpelier. Four days later the entire regiment was in camp. The 6th Vermont Infantry Regiment was mustered into service on October 15, 1861. To command this regiment Governor Fairbanks selected 29-year-old Nathan Lord, Jr., who was at the time the lieutenant colonel of the 5th Vermont. Nathan Lord,

Jr., a New Hampshire native, was the youngest son of Nathan Lord, the president of Dartmouth College. Nathan Lord, Jr., was a graduate of Dartmouth College and at the outbreak of the war was working in a foundry in Lawrenceburg, Ind. There he enlisted in the 7th Indiana Infantry, a three-month regiment, and was chosen as captain of Company G. He saw active service in western Virginia. After his time in the 7th Indiana Lord returned to Vermont and offered his services to Governor Fairbanks.[54]

Asa Peabody Blunt from St. Johnsbury, Vt., was Governor Fairbanks' pick for the lieutenant colonel of the 6th Vermont. Blunt was born in Danville, Vt., on October 19, 1826. When the war broke out he was working for E. & T. Fairbanks & Co. in St. Johnsbury. Blunt had been commissioned as the adjutant of the 3rd Vermont on June 6, 1861, but the governor wanted him as second in command of the 6th Vermont and he was so commissioned on September 25.[55]

Asa P. Blunt, the first lieutenant colonel of the 6th Vermont Infantry Regiment. Blunt was promoted to colonel on September 19, 1862, and selected for command of the 12th Vermont Infantry Regiment (Vermont Historical Society).

Four days after being mustered into service the 6th Vermont was on trains moving south to Washington where it arrived on Tuesday, October 22. After a few days needed to get their equipment offloaded and to get organized, the regiment marched on October 24 to Camp Griffin. With the arrival of the 6th Vermont in camp the formation of the Vermont Brigade was complete.[56]

While all the Vermont regimental commanders had military training, only Colonel Nathan Lord had actually been in combat. However, the Vermont regiments were better off than the majority of Union Civil War regiments raised at the beginning of the war whose officers were appointed for political reasons or because they were successful in civilian life.

The Vermont Brigade would, later in the war, make a name for itself as one of the best fighting and fastest marching brigades in the Army of the Potomac, but in the winter of 1861–1862 it was better known for having the largest number of men on sick roles in the army. The army's medical staff was bewildered. The predominate diseases were measles, remittent and intermittent fevers, typhoid, pneumonia, and diarrhea.[57]

This phenomenon began in November and grew steadily worse as winter progressed. In November a report by the Surgeon Charles S. Tripler, medical director for the Army of the Potomac, indicated the 5th Vermont had 271 men out of 1,000 sick; the 4th Vermont,

244 out of 1,047; while the 2nd Vermont had 87 out of 1,021, and the 3rd Vermont, 84 out of 900. The lower figures for the 2nd and 3rd Vermont regiments were probably the result of having been in the field longer and thus exposed to disease in warmer weather. Why the other Vermont regiments fared worse than those from other states was never determined. Particularly curious was the case of the 5th Vermont, which lost more men than any of the other Vermont regiments.[58]

On February 6, the medical director reported that he had sent a large detachment of convalescents to Philadelphia to make room for sick Vermonters in the field hospitals at Camp Griffin. He hoped the other patients might benefit from not seeing so many sick men from one organization. The governor of Vermont sent five additional assistant civilian surgeons to tend to the brigade. Log houses were built and the sick men were moved out of hospital tents. Unit officers attempted to ensure a good policing of the camps and inspected their men for personal cleanliness. The health of the Vermont Brigade did finally improve and the depression that had set in began to lift as winter drew to a close.[59]

2

The Peninsula Campaign

While McClellan's men were busy in their camps of instruction around Washington, Maj. Gen. Joseph E. Johnston's Confederate troops were doing the same 15 miles away at Centreville and Manassas. For months Lincoln had been pressuring McClellan to attack, but McClellan did not think his men were ready. McClellan mistakenly believed he faced 115,000 rebels at Manassas instead of Johnston's army of only 50,000. Where McClellan got his information on the size of Johnston's army is unknown, but whatever the source he apparently truly believed it. To make matters worse, McClellan's army had by now swollen to approximately 150,000 men and would have easily defeated Johnston if he had attacked him. Lincoln finally lost patience and on January 17 he ordered a general advance of all U.S. armies to begin on or before February 22. Four days later he issued an order directing McClellan to occupy a point on the Orange & Alexandria Railroad southwest of Manassas Junction.[1]

McClellan rejected the plan and countered with one of his own, which called for his army to be transported down the Potomac River to the Chesapeake Bay and up the Rappahannock River to Urbanna, Va. From there he would push quickly to West Point, at the head of the York River and the terminus of the Richmond & York River Railroad, then with two supply bases established, he would push toward Richmond which was only 40 miles away. McClellan told Lincoln that his plan would threaten Johnston's lines of communications forcing the evacuation of Manassas without a fight and move any fighting to Richmond instead of in the vicinity of Washington, D.C. By mid–February Lincoln finally gave in to McClellan's plan.[2]

Without consulting McClellan President Lincoln directed that the Army of the Potomac to be organized into four army corps on March 8. The I Corps was to be commanded by Maj. Gen. Irwin McDowell; the II Corps to be commanded by Maj. Gen. Edwin V. Sumner; the III Corps to be commanded by Maj. Gen. Samuel P. Heintzelman, and the IV Corps to be commanded by Maj. Gen. Erasmus D. Keyes. A V Corps was organized from the two divisions currently serving in the Shenandoah Valley which was to be commanded by Maj. Gen. Nathaniel P. Banks. Baldy Smith's division became the second division of the IV Corps. Brig. Gen. Stebens' brigade was transferred from Smith's division and was replaced by the brigade commanded by Brig. Gen. John Davidson.[3]

On the evening of March 9 the Army of the Potomac had orders to have two days' rations cooked and be ready to march at 3 a.m. the next morning. At sunrise the next morning McClellan's exuberant army moved southwest toward Manassas. After months of training the Union troops were finally going to have a crack at the rebels. By the afternoon the Army of the Potomac came to an abrupt halt. It was not long before word ran through the ranks that the rebels had already left Manassas. The next morning the rumor was confirmed. General Johnston and his army had retreated beyond the Rappahannock River.[4]

McClellan called a council of war on March 13 to modify his Urbanna campaign plan. With Johnston behind the Rappahannock River and nearer to Richmond, debarkation at Urbanna was too risky because after landing at Urbanna the Army of the Potomac would be farther from Richmond than Johnston. Because of this McClellan modified his plan by moving to two new debarkation points, Fort Monroe in Hampton and Ship Point in York County. From there the army would march up the Virginia Peninsula between the York and James Rivers toward Richmond. Lincoln approved the revised plan the same day, with the proviso that McClellan had to leave a sufficient force at Manassas to keep the Confederates from reoccupying it and leave enough troops behind to protect Washington. McClellan issued orders for his army to start loading aboard ships in Alexandria on March 17.[5]

Smith's division arrived at Fort Monroe during the night of March 24 and debarked at 10 a.m. the next morning. By the time Smith's men were off the ships Fort Monroe was already full of troops and Smith was ordered to march his men to the tip of the Peninsula at Newport News Point. After getting organized Smith's division started its march for Newport News. The division marched three or four miles toward Newport

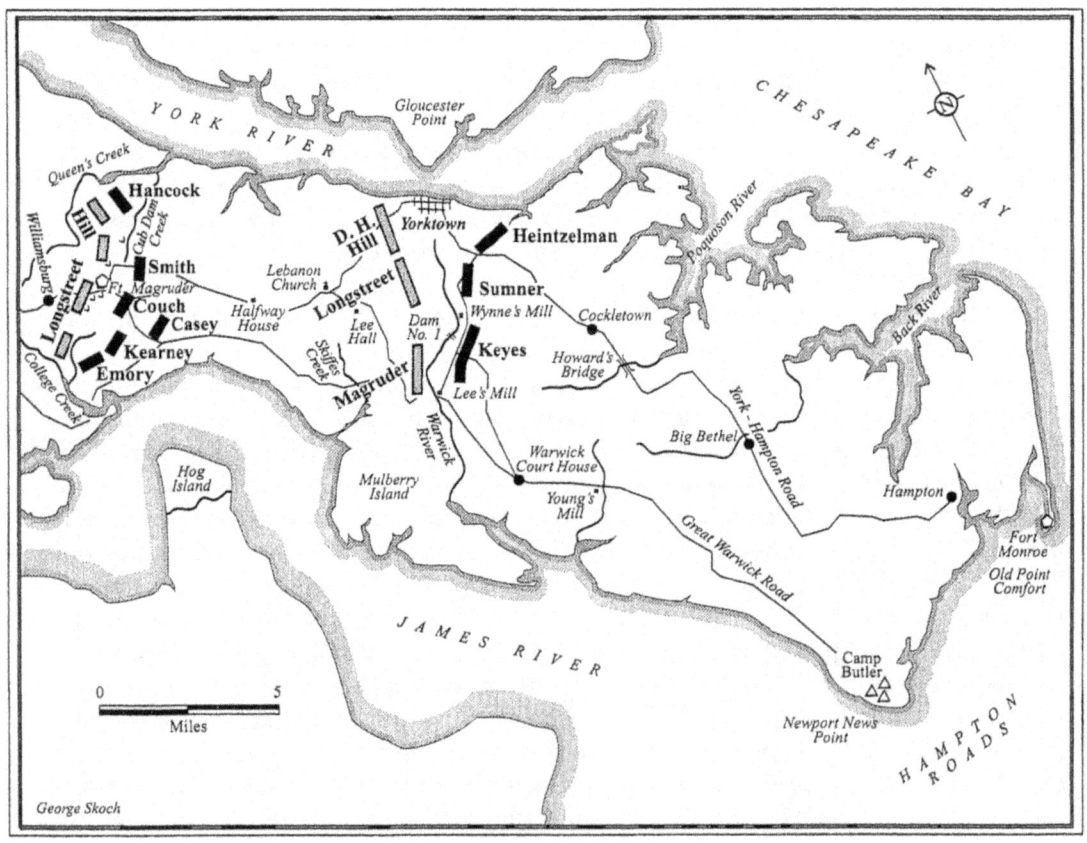

Lower Virginia Peninsula.

News before halting for the night on a plantation about three-quarters of a mile from the James River. Here it remained for two days.[6]

On March 26 Smith's and Maj. Gen. Fitz-John Porter's divisions were ordered to make a reconnaissance in force up the Peninsula the next day. As ordered the two divisions moved out not long after sunup. After making about 10 miles, Brig. Gen. Winfield S. Hancock's brigade, which was leading Smith's division, ran into the enemy's pickets. Smith halted his division and prepared to encounter the enemy which was supposed to be in force.[7]

The pickets that Hancock encountered left after firing a few shots and Smith had his division camp where it was and the next morning he marched it back down the Peninsula and went into camp about two miles above Newport News Point. The Vermonters were

Brigadier General Winfield S. Hancock (Library of Congress).

infuriated. They could not believe they had been ordered to retreat after only running into a couple of rebel pickets.[8]

McClellan arrived at Fort Monroe on April 2 and immediately launched his campaign. He planned to send two columns up the Peninsula to confront Maj. Gen. John B. Magruder who commanded the Army of the Peninsula and whose troops were entrenched in and around Yorktown. The IV Corps was to proceed up the James River side of the Peninsula to the "Half-way House," located between Yorktown and Williamsburg and serve as a blocking force. The II and III Corps were to march directly from Fort Monroe to Yorktown and attack. McClellan expected the U.S. Navy to protect his left flank on the James River and, in concert with the II and III Corps, bombard Confederate defenses at Yorktown. With his back to the York River and his escape route blocked, Magruder would be trapped in Yorktown and be forced to surrender as Cornwallis had been in the Revolutionary War. If Johnston attempted to move from Gordonsville to reinforce Magruder, McDowell's I Corps, still in Alexandria, would land on the Gloucester side of the York River to intercede.[9]

General McClellan's plan was sound but immediately started to unravel. There was only a limited amount of units ready to move. They were the second division of the II Corps, the first and third Divisions of the III Corps and the first and second divisions of the IV Corps, plus Brig. Gen. George Sykes' brigade of regulars, the reserve artillery, and about nine cavalry regiments, and the division artillery. About 58,000 men and 100 guns in all. The third division of the IV Corps had debarked but was grounded at Fort Monroe awaiting wagons. The U.S. Navy which had never been fully bought into McClellan's plan was getting cold feet. It feared the CSS *Virginia* in the James River and, after second thought, felt that Yorktown and Gloucester Point, at the mouth of the York River, were too well fortified to attack. Also, prior to leaving Alexandria the War Department had given McClellan control of the 10,000 troops under Brig. Gen. John E. Wool's command at Fort Monroe, but on the evening of the April 3, Lincoln sent a telegram denying him their use. Lastly, although he did not know it yet, the maps of the Peninsula he had been issued were grossly inaccurate.[10]

The Confederates were well aware that the Peninsula would more than likely be invaded and had started fortifying an area just below Williamsburg not long after the state had seceded. On May 21, 1861, Colonel John B. Magruder was given command of all the troops on the Virginia Peninsula and was ordered to make his headquarters in Yorktown. In addition to being the senior commander in the area he was also charged with finishing the line of entrenchments and forts below Williamsburg that stretched from where College Creek empties into the James River on the west to Queen's Creek, an inlet on the York River, on the east.[11]

John Bankhead Magruder, the son of Thomas and Elizabeth (Bankhead) Magruder, was born in Port Royal, Va., on May 1, 1807. He graduated from the U.S. Military Academy in 1820 and was commissioned as a second lieutenant in the infantry. He served in the Mexican War where he was brevetted three times for gallantry and meritorious service. He was known as "Prince John" in the old army because of his courtly manner and reputation for lavish parties. He also had the reputation for being overly fond of liquor.[12]

Major General John B. Magruder (Library of Congress).

At the outbreak of the Civil War Magruder resigned from the U.S. Army, and joined the Confederacy and was commissioned as a colonel. John Magruder was in his prime and was the right man for the job. At age 54 he was tall, erect and handsome. He continued his reputation as Prince John by always being perfectly uniformed and riding everywhere at a gallop. Despite his flash he took the assignment seriously and went at it with a vengeance knowing that time was not on his side. Leaving the completion of the Williamsburg defensive line to Col. Benjamin S. Ewell, whom he superseded, Magruder looked for a more forward line of defense further down the Peninsula. He found what he was looking for in Warwick County (today the Denbigh section of Newport News). When completed the "Warwick Line" would stretch from Yorktown to the James River.[13]

Around the village of Yorktown, the British redoubts from the Revolutionary War were rebuilt and just west of the village two new ones were constructed. A couple thousand yards west of the new redoubts, at the headwater of the Warwick River, the Warwick Line commenced. From its headwater to Lee's Mill, the Warwick River was no more than a sluggish creek, meandering through a swampy forest. At Lee's Mill the river deepened and the banks became steep, in places rising 30 to 40 feet straight up from the water. In places the river became several hundred yards wide. Magruder had constructed three additional dams between the already existing dams at Wynne's Mill and Lee's Mill to deepen and widen the water into a series of ponds. From below Lee's Mill to the mouth of the Warwick River the water was tidal and at times quite swift. From Yorktown to the James River, the Confederate side of the Warwick Line was laced with a continuous network of trenches and rifle pits and fortified with redoubts at vulnerable points. The Warwick Line was not completed until the spring of 1862 and Magruder would make it his main line of defense.[14]

The Army of the Potomac started its move up the Peninsula early in the morning on April 4. The IV Corps was to move up the Great Warwick Road at 6 a.m. and to proceed as far as Young's Mill and camp for the night.[15]

With Hancock's brigade leading the way, the IV Corps began moving up the Peninsula. Around noon, the skirmishers met Confederate pickets at Waters Creek, but they quickly fled. General Keyes stopped the column at this point and closed up his two divisions. During the halt he received a report from his cavalry scouts that strong fortifications occupied by two enemy regiments had been sited at Young's Mill.[16]

The obstacle Keyes encountered was Magruder's first of three lines of defense. This first line was more of a screen used to slow down, rather than stop, a force as large as McClellan's. The line stretched from Young's Mill, at the head of Deep Creek, across the Peninsula to Harwood's Mill at the head of the Poquoson River. The only major fortifications were at either end blocking the two main roads running up the Peninsula with only a few minor works in between.[17]

Keyes resumed the march at a cautious pace. After proceeding about two more miles, the skirmishers came upon a cleared plain about 1,000 yards wide, and the column stopped. On the other side of the plain were the rebel fortifications sitting atop a 20- to 30-foot rise above Young's Mill. Below the brow of the rise, the road dropped into a ravine and crossed a mill pond dam. On the right of the dam was the millpond and on the left a swamp. Where the road started to rise up the other side of the ravine, the rebels had erected a stockade wall with a large gate made of logs. The embankments below the fortifications were littered with felled trees.[18]

Smith sent the Vermont Brigade forward to clear the works, but all it encountered were several enemy cavalry pickets who put up a bit of a fight before leaving. One of the bullets fired by the rebels barely missed hitting the commander of the 5th Vermont, Colonel Henry A. Smalley, in the head, but did wound one of his men. Private Peter Brady of the 5th Vermont's Co. G took the mine ball in the left shoulder joint and had the unpleasant distinction of being Vermont's first combat casualty in the Peninsula Campaign. He would remain in army general hospitals until given a disability discharge from the army on November 29, 1862.[19]

The works at Young's Mill were extensive and within its perimeter were barracks made of pine slabs that had housed several thousand rebels during the previous winter. The Federals found the rebels had, in making their hasty getaway, left their evening meals cooking on campfires and made good use of both the cooked meals and the barracks.[20]

In a driving thunder storm, Keyes' IV Corps moved out at 6 a.m. toward the Half-way

Sketch by Vermont artist and newspaper reporter Larkin G. Mead of the Vermont Brigade attacking Young's Mill (George Houghton Album, University of Vermont Special Collections Library).

House. The roads, which McClellan had been assured were well drained and sandy, were not. They were soon transformed into a morass of deep, sticky, clay mud. Forward movement of troops and artillery was slowed to a crawl, and the supply wagons were at a virtual standstill; however, the men pressed on and passed Warwick Court House at about noon. Warwick Court House, consisting of a dilapidated brick courthouse, a jail, a store, a tavern, and two houses, would serve as the IV Corps headquarters for the next month.[21]

When the Vermonters left Young's Mill the 5th Vermont's surgeon, William P. Russell, and a small medical staff, were left there to set up a hospital for the IV Corps soldiers in the abandoned rebel barracks.[22]

About three miles past the courthouse, Smith's division, which led the Corps, halted at Lee's Mill. Facing them across the Warwick River were Confederate fortifications bristling with cannons and muskets. This was quite a shock for the high command. The maps the army had been given showed the Warwick River running parallel to the Peninsula, not across it. Also intelligence failed to indicate the area was fortified. General Brooks wrote to his father, "Our knowledge of the country was '0.' Our maps worse than none for they were entirely wrong and served only to mislead us." Reaching the Halfway House as ordered was now out of the question.[23]

Smith deployed his division with Davidson's brigade on the left of the Great Warwick Road and Hancock's on the right. Brooks' Vermonters were put in reserve and headed to the right of the road into the woods behind Hancock's men. Firing by the skirmishers began immediately. By 2 p.m. Federal artillery was in position and joined the fray. By now the thunderstorm that had started in the morning was so violent that, at times, it drowned out the roar of the cannons.[24]

Unable to position his units as originally planned McClellan decided to set siege to Yorktown. Near Warwick Court House hundreds of men in the rear brigades were brought up to corduroy the roads which General Brooks described as "without bottom." Before the corduroy roads were completed, supplies had to be transported on the backs of soldiers.[25]

With his left flank unexpectedly halted at the Warwick River, McClellan moved his right flank nearer the fortifications around Yorktown. Artillery was sent forward and artillerymen and infantry skirmished with the rebels all afternoon with little loss.[26]

As afternoon of April 5 turned into evening, the Vermonters saw the wounded men from Davidson's and Hancock's brigades being carried through their lines as they were evacuated rearward to the IV Corps hospital at Young's Mill. The skirmishing and artillery duel continued until dark, when it gradually subsided, as did the rain. That night Smith's men, including Smith himself, slept on the soaking wet ground without tents wherever darkness found them. Some buildings across the Warwick River had caught fire from the shelling and burned brightly most of the night, casting an eerie glow over the battlefield. These sights along with being soaking wet, tired, hungry, and without a dry place to sleep only added to the anxiety of what tomorrow might bring.[27]

April 5 had been a day of surprises for McClellan. The weather, road conditions and the Warwick Line had been bad enough, but that afternoon he had received a telegram informing him that the president was retaining McDowell's I Corps. To keep McClellan from being reinforced, Maj. Gen. Thomas J. "Stonewall" Jackson attacked Brig. Gen. John Shields' division at Kernstown, Va., in the Shenandoah Valley on March 23. Although it was a defeat for Jackson, the Lincoln Administration became jittery and ordered the I Corps to the Shenandoah Valley to defeat Jackson. McClellan was incensed at losing an entire Corps and started a feud with Washington that would last through the entire campaign.[28]

The next day, Sunday, April 6, the men of the IV Corps awoke before dawn to the sound of reveille in the Confederate camps across the river. After sunrise, the firing commenced again and continued throughout the day. An occasional artillery shell came crashing through the treetops, but no one in the Vermont Brigade was hurt.[29]

The troops in reserve, such as the Vermont Brigade, continued the task of corduroying the roads and constructing emplacements for the artillery pieces. In some areas the men had to carry the logs on their shoulders for over a mile. Even though the roads would be greatly improved over the next week, the artillery and ammunition trains would have priority. The wagons with rations would not move for several more days.[30]

Manning the Warwick Line were about 11,000 Confederate soldiers. Roughly 6,000 defended the anchors on the York and James Rivers and about 5,000 were spread in between for eight or nine miles, defending its weakest points. For the next two weeks Magruder totally misled McClellan as to his troop strength by military theatrics until he could be reinforced. At morning roll call, Confederate officers would shout orders, within earshot of the Union lines, to nonexistent units. Companies and regiments would be marched over and over again through breaks in the forest visible to McClellan's scouts causing them to believe they faced up to 100,000 Confederates.[31]

Early in the morning on April 6, Smith sent Hancock's brigade up stream on a reconnaissance to find a weak spot in the Confederate line. If he could find one, he was to hold it until Smith could reinforce him and then attack. Knowing Keyes was not one to take responsibility, Smith rode to Keyes' headquarters to inform him of what he had done. In the middle of their conversation, an orderly handed Keyes a message from McClellan. Keyes quickly read the order and handed it to Smith. The message directed all McClellan's commanders not to undertake any offensive operations until the line had been thoroughly examined by engineers. Smith related in his autobiography, "Very much chagrined, I rode back to my camp to find a message from Hancock that he had found a place at 'Dam Number 1' where he could cross. I had only to reply to him to come back to camp."[32]

On Monday evening, after having been under fire for two days and nights, the Vermonters were moved a little rearward near the Garrow Farm, where they remained for several weeks. As the Vermonters started to move, the rain began again and did not let up, day or night, until April 10.[33]

By the time the rain stopped on April 10, McClellan had most of his army or at least all that Lincoln was going to give him. Heintzelman's III Corps covered the Yorktown end of the line from the mouth of Wormley's Creek to a point little more than two miles below Yorktown toward Wynne's Mill. The II Corps held the center with Sedgwick's division. Brig. Gen. Israel B. Richardson's First Division of the II Corps would not get forward until April 16. The IV Corps held the left.[34]

By April 15 the area was starting to dry out. With drier weather and the newly corduroyed roads, rations were finally coming forward. More importantly, the sutlers were now in camp and Pvt. Charles M. Hapgood of the 2nd Vermont's Co. A happily noted in his diary, "Got some tobacco and cookies." The majority of the Vermonters were off duty for the day, and along with visiting the sutler, the men spent most of the day playing baseball. The day of rest was cut short in the evening with orders to be in light marching order the next day with two days' rations.[35]

The marching orders were the result of a directive from McClellan to make a reconnaissance at Dam No. 1 which spanned the Warwick River midway between Lee's and Wynne's Mills. On the Confederate side of the river was a small exposed redoubt with a 24-pounder howitzer, known as the "one-gun battery," flanked with trenches and rifle pits. Two hundred yards to the rear near the tree line, were two more redoubts, each with one gun. The redoubt on the Confederate right held a six-pounder smoothbore and the one on the left a 24-pounder howitzer. The artillery positions were protected by the 2nd Louisiana Infantry on the upstream side of the dam and by the 15th North Carolina Infantry on the downstream side. Intelligence reports from the pickets indicated that the Confederates were strengthening their fortifications. McClellan did not want the enemy to reinforce its positions anywhere along the line. He sent an order to Keyes to put a stop to the Confederate's work and to silence their guns. Keyes passed the order down to Baldy Smith to execute. Smith assigned the task to Brooks' Vermont Brigade.[36]

On the Federal side of the river opposite Dam No. 1, was a clearing, several hundred yards wide and 600 to 700 yards deep on the high ground just above the river. In the clearing stood three burned chimneys, the only remains of the Garrow house known as Merry Oaks. The Confederates had burned the house two weeks prior to the arrival of the Federals on April 5. The burning of the house was another great loss for the Garrow family. The owner, John Toomer Garrow, who served as a private in Co. B, 32nd Virginia Infantry Regiment, had died from a fever in November 1861 leaving a widow and five children. The house site was referred to by several names in Federal reports, "Garrow Chimneys," "Three Chimneys," and "Burnt Chimneys" for the three stark chimneys left standing. The most commonly name used was "Burnt Chimneys." With the exception of the several hundred yards of cleared land, known locally as Garrow's field that bordered

Photograph of Confederate earthworks at Dam No. 1. Supposedly taken while the works were still occupied by the Confederates (George Houghton Album, University of Vermont Special Collections Library).

the Warwick River, the rest of the bank above and below the dam was covered with a fairly dense growth of woods. Smith's division had been picketing this area since its arrival on April 5.[37]

General Brooks had his brigade up before daylight on April 16 and moved his regiments out at 6 a.m. General Smith accompanied General Brooks and directed the disposition of the troops. As the Vermont Brigade approached the Garrow farm, General Brooks sent the 3rd Vermont forward through the woods on the lower (down river) side of the opening, and the 4th Vermont through the woods on the upriver side. Orders for both regiments were to send skirmishers to the water's edge below and above the dam and open fire on any working parties of the enemy in sight about their works.[38]

Hancock's brigade, with two batteries, secured the Lee's Mill road and Davidson's brigade, with one battery, was held as a general reserve.[39]

Meanwhile, Capt. Thaddeus P. Mott's 3rd New York Artillery was posted in the edge of the woods along the road in the rear of the field.[40]

The 4th Vermont was the first regiment to get into position where it halted in the woods a few rods from the river. Companies B and G were deployed as skirmishers and advanced to the swampy edge of the pond above the dam concealing themselves in the bushes. It was now about 7:30 a.m. and the Vermonters could hear the Confederates on the other side of the river holding their guard mount with their band playing the tune "Rosa Lee." Colonel Stoughton, who had accompanied his skirmishers, took a musket from one of his men and fired it into the nearest opening in the rebel fortification. Instantly after Stoughton's shot his men followed suit. The rebels stopped their morning activities and returned the fire with their artillery. The first shell passed over the 4th Vermont and struck a pine tree under which their assistant regimental surgeon, Willard A. Child and chaplain, Salem M. Plympton, were sitting under a large pine tree watching the 4th Vermont engage the enemy. The shell cut off the top of the pine tree and covered Child and Plympton with fragments of bark and pine needles.[41]

As soon as the rebel artillery opened up, one of Mott's sections moved in the open to the right rear of the chimneys and unlimbered. As soon as the artillery was in position and ready to fire, the 3rd and 4th Vermont, as well as Mott's guns opened fire on the 2nd Louisiana's sector in earnest. By now it was about 8 a.m. The Southerners replied in equal measure with rifle and artillery fire. As the rebel artillery returned fire, Mott brought forward his other two sections, and quickly started pounding the Confederate positions. The Confederate's fire was not as strong as the Federal's since the rebel's 24-pounder on the upriver side of the dam was in a position to do more damage to their own troops than the Federals and ceased firing.[42]

While the artillery was banging away at one another, the 3rd Vermont got into position on the left of the field. Having a longer front to cover, six companies were deployed by Colonel Hyde as skirmishers and advanced to the edge of the swampy area. With any protection as they could get from logs and stumps, the 3rd Vermont skirmishers opened a hot fire on the rebels in the rifle pits across the creek and received a sharp response. During this exchange of fire several men in the 3rd Vermont were wounded. Over the next hour the Confederate rifle fire slowly receded, but their artillery in the upper earthworks stayed very active. One of the enemy's shells struck the wheel of one of Mott's pieces, exploded and killed three of the cannoneers and wounded several others.[43]

As Mott's and the Confederate artillery were pounding each other, Colonel Smalley was ordered to send a detachment of the 5th Vermont, composed of the best marksmen in his command, to the river front where the enemy's guns could be reached at shorter range. For this mission 10 of the best shots in each company were selected. Captain Charles P. Dudley, a 25-year-old law student from Manchester, Vt., and commander of Company E, was placed in command the sharpshooters. Thirty-six-year-old Montpelier native, First Lt. Charles C. Spaulding was detached from Co. D to assist Dudley. With the privates and noncommissioned officers combined Dudley had a total of 65 sharpshooters. The detachment moved down through the Garrow field toward the water. In the process, two men were wounded by shell fragments. After passing the chimneys they started receiving fire from the rifle pits across the creek. Dropping to the ground they crawled down the slope to the water's edge seeking shelter behind undulations in the ground. After getting into position they opened fire on the Confederate artillerymen and any of the enemy infantrymen who showed themselves above the tops of their rifle pits.[44]

Later in the morning the Confederate 24-pounder near the end of the dam was disabled by a shot from one of Mott's guns. The other rebel guns were kept silent by the 4th and 5th Vermont's sharpshooters. The rebel rifle fire finally ceased, with the exception of occasional scattered shots and General Smith ordered the firing on his side to cease. The first phase of the operation was complete.[45]

Earlier in the morning while the Vermonters and the rebels were busy firing at each other one of Brooks' aides, First Lt. Edwin M. Noyes of the 3rd Vermont's Co. C, reconnoitered below the dam to determine if it was possible for troops to cross the stream.

With the combatants concentrating on each other, Noyes not only crossed the waist deep stream, but got to within 50 yards of the rebel trenches without being seen.⁴⁶

The area Noyes reconnoitered was guarded by the 15th North Carolina Infantry Regiment, but on this day the rebels were back from the river, just inside the tree line, working on their fortifications. Their forward rifle pits were manned by a light force of pickets reinforced by Co. D of the 16th Georgia Infantry Regiment.⁴⁷

Lieutenant Noyes got back to Generals Smith and Brooks about the time the firing ceased and at the same time that General McClellan arrived. Noyes reported that the stream was not more than waist deep and the trenches on the other side were very lightly defended. Furthermore, some wagons had been seen in the rear of his works which seemed to indicate that the rebels were removing supplies. To Smith and Brooks it seemed that maybe the enemy was demoralized and preparing to vacate its position.⁴⁸

First Lieutenant Edwin M. Noyes, Co. C, 3rd Vermont Infantry Regiment (Vermont History Society).

After hearing Noyes' report, McClellan told Smith to send a force across the stream, but not to bring on a major engagement and to withdraw his troops if serious resistance developed. Baldy Smith tapped Colonel Hyde to pick two companies from the 3rd Vermont for the attack.⁴⁹

In carrying out this plan Smith withdrew Dudley's skirmishers and moved them to the woods on the left. In their relocation they came under sharp rifle fire indicating that the rebel rifle pits were still manned. Companies K and E of the 4th Vermont relieved companies B and G on the skirmish line above the dam. The 3rd Vermont's skirmish line, under the command of the 3rd's Major Thomas O. Seaver, was maintained in the edge of the woods on the river bank below the clearing.⁵⁰

At about 2:00 p.m. the 2nd Vermont was sent into the woods on the right, in the rear of the 4th Vermont. In the process of crossing the cleared area in the rear of their artillery the 2nd Vermont was hit by enemy artillery fire. A fragment from one of the artillery shells hit 21-year-old Pvt. William Fuller, a farmer from Vergennes, Vt., in Co. F, in the head and killing him instantly. Within minutes the 2nd Vermont was across the cleared area and in the relative safety of the woods. Fuller was the 2nd Vermont's only casualty for the day.⁵¹

Colonel Hyde picked companies D and F to lead the attack, but a number of men from both companies had been placed on picket duty earlier in the day leaving the two companies short-handed. After discovering this Hyde reinforced the first companies with companies E and K. If the four-company task force succeeded in carrying the rifle pits near the water's edge, the men were to announce the fact by cheering loudly and waving a white handkerchief. Colonel Hyde gave Corporal Alonzo Hutchinson, a 26-year-old, six-foot-tall carpenter from Charleston, Vt., of Co. D his white handkerchief to signal with. Upon seeing the waving white handkerchief signal more troops would be sent across the river to support the four companies in attacking the earthworks beyond.[52]

Captain Fernando C. Harrington of Company D and Capt. Samuel E. Pingree of Company F formed their two companies near the river bank. Then men were ordered to unhook their waist belts and hold their cartridge boxes above their heads with one hand and hold their rifles high with the other. Companies E and K were formed up behind companies D and F waiting for their turn to cross the swampy low land. Captain Harrington was the senior captain and was put in command of the operation, but just before Colonel Hyde gave the order to charge Harrington turned over the command to Captain Pingree claiming that he was too sick to make the charge. Harrington was a poor leader and was dismissed from the service on July 23, 1862, for being absent without leave the month prior. The dismissal was overturned in 1870 and he was given an honorable discharge.[53]

Around 3:00 p.m. Mott's, Wheeler's and Kennedy's batteries opened a vigorous fire on the Confederate fortifications on the other side of the river. The enemy's artillery immediately responded, but their fire soon slackened under the storm of shot and shell from the Yankee artillery. That was the signal for Pingree to advance. Pingree, standing in front of his men, yelled the order "Forward!" and companies D and F started for the other side of the river. The men hurriedly struggled across the stream though they were under sporadic rifle fire. Most of the way the swampy bottom was covered with fallen trees and cut limbs that caused the men to trip and fall getting both their weapons and ammunition wet in the water that ranged from two to five feet deep. As the Green Mountain Boys struggled through the water the Confederates started picking them off. One of the first men to be hit was Corporal Hutchinson. As he struggled to stay on his feet he uttered, "I cannot wave the flag after all" and passed Col. Hyde's handkerchief off to another man. Hutchinson died two days later. Just as Hutchinson was wounded, Co. D's Pvt. Jeremiah Bishop, a 40-year-old farmer from Brighton, Vt., took a rebel minie ball in the hip and was carried back to the Union side of the river. Jeremiah's 17-year-old son Pvt. Jerome Bishop was also wounded, only not as severely as his father. Jerome was given a disability discharge from the army the following July for failing health. In addition to the Bishops, a number of other men were killed or wounded while crossing the river.[54]

In spite of the obstacles in the water the two companies reached the opposite bank and dashed straight for the rifle pits. The rebel soldiers, numbering about the same as the Vermonters, quickly retreated to their larger earthworks to the rear. The Green Mountain Boys now had their dander up. Cheering loudly the Vermonters ran across the rifle pits chasing after the gray backs. Captain Pingree, whose orders were to occupy the rifle pits at the water's edge and wait for reinforcements, had his officers get the men stopped and returned to the rifle pits.[55]

Just after Captain Pingree got his men back to the safety of the rifle pits he was shot in the left buttock. Although bleeding profusely, he refused to be taken back across the river and remained with his men. Not long after Pingree was hit his second lieutenant, 24-year-old Edward A. Chandler from Pomfret, Vt., was hit by a rebel bullet that went through his right hand shattering three bones and then boring into his right thigh. Fifteen minutes after his first wound Captain Pingree had his right thumb was shot off, again he refused to leave his men.[56]

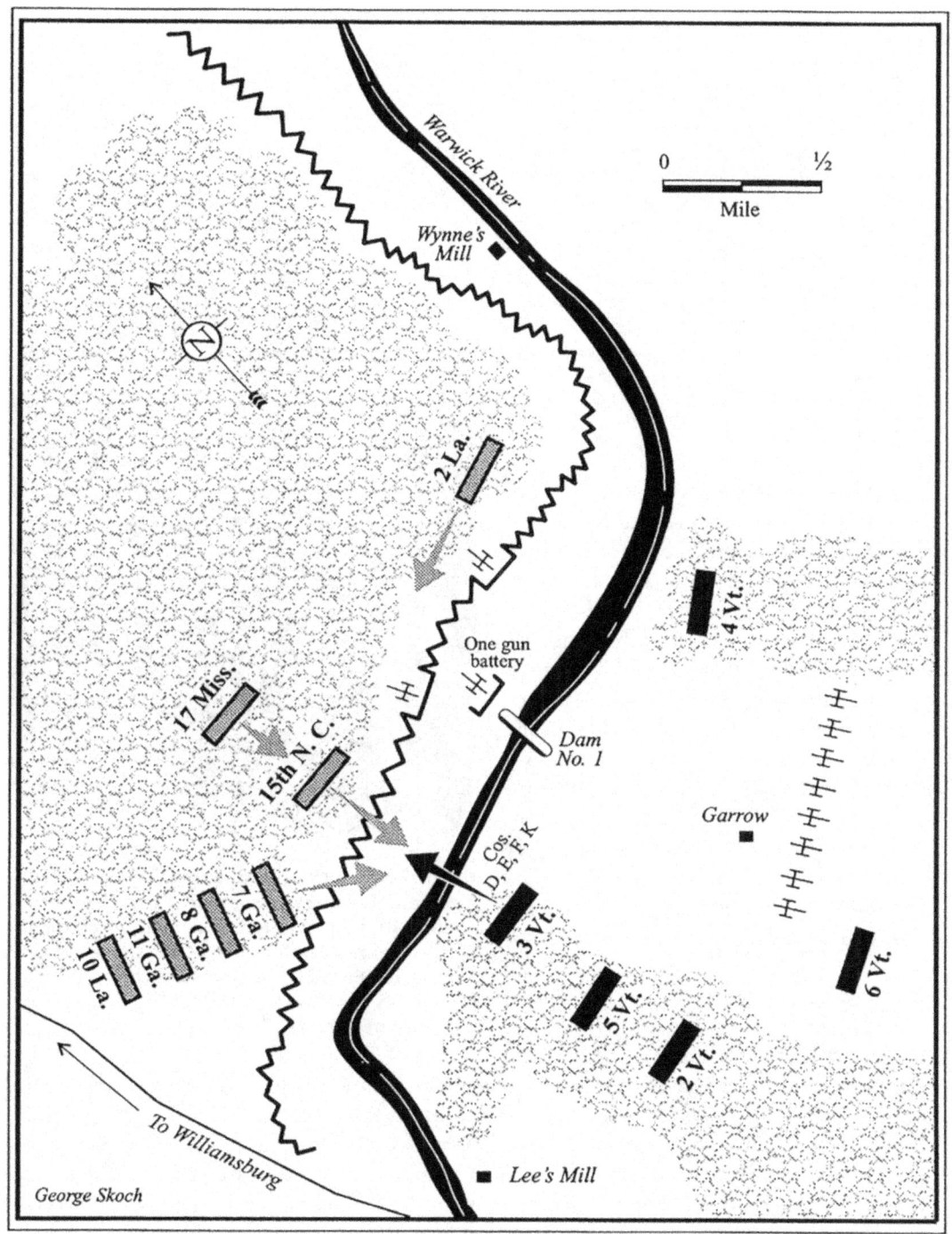

Battle of Dam No. 1.

As companies D and F were getting back to the rifle pits, companies E and K charged across the river as told by 23-year-old Corporal George Q. French, from Johnson, Vt., in Co. E:

Before us was the creek—twenty, some say forty rods in width—& just on the other shore a dense woods filled with rifle pits & rebels without number. Into the water we plunged, fixing our bayonets capping our pieces as we went. On we pushed, climbing over logs, roots and every kind of impediment which floated in the water or rested on the ground, firing as we had opportunity, until the channel of the creek was past & the depth of the water began to diminish. Then the gleam of our steadily advancing bayonets began to strike a terror to the rebel hearts & one by one they leaped from behind their breastworks & took cover in the thickets behind. Now commenced a scene which beggars all description. Firmly grasping our trusty rifles we rushed on, shouting, firing, yelling— & ere we set foot on dry land every rebel had left the pits in front of us.[57]

After Captain Pingree got his men back into the rifle pits they started shouting as ordered to indicate they had been successful. Also, the man that Corporal Hutchinson had given the white handkerchief to started waving it with all he was worth, but no reinforcements were sent. The situation did not look good. The Confederate troops were visibly rallying. The first counter-attack was made by the 15th North Carolina, which came on the double quick from its camp over the crest of a low hill and charged the rifle pits. They were met with a hail of bullets from the Green Mountain Boys that took down the 15th North Carolina's commander, Colonel William McKinney, with a minie ball in his forehead. Some forty of his men were killed and wounded. With their revered commander dead the Tar Heel's

Samuel E. Pingree, commander of Co. F, 3rd Vermont Infantry Regiment. Pingree would eventually be promoted to lieutenant colonel of the regiment before being mustered out of service in 1864. He was awarded the Medal of Honor for his action at the battle of Dam No. 1 (Vermont Historical Society).

retreated in a panic. Just as the North Carolinians were starting to retreat their brigade commander, Brig. Gen. Howell Cobb, arrived and took control. General Cobb got the 15th North Carolina reorganized and with elements of the 2nd and 10th Louisiana and the 7th, 8th and 16th Georgia Infantry Regiments the Confederates started charging toward the Vermonters. The four companies of the 3rd Vermont were now in serious trouble. During this time Captain Pingree sent several messengers back across the river to ask Colonel Hyde to send over reinforcements or give the order for Pingree's command to retreat, but no answer was received.[58]

The Vermonters were holding their ground but were paying quite a high price. Private Emerson E. Whitcomb, a farmer from Springfield, Vt., in Co. B was wounded severely in the hip. Company D's Pvt. Wesley Davis was hit in the left shoulder. Another Company D man, Pvt. Jason D. Niles, a 24-year-old farmer from Charleston, Vt., was shot in the chest. Company E's first sergeant, Hiram C. Holmes from Waterville, Vt., was slightly wounded in the ear. Although the wound was considered slight, it was bad enough for him to be sent to Carver U.S. General Hospital in Washington, D.C. Sergeant Holmes apparently got a furlough while in the hospital to see the sights in Washington. While he was out and about he must have visited one of Washington's many houses of ill repute as he was given a disability discharge from the army on June 4 for symptoms of secondary syphilis. Pvt. Charles Turner, a 19-year-old farmer from Johnson, Vt., sustained a horrible wound. A rebel minie ball hit him in the right groin, went through the upper portion of his pelvic bone and exited out his back two inches from the right side of his spine. After recuperating from his wound Turner's military days were over and he was given a disability discharge on October 15, 1863. Charles H. Page, a 23-year-old from Barre, Vt., had a severe wound in the arm. The wound was more than the doctors could repair and his arm was amputated the next day. Page left the army on February 28, 1863, with a disability discharge and returned to his home in Westminster, Mass. Company F's Pvt. Richard H. Rowell from Brighton, Vt., had his time in the military ended when he was shot in the buttocks producing lameness in his legs and paralysis of his bladder. The luckiest man in the four 3rd Vermont companies was Captain Leonard E. Bennett, the commander of Co. K. He was hit by eight bullets that pierced his uniform without making one scratch on his skin.[59]

The Vermonters finally started to run out of ammunition as the rebels were starting to close in on both flanks, Company D's Second Lt. Erastus Buck made a difficult decision as he described later:

> We were bound to die rather than retreat without orders. Something desparate had got to be done. A charge was our only show, and charge we did. We jumped the works and gave a loud yell. The rebels supposed a brigade was charging them and ran like sheep. But when they saw it was only a ruse, they rallied. I saw whole regiments marching against us, and we retreated, never expecting to recross the fatal stream.[60]

Lieutenant Buck's men were just scurrying back to the rifle pits when a messenger from Colonel Hyde ran up to Captain Pingree with the order to retreat back across the river. While this order brought some relief to the beleaguered Vermonters, it brought a whole new problem, retreating across the river while the infuriated Confederates were firing at them. Although wounded and in pain, Captain Pingree saw to it that as many of the command as possible were gotten back across the river to safety. Seeing his men heading to safety, Pingree, suffering from the loss of blood, finally allowed several of his men to help him back across the river.[61]

While crossing the river Lt. Erastus Buck said the rebels "made the water boil with their bullets." Referring to his group of men, Lt. Buck continued:

> As providence would have it, we escaped unharmed to the opposite shore. Sgt. [William H.] Currier and I. [Isaac H.] Clough in our Co., a Lieut. in Co. E got part way through the water and the fire came so hot they sunk themselves into the water behind a tree and remained for two hours and then made their escape. We had given them up for lost, but we were thankful to see them. I feel sad to relate that Lucius Briggs was shot dead on the ground. He fought brave.[62]

Most of the wounded men were helped back across the river by their comrades as observed by the 2nd Vermont's, Pvt. Wilbur Fisk, "Within a few minutes squads of men were seen emerging from the woods with their wounded comrades, carrying some of them on their backs, some on stretchers, and others were assisted hobbling along as best way they could; and many alas! Were left that could not be recovered." A number of the dead and wounded men were in fact left behind. The wounded that could not be recovered were taken prisoner by the Confederates. One of those men was Pvt. John Roe, a 22-year-old farmer from Morristown, Vt., in Co. E. He was taken to Richmond several days later and placed in a prisoner of war camp. He was paroled the next month on May 11.[63]

One of the most well-known men in the Vermont Brigade that was wounded was the "sleeping sentinel," Pvt. William Scott. Whether he made it back under his own power or was assisted by his comrades is not recorded, but he had been shot through his left lung. After crossing the river he was taken to the field hospital where he died the next morning. Scott was buried in the 3rd Vermont's regimental cemetery on the Garrow farm. Interestingly, as Scott's grave was being dug in a grove of holly and wild cherry trees the men uncovered the remains of an American soldier buried during the siege of Yorktown 80 years earlier. The side he fought for was determined by buttons and a belt clasp that were uncovered. In 1867 the U.S. government reinterred all of the Union remains in the Yorktown area in what is now the Yorktown National Cemetery. Private Scott is buried in grave number 351.[64]

Corporal James Fletcher of Co. E, a 20-year-old college student from Johnson, Vt., was in the regimental hospital with a fever when preparations were made for the charge across the Warwick River. Instead of remaining in relative safety, he went across the river with his company. He came out unscathed and helped wounded survivors back across the river. After saving a number of men Fletcher went back to the hospital. By war's end he had been promoted up through the ranks to first lieutenant.[65]

While the wounded men were struggling back across the Warwick River in a hail of bullets, Julian A. Scott, a 16-year-old fifer from Johnson, Vt., and 25-year-old Pvt. Ephraim Brown, both in the 3rd Vermont's Co. E, rushed into the water and helped pull men to safety. The first man they came to was Pvt. John Backum, a 19-year-old farmer from Johnson, Vt., who was shot through the left lung. Scott and Brown had just reached Backum when Brown was shot in the thigh. Scott carried Backum across the river on his back and then returned and helped Brown to safety. Young Scott carried no less than seven more men to safety. After the battle of Dam. No. 1 both Brown's and Backum's days in the army were over and each was given a disability discharge after their wounds healed.[66]

For their selfless and heroic acts during the battle of Dam No. 1 both Musician Julian A. Scott and Capt. Samuel E. Pingree were awarded the Medal of Honor.[67]

About 4:30 p.m. orders came down from General Smith for another assault on the Confederates across the river. The reason for this attack remains a mystery to this day. This time Brooks chose the 4th and 6th Vermont to make the charge with four companies each. Colonel Stoughton chose companies A, C, F and I for the attack. Colonel Lord, for some reason, chose five companies. They were companies A, C, D, F and I. The 4th Vermont was to charge across the dam and the 6th Vermont was to charge across the river below the dam where the 3rd Vermont had crossed earlier in the day.[68]

At 5 p.m. both regiments charged toward the river at the double quick. The 4th Vermont got as far as the dam when the Confederate fire became so intense that Col. Stoughton recalled his four companies. Before the companies could get off the dam and back into the woods Privates David J. Dibble and Stephen B. Niles both of company I were laying on the ground dead. Both men were shot in the head. Ten other men were wounded and were carried to safety by their comrades. Private Franklin N. Grimes of Co. C. sustained a serious wound in his lower right leg from a shell fragment. On April

20 he was admitted to the U.S. general hospital at Fort Monroe, Va., where his lower leg was amputated at the knee joint. Unfortunately, gangrene set in and Private Grimes died on April 28. Another one of the wounded, Capt. Henry B. Atherson, the commander of Co. C, was shot in the right groin and because of the wound he resigned on August 12, 1862. Casualties in the 4th Vermont were kept fairly low in the cleared area they had to cross by the men jumping up and running a few steps and then throwing themselves flat to the ground again. In this manner they worked their way back to the cover of the woods.[69]

The sight selected for the 6th Vermont's crossing was near where the 3rd Vermont had made its charge several hours earlier, eight or 10 rods below the dam. By now though, the river had been widened and deepened by the Confederates closing the sluice of another dam downstream. The water now was about 20 rods wide, extending nearly up to the enemy's rifle pits. As the five companies entered the water the rebels opened up on them with a withering fire. Without returning a shot the Green Mountain Boys pushed on, forded the waist deep channel, and tried to charge the rebel rifle pits.

During the charge through the water Capt. Edwin F. Reynolds, a machinist from Rutland, Vt.; and commander of Co. F, received a serious wound in the hip, but in spite of his wound he pressed on at the head of his company. As he neared the opposite shore Reynolds was hit in the chest by a bullet that killed him instantly.[70]

As the five companies of the 6th Vermont reached the opposite side of the river they got within 20 yards of the rifle pits, but the high volume of fire from the rebels stopped them cold. Fortunately for the Vermonters, the well ensconced rebels held their rifles at an angle that was a little too high causing most of their shots to pass over the 6th Vermont's men's heads. If that had not been the case none would have probably survived. As it was, officers and men were dropping fast. The commander of Company H, Capt. David B. Davenport, a boot and shoe dealer from Roxbury, Vt., took a flesh wound in his thigh. Company D's second Lieutenant, Charles F. Bailey was knocked down by a lead round ball in the left groin. The ball passed through his pelvis coming to rest on the left side of his rectum. His men helped him back across the stream. Lieutenant Bailey was admitted to Harwood U.S. Army General Hospital in Washington, D.C., on April 22 where he died of his wound on May 1.[71]

While the officers were taking casualties, the enlisted men were taking their share of wounds. Both of the Graves brothers from Cavendish, Vt., in Company C were wounded. Twenty-four-year-old Luther Graves was hit in the head. He was admitted to the army hospital at Fort Monroe, Va., on April 20. From the shape of the wound the doctor originally thought Luther had been hit by a piece of shrapnel. The doctor tried to find the object by inserting his finger, but it was out of his reach. He also tried using a probe, but still could not find whatever it was that had hit Luther. All of this was done while Luther was still conscious without it hurting him. Whatever the object was it was beyond the doctor's reach. On April 24 Luther sank into a coma, started having convolutions, and died. After Luther's death the doctor was able to remove the object from his head. It was a round lead musket ball. Luther Graves was buried in what is now the Hampton National Cemetery in Hampton, Va., in grave 4999. Luther's younger brother Nathan, a strapping, six-foot-tall blacksmith, also in Company C was also wounded. Nathan was shot in the left leg by a rebel minie ball that shattered both his tibia and fibula. After his wound healed he was so lame he could no longer serve in the army and was given a disability discharge on April 20, 1863.[72]

Two other Company C soldiers were hit. Private Dana C. Ayers, a farmer from Mt. Holly, Vt., was shot in the knee. He spent over a year in army hospitals before being transferred to the Invalid Corps. Private Elisha M. Goddard from Mt. Holly was wounded in the right hamstring muscle causing paralysis of the right foot. He was given a disability discharge on October 31, 1862. Private Henry White, an artist from Montpelier, Vt., in Company F was wounded in the left knee by a small lead ball causing partial paralysis of his leg. He was given a disability discharge at Fort Monroe, Va., on November 14, 1862.[73]

Seeing his men falling like leaves, Colonel Lord sent them an order to retreat. Needless to say, the order was obeyed without hesitation. The return was more dangerous than the advance with the survivors carrying their rifles and dragging or carrying the wounded. Six-foot, one-inch Corporal Ruluf L. Bellows of Co I. was carrying the 6th Vermont's colors and nearly reached the rebel rifle pits when the order to retreat came. It was then that he was mortally wounded by a gunshot to the knee. As the colors fell from his failing grasp into the water, they caught the eye of Company I's First Sgt. Edward A. Holton. He shouted to some of his soldiers to rally on the colors. Holton ran back, rescued the flag, and carried it safely back across the stream, while the other men carried Corporal Bellows back through the water to the Vermont side of the river.[74]

Corporal Alexander W. Davis of the 6th Vermont's Co. D gives a verbal picture of what the charge and the retreat were like:

> We started to the rear to find the water almost up to where we stood, and over all the interval between us and the opposite shore. In the turbid current was a mass of men, struggling to the rear. Such a sight never again met my gaze during the war. Wounded men, on reaching the old bed of the stream sank with cries of despair, to be found later in the swamps down the stream, where their bodies had lodged. I saw two men ahead of me carrying a wounded man, when they were struck by rebel bullets and one or both sank. I saw two others assisting a wounded man, when a bullet passed through the latter's head and he pitched forward and was gone. The muddy water literally boiled with bullets.[75]

When Captain D.B. Davenport of Company H, who had received a flesh wound in the thigh, reached the safety of the riverbank on the Union side when he was met by his 11-year-old son, Henry, one of Company I's drummer boys. Once Captain Davenport was taken from the water's edge to the woods, Henry went back down to the river with a tin cup to get his father some water. As Henry squatted down to fill the cup it was shot out of his hand. Captain Davenport survived his wound, but died of disease on September 20, 1862. After his father's death Henry Davenport was discharged from the army.[76]

By the time the five companies returned they had suffered a loss of 23 men killed or mortally wounded and 57 wounded. It was now near nightfall and the futile battle of Dam No. 1 was finally over. In all, the Vermont Brigade lost 44 men killed, 21 mortally wounded and 148 wounded. Seven of the wounded were taken as prisoners.[77]

As night fell over the battlefield, the Vermont regiments quickly started digging trenches and rifle pits to secure their side of the river. Rifle fire finally subsided and all was quite except for a Federal cannon that lobbed shells randomly across the river every half-hour or so to keep the rebels awake and to prevent them from repairing their damaged works.[78]

At daybreak on April 17, rifle fire between the pickets commenced again. A number of Berdan's sharpshooters were sent over from the Yorktown end of the line to add their firepower. Some of the sharpshooters were armed with rifles with telescopic sights that were deadly accurate. They were so effective that by April 19 Magruder was complaining to Richmond about them:

> I beg leave to call attention of the commanding general to the great difficulty in carrying on the exhausting defense at the dams assigned to my command, particularly dam No. 1. Sharpshooters of the enemy have been pushing their way forward causing it to be extremely dangerous to relieve troops except in the night.... Troops at the dams are almost constantly under fire, and that though they exhibit fine spirit they must inevitably become exhausted.[79]

The Yankees also had trouble with sharpshooters. Twenty-three-year-old Pvt. Francis D. Hammond of the 5th Vermont's Co. D told of his experience:

> I went out to our breast works yesterday it but a few rods from here out of the wood a little ways. It is not safe to leave the bushes. The sharp shooters are on the lookout every minute throughout the day on both sides. They lay all along the edge of the woods and as soon as they see a man stirring they will surely fitch him. Just after I left the breast work and stepped into the bushes there was a man coming along behind me. The enemy saw him just before he entered the bushes. A rifle ball went through his body he died within a short time after and the same day while we were out getting some bushes to make us a tent there was a bullet whistled by my head but that is nothing. It didn't touch me...[80]

With the majority of the Army of the Potomac facing him Magruder pleaded with Richmond for reinforcements. Major General Robert E. Lee, President Jefferson Davis' military advisor, started pulling regiments piecemeal from Johnston's army stationed behind the Rapidan River. By April 4 Lee had slowly pulled a total of three divisions from Johnston. On April 9 President Davis ordered the final movement of Johnston's troops south. On April 17, Johnston arrived on the Peninsula. Being the senior commander, he assumed command of all Confederate forces which by now numbered about 53,000. He quickly reorganized his army into four divisions commanded by Major General Magruder, Maj. Gen. James Longstreet, Maj. Gen. Daniel H. Hill, and Maj. Gen. Gustavus W. Smith. Magruder was assigned command of the right wing of the army, Longstreet the center, and Hill the left wing. Gustavus Smith's division was held in reserve.[81]

For the next several weeks the Vermont Brigade exchanged shots with the rebels during the day and dug fortifications at night. Men not employed in digging or on picket were denied a decent night's sleep by being called into line of battle several times a night, only to find it a false alarm.[82]

A white flag of truce was hoisted on the Confederate side of the Warwick River on Saturday, April 19. The rebels wanted a cease-fire so the Vermonters could retrieve their dead left behind during the battle of Dam No. 1 and so the rebels could gather up their dead killed by the Yankee sharpshooters. One of the Federal soldiers reported, "Our sharpshooters had shot lots of them since then [April 16] and there they had to let them lie, until they smelt very badly...." As soon as the flag of truce was acknowledged by the Vermonters, the rebels came out of their trenches and as one witness described it, "you should have seen the heads pop up over their breastworks. they looked just like the bees when they swarm on the outside of a hive." Col. William M. Levy, commander of the 2nd Louisiana, walked halfway across the dam and was met by Captain Currie of General Smith's staff and a truce was negotiated. The rebels brought the dead Vermont soldiers across the dam, where their comrades received them. Due to the rapid decomposition from lying in the hot sun for several days, the bodies of the dead men were unidentifiable. They were carried away and interred with the rest of the fallen Vermonters on the Garrow farm.[83]

After several hours the truce ended and the Federal sharpshooters and pickets went back to work shooting at the rebels as though the friendly visit had never happened.[84]

Being at the bottom of the chain of command, the Vermonters were totally unaware that McClellan was finally ready to commence his bombardment of the Confederate lines on May 5. General Johnston, however, was not. From observing the progress of the Federal's work and the intelligence gained from Union prisoners and deserters, he knew it was time to pull back from his untenable position on the Peninsula. The Confederates unleashed a furious cannonade along the Warwick line that lasted most of the night of May 3 as their troops filled the roads on their march toward Richmond. As the Federal observation balloons ascended in the early morning hours of May 4, the rebel's tents could be seen, but there was not a soldier in sight. Scouts were sent into the rebel lines near Yorktown and found them deserted. McClellan immediately sent orders to all his commanders to pursue the retreating rebels.[85]

As the Green Mountain Boys went about their daily morning routines they were unexpectedly ordered into formation and told of the rebel's departure. The 5th Vermont was immediately sent across Dam No. 1 to secure the area. After the area was secured, other Vermonters wandered over to see the forts. They were amazed at the extent of the damage they had inflicted over the past month. Destroyed equipment lay everywhere. The only things left behind of any value were the tents that were left up to deceive the

Captain Romeyn B. Ayres' battery crossing Dam No. 1 on the morning of May 4, 1862 (George Houghton Album, University of Vermont Special Collections Library).

Yankees. There was hardly a tree in the area that did not have bullet holes in it or branches torn off by artillery shells, and the ground was furrowed by cannon balls. Because of half-buried horses and mules, open latrines and rotting food, the stench was intolerable. After looking around everyone was sent back to camp to pack up and be ready to move.[86]

General Baldy Smith's and Maj. Gen. Joseph Hooker's divisions were ordered as lead elements to follow Brig. Gen. George Stoneman's cavalry in pursuit of the rebels. Smith's division pulled out at 8 a.m. with orders to take the Great Warwick Road and Hooker was to take the road from Yorktown to Williamsburg. To get to the Great Warwick Road, on the other side of Lee's Mill, Smith had to cross the Warwick River at Dam No. 1, pass through the Confederate trenches and then veer left. While traversing the trenches, a man in the 77th New York stepped on what appeared to be a rag laying on the ground, but it emitted a report like a pistol shot. The regiment's commander lifted the rag with his sword tip exposing a torpedo (Civil War term for a land or waterborne mine). The torpedo consisted of an artillery shell planted vertically in the ground topped with a fuse that would ignite when stepped on. Luckily, this one did not explode. This was not the case for a number of Federal soldiers on the Yorktown end of the line. Smith's men were now cautious where they stepped, avoiding any scrap material lying on the ground. Later in the day, Smith included the following line in a note to McClellan, "Our road through the fort was lined with torpedoes, but happily none went off."[87]

For the rest of the morning and afternoon the Union column trudged on toward Williamsburg. During the march the Vermont Brigade was starting to develop the gait that they would become famous for as the war wore on. Smith's division, with the Vermont Brigade in the lead, was to make a halt at the Halfway House to allow Keyes' other two divisions to close up, but Smith pressed on. Keyes called for one of his orderlies and said, "If your horse has bottom enough to catch up with the Vermont Brigade, I want you to overtake them and order a halt. Tell them we are not going to Richmond today."[88]

Major General Edwin V. Sumner (Library of Congress).

The two roads the Federal troops were following came together two miles from Williamsburg. Here lay Magruder's third and final line of defense stretching seven miles from College Creek on the James River to Queen's Creek on the York River. The line consisted of a series of 14 redoubts. Near the center of the line, where the two roads converged, was redoubt No. 6 known as Ft. Magruder.[89]

By the time Smith's division

arrived on the right of the Union line it was nearly 5:30 p.m. Under orders from General Sumner, who McClellan had put in charge, Smith formed his command for an assault with Hancock's Brigade in the lead and the Vermont Brigade in support. It was 6:30 p.m. before the lines moved forward, but as soon as the division entered woods, Smith found it too thick with underbrush, and with the increasing darkness, called off the advance. The troops bivouacked in place for the night. Around midnight it started raining, but the men were so tired they hardly noticed. As Pvt. Charles M. Hapgood complained that night, "I am almost tired to death."[90]

The next day Smith had his division up early. Although somewhat refreshed, the men were stiff and sore from the march the day before and from sleeping on the cold, wet ground. Smith had the division in line of battle early ready to assault the Confederates, but Sumner held it in place fearing an attack on his center.[91]

Hooker, however, took matters into his own hands. Without a plan of battle, and without consulting Sumner he assaulted Fort Magruder at 7:30 a.m. As the battle intensified General Longstreet brought in three more brigades and started pushing Hooker backwards. Hooker asked Sumner for reinforcement, but was denied. His only hope now was that Brig. Gen. Philip Kearny's division of the III Corps, that was slogging through the mud on the Hampton road, would arrive in time to help him.[92]

During the morning, Baldy Smith had not been totally idle. He had sent his engineer to reconnoiter the rebel works in his front. The engineer returned and reported that a deep ravine that was not conducive to an assault protected the redoubts. But a black man he had met told him that two miles to the right there was a road that crossed a dam in the ravine that would allow an approach to the rear of the redoubts. Smith dispatched four companies of the 4th Vermont to verify the intelligence. The four companies returned around 10:30 a.m. with great news. Not only did the road and dam exist, but the redoubts on the other side of the dam were unoccupied. With that information in hand, the overly cautious Sumner allowed Smith to send one brigade to seize the redoubts. Smith chose Hancock's Brigade for the mission. Without Sumner's knowledge Smith reinforced Hancock with two additional regiments from Davidson's brigade, Wheeler's battery, and a company of cavalry.[93]

Around noon Hancock started and in a short time had secured the redoubts. Now the Federals had effectively flanked the enemy. Once in position Hancock was ready to attack the two manned redoubts between him and Fort Magruder as soon as Smith could send reinforcements.[94]

While Hancock was making his end run, Sumner changed his mind about supporting Hooker and ordered Smith to send a brigade to help him. Fearing Hancock would need reinforcement more than Hooker, Smith got Sumner to change the order. The Vermont Brigade was up and formed in the road ready to move when Sumner changed his mind again and ordered them to stay in their current position.[95]

From their position the Vermonters could see Hancock pushing the rebels back toward Fort Magruder with his skirmishers and artillery, but he hesitated to occupy the works without being reinforced. They could also see Brig. Gen. Jubal Early's brigade advancing on Hancock and knew he was in trouble.[96]

Smith asked Sumner several more times to allow him to aid Hancock. Twice the Vermont Brigade was sent to the right only to be recalled. The last time it got as far as the dam before being recalled, and as Smith said in his autobiography that he and the Vermont Brigade "turned backwards to the field of nincompoops." Brooks, apparently more upset than Smith, broke into a swearing rage.[97]

Hooker was barely holding his portion of the line when Kearny finally arrived around 3 p.m., in time to reinforce him. Together, Hooker and Kearny stopped the rebel advance and regained most of the ground that Hooker had lost.[98]

The rebels assaulted Hancock's position and were repelled with terrific loses to include Early himself, who was wounded twice. By 6 p.m., the rebels pulled back leaving Hancock in possession of their left flank. The battle of Williamsburg was now over.[99]

As the firing ceased and the smoke lifted, the Vermonters could see that Hancock's command was still intact and in possession of the flank. Their pent-up emotions poured forth like water from a ruptured dam. They started cheering at the top of their voices. The cheering, however, galled the rebels who lobbed several shells at the Vermonters, inflicting no casualties, and causing them to only cheer louder. After dark, the Green Mountain Boys tried to get some rest as best they could.[100]

That night, the Confederates withdrew from Williamsburg and continued their retreat toward Richmond. If there was a victor of the battle it would have to be the Confederates. They suffered 1,682 men killed, wounded or captured to the Federal's 2,283. The biggest victory for the Confederates was they bought enough time for the rest of their army to continue its retreat unmolested.[101]

Second Lieutenant Chester K. Leach, Co. H, 2nd Vermont Infantry Regiment (U.S. Army History and Education Center).

Tuesday, May 6, dawned clear and pleasant after a night of near torrential rain, and the scene of two days earlier was repeated. Yankee pickets edging forward at first light discovered the rebel lines deserted. Smith's division, following orders received the night before, marched around to the right to where Hancock had fought expecting to pursue the rebels, but instead was ordered to go into camp. For the next three days, the Federal army sat idle while the rebels marched closer to Richmond.[102]

Lieutenant Chester K. Leach of the 2nd Vermont's Co. H described the aftermath of the battle at Williamsburg in a letter to his wife:

> The dead are not all buried yet, but the men are burying them as fast as possible. Our dead are mostly buried, but the ground is strewn yet with the Rebs. There is hardly a tree in the woods where they fought, however small, but has one or more bullet holes in it. The woods is full of rebel guns, which are Springfield muskets, smooth bore, which once belonged to the U.S.[103]

3

The Battles of Garnett's Hill and Gouldin's Farm

McClellan's army started leaving Williamsburg in piecemeal fashion on May 6. Smith's division however, did not leave until Friday morning May 9 at sunrise. The pace up the Peninsula was rather leisurely making only 10 to 12 miles a day. The first day's march took Smith's division to Burnt Ordinary (present-day Toano). On May 10, after passing through Barhamsville, Smith stopped at about noon near Slatersville where the division remained until May 12. Slatersville, strictly speaking, was not a village, but a small cluster of homes belonging to the Slater family at the intersection of modern day Virginia routes 249 and 627.[1]

On the march from Williamsburg the supply wagons were slowed by the muddy roads and by the time the Vermont Brigade reached Slatersville the men's haversacks were empty. Although McClellan had issued orders to the army to respect southern civilians and their property, the Vermonters were not going to go hungry. Although the Confederates had pretty much stripped the country during their retreat, the Vermonter's still found enough chickens, turkeys and hogs they could steal to subsist on. Under these circumstances the officers turned a blind eye to these flagrant violations of orders.[2]

On Sunday, May 11, while at Slatersville Pvt. Wilbur Fisk of the 2nd Vermont's Co. E noted in a newspaper article he wrote:

> Sunday we had entirely to ourselves. No marches or fatigues are required of us on this day, unless absolutely necessary. Gen. McClellan respects the Lord's day, as do a large proportion of his men. Many of them respect it more because *he* does than from any other consideration. Divine services were held in our regiment, the first we have enjoyed the privilege of attending since we left Camp Griffin.[3]

Around 4 p.m. on May 12 Smith's division moved to New Kent Court House, a distance of four miles. Early the next day Smith was ordered to move to Cumberland Landing. The route of march for some reason was cross-country through the woods "with only little signs of a road." Although it was only a four or five-mile trek, it was a very difficult trek.[4]

On the morning of May 14 Baldy Smith ordered his division to fall in, and along with Major General William B. Franklin's and Fitz John Porter's divisions, moved five miles up the Pamunkey River to White House. The muddy road slowed the movement to a crawl. McClellan noted in his report of the campaign, "So bad was the road that the [wagon] train of one of the divisions required thirty-six hours to pass over this short distance."[5]

3. The Battles of Garnett's Hill and Gouldin's Farm

Army of the Potomac camps at White House Landing. The tents in the foreground are supposed to be those of the Vermont Brigade (Vermont Historical Society).

After reaching White House, Smith's division camped in a 300-acre clover field. The Vermont Brigade got its tents up around 4 p.m. just as it started to rain. Private Kirk Rand of the 2nd Vermont indicated the men made themselves at home on the Lee property, "the folks that owned the farm here had just fenced it with new rails but there is not a rail to be seen now. When a division marches on to a field you will see a nice clean field. The next morning when they leave it will be all covered with pieces of rail sticking up in the ground where we have put our little tents." Here the Vermont Brigade remained until May 19.[6]

White House had originally been the plantation of Daniel Parke Custis and his wife, Martha Dandridge Custis. When Daniel died in 1757, Martha became one of the richest widows in Virginia. After a brief courtship, the Widow Custis married George Washington on January 6, 1759. For a brief time George and Martha lived at White House, but Martha wanted a larger house on the Potomac River, so George enlarged his home at Mount Vernon. In 1859 White House was inherited by Robert E. Lee's second son, Col. William Henry Fitzhugh "Rooney" Lee, who was currently leading the 9th Virginia Cavalry Regiment in the Confederate army.[7]

Lt. Col. Wheelock G. Veazey, who had replaced Breed Hyde as the 3rd Vermont's lieutenant colonel, was quite impressed with White House as he noted in a letter to his wife:

> This morning we came to this camp, still on the Pamonkey, and on the Whitehouse farm, the house where Washington found his wife. The property is now owned by the descendant of her family. It was

White House, the home of President George Washington's wife, Martha D. Custis (Library of Congress).

& is one of the largest estates in Va. The original estate was I think 14000 acres, now divided between two men by the name of Lee. The owner of this farm is an officer in the rebel service. I think it is the finest estate I ever saw. The house is in good condition & most beautifully located. The river navigable for our gun-boats & transports, runs within a few rods of the house and has a good landing. There are fine lawns and gardens about the house, and drives for miles on the plantation—large fields running back from the house perfectly level & in good cultivation—clover in blossom & wheat three feet high in fields of 700 acres. There are 120 servants here and hundreds elsewhere on the plantation. It seems as tho the human heart could scarcely desire anything more than this estate affords. Yet its lordly owner has left it all for a false idea. This is but one illustration of the zeal & earnestness of these people. The mass of our forefathers made no such sacrifices as the mass of these Southerners are making now. How we succeed so well ag'st them is a mystery. Of course the memory of Washington is enough alone to make us guard everything with even a tender care. Not a tree, nor shrub, nor a fence is allowed to be touched about the house. Nor is anyone allowed to enter the grounds about it. I have charge of all property, therefore I went all over the premises. We dont allow the men to mingle with the negroes even, or go into their houses.[8]

Just prior to the arrival of the Yankees, Mrs. Robert E. Lee had been living at White House. As she left the property she pinned the following note to the door of the house that read, "Northern soldiers who profess to reverence Washington, forbear to desecrate the home of his first married life,—the property of his wife, now owned by her descendants.—

A Grand-daughter of Mrs. Washington." McClellan obligingly had a guard posted on the house and prohibited its use by the army.[9]

White House was of particular strategic importance to McClellan. The Pamunkey River was navigable for Federal supply transports to reach White House and the Richmond & York River Railroad, running from West Point to Richmond, crossed the Pamunkey River there. It was not long before White House became an enormous supply depot.[10]

Before continuing the advance on Richmond, McClellan reorganized his army on May 18 by forming two new corps. A fifth Corps was formed under the command of Fitz John Porter, from Porter's first division of the III Corps and George Sykes' regular infantry division. A sixth corps was formed under the command of William B. Franklin, from a division Franklin's I Corps and Baldy Smith's second division of the IV Corps.[11]

William Buel Franklin, born on February 27, 1823, graduated first in his class from the U.S. Military Academy in 1843 and was commissioned in the Corps of Topographical Engineers. He had performed engineering duties on the frontier, supervised harbor improvements, and taught at the U.S. Military Academy. Franklin served in the Mexican War where he won two brevet promotions. On May 17, 1861, he was promoted to brigadier general of volunteers and given command of a brigade in Heintzelman's division which he led in the first battle of Bull Run. In September of 1861 Brigadier General Franklin was given command of a division in the defenses of Washington. After the battle of Williamsburg, Franklin led his first division of I Corps at the battle of Eltham's Landing. Franklin was promoted to major general on July 4, 1862.[12]

After several false starts Smith's division finally moved out of White House Landing on May 19, but only marched up the Richmond & York River Railroad about five miles to Tunstall's Station. After it reached the station it turned right and camped on the high ground above the station for the night. Two more days of marching brought the division near New Bridge where it camped on a low ridge of pines in the vicinity of Cold Harbor. It remained here until May 24, when Smith moved forward three-quarters of a mile closer to the Chickahominy River and camped on Dr. William Gaines' farm, known as Fairfield.[13]

The grounds around the Gaines' house were so beautiful that General Smith made his headquarters there. He wrote later, "Our tent was under a magnificent tulip tree filled with flowers, and for days no sound of war entered into our quite."[14]

Major General William B. Franklin. He was selected for command of the newly formed VI Corps in May 1862 (Library of Congress).

Dr. Williams Gaines' house, Fairfield, which Brigadier General Smith used as his headquarters (Vermont Historical Society).

McClellan now had Franklin's VI Corps on the right of the Union line, three miles from New Bridge, supported by the V Corps. Stoneman's cavalry was on the right of Franklin, and within about a mile of New Bridge. The II Corps occupied the center, near the Tyler House, and connected on its left with Keyes' IV Corps, which held the left of the line near Bottom's Bridge. The III Corps was held in reserve.[15]

The Vermont Brigade would remain on the Gaines farm until June 5. During this time it was kept busy with picket duty, corduroying roads and building bridges across the Chickahominy River. Some of the more mechanically minded Vermonters brought one of Dr. Gaines' mills back into working order and were soon producing flour for the entire division. The troops also helped themselves to the doctor's tobacco that was drying in his barns.[16]

Guard duty could be a little exciting at times according to Pvt. Wilbur Fisk:

An extra regiment goes with the workmen to protect them. Batteries, too, are stationed at every available point to command the bridge. Once, while our regiment was acting as guard, and when we were quietly passing away the time, as unconscious of danger and as unmindful of the presence of an enemy as if we had been playing with the kitten under the parental roof in old Vermont, we were suddenly startled into the liveliest activity by a well-directed cannon ball which passed just over our heads and planted itself in the ground a short distance from us, followed by the second and third shot in almost the same place. There was a lively bustling among the boys just then. The thread of many an animated discussion was suddenly broken; papers were thrown aside by those lucky enough to possess them; cards were rejected without the least regard for their loss,—for it is quite noticeable that card-players, gamblers especially, have an instinctive dread, a superstitious fear of cards in moments of alarm and peril,—all were quickly on their feet ready to run, or dodge, or look out for themselves the best way they could. Soldiers, when they are not in the ranks armed and equipped and under the influence of discipline, and not directly under the control of a leader, feel just as other people are supposed to in times of danger, and when one shot has barely missed them, and they have reason to believe another is about to be fired, with no chance on their part to return it, or for concerted action to resist the foe, it is the most natural thing in the world for even soldiers to feel inclined to run, and to any one who would attribute this inclination to cowardice, I would say it is a great pity, the Army of the Potomac should be deprived of *their* services. However, there was no running of any consequence here; many of the boys never so much as stirred out of their tracks. Our batteries promptly accepted the rebel challenge and silenced their saucy demonstrations in short metre. The workmen kept right on their work, without scarcely deigning to notice anything but their own legitimate business.[17]

Not long after arriving at the Gaines' farm, Lt. Col. Wheelock G. Veazey of the 3rd Vermont was put in temporary command of the 5th Vermont. All three field officers, Colonel Smalley, Lieutenant Colonel Grant and Major Redfield Proctor, were on leaves of absence due to illness. Veazey would remain in command until the first week of June when Grant returned to duty.[18]

Brigadier General William T.H. Brooks and staff. Left to right: Harry the cook; Captain Thomas Read, assistant adjutant general; Edward E. Phelps, brigade surgeon; Brigadier General William T.H. Brooks; First Lieutenant Edwin M. Noyes, aide de camp and First Lieutenant Abel K. Parsons (Vermont Historical Society).

Top: The 2nd Vermont's senior officers. From left to right: Lieutenant Colonel George J. Stannard, Colonel Henry Whiting and Surgeon Benjamin W. Carpenter. *Bottom:* The 4th Vermont's leadership. Left to right: Major Charles B. Stoughton, Colonel Edwin Stoughton and Lieutenant Colonel Harry N. Worthen (both photographs Vermont Historical Society).

The 6th Vermont's staff. Seated from left to right: Lieutenant Colonel Asa P. Blunt, Colonel Nathan Lord, Major Oscar L. Tuttle and Surgeon Charles M. Chandler. Standing from left to right: Chaplin Edward P. Stone, Quartermaster John W. Clark and Assistant Surgeon Lyman M. Tuttle (Vermont Historical Society).

A tragedy occurred in the 4th Vermont on May 23. The body of 32-year-old Sgt. Charles Whitwell of Co. B was found in the woods outside of camp. He had committed suicide by shooting himself in the head with his rifle. Charles Whitwell had an interesting history. He was born on March 7, 1829, to Francis and Elizabeth Whitwell in Shrewsbury, England, and was christened in Shrewsbury's Saint Alkmunds Anglican Church on March 24, 1829. Charles' father was a furrier and the family must have had a fairly comfortable life and Charles must have gotten a good education because in 1851 he was a schoolmaster in Leighton. Sometime between 1851 and 1860 he immigrated to the United States and settled in Hanover, N.H. Because of his education and teaching experience he may have been associated with either Dartmouth College in Hanover or Kimball Union Academy in nearby Meriden. On April 19, 1861, Whitwell enlisted as a private in Co. K, 1st New Hampshire Infantry Regiment. The 1st New Hampshire was a three-month regiment that saw no action and was mustered out of service on August 9. Eight days later on August 17 Whitwell enlisted in Co. B of the 4th Vermont in Chelsea, Vt. Probably because of his maturity and his experience in the 1st New Hampshire he was selected as one of the company's sergeants. On November 10, 1861, while the 4th Vermont was at Camp Griffin, Va., Whitwell submitted a letter to his company commander requesting to be relieved from "the onerous duties of sergeant." Apparently he and his commander worked out whatever was bothering him because he retained his stripes. On January 2, 1862, Whitwell submitted a letter to his company commander requesting to be included in a group of men going back to Vermont to recruit, but he was not selected. According to Carleton Young's *Voices from the Attic: The Williamstown Boys in the Civil War*, Sergeant Whitwell had gotten his first sergeant, William Henry Martin, to promise to settle his financial affairs in case of his death. It is possible that Whitwell could not cope with military life and with his mind at ease with First Sergeant Martin promising to deal with his estate, he left camp and shot himself.[19]

Just as darkness was nearing on May 29 the sky opened up with violent lighting and a terrific rainstorm. By morning the rain had stopped, but the Chickahominy River, which usually was not more than 20 feet wide and a few feet deep, was now a wide raging torrent. The Army of the Potomac was now split into two pieces with no way to reunite and would remain so for a week.[20]

May 30 was a sad day for the 2nd Vermont. That day Lieutenant Colonel Stannard left for Vermont to command the newly formed 9th Vermont Infantry Regiment. He had been promoted to Colonel on May 21. Stannard was a favorite in the regiment as Pvt. Kirk Rand of the 2nd Vermont's Co. C wrote in a letter to his girlfriend, "I am afraid that the 9th and 10th Regts. will fill up slow but they have got a good Col. in the 9th. he does not know the name of fear. we miss him a good deal here." Major Charles H. Joyce, of Northfield, Vt., was promoted to fill Stannard's vacant position.[21]

The 2nd Vermont's second lieutenant colonel, Charles H. Joyce. After the war he returned to his law firm. From 1875 to 1883 he was Vermont's U.S. representative (Vermont Historical Society).

Also on May 30, the 5th Vermont was sent up the Chickahominy River to guard a party of engineers that was building a bridge. While there the regiment was shelled for about two hours by rebel artillery. During the shelling Lt. Col. Veazey had a narrow escape when a shell fragment knocked off his hat, but left him unscathed. First Sgt. Orlando B. Reynolds of Co. B, from Chazy, N.Y., was the only real casualty and he was only lightly wounded. Reynolds was promoted to second lieutenant in

3. The Battles of Garnett's Hill and Gouldin's Farm 55

Co. B on July 6, but fell from grace on February 22, 1863, when he was dismissed from the service for being AWOL.[22]

Determined to take advantage of the Army of the Potomac's being split with no way to reunite, General Johnston attacked the two Federal Corps on the south side of the Chickahominy during the afternoon of May 31 at Fair Oaks. But Keyes and Heintzelman, reinforced later by Sumner, made a good fight against superior numbers and by nightfall still held their ground. In addition to the fact that the attack by the rebels was badly handled from the beginning, they lost their commander, General Johnston, who received a severe bullet wound in the shoulder and was knocked from his horse by a shell fragment. Major General Gustavus W. Smith assumed temporary command after Johnston was wounded. That night Confederate President Jefferson Davis selected Maj. Gen. Robert E. Lee, his military advisor, to replace Johnston. To the southerners, the loss of General Johnston seemed like a terrible tragedy at the time, but the selection of Robert E. Lee to replace him would change the course of the war. The battle renewed the next morning, but after two or three hours it ended when General Lee ordered his units back to their original positions. The constant rains had left the roads almost unusable giving Lee several days to reorganize his army. Losses for the two-day battle were quite heavy with the Federals losing 5,031 men and the Confederates 6,134.[23]

While the struggle of the 31st was in progress, the Vermonters, with the rest of General Smith's division, were under orders to be ready to move at a moment's notice. The Green Mountain Boys watched and listened with great interest to signs and sounds of the battle as the roar of artillery drew nearer. During the afternoon the sound of musketry was added to the din and for a while after dark the flashes of cannons and exploding shells were visible. There was little sleep for any of Smith's troops that night. The men of the Vermont Brigade were under arms most of the night and before daylight the next morning they headed out with three days' rations and 60 rounds of ammunition to cross the river at New Bridge to take part in the day's fight. But high water slowed the construction of the pontoon bridge which was to replace the bridge burned by the enemy so the Vermonters waited on the riverbank until 10 a.m. At that time word came that Smith's division was not needed and it marched back to camp except for the 6th Vermont which was left to guard the bridgehead.[24]

The pause in fighting following the battle of Fair Oaks allowed McClellan to push his lines even nearer to Richmond. As part of this movement, Franklin's VI Corps crossed the river and was posted on the right of the Union lines, leaving only Porter's V Corps on the north bank. Moving with the VI Corps, Baldy Smith's division packed knapsacks at three a.m. on the morning of June 5, and marched down the Chickahominy River.[25]

Private Quincy F. Thurston of Co. D, 2nd Vermont, a 23-year-old mechanic from Huntington, Vt., gives a glimpse of the move when he wrote a friend in Vermont:

> Yesterday we took up our line of march and after a very roundabout course of five or six miles we arrived near the site of the grape vine bridge, built by Gen. Sumner before crossing last Sunday. The rains since that date have erased the said bridge and our troops have been employed in building a more permanent structure. I had the pleasure of assisting in the matter by carrying one rail to the pioneer engaged in the work. This amount of work performed by a large detail of men was more than sufficient to furnish material for what was wanting when our Brigade arrived. The "corduroy" extends over half a mile. Towards night, we shouldered our knap-sacks again, and crossed the "Rubicon" as we supposed, but found another body of water a branch of the Ch-[ickahominy] which had flooded the meadow. This was bridged the most of the way only by string pieces and we found it rather "skittish" business crossing. We all reached the Richmond side, safe and sound, and after ascending a long

sloping bank, proceeded to pitch our tents in a clover field on the summit. It was then about five o'clock and we had just arranged ourselves for a nights rest, when the order came to pack up and prepare for another march. Such is a soldier's life. We were consoled however by the reflection that we were on the road to Richmond. A further march of some miles through mud which you know all about, and we arrived in a wheat field, situated somewhat like the bed of clover we left. It was about dark and we made ourselves busy in preparing for the night. So here we are, and we know not how long we shall stay in here or what may happen from one hour to another.[26]

After crossing into Henrico County, the VI Corps moved up the river to a hill near Simon Gouldin's house about a mile north of Fair Oaks Station and half a mile south of the river. Simon Gouldin's farm, Elmwood, consisted of 552 acres of which about one half was cultivated and the other half was covered with timber. It was situated on a high plain that was bordered on the north side by the Chickahominy River. The Vermont Brigade remained in this camp for the next 19 days. Since the time the Federal troops arrived on Gouldin's farm it has been called Golding's farm. The cause of this may have been the way the Yankee ear heard Southerners pronounce Gouldin, but for whatever reason the name stuck. In 2011 the Richmond National Battlefield Park changed the name back to Gouldin's farm on their maps and in their literature and that is the way it will be referred to in this work.[27]

Between Gouldin's farm and the farms of Dr. John R. Garnett and his son, Dr. James M. Garnett, to the west, ran Labor in Vain Ravine through which ran the two branches of Labor in Vain Creek. As the creek flowed toward the Chickahominy the ravine widened and its sides steepened. Upstream, the main branch of Labor in Vain Creek had been dammed up to create a millpond from which a canal carried water over a waterwheel. The waterwheel had run a gristmill which was no longer in operation. James M. Garnett's house, also referred to as the "brick house," was located on the high ground just west of the millpond in Labor in Vain Ravine. Dr. John R. Garnett's house, on the New Bridge Road, was three quarters of a mile west of James M. Garnett's house. Just west of James M. Garnett's house was an overseer's house which was located beside a farm road that ran from the intersection of Nine Mile Road and New Bridge Road over the mill dam to the Gouldin House. The area around the two Garnett farms was known as Garnett's Hill.[28]

Private Wilbur Fisk explained how the Union and Confederate forces were positioned on the Gouldin and Garnett farms:

> We are now encamped on what appears to me rather a worn-out farm, though of respectable dimensions, owned of course, by a loyal secessionist. It is enclosed on all sides, as nearly all the farms are, by woods, while on the North side flows the famed Chickahominy. West of us there is a sort of ravine, the opposite side rising abruptly, and is covered with timber. Here we have our picket reserve. At the top of this bluff the table-land stretches off to the West, covered with a handsome a crop of oats I ever saw wave before a passing breeze. Just beyond this oat-field, in the edge of which are the rebel pickets, while we are stationed behind stumps and trees on this side.[29]

Facing the Federals was Prince John Magruder's command consisting of three two-brigade divisions. From a fort on Mrs. Charles L. Price's farm on the north side of Nine Mile road to the railroad tracks of the Richmond & York River Railroad, the Confederate line was held by Prince John Magruder's command consisting of Magruder's division along with the divisions of Maj. Gen. David R. Jones and Maj. Gen. Lafayette McLaws. Brigadier General Jones was on the left of the line with the brigades of Col. George T. Anderson, on the left, and Col. Robert Toombs on the right. These two brigades had the

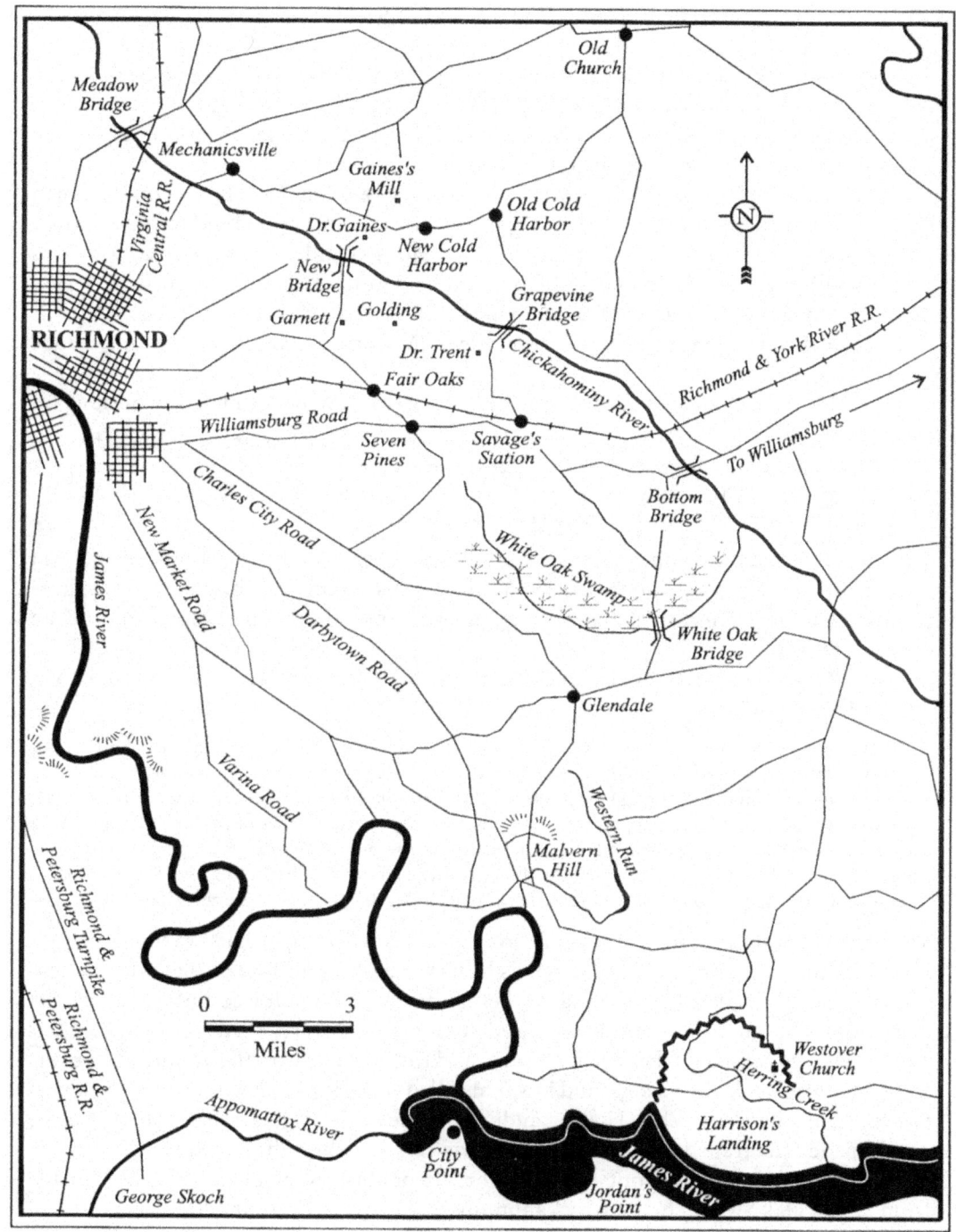

Richmond and vicinity map.

important mission of observing and defending against enemy movements at New Bridge and across Dr. James M. Garnett's wheat field. Brig. Gen. Richard Griffith's brigade of Magruder's division, on the right of Toomb's brigade, extended Magruder's line to the Nine Mile Road. Encamped between the Nine Mile Road and the Richmond & York River Railroad was Howell Cobb's brigade of Magruder's division and Brig. Gen. Paul J.

Semmes' and Brig. Gen. Joseph B. Kershaw's brigades of McLaws' division. Since Magruder was in command of the entire line he delegated field command of the two brigades of his division to Lafayette McLaws. South of the railroad the three brigades of Maj. Gen. Benjamin Huger's division extended the line to White Oak Swamp.[30]

McClellan had Porter's V Corps at Beaver Dam Creek and New Bridge on the north side of the Chickahominy River securing the right flank and protecting the railroad, as well as Brig. Gen. Silas Casey's division at White House Landing. On the south side was Franklin's VI Corps with Sumner's II Corps on his left flank. Sumner's left flank rested on the Richmond & York River Railroad where it connected with Heintzelman's III Corps which stretched to the White Oak Swamp. Keyes IV Corps remained at Bottom's Bridge as the reserve.[31]

Pvt. Daniel A. Cooledge of the 2nd Vermont's Co. A wrote in his diary on June 6:

> We find that we are near the bridges which we have been building [while on the other side of the river]. We were sent on fatigue at the bridge. Carried poles for the bridge which was in danger of being carried off by the water. When we got through there we went on over half a mile farther to bring up some commissary stores. I helped bring some bacon.[32]

The men of Smith's division would work on bridges, roads and fortifications for the next two weeks. To add to the men's misery Smith had his regiments stand at arms at three a.m. every morning and remained in line of battle until after sunrise ready to repel an enemy attack.[33]

Pvt. Warren E. Bliss of Co. G, 4th Vermont, a 21-year-old farmer from Calais, Vt., wrote of the situation:

> We have to form & stand in line of Battle every morning from 3 o'clock till 5 and are called up about every night in to line as there will be some trouble (either imaginary or real) among the Pickets. There is a great deal of fast riding being done to day about the Camps by Officers & Orderlys, & the appearance is that something important is about to be done. every man has been ordered to have his canteen filled with Tea or Coffee to night, & have 20 extra rounds of Cartridges to carry in his pocket And the sick are all being carried to Hospitals across the Creek to the rear & pioneers & fatigue partys are cutting roads through the timber as far as our picket Line for the Artillery &c. &c.[34]

This continued until it became evident from the ever-growing sick list the men needed rest. Realizing the men could not go on as he had ordered, Smith required only one regiment in each brigade to be under arms before daylight. This slowed the rising sick list to an extent, but the sickness still increased, due to the rain-drenched clothing, blankets and provisions caused by the frequent rains, and the malaria from the swamps and overflowed bottom lands. The camps and hospitals filled with sick men, and hospital steamers ran constantly between White House Landing and the hospitals in Washington, Baltimore and Philadelphia transporting thousands of victims of "Chickahominy fever."[35]

To protect the Union front a series of forts, redoubts and rifle pits were constructed from White Oak Swamp to the Chickahominy River on the Gouldin Farm. The redoubt on the Gouldin Farm anchoring the line at the Chickahominy River was built by Baldy Smith's third brigade. When completed it was named "Fort Davidson" after the brigade commander Brigadier General Davidson.[36]

While McClellan's troops were corduroying roads and building bridges, Lee, wanting to take the offensive was reorganizing his army. On June 11, anxious to learn of McClellan's intentions, Lee ordered 29-year-old Brig. Gen. James Ewell Brown "Jeb" Stuart, commander of all of the Army of the Northern Virginia's cavalry, to lead a reconnaissance north of the Chickahominy to gather information on McClellan's right flank and the road network between the Chickahominy and Pamunkey Rivers. Stuart told Lee that he believed that he could ride all the way around the Federal forces. Lee, however, did not want to unnecessarily risk any of his cavalry and told Stuart to be content with accomplishing the reconnaissance.

Stuart picked 1,200 men for this expedition, including Lee's son, Rooney who was the commander of the 9th Virginia Cavalry Regiment. Stuart and his troopers left the next morning riding up the Brook Turnpike as though they were going to reinforce Jackson in the Shenandoah Valley. Then, after reaching the Pamunkey River Stuart turned the column and proceeded down the south bank of the river. When Stuart reached Tunstall's Station, on the Richmond & York River Railroad, he was only four miles from the Federal supply base at White House Landing. He was tempted to destroy it, but with Union cavalry nipping at his heels, he decided the risk was too great. He continued on to Providence Forge where the command was barely able to cross the swollen Chickahominy to safety on June 14, before being attacked.

In Stuart's absence Lee had some anxious moments. Besides worrying about Stuart, he received intelligence that McClellan was being reinforced, but did not know to what extent. Also, the muddy roads that had brought McClellan to a standstill were quickly drying up which would allow him to bring his siege artillery up from White House Landing. As soon as Stuart crossed the Chickahominy River to safety he sent a messenger to Lee to report his success.

In three days Stuart and his men traveled nearly 150 miles, destroyed a considerable amount of Union property, captured 165 prisoners, and lost only one man. Stuart reached Lee's headquarters on June 15. He informed Lee of the roads and terrain between the rivers and let him know that McClellan seemed content to supply his army from White House Landing. The most important news was the Union Army's right flank, Porter's V Corps, was all alone on the north side of the Chickahominy with nothing between it and Fredericksburg. This left Jackson's route to the Federal rear wide open. Of particular importance was that the roads behind the Federal lines had not dried up as quickly as they had behind Confederate lines, meaning McClellan would be stymied for several more days. With this intelligence Lee now had time to formulate his plan of battle.[37]

The obvious course of action for Lee was to attack McClellan's isolated V Corps. If successful Lee could interdict McClellan's supply line, a combination of the Richmond & York River Railroad and a network of country roads, from White House Landing which McClellan needed to supply his forward positions. This transportation network supplied ammunition and equipment to the army as well as daily meals for the 117,000 soldiers and forage for 10,000 horses and mules.[38]

Lee planned to keep Magruder's and Huger's divisions of 25,000 men on the south side of the Chickahominy to confront McClellan's 70,000. In the meantime, Lee, with the rest of his army, would hit Porter's V Corps, however; to do so Lee needed the support of Stonewall Jackson's Army of the Valley. During May Jackson defeated Union Forces in the Shenandoah Valley at McDowell, Front Royal, and Winchester. On June 8–9 he defeated the Federals at Cross Keys and Port Republic. At that point Federal troops were withdrawn from the Valley and Jackson was free to reinforce Lee. Jackson's army would add 18,000 more men to Lee's 47,000-man attack force which would be more than enough to destroy Porter's 30,000-man V Corps. Leaving his troops to be loaded aboard trains, Jackson headed for Richmond. He arrived at Lee's headquarters on the June 23. Shortly after Jackson's arrival, Major Generals Longstreet, A.P. Hill, and D.H. Hill arrived and went into Lee's office where Lee laid out his plan of attack.[39]

Jackson was to move to Ashland, 16 miles north of Richmond. Then, on the day before the battle he was to march southeast with Stuart covering his left flank. Marching south Jackson would attack Porter's right flank and rear. As Jackson's march would be at some distance from the Chickahominy River, A.P. Hill, whose division would be opposite the Meadow Bridges, was to send Brig. Gen. Lawrence O'Bryan Branch's brigade up the Chickahominy to a place called Half Sink. When Jackson started his march, Branch was to move to the enemy's side of the Chickahominy and advance parallel to the river toward Mechanicsville. This way he could eliminate any enemy outposts that might threaten Jackson' right flank and clear out any Yankees on his side of the Meadow Bridges giving A.P. Hill an uncontested crossing.[40]

After crossing the Meadow Bridges A.P. Hill would advance on Mechanicsville. There he would clear out any Federal troops and open the Mechanicsville Bridge for D.H. Hill and Longstreet. After crossing the Chickahominy D.H. Hill would march past A.P. Hill's rear and support Jackson. Longstreet would cross the Chickahominy River and support A.P. Hill.[41]

Lee's units would roll down the Chickahominy and attack the Federal position in front of New Bridge. After defeating Porter contact would be reestablished with the Confederate divisions on the south side of the river. The advancing column would press on toward its final objective: the Richmond & York River Railroad. After explaining his plan Lee left his division commanders alone to finalize the details. June 26 was the date they set for the attack.[42]

Back on Gouldin's farm, on June 20, one of the inevitable sort of accidents that happen in military units occurred in the 4th Vermont. Corporal Silas H. Stone, a 23-year-old house painter from Danville, Vt., in Co. A was on picket duty. After he had been relieved of his post and returned to the reserve camp he remembered that he had not removed the cap from his loaded rifle. In the process of pulling back the hammer to remove the cap his thumb slipped and the hammer came down on the cap discharging the weapon. The ball went through the top of his left foot and out the bottom, breaking several bones along the way. He was taken to the regimental hospital where his foot was patched up and the next day he was sent to the large army hospital located at Savage's Station south of Richmond. Stone would return to his regiment only to be wounded again in the battle of the Wilderness.[43]

Senseless accidents also happened on the Confederate side on Garnett's Hill as remembered by Pvt. William T. Fluker, a 17-year-old soldier in Co. D, 15th Georgia. On June 16 while the 15th Georgia was on picket duty near the John R. Garnett house, a Pvt. John McCluskey accidentally discharged his musket and killed his mess mate Pvt. Jesse M. Hackney. Overcome with grief McCluskey pleaded with his regimental commander to have him shot. Naturally the colonel refused his request. Ironically, one week later at the battle of Garnett's Farm, on June 27, Pvt. McCluskey was mortally wounded within several yards from the spot where he had shot his friend. Fluker described McCluskey as a typical Irishman with a jolly nature, full of Irish songs and wit, but no one ever saw him smile after the accident. When McCluskey was killed, he fell on top of Pvt. Fluker. First Lt. John Tilley pulled McCluskey off Fluker and was himself killed by the enemy while doing so.[44]

While on the picket line enemy sharpshooters were a constant threat. Finally, on

3. The Battles of Garnett's Hill and Gouldin's Farm

June 13 an unofficial truce was worked out on the front lines as the 2nd Vermont's Private Cooledge noted in his diary, "We came out at nine. A flag of truce was sent in by our officers and it is agreed that there shall be no more picket firing. This is a wise arrangement as we can rest better and there will not be much chance for a false alarm."[45]

George H. Randall of the 3rd Vermont's Co. A wrote about what he had witnessed:

> I suppose when I tell you that our pickets and the rebel pickets are so near each other that they can talk with each other and I am so near I hear them talking this very moment but the two partys have agreed not to fire on pickets so they have some funny talks with each other.... I shall stay on picket till morning. I have to go once in 15 days and cary a stretcher so if any one gets wounded I help cary them to camp.[46]

Apparently not everyone abided by the truce. On June 23 Pvt. Eleazer Wells Bartholomew, a 36-year-old bachelor farmer in Co. E, 4th Vermont, went to the 5th Vermont's camp to purchase some items from the sutler. While Bartholomew was talking with a small group of men a rebel sharpshooter spotted them and fired. Bartholomew was hit in the left groin. The bullet went through him and slightly wounded two other men in the group. After being treated in the field Bartholomew was sent home on furlough to recuperate. Surprisingly, he was back with his company in August, but was on light duty the rest of his time in the army. The rebel that shot Bartholomew was killed later that day by a sharpshooter from the 4th Vermont.[47]

In an attempt to reduce the number of men getting sick in the 3rd Vermont Major Thomas O. Seaver published General Order No. 16 on June 21 which read:

> Company commanders will have their men bathe at least three times a week. The men will be put in charge of efficient noncommissioned officers. Company commanders will use all proper means to promote the cleanliness of their men in order to avoid the appearance of all vermin common to camp life.

Whether or not the General Order had any effect on the men's health remains unrecorded.[48]

On June 24 Baldy Smith asked General McClellan to come to his line of defense. Upon arrival McClellan was taken forward and shown the terrain. In the distance across Nine Mile Road was the site of an old tavern that was a key position. If McClellan could take the position it would be much to his advantage. From there he could turn Magruder's left flank which would allow him to bring his siege guns closer to Richmond and he could shorten his line of communication with Porter. Smith assured McClellan that his division could capture the position if he was supported by Sumner's II Corps on his left. McClellan agreed to Smith's plan, but said that he wanted his reserve artillery to have a chance to distinguish themselves before an infantry assault.[49]

Also on June 24, the roads were finally dry enough that McClellan started slowly bringing his siege guns forward clogging the roads as the 2nd Vermont's Pvt. Daniel Cooledge noted in his diary, "Our comassary stores are with difficulty brought up. The road is taken to a great extent with trains loaded with siege guns."[50]

During the evening of June 24 McClellan ordered General Heintzelman, whose III Corps stretched from Fair Oaks south to the White Oak Swamp, to "take advantage of the weakness of the enemy and push your pickets at least to the edge of the next clearing." McClellan hoped to gain possession of James M. Garnett's field on the night of June 25. Once taken, McClellan planned to move the next day to Old Tavern. There he would have high ground that would allow his siege guns to rake the Confederate left as well as securing New Bridge and he wanted Heintzelman's and Sumner's Corps a little closer for support. Heintzelman kicked off the attack at 8 a.m. the next morning. This battle variously known as Oak Grove, French's Field, King's Schoolhouse, and The Orchard, lasted until almost dark with Union troops advancing their line only a quarter to a half mile while losing 626 men to the Confederate's 441. This was the first of a series of battles that would be known as the Seven Days' Battles and would be McClellan's last offensive action.[51]

Word of the battle soon reached General Lee which concerned him as to his own plan of battle and he rode to the Williamsburg road to examine the situation for himself. Surveying the situation Lee felt that McClellan was not attacking because he was aware of Jackson's advance, but it appeared that he would be on the offensive soon.[52]

On the morning of June 26 Lee woke to a perfect day for battle, no rain and moderate temperatures. Then came a message from Jackson and the day started to fall apart. Jackson informed Lee that he had been delayed and would not be at his jump-off point, the Central Railroad between Ashland and Richmond, until 6 a.m., three hours late. Although disappointed Lee decided to continue on. A.P. Hill's division was on its way to the Meadow Bridges and Longstreet and D.H. Hill were moving on the Mechanicsville Turnpike toward the bridges they were to cross. By 8:00 a.m. A.P. Hill, D.H. Hill, and Longstreet were in position. Now the wait for Jackson began. Jackson sent Branch a message about 9:00 a.m. that his lead elements were crossing the Virginia Central Railroad. This meant that Jackson was already six hours behind schedule. Finally, near 3 p.m. the sound of musketry came echoing down the Chickahominy. Surely Jackson was about to flank the Union position on the other side of Beaver Dam Creek. All was excitement as A.P. Hill's men pushed the union troops east through Mechanicsville clearing the way for D.H. Hill's division to cross the Chickahominy and support Jackson. It was now 4 p.m. and there were still three hours of daylight left. Maybe the day could be saved after all.[53]

When Lee arrived at Mechanicsville he discovered the truth. A.P. Hill had not waited for Branch and Jackson at the Meadow Bridges. Disregarding orders he started the attack on his own. While he had secured the bridges and Mechanicsville, his troops were in the open being hammered by the Union artillery on the hill across Beaver Dam Creek. Opposite Lee was Brig. Gen. George A. McCall's division, which had been released from the I Corps and arrived on June 10, on the high ground. A direct frontal assault on the Federals would be suicidal. In an attempt to fix attention on Beaver Dam Creek and occupy McCall specifically and McClellan generally, Lee's maneuvering got out of hand and became a real attack. The gray-clad troops did their best, but were cut to ribbons. Darkness finally fell and the rebels pulled back. The battle of Mechanicsville had cost the Confederates 1,484 casualties versus the Federal's 361.[54]

During the afternoon of the fighting at Beaver Dam Creek, McClellan had his chief engineer search for a new position for the V Corps. McClellan wanted a new position that would not only give Porter a good line of defense, but would also allow him to guard the Grapevine, Alexander's, Woodbury's, and Duane's Bridges across the Chickahominy. The site chosen was a fairly large open plateau, called Turkey Hill, varying in height from 40 to 80 feet, approximately two miles wide and a mile deep. On Turkey Hill were three dwellings, the Watt, McGhee, and Adams Houses, but the battle fought there the next day would forever be called the battle of Gaines' Mill. Although almost a mile away, Dr. Gaines' mill was the most familiar place name to all involved.[55]

During the fighting at Mechanicsville and Beaver Dam Creek the troops in Smith's

3. The Battles of Garnett's Hill and Gouldin's Farm   63

division could see a lot of the battle from their position overlooking the Chickahominy. To be ready to reinforce Porter if necessary, Smith had his men wear their equipments all day and stack their weapons within easy reach, but the call never came.[56]

That evening McClellan received intelligence that Jackson's army had arrived and would threaten Porter's right and rear. Not only would Porter be threatened, but the railroad to the huge supply base at White House Landing would be vulnerable. Under the false impression that he was facing 200,000 Confederates, McClellan decided to change his base of supply to the James River leaving Porter one day more on the north bank of the Chickahominy River to hold back Lee and cover the start of the Army of the Potomac's "change of base."[57]

Also on the evening of June 25 Smith again received a note from McClellan postponing the attack at Old Tavern until the next night. Then, the next night, June 26, Smith received another note from McClellan ordering him not to bring on a general engagement at all and was ordered to go to work that night and construct a redoubt on Garnett's Hill. McClellan said the guns would be ready to be mounted the next morning. Although within 30 paces of the rebel pickets, Col. Barton S. Alexander, of the engineers, started to work that night with troops from the Vermont Brigade. Some of the regiments were on guard while others dug a large redoubt and rifle pits along the east rim of Labor in Vain Ravine. The men dug so quietly that the rebels were unaware of the works existence until daylight. The 2nd Vermont's Pvt. Wilbur Fisk described the operation:

> That night there was a detail of picked men sent to dig a rifle-pit close up to the rebel line. This was rather delicate and dangerous business; the men selected were those that could work rapidly, keep quiet, and fight if necessary. The rest of the regiment—and I don't know but that other regiments were sent out on the same business—went as guard. Very cautiously we crept up to the place we were to occupy, as a hunter would approach a sleeping lion, and all night we lay there giving the officers all the annoyance imaginable to keep us from falling asleep. The muffled sound of the picks, spades and shovels was all that disturbed the silence of the night. At first appearance of daylight, the guard withdrew and were relieved by the regiments.

When complete the redoubt was named Fort Lincoln and was large enough to hold 30 pieces of artillery.[58]

The morning of Friday, June 27, promised another hot and sultry day and another day of wholesale bloodletting. When A.P. Hill renewed his attack along Beaver Dam Creek early in the morning he encountered a delaying force that slowed his advance until he was finally stopped completely at about 2 p.m. by Porter's main defensive line located on the bluffs overlooking Boatswain Swamp. Charges by a number of other Confederate brigades also failed to get through the fire-swept swamp to attack the Federal line. Longstreet, arriving on A.P. Hill's right, saw that he would face the same difficulties, so Lee ordered him to delay his attack until Jackson could get into position to hit the opposite flank. As had happened the day before, Jackson's arrival was delayed. Meanwhile Longstreet was ordered to conduct a diversionary attack to relieve the pressure on the Confederate right until Jackson could attack.[59]

A guide, misunderstanding Jackson's destination, led him down a wrong road. Felled trees across the road caused further delay. It was late afternoon before Jackson's three divisions arrived, but Lee finally had all of his 56,000 men on the battlefield and in position to attack.[60]

During the afternoon Porter was reinforced with 5,000 more troops. Around 7:00 p.m., Lee, hoping to finish off Porter, ordered an all-out assault. The main effort was aimed at Brig. Gen. George W. Morell's division over the same ground that A.P. Hill had failed to carry earlier in the day. This time Brig. Gen. John B. Hood and Col. Evander Law spearheaded the attack. Hood cheered his men on as Federal artillery fire tore through his ranks, but the gray line never faltering streamed down the wooded slope and across the shallow creek. Morell, reinforced by Slocum's division, could not stop the Confederate attack. Hood and Law's men charged up the slope and forced a retreat along the entire Federal front. With darkness approaching, Porter's reinforced Corps began a withdrawal toward the Chickahominy. Nightfall brought an end to the carnage. The day's fight had cost Lee about 9,000 casualties and Porter about 6,800.[61]

As Lee was opening the battle on the north side of the Chickahominy, Magruder, on the south side, had orders to hold his position in front of the enemy against attack at all costs and to conduct demonstrations to discover the Federals' intentions and to keep them on the south side of the Chickahominy River.[62]

On the Union side of the line opposite Magruder, June 27 started off quietly enough, but that soon changed. About 8 a.m. the Green Mountain Boys were relieved from the front line and returned to camp. Hancock's orders were to complete the redoubt and rifle pits and be prepared to defend them. Hancock positioned his regiments with the 43rd New York on the right flank toward the Chickahominy River. Next was the 5th Wisconsin with the 6th Maine on its left. On the left of the 6th Maine was the 49th Pennsylvania located in the rear of the newly constructed Labor in Vain Redoubt. In the redoubt were two companies of the 1st U.S. (Berdan's) Sharpshooters.[63]

Not long after Hancock got into position Smith could see the rebels forming on the Nine Mile Road and in the rear of John R. Garnett's house, but while moving his units to defend his position he received an order from Franklin to do nothing to bring on a general engagement. To obey this order, and yet defend his division, Smith ordered Hancock to fall back to the woods about a 100 yards back from the east bank of Labor in Vain Ravine while keeping a strong picket force in the rifle pits that were being constructed. Hancock left the 49th Pennsylvania in place and pulled back his other three regiments. Meanwhile, Capt. J. Howard Carlisle's Battery E, 2nd U.S. Artillery and First Lt. Adelbert Ames' Battery A, 5th U.S. Artillery, under the command of Col. George W. Getty, and five 30-pounder Parrotts of the 1st Connecticut Heavy Artillery, were placed in position on a high mound on the east side of the ravine to cover Hancock's left flank and to be able to lob shells in the direction of Old Tavern.[64]

Although the rebels did a considerable amount of maneuvering no advance was made. Then, somewhere between 10:00 a.m. and noon, the reports differ widely, the rebels opened up on Smith's artillery and infantry with some three or four batteries from the crest of the hill near the overseer's house between Dr. John R. Garnett's and James M. Garnett's houses. The Union guns quickly replied. Captain Carlisle mentioned the intensity and destruction of the Confederate artillery in his after-action report:

> At about 12 p.m. the enemy opened fire on us, which was returned, and the firing soon became hot on both sides. The position of the enemy's guns commanded ours, and they had the advantage of being nearly concealed by the crests in the field. Their guns were 6-pounders, 12-pounders, and rifled pieces of unknown caliber, and their firing rapid and true. Their fuses were also well timed, shell and shrapnel exploding among and around our guns with rapidity and precision. Our fire soon caused them to change position, but they immediately reopened fire from a new position, firing probably from about twenty-four guns from their redoubts, placing us under a fire from the front and two oblique fires. Our limber-boxes being exhausted, two caissons were brought up and the fire kept up with as much rapidity, but with deliberate aim. We were crowded close together, owning to the nature

A masked battery of 10-pounder Parrott rifles on the Gouldin farm (Vermont Historical Society).

of the ground, making us a fine target. The enemy also frequently changed position. The fire was very hot for about an hour and a half and then quickly died away. During the last twenty minutes of the firing the enemy used but little shell. Our range varied from 900 yards to 1,700 yards with the enemy's change of position. Two men were killed at the guns and 2 wounded. Four horses were killed and 3 disabled. One wheel was broken by a shot; also a sponge staff and a maneuvering handspike shot from the trail. Two of the other gun-carriages were marked by shot, but not injured, and our guidon torn and burned by shrapnel.[65]

During the bombardment the Vermont Brigade's camps were hit and several men were killed or wounded. The first Vermont casualty was Private Andrew Laffie of the 5th Vermont's Co. H who was killed outright. The 18-year-old farmer from Brandon, Vt., was hit in the right shoulder by a cannon ball and killed instantly. He left a mother and disabled father that depended on him for their support. Several years after Andrew's death his mother, Mary, applied for and received a dependent mothers' government pension of $8 a month.[66]

Another 5th Vermont casualty was Company A's Corp. George H. Parker from Montgomery, Vt. Corporal Parker was severely wounded on the left side of his back just below the shoulder blade by a shell fragment. The fragment gouged out an ugly wound measuring five inches long, two inches wide and one-half inch deep. The missile also fractured several of his ribs that never healed properly and were left deformed. Although he would survive his wound, Parker suffered from it the rest of his life.[67]

Private Samuel A. Shattuck from Winhall, Vt., in the 2nd Vermont's Co. I was also hit by a shell fragment. The hot piece of steel hit him in the lower right arm causing a compound fracture of his radius. He returned to his regiment at the end of June of 1863, but the wound broke open again soon afterward. Shattuck was finally given a disability discharge from the army on December 30, 1863.[68]

Sergeant Frederick M. Kimball of the 6th Vermont's Co. D provided a description of what the cannonading was like in his regiment's camp in a letter to the editor of the *Vermont Standard*:

> The enemy had got our position, and opened a battery upon us. This made some scattering of the boys, yet it did not last long. One shell, as we were in line of battle, in our street, struck the ground but a few feet behind the rear rank man, and had we not been lying on the ground, or had it burst, it would doubtless have mowed our ranks; but it bounded and passed harmlessly away. Another passed through Captain [Oscar A.] Hale's tent, and thus they came among us.[69]

After about an hour-and-a-half of firing the Federal artillery finally silenced the rebels' guns. During the day Magruder continued to maneuver his units, as he had on the Peninsula, and had his pickets fire on the Yankees fooling the Union generals into believing an all-out attack was imminent. That afternoon Franklin was ordered by McClellan to

The 3rd Vermont's Capt. Oscar A. Hale at his tent after it had been hit by a Confederate shell (Vermont Historical Society).

Opposite: **Battle of Garnett's Hill, June 27, 1862.**

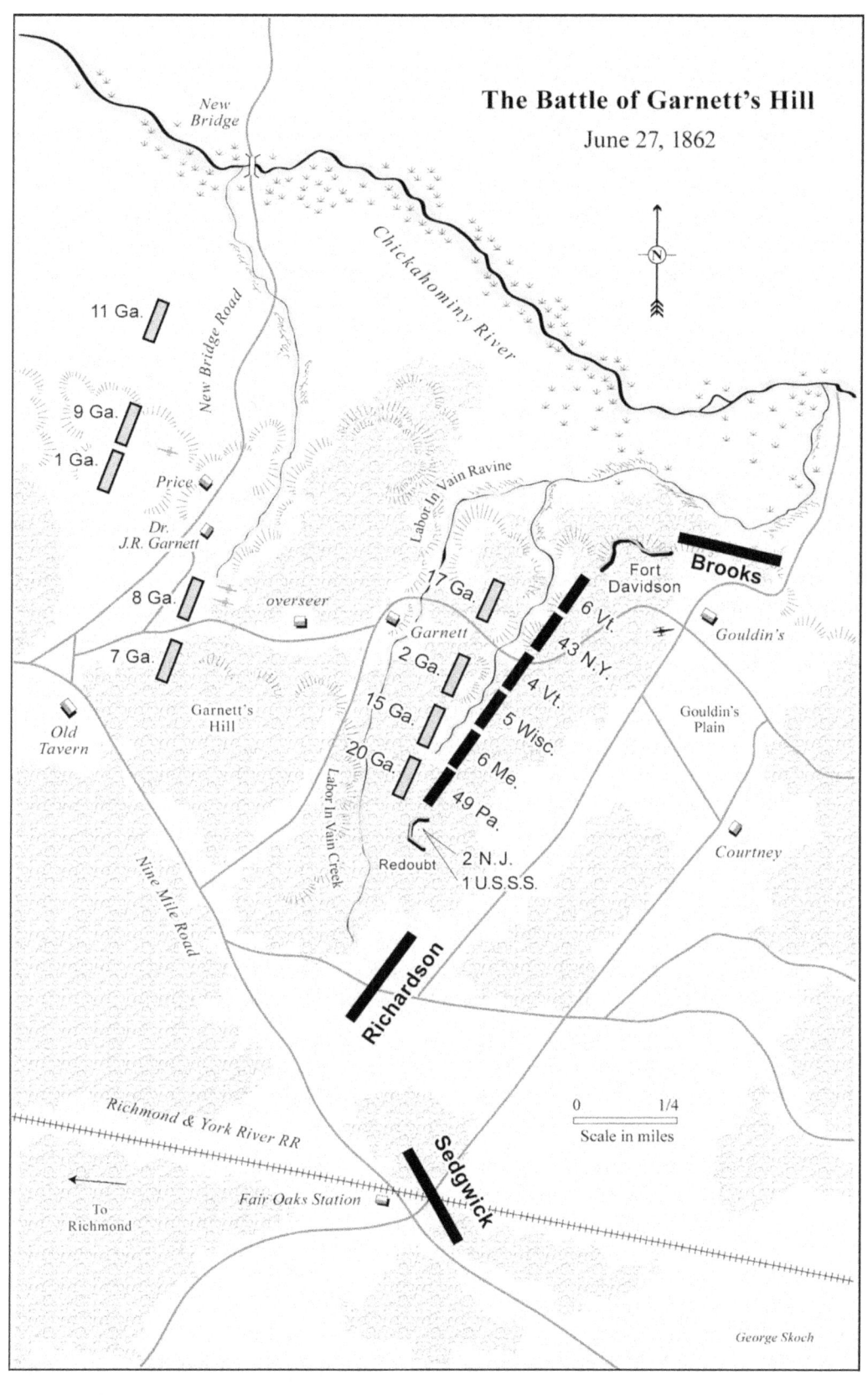

send Slocum's division to the north side of the Chickahominy to support Porter. That left Smith's line stretched thinner than ever.[70]

In the early part of the afternoon, having probably discovered that half of Franklin's VI Corps had been sent across the Chickahominy River, General Magruder notified his division commanders of his intention to "feel" the enemy along his entire front and directed them to issue the necessary orders; however, confusion and delay in implementing Magruder's "intention" resulted in a delay of the advance until late afternoon. The 2nd and 17th Georgia regiments of Robert Toombs' brigade were to move forward from James M. Garnett's house. The 13th Mississippi of Griffith's brigade and the 7th South Carolina of Kershaw's brigades were to advance across Garnett's wheat field north of Nine Mile Road. The 8th South Carolina of Kershaw's brigade was to feel the enemy line between Nine Mile Road and the railroad.[71]

At about 3:00 p.m., seeing the rebels maneuvering as though they might attack, Baldy Smith ordered General Brooks to send one of his regiments forward to reinforce Hancock. Brooks, whose brigade was under arms in their camps, sent the 4th Vermont. The Green Mountain Boys were inserted between the 5th Wisconsin and the 43rd New York pushing the 43rd closer to the Chickahominy River. General Brooks also offered to take charge of the right of Hancock's line, which Hancock readily agreed to.[72]

On the west side of Nine Mile Road the commander of the 7th South Carolina formed his men and waited for the attack order from Col. Barksdale. The word did not come until 4:30 p.m. The 7th South Carolina quickly deployed its skirmishers and prepared to advance, but before ordering an advance the 8th South Carolina arrived on the field. The commander of the 8th South Carolina ordered the 7th South Carolina to advance with the 8th South Carolina. The 7th South Carolina moved across Nine Mile Road and formed on the left flank of the 8th South Carolina and the two regiments moved forward together. On the east side of Nine Mile Road, the 1st Georgia Regulars and the 9th Georgia of Col. George T. Anderson's brigade threw out skirmishers and prepared to advance. The South Carolinians and Georgians were about to meet Brig. Gen. William W. Burns' and Brig. Gen. Willis A. Gorman's brigades of Richardson's division of Sumner's II Corps.[73]

Pickets from Toombs' brigade were near Hancock's brigade along Labor in Vain Ravine east of James M. Garnett's house. Realizing that when the South Carolinians and Georgians made contact with Richardson's brigades Toombs' pickets would take heavy fire from the Yankees in their front, General Jones sent the following order to Toombs:

> The divisions to your right have been ordered by General Magruder to feel the enemy in their front with strong pickets, and to follow up to the utmost any advantage which may offer or success which may issue. You are ordered to do the same, taking as your signal for advance the commencement of the movement on your right.[74]

The South Carolinians had just started to advance when the Union pickets opened fire on their skirmishers which the rebels returned in kind. Then the Yankee artillery opened up on the woods through which the South Carolinians were advancing with shells and canister. The rebels then ran in front of Richardson's entrenchments. With the incoming rifle fire and artillery from the Yankees the South Carolinians were halted and ordered to lie down to avoid annihilation. After the commander of the 8th South Carolina was satisfied that further advancement was futile he ordered both regiments to fall back.[75]

On the east side of Nine Mile Road the 1st Georgia Regulars and the 9th Georgia advanced beyond the 7th and 8th South Carolina. As the 1st Georgia Regulars was advancing, Pvt. William H. Andrews of Co. M witnessed the gruesome effect of the Yankee artillery:

> On going in, we passed one of our batteries. Just before we got to it, met two men bearing between them a wounded soldier with both legs shot off just above his ankles. A small piece of skin held his feet on. It was a sickening sight to see his feet as they twisted and dangled to his legs. Death would be preferable to such a wound as that.[76]

The Georgians charged forward pushing the Yankee pickets before them before being stopped by the Union artillery; however, before being stopped the Georgians got as far as the Union picket's reserve bivouac area where they picked up knapsacks and canteens, as well as other military and personal items. At this point the fire was so intense the Georgians could go no further and remained in the Union camp until ordered back later that night.[77]

Hearing heavy firing on his right, General Toombs ordered the 2nd Georgia to advance and take a position in the Labor in Vain Ravine in front and to the left of the James M. Garnett house. This put them almost exactly opposite the 6th Maine. The time was between 6:00 and 7:00 p.m. The 2nd Georgia moved into position in Labor in Vain Ravine.[78]

While the South Carolinians and Georgians were advancing rebel batteries in Garnett's field opened on the Union batteries behind Hancock's line, as well as the troops in the Labor in Vain Redoubt and the rifle pits. Union counter-battery fire and rifle fire from Berdan's Sharpshooters in the redoubt soon forced them to retreat.[79]

At approximately 7:30 p.m. the 2nd Georgia advanced rapidly across a wheat field directly at the 6th Maine. The 6th Maine's commander, Col. Hiram Burnham, described what happened next in his after action-report:

> In front of the line occupied by my regiment was a narrow strip of wheat field, perhaps 100 yards wide. This field was most elevated in the center, from which it declined slightly to the woods on either side, the opposite side being skirted by a piece of timber similar to the one we occupied. It was quite dark in the woods; when a few scattering shots from our pickets, posted along the crest in the center of the field, instantly followed by a heavy volley all along our front, brought everyone to his feet. The volley was instantly returned, but the attack came suddenly, and though somewhat surprised, it did not find us off our guard. The firing from both sides was rapid and heavy, and was kept up nearly an hour by the enemy.[80]

When he heard the firing Lieutenant Colonel Buck, of the 2nd New Jersey, moved his reserves into the rifle pits to the right of the redoubt. Together with the two companies of Berdan's Sharpshooters, the men of the 2nd New Jersey opened on the right flank of the 2nd Georgia. Additionally, the 49th Pennsylvania had two hand-cranked Ager machine guns. These guns were not issued by the Federal government, but rather purchased by the governor of Pennsylvania. The Ager was commonly called the "coffee mill gun" because the hopper that held and fed the bullets looked like a coffee grinder. The Ager could spit out 120 58 cal. bullets per minute. The Georgians made several attempts to hit Hancock's line, but the withering fire from muskets, machine guns and artillery finally brought them to a halt leaving many of their men dead and wounded. The 2nd Georgia then protected itself by taking a position behind the crest in the middle of Garnett's field.[81]

Private John P. Humphrey of the 49th Pennsylvania's Co. B, recounted what happened in his regiment in a letter to his cousin:

A heavy body of rebel infantry was on our front, and they swept over the skirmishers and attacked our position. General Hancock was ready and waiting for them. We opened fire on them and our line was a sheet of fire from one end to the other. The rebels struggled manfully to gain our position, but in vain. Our brigade was supported by the gallant 4th Vermont and though the rebels rallied time and again to the assault, they could not stand the fusillade of leaden pellets that swept the crest and piled their dead on the field.[82]

Toombs quickly ordered Col. William M. McIntosh to move his 15th Georgia forward to reinforce the 2nd Georgia. The 15th Georgia crossed the field at the double quick under heavy fire and quickly formed on the 2nd Georgia's left flank. While McIntosh was in front of his regiment cheering on his men he fell mortally wounded with a minie ball in his thigh and was carried from the field. The engagement now became general and fierce all along the line. For a few minutes the 15th Georgia punished the 4th Vermont and the 43rd New York. The 17th Georgia was in line of battle along the fence near Garnett's spring when Toombs ordered it to send a strong picket force to the left of the 15th Georgia.[83]

An unnamed soldier in the 4th Vermont wrote of the rebel attack:

Suddenly the Georgia Brigade before mentioned, advanced in line of battle, through the belt of forest on their side of the line, and as they came on were fired upon by our videttes, who immediately threw themselves into a ditch running through the oat field. Coming into the field out of their cover, the rebel line opened their fire upon the 4th Vermont. Fortunately our men were kneeling, and the bullets passed over us. Rising at once, the 4th poured a deadly fire into their ranks, which told with great power and drove them back into cover, and for two hours we kept them there. Their batteries were also playing at the time, and were answered by ours—the shells from both sides passing over our heads, and making loud, if not harmonious music.[84]

Private Harlan P. Paige, Co. E, 4th Vermont. He finished the war as a first lieutenant (University of Vermont).

As the battle heated up General Brooks brought up the 6th Vermont and placed it on the far right of the line on the right of the 43rd New York. Colonel Lord brought his regiment at the double quick. As the 6th Vermont neared the firing line men began to drop. First Sgt. Oscar G. Kelsey, of Co. G from Warren, Vt., was struck by a minie ball in the right leg just below the knee which broke both leg bones. Kelsey died of his wound on July 9 leaving a 19-year-old widow. Private George A. Shonio, a 21-year-old farmer from Duxbury, Vt., was hit with two minie balls almost simultaneously. The first bullet hit him on the right side of his abdomen and came to rest near the surface of the upper part of his right hip. The second bullet entered near the first and lodged in his groin. It was never removed and he never returned to his company. Pvt. James Clark of Company A took a minie ball in the shoulder. He died in Troy, N.Y., on July 19, while his father was bringing him back to Vermont

3. The Battles of Garnett's Hill and Gouldin's Farm　　　　　　　　71

to recuperate. Once the 6th Vermont got in place, Hancock's line extended from the Labor in Vain Redoubt to the bluff overlooking the Chickahominy River. Companies C and I of the 5th Vermont were also on the picket line in the low ground on the right.[85]

As soon as the 6th Vermont got into position the 43rd New York's skirmishers ran out of ammunition and a portion of the 6th Vermont took their places on the skirmish line while two companies, under the command of Major Oscar L. Tuttle, were sent farther to the right to protect the right flank.[86]

The fighting between Toombs' and Hancock's brigades was now taking place in earnest. Private Harlan P. Paige of the 4th Vermont's Co. E, described his portion of the battle in a letter home:

> Our Reg. was in one row on the picket line in front of Camp Lincoln but we were in the edge of one wood and secesh in the edge of another wood across the field so that neither could see the other but we could see the flashes of their guns and fired accordingly. Secesh fired too high and killed none of us but wounded a very few.[87]

Three of the men wounded in the 4th Vermont were George W. Gibson, Frederick C. Rogers, and William J. Camp. Private George W. Gibson was only 5 feet and four and one-half inches tall, but his small stature did not save him from becoming a target for some rebel. A minie ball struck him in his left cheek shattering his jaw bone. The ball then traveled down his neck near the windpipe and jugular vein exiting over the top of his left shoulder blade. Miraculously, he lost no teeth. In its path of destruction the ball damaged some of the nerves in his left shoulder causing partial paralysis of his left arm. He received a disability from the army the following October. Company A's first sergeant, Frederick C. Rogers, was shot in the left leg. The bullet hit about four inches below his knee joint and damaged his fibula. He survived the wound, but did not return to his company until March of 1863. Twenty-three-year-old Pvt. William J. Camp in Co. A was shot in the left wrist. He was given a disability discharge from the army on August 9.[88]

As the rebel bullets flew over the heads of the men in the 4th Vermont causing leaves and twigs to rain down on them, Company I's Sgt. Marshall H. Twitchell ran up and down the firing line carrying orders from his company commander, Capt. Leonard A. Stearns, to subordinates while Stearns remained hiding behind a tree. Although Twitchell did not like the duty he did as he was told. After the battle several of Twitchell's comrades told him that it appeared that Stearns was trying to get him killed. Twitchell wrote in his autobiography, "I knew he was bad but did not think until then that he was mean enough to try to get me killed for the purpose of closing my lips that I might not divulge secrets damaging to him, which he knew I possessed." Captain Leonard A. Stearns resigned from the army less than a month later on July 28, 1862. Colonel Edwin Stoughton's endorsement for approval of Stearns' resignation included the statement, "This officer has of late become perfectly useless."[89]

Just after dark Toombs was afraid his left flank was in danger of being turned and he sent the remainder of the 17th Georgia forward. Colonel Henry L. Benning positioned his 17th Georgia on the left of the 15th Georgia, but by that time it was so dark Benning stated that, "We could see no enemy." Toombs then ordered the 20th and the 7th Georgia regiments forward. The 20th Georgia came to within 75 yards of the 15th Georgia when it had to ground to avoid the Federal fire that overshot the Confederate front line. The 7th Georgia surged forward, but heavy fire from Berdan's Sharpshooters and the 2nd New

Jersey soon halted them. By now the opposing lines were only 40 yards apart, but it was so dark that neither side could see each other. For a while, however, they continued to fire in the direction of each other's muzzle flashes. Within about an hour and a half after the battle commenced it got so dark that the firing started fizzling out and finally stopped. Thus ended the battle that would be known as the battle of Garnett's Hill.[90]

After the battle the 6th Vermont relieved the 5th Maine and 49th Pennsylvania and held the picket line in the center through the night. The 4th Vermont was withdrawn from the line just before midnight. The rest of the Vermont Brigade lay on their arms in supporting distance of the firing line throughout the night.[91]

During the battle the 4th Vermont had eight men wounded. The 6th Vermont lost one killed, six wounded and one missing. Hancock's brigade, including the Vermont losses, had seven men killed and 111 wounded and missing. While Confederate casualties are sketchy, their loss is estimated to be about 400 killed and wounded.[92]

Around 11 p.m. McClellan gathered his corps commanders together at his headquarters and informed them he intended to abandon his supply base at White House Landing and reestablish it along the James River. Each Corps commander was furnished with a map detailing the respective positions each was to hold to until the next evening. The meeting broke up at about 2 a.m. Sumner's II Corps, Heintzelman's III Corps and Franklins VI Corps would protect the rest of the Army of the Potomac while it made its way to the James River. Sumner would be the overall commander on the ground and Franklin's Corps would be the rear guard. Smith's division was designated as the rear guard to protect the VI Corps as it marched to the James River. Accordingly, Smith had his division up at 3 a.m. on June 28 and in line of battle ready to repel an early morning attack. With no attack forthcoming, the men were released at daybreak to fix their breakfast. They were also informed that right after breakfast they were to pack up and move their camps nearer Fair Oaks Station on the Dr. Robert Courtney farm. Smith's task was to shift his position so that instead of facing to the northwest, his defense line would face the enemy in a more northerly direction across the Chickahominy River. But to be able to have clear fields of fire to the north a large amount of trees had to be felled. Smith put several of his regiments to work felling these trees as he wrote years later in his autobiography:

> The next morning [June 28] I received notice that a movement for a change of base would begin that night, and I was to command the rear-guard. In fact the troops began to move that day, and to make ready for my move I had to make a change of front to the rear and almost at right angles to the line I had held; so that I would look across the Chickahominy instead of looking up it as before.... To change my front and have an open view of the Chickahominy I had to cut down a large forest. In my division I had the 6th Maine and the 5th Wisconsin regiments made up of lumbermen, and all my Vermont regiments were experts with the axe. I formed them all in line facing the front and they went to work. I am sure no such wood cutting ever took place before or will ever again, and I stared in wonder, and almost in awe to see these mighty trees go down like grass before mowers. I learned afterward that they would cut trees only half down and in such a way that the falling of the trees then carried in turn all the others, so that what seemed marvelous to me was only the skill of the lumbermen. This soon allowed me to change my front and I waited results.[93]

While the tree-cutting was taking place all of the sick and wounded in the regimental and brigade hospitals in Smith's division were transferred to the hospital that had been established at Savage's Station on the Richmond & York River Railroad. McClellan had moved his headquarters there during the night.[94]

Observing the movements on the Federal side, Brig. Gen. David R. Jones went to

3. The Battles of Garnett's Hill and Gouldin's Farm

Magruder's headquarters to ask for help from long range guns on the north bank of the river to support an attack on the Yankees who he mistakenly thought were evacuating. Magruder, however, was not at his headquarters so Jones sent an aide across the river to ask Lee for artillery support and then returned to his own lines. In light of this new development Jones had six long range guns brought up near Dr. John Garnett's house and had two shorter range batteries moved into the field near James M. Garnett's house.[95]

To protect Smith's left flank about 100 men from the 49th Pennsylvania were on picket duty in the rifle pits from the right of the Labor in Vain Ravine Redoubt and northward. A portion of the 33rd New York and a detachment of the 77th New York were ordered forward as a reserve for the 49th Pennsylvania pickets. Just as the picket reserve got into position the rebel artillery unleashed a terrific cannonade on Smith's division, mainly on the camps. The time was somewhere between 11 a.m. to 12 p.m., personal accounts vary.[96]

The effect on the Vermont Brigade was electrifying and men scattered as noted by Pvt. Casper H. Dean, a 20-year-old farmer from Monkton, Vt., in Company A of the 6th Vermont:

> About 12 o'clock on the 28th Ult. the rebels run a battery out of a piece of woods in front of us into an open field and commenced shelling our camps very briskly. The Vt. Brigade soon skedaddled down the west bank of the Chickahominy to get out of range. Many shells struck among us but did not kill any of us. Some were wounded. One shell struck a tree and dropped down on one man's knapsack while he was lying down. After being shelled a while, we rec'd orders to march back into a large piece of woods where we formed a line of battle.[97]

During the shelling, according to Dr. Sawin, assistant surgeon of the 2nd Vermont, the Vermont Brigade had two men killed and six wounded. Captain John S. Tyler of the 2nd Vermont's Company C described one of those casualties that occurred in his company:

> The rebels open on us with both infantry and artillery. We remain close to the ground, as a support to the pickets in front. Soon the rebel infantry is repulsed, but their artillery keeps up a galling fire. Then it was that Corpl. Paddleford of my company, with whom I was conversing at the time was struck in the left shoulder by a piece of shell. His wound is not dangerous, but being unable to march he had to be left to the tender mercies of the rebels.[98]

Captain John S. Tyler, Co. C, 2nd Vermont, pictured here as a lieutenant colonel. He was promoted to lieutenant colonel of the 2nd Vermont on April 2, 1864. He became the commander of the 2nd Vermont on May 5, 1864, when the commander was wounded in the Battle of the Wilderness. Tyler was in command less than an hour when he was mortally wounded (U.S. Army History and Education Center).

Corporal Frank G. Paddleford was injured a little more seriously than Captain Tyler initially thought. After being treated in his regiment he was sent to the hospital at Savage's Station. When the hospital at the station was captured on June 30, the day after the battle there, Paddleford became a prisoner of war. He was paroled on September 13 and spent the next month-and-a-half in U.S. Army hospitals. He would not return to his company until the middle of November.[99]

The Green Mountain boys grabbed their knapsacks, haversacks and rifles and headed a half a mile through the woods to the safety of Dr. Courtney's farm.[100]

The historian of the 33rd New York wrote of the rebel artillery fire:

> Shot and shell flew in every direction, crashing through the trees, ploughing up the ground, completely riddling the tents, firing the baggage and commissary stores, and rendering every foot of the camp enclosure untenable. The camp guard, prisoners, sick, convalescents and, others, seizing their arms, immediately sought refuge behind the earthworks, consisting of ditches and the breastwork in front, which had afforded such good protection on the Thursday previous.[101]

While the shelling was taking place General Jones mistook Smith's men scattering as a retreat and ordered General Toombs to get ready to attack. Instead of attacking with his own regiments Toombs ordered Col. George T. Anderson, commanding Jones' third brigade to attack and Toombs would support him. Anderson selected the 7th and 8th Georgia regiments and moved them forward. In the meantime, General Jones set off again to find Magruder, which he did in a short time, and told him about the attack he had ordered. In compliance with Lee's order to initiate no assault except in coordination with a general advance, unless absolutely assured of success, Magruder ordered him to call off the attack at once. General Jones sent one of his aides back to stop the attack, but it was too late.[102]

The shelling only lasted about 45 minutes and taking advantage of the shells raining down on the Yankees, Anderson moved his two regiments toward the jump off point on the west side of Labor in Vain Ravine. About this time the shelling stopped. As the Georgians reached the edge of the ravine the 49th Pennsylvania's pickets on the east side opened fire. Undeterred the 7th and 8th Georgia plunged into the ravine and up the other side into Gouldin's wheat field. Farther to the east the Pennsylvanians could see two more rebel regiments approaching. They were Toombs' 15th and 20th Georgia regiments which also crossed through the ravine and into the wheat field. After climbing up out of the ravine the 20th Georgia was on the far north end of the line with the 15th Georgia on its right followed by the 8th and then the 7th Georgia.[103]

The 33rd New York fell back to its entrenchments not long after the Georgians got a footing on the east side of the ravine. The 49th Pennsylvania's pickets gave the Georgians a couple of volleys before following the 33rd New York. Now the 49th Pennsylvania, 33rd New York and the 77th New York were reunited behind their fortifications. A member of the 33rd New York remembered later:

> The defenses gained, and the co-operation of the remainder of the Regiment secured, a most gallant stand was made. Colonel Taylor [commander of the 33rd New York] had hardly stationed the men in their places before the rebels, flushed with their first success, and confident of easily storming the defenses and capturing the defenders, came charging furiously down upon them. All became hushed along the line as the men nerved themselves for the encounter. The orders to "reserve fire," "fire low," &c., were given in a quiet undertone, and the soldiers, bringing their firelocks to their shoulders and

Opposite: **Battle of Gouldin's Farm, June 28, 1862.**

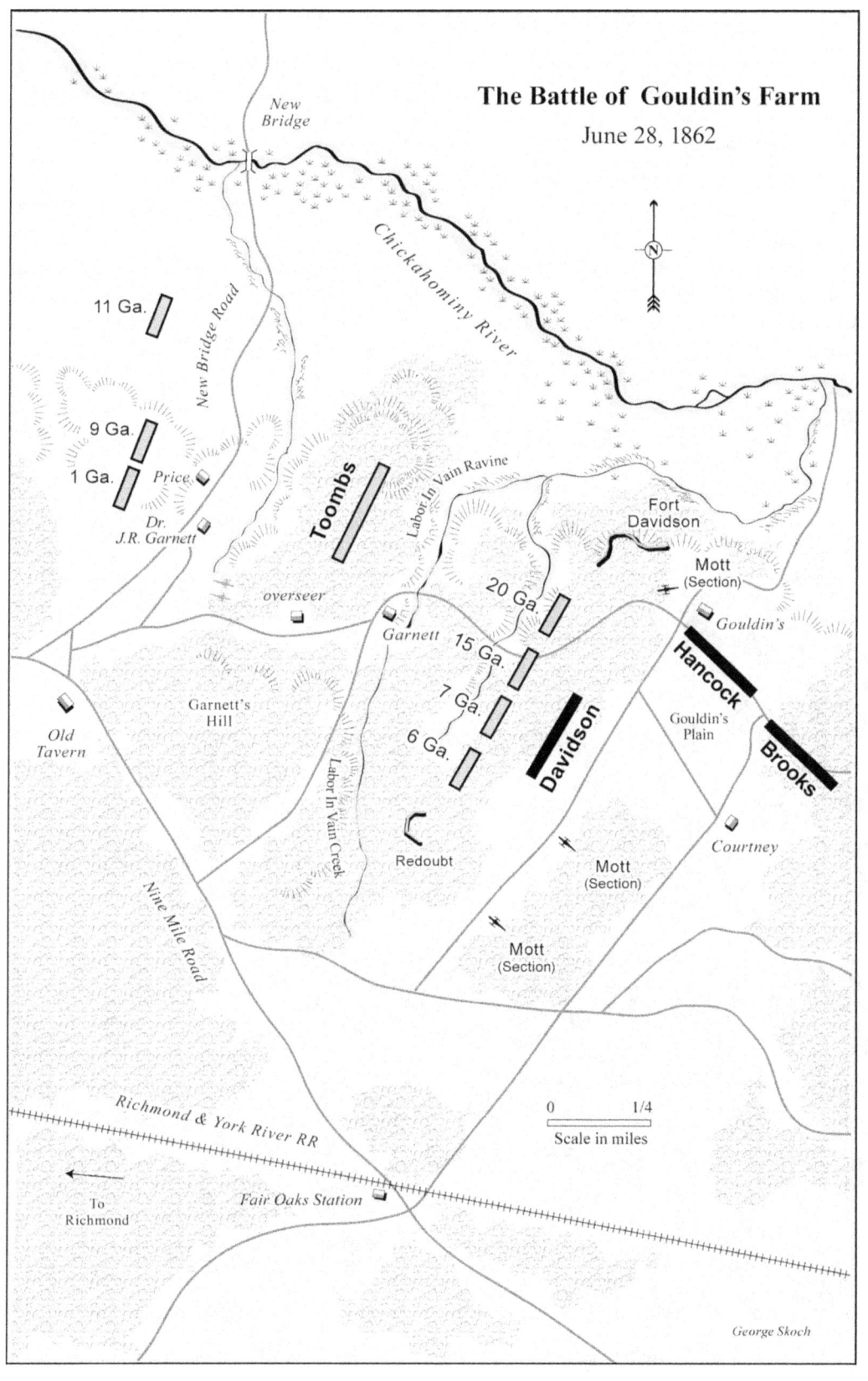

resting them over the top of the parapet, calmly waited the approach of the enemy. On they came, yelling and shouting like demons, till within a few yards of the breastwork when there instantly shot forth from behind it a sheet of flame, followed by another and another, until, staggered by the galling fire, the rebels wavered, broke and fled in great disorder from the field.[104]

In the meantime, the 15th and 20th Georgia had advanced only 30 or 40 paces when a courier arrived and gave them an order from General Toombs to halt in place and support the withdrawal of the 7th and 8th Georgia.[105]

Before the 7th and 8th Georgia received the order to withdraw, Col. Lucius Mirabeau Lamar, commander of the 8th Georgia, and field commander of both the 7th and 8th Georgia, reformed his lines and attacked again. The two Georgia regiments were no match for the entrenched Federals with their muskets and Ager machine guns, and enfi-

The remains of White House after being burned by Union soldiers (Library of Congress).

3. The Battles of Garnett's Hill and Gouldin's Farm   77

lading artillery fire. The Georgians were cut to pieces and had to fall back again. Lamar put his hat on his sword and waved it aloft trying to rally his men for a third time. Making a very conspicuous target Lamar went down with a serious wound in the groin. The Georgians did rally and made a third charge, but as Capt. George O. Dawson, the ranking officer in the 8th Georgia after the battle, wrote in his after-action report, "the enemy made sad havoc in the ranks." The 7th and 8th Georgia retired for the third and final time. The 8th Georgia's lieutenant colonel, John R. Towers, was captured while trying to get Lamar off the field. Also the 8th Georgia's major, Edward J. Magruder, had part of his nose shot off and was captured along with Towers. In addition to the three men already mentioned the 8th Georgia lost one officer killed and three wounded, along with 23 enlisted men killed, 55 wounded and 9 missing. The 7th Georgia lost their lieutenant colonel and one captain wounded. They also had 7 enlisted men killed, 60 wounded and 15 captured.[106]

After the Georgians retreated back across the ravine, the New Yorkers and Pennsylvanians went forward to police the battlefield. They returned with Col. Lamar, Lt. Col. Towers, Maj. Magruder and 9 enlisted men of the 8th Georgia, along with the regiments colors. They also brought in 15 enlisted men from the 7th Georgia and 200 muskets. By 2:00 p.m. the Union picket line was reestablished in the rifle pits on the east rim of the ravine. Magruder's and Smith's lines were quiet the rest of the night.[107]

On June 28, while Smith was being attacked, parts of McClellan's army started moving toward the James River. First 5,000 wagons, loaded with supplies and ammunition, and 26 siege guns left White House Landing and made their way to the river. The herd of cattle was moved on to the James River the next day. What supplies that could not be taken from White House Landing by ship or wagons were destroyed. About noon Keyes' IV Corps started moving toward the White Oak Swamp. Keyes was followed by Porter's V Corps. Finally, Slocum's division of Franklin's VI Corps brought up the rear. Slocum's division was to stop on the south side of White Oak Swamp and serve as the rear guard for the other units.[108]

A casualty of abandoning the supply base at White House Landing was White House itself. During the burning of the supplies, an overzealous Union soldier set fire to the house itself and it burned to the ground, even though McClellan had ordered that it remain untouched.[109]

4

The Battle of Savage's Station

The night of June 28–29 was a tense one for everyone in Smith's division. Smith expected another attack at any minute and had his troops sleep on their arms. In the middle of the night he received his orders for the next day which was to follow the army as the rear guard to the Trent house and then to Savage's Station. Before daylight Smith had his men up and getting their breakfast. The rifle pits on the eastern side of Labor in Vain Ravine remained manned and would remain that way until the division moved out. Smith's mission was to cover the departure of the last wagon train and hold the line against any rebel movement from the Grapevine Bridge area. The wagon trains moved out for Savage's Station and Smith's men followed suit at about 5:00 a.m.[1]

When Smith's division left Gouldin's farm it was nothing like the farm they first camped on earlier in the month. An advertisement for the sale of the Gouldin farm in the September 18, 1862, edition of Richmond's *The Daily Dispatch* tells the sad tale so familiar around Richmond after the withdrawal of McClellan's army:

> **Valuable farm of 552¼ acres in Henrico County**, on the Chickahominy, seven miles east of Richmond, **for sale**. At the request of Mr. Simon Gouldin we offer for sale his valuable farm, located as above, adjoining the farms of Dr. Peterfield Trent and Mr. James Garnett. It contains 552¼ acres, of which about half are cleared, and in a state of fine cultivation. The other half in in heavy, original timber, of which a portion has been cut down by the late army of the invasion, and now supposed to be worth several thousand dollars on the land. The dwelling has five rooms; but all the other buildings have been injured or destroyed by the enemy. As the owner has lost much of his working force, and all his crops, stock, etc., he is unable to work the farm, and hence has concluded to offer the same for sale, and will sale at a reduced rate. The terms of payment can be made most liberal. Mr. Gouldin will be at the farm for the next week, and will take pleasure in showing it to those who may call on him.

The Gouldin house survives to this day, although over the years it has received several modifications.[2]

On the march to the Trent House 38-year-old Tunbridge, Vt., native Pvt. Harvey K. Goodwin of Co. E, 2nd Vermont, fell out of the ranks and sat down against a tree refusing to go any further. First Sergeant Henry R. Hayward said to Goodwin, "Harvey, you will be taken in five minutes if you don't move." But Goodwin would not budge. He just shook his head no and said he did not care. With that Hayward moved on and that was the last he ever saw of Goodwin. Goodwin died in a prisoner of war camp in Richmond the following month on July 7.

Harvey had always been considered eccentric by the people of Tunbridge. He owned a farm of a little over 100 acres where he made the majority of his living, but he also was a part time preacher, poet, penmanship teacher, and portrait painter. Several years prior to the Civil War Harvey was a member of the Tunbridge Militia. After the outbreak of the war Goodwin enlisted in Co. E, 2nd Vermont, as a drummer. It did not take long for Harvey's eccentricity to become evident to everyone in his company. When the regiment was mustered into service in Burlington on June 20, 1861, Harvey initially refused to take the oath but was finally persuaded do so by his comrades.

A month after the Union defeat at Bull Run Goodwin accidentally shot off the end of his right forefinger while cleaning his pistol. He was given a 30-day furlough four days later to go home to Tunbridge to heal up. After returning to his company Goodwin again displayed his bizarre behavior. First Sergeant Hayward stated later, "He would sit for some time with his head between his hands and his elbows on his knees. At those times you could hardly get a word out of him. He would not make any conservation with you at all. Did not do it every day, but often." But worst of all was Goodwin's refusal to beat the army's drum calls. He wanted to use his own. It finally got to the point his drum was taken away from him and he was given a fife to play. Harvey Goodwin left a widow and two children.[3]

After marching for two hours or so on the Fair Oaks Station-Grapevine Bridge Road Smith's men reached Dr. Peterfield Trent's house. After the wagon trains left the Trent house area, Smith sent Hancock's brigade to cover the approach at Sumner's Lower Bridge, downstream from the Grapevine Bridge. Davidson's brigade moved a short distance to the east, going into line near the Dudley farm, again to cover a possible avenue of Confederate approach. General Brooks' Vermonters remained at the Trent house blocking the road they had moved in on. Smith now had all the approaches to Savage's Station from the north covered.[4]

Smith was supposed to have Sumner's II Corps on his right and Slocum's division on his left, but for some unexplained reason McClellan had sent Slocum's division on to White Oak Swamp Bridge without telling Franklin. Sumner was unaware that he was supposed to connect with Smith, thereby leaving both of Smith's flanks exposed. Generals Franklin and Smith rode on to Savage's Station to find out what was going on. Thankfully for the Army of the Potomac the Confederates were unaware of the gaps on Smith's flanks. If they had, the result could have been disastrous.[5]

Early Sunday morning, June 29, Magruder sent scouts forward to the Yankees' earthworks all along his line to determine if they were still manned. Of course, they returned to report that the trenches were empty of Union soldiers. At almost the same time one of General Lee's aides arrived to tell Magruder that two of Longstreet's engineers had also examined the trenches and reported the Yankees' departure to the general. Through intelligence reports he had received Lee was able to piece together the fact that McClellan was moving his army toward the James River rather than back down the Peninsula. To get to the James River McClellan had to move the army to Savage's Station and then down the Williamsburg Road a few miles to White Oak Swamp Road which ran south to White Oak Swamp Bridge. After crossing the swamp the road ran up hill about a mile where it reached the Long Bridge Road. A half-mile west on Long Bridge Road was Glendale, the intersection of the Charles City, Long Bridge, and Willis Church Roads. At Glendale the Union columns would take the Willis Church Road to Malvern Hill. Down the other side of Malvern Hill the Willis Church Road intersected with the River Road where moving a few miles southeast the Army of the Potomac would establish its new base at Harrison's Landing. Harrison's Landing was the name of the wharf on Benjamin Harrison IV's, plantation known as Berkeley.[6]

To have a chance of destroying the Army of the Potomac, Lee would have to bottle up McClellan's column before it reached the naturally strong defensive position on the top of Malvern Hill. If Lee could get troops on Malvern Hill first and Jackson on the Yankees' heels on the White Oak Swamp Road the rest of Lee's divisions could flank the strung-out Yankee column at Glendale. Lee's plan was seemingly sound, but it had a number of ifs. McClellan's most advanced unit, Keyes' IV Corps, was seven miles closer to the James River than Huger's division. The majority of Lee's other divisions, except Magruder's, were north of the Chickahominy River. To have any chance of bagging McClellan, Lee's units would have to move and move fast and he had to have a way to slow McClellan down.[7]

Lee's plan of action was fairly simple. Huger's division was to move down the Charles City Road attacking any Federal units it might encounter and flank any that were on the Williamsburg Road. If no Yankees were found, he was to cross the White Oak Swamp and hold up at Glendale. Major General Theophilus Holmes, on the south side of the James River, was to cross his division to the north side of the river and march to Malvern Hill. He was to be in position the next day, June 30. In order to slow McClellan's rate of march, Magruder was to move out immediately and follow the Federals down the Williamsburg Road and attack his rear guard as soon as he made contact. Lee felt that Magruder's attack, along with McClellan's large and cumbersome wagon train, would slow him down enough that Lee could get his units into position to destroy the enemy forces. Jackson, with D.H. Hill's division still attached, after repairing the Grapevine Bridge, was to cross the Chickahominy River and turn east toward Savage's Station and support Magruder. Longstreet and A.P. Hill had the toughest assignment. They were to cross the Chickahominy River at New Bridge and follow Nine Mile Road to a north-south road that would take them to the Darbytown Road. Then they would follow the Darbytown Road and be in position at Glendale by June 30. General Ewell's infantry and Stuart's cavalry were to stay in position on the north side of the Chickahominy River at Bottom's Bridge to challenge McClellan if he decided to strike out for the lower Peninsula instead of heading to the James River. Again, the plan was fairly simple, but the difficult part would be getting all the units in position at the right place and at the right time.[8]

After sunrise Lt. Col. Robert H. Chilton, of Lee's staff, rode into Magruder's camp and told him that he was to meet General Lee on Nine Mile Road. They left in such a hurry that Magruder had to give orders to his commanders from the saddle, "to put in motion my whole command, which extended over a distance of some miles, directing Brigadier General Griffith's brigade, which was nearest to the road, to advance at once from the center, and ordering Brigadier General Jones' division in advancing to incline toward Fair Oaks Station, as I had been informed that Major General Jackson had crossed or was crossing the Grapevine Bridge, and would operate down the Chickahominy." Upon meeting, Lee filled Magruder in on the plan of attack. Lee and Magruder rode on to Fair Oaks Station where Lee repeated the plan again to Magruder and then left to see Huger.[9]

When Smith's division left the Courtney farm, Sumner's II Corps left the Fair Oaks area and moved down the Richmond & York River Railroad toward Savage's Station. Sumner moved his corps to Mrs. Eliza Allen's farm about a mile east of Fair Oaks Station and took up a position in abandoned Union earthworks on the north side of the railroad

4. The Battle of Savage's Station

that had been constructed after the battle of Fair Oaks and was referred to as the second line of defense. There he formed his corps in line of battle facing west with Brig. Gen. Israel B. Richardson's division on the right and Brig. Gen. John Sedgwick's division on the left. Major General Heintzelman's III Corps marched down the Williamsburg Road and pulled in on Sumner's left on the south side of the railroad.[10]

By the time Lee left Magruder a portion of Kershaw's brigade was arriving at Fair Oaks Station. Magruder directed Maj. Gen. McLaws to consolidate Kershaw's brigade and place it on the south side of the railroad. Then he ordered two regiments of Griffith's brigade to take position in reserve behind Kershaw's brigade, leaving the Williamsburg Road, still farther on the right, unoccupied and open for Huger. Here is where Magruder misunderstood Lee both times Lee explained the plan of attack to him. Magruder understood Lee to say that Huger would be on his right flank on the Williamsburg Road, when in fact, Huger was to take the Charles City Road. Later when Magruder discovered his mistake he sent a message asking for support on his right flank from Huger. Lee had two of Huger's brigades move over to the Williamsburg Road, but told Magruder if they were not needed by afternoon he would recall them.[11]

Magruder then formed the other two regiments of Griffith's brigade on the left of Kershaw with their right flank on the railroad. As soon as Howell Cobb's brigade arrived, it was placed on Griffith's left. Magruder then dispatched an aide to locate Brig. Gen. David R. Jones' division and directed it to form on the left of Cobb's division. Now that his units were for the most part in position, Magruder sent out a detail to clear obstructions from the Richmond & York River Railroad for a rail-mounted gun. Then he sent a staff officer toward Grapevine Bridge, some three miles off, to locate Jackson's troops which he thought had already crossed the Chickahominy River.[12]

The Confederate rail-mounted gun was the first railway battery ever used in warfare. After taking command of the Army of Northern Virginia General Lee was concerned about McClellan bringing up his siege guns from White House Landing. Because of the size of the guns most of them had to be transported by rail on the Richmond & York River Railroad. On June 5, Lee fired off a note to his chief of engineers, Major Walter H. Stevens, asking if he could build a battery to challenge any train bringing McClellan's artillery toward Richmond. In the same note he wondered if a mobile railroad battery would be better than artillery in a fixed position. Next, he wrote Colonel Josiah Gorgas the Confederate Chief of Ordnance if there was a possibility of constructing an iron-plated battery, mounting a heavy gun, on trucks, the whole covered with iron, to move along the Richmond & York River Railroad. Lastly, he sent a note to Captain George Minor, the Confederate Navy Chief of Ordnance and Hydrography, if he could put a large cannon on a railroad flat car protected with an iron apron in front to protect the gun and crew.[13]

The navy complied with Lee's request and put Lieutenant John Mercer Brooke to work on the design. Brooke had already gained fame in the Confederate Navy by designing the conversion of the burned-out hull of the USS *Merrimac* to the Confederate ironclad CSS *Virginia*. The car selected for the battery was a seven-axle flatcar. Not surprisingly the armor protection for the gun was very similar to that of the CSS *Virginia*. The armored shield in front of the car angled back toward the rear at an angle of about 36 degrees. The base of the shield was a layer of 12-inch thick pine covered with a layer of 8-inch thick pine and on top of that a layer of four-inch thick oak. On top of the wood were two layers of steel planks two inches thick and eight inches wide attached with countersunk bolts. A port was cut in the center of the armored shield to allow the muzzle of the gun to protrude. The armament was a single 32-pounder banded rifled gun. The flatcar was pushed by a single steam locomotive. The battery was built near the Richmond & York River Railroad depot in the Rocketts section of Richmond at the base of Chimborazo Hill near the Williamsburg Road. It was delivered to the army on June 22 with 200 rounds of ammunition including 15-inch solid bolt rounds. The southerners often referred to the railroad battery as the "Dry-Land Merrimac" or the "Land Merrimac." As massive and well-constructed as the battery was, it had two flaws. First the gun crew only had protection from the front and were quite vulnerable to small arms fire from the sides and rear. Secondly, the gun had a limited ability to traverse from side to side because it was built to shoot straight down the track at another train.[14]

Forty-eight-year-old First Lt. James E. Barry of the Norfolk United Artillery and 14 of his men volunteered to man the battery. The Norfolk United Artillery was organized in Norfolk several days before the burning of the Portsmouth navy yard by Federal forces in April of 1861. The company was called into service on April 19, 1861, under the command of Captain Thomas Kevill and was stationed at Fort Norfolk.[15]

The company took its name from Norfolk's United Fire Company, of which most of

Library of Congress photograph labeled "Robert E. Lee's railroad battery. (Source: David H. Schneider, "Lee's Armored Car," Civil War Times, Feb. 2011.) Photograph from the main eastern theater of war, the siege of Petersburg, June 1864–April 1865." The photograph was probably taken in the Richmond area as there is no record of the battery being taken to Petersburg in Confederate records (Library of Congress).

Rear view of Lee's railroad battery. The cannon is a 32-pounder Brooke which was designed by Lieutenant John Brooke who also designed the railroad battery (Library of Congress).

its men had volunteered for military service. At Fort Norfolk the company was furnished with muskets and was also placed in charge of four light guns. The company drilled both as infantry and artillery. They also had charge of a battery of heavy guns. When the 41st Virginia Infantry Regiment was formed on May 23, 1861, the United Artillery became its Company E.[16]

When the ironclad CSS *Virginia* was ready for service it was found that she was short 31 men of a full crew and because his men knew how to fire large guns, Captain Kevill was asked for volunteers to make up the difference. When he asked for volunteers the entire company stepped forward. Knowing the strength required to man the large guns on the vessel, Kevill picked 31 of the strongest men in the company. Captain Kevill and his men served on the CSS *Virginia* until she was scuttled in the Elizabeth River on May 11, 1862.[17]

After the fall of Norfolk the Norfolk United Artillery was stationed at Drury's Bluff on the south side of the James River below Richmond. There the unit manned the large guns defending Richmond from Union gunboats. Such was the situation when the company was asked to supply volunteers for the railroad battery.[18]

On its maiden run a timber under the gun broke and the battery had to be repaired. It was finally ready for action on Saturday, June 28, and it was sent down the line to Fair Oaks Station to await action. Between the flatcar with the rifled gun on it and the engine another flatcar was added with cotton bale walls on each side to protect the ammunition for the gun and its sharpshooters assigned to protect the gun crew. The next day, as soon as the tracks were clear, the gun was moved toward Orchard Station and started lobbing shells at the Yankees.[19]

No sooner had the staff officer left to find Jackson than a messenger arrived from Kershaw reporting that the Union troops were in his front and that they were fortified. Magruder ordered Cobb to send a scouting party forward to determine if Union troops were also in front of Magruder's own division. While this was happening, the staff officer returned with Jackson's engineering officer in tow and reported that Jackson had not crossed the river because he was having to rebuild the Grapevine Bridge, but that would be completed in two hours. Meanwhile, Gen. Jones pushed his division forward with the 1st Georgia Regulars deployed as skirmishers. The Georgians advanced about 400 yards when they came under fire from the Union picket line, which they drove back to the main Union line. As soon as the Yankee pickets were safely back among their comrades their artillery opened up on the Georgians. Jones now found his division had advanced too far with no support on either flank and therefore halted his command. He brought up two artillery batteries and started dueling with the Yankees. During the cannonading General Griffith was knocked from his horse mortally wounded by a shell fragment in his thigh. He was transported to Richmond where he died the next day. Colonel William Barksdale, commander of the 13th Mississippi, assumed command of Griffith's brigade.[20]

The sparring between the pickets and the artillery lasted from 9:00 to 11:00 a.m. with Sumner's Corps receiving most of the fire. At that time both sides backed off. Magruder's units remained in place waiting for Jackson's arrival. The Union II and III Corps continued retreating to Savage's Station. At 2 p.m., with Lee's permission, Huger recalled his two brigades on the Williamsburg Road. The casualties in the battle of Allen's Farm [also known as Orchard Station or Peach Orchard] were low, Magruder losing 28 men to the Union's 119. Now Magruder felt that he was in a real fix. He was about to engage a Federal force larger than his own with no support on either flank so he decided to wait for Jackson before moving forward. Magruder thought that he was facing a Federal division when in fact he was facing two and one-half corps, pitting his 13,000 men against 27,000. Magruder kept his units in place waiting on Jackson. Later that afternoon Magruder found out that Jackson would not be crossing the Chickahominy River until the next day. Exhausted and frustrated Magruder finally told his division commanders to proceed on toward Savage's Station and attack any Union units they ran into regardless of size.[21]

The name Savage's Station is somewhat of a misnomer. The site was not a railroad station on the Richmond & York River Railroad with a depot, but merely a turnout switch and a siding on the farm of 49-year-old George Morton Savage. The Richmond & York River Railroad ran through the farm. The siding allowed for rail cars to be dropped off and filled with farm produce and timber to go to market. The Richmond & York River Railroad was charted by the Virginia Assembly in 1853 and when completed in March of 1861 it stretched 38 miles from Richmond to West Point on the York River. Between Richmond & West Point there were 13 stations: Fair Oak, Orchard, Savage's, Meadow, Dispatch, Summit, Tunstall's, Bromley's, White House, Fish Hall, Cohoke, Sweet Hall, and Romankoke. There were actual depots at Richmond, Meadow Station, Dispatch Station, Tunstall's Station, and West Point. All the other stations, like Savage's, were merely stops along the line.[22]

Savage's house was a two-story white frame house that sat on a knoll on the north side of the railroad near the siding. Near the house were barns and slave quarters. Behind the house was a large peach orchard. The farm, named Laurel Grove, consisted of 864 acres of which about half was cleared farm land while the remainder was wooded. Some of the farm land on the north was bordered by the Chickahominy River.[23]

While many citizens in eastern Henrico County left when the Yankees were approaching, George Savage and his family decided to stay. To keep the Yankees from freeing their slaves, most farmers either sent their slaves to Richmond, leased them to other farmers west of the city, or sent them to other farms owned by their masters. Since there is no mention of his slaves in the surviving records, George Savage must have sent his slaves away. Savage's first contact with Union soldiers occurred on Friday, May 23, 1862, when two blue-clad soldiers showed up at his house looking for some milk and butter. He told them he had none to spare. Then they asked him when the rebel pickets had left and Savage told them he did not know. One of the soldiers replied the rebels were cowards and with that they left. The next day more soldiers arrived. Some forced their way into the house and verbally insulted the family. A day or two later there was a skirmish about a mile from Savage's house and the wounded Yankees were brought to Laurel Hill. Savage was asked if they could establish a hospital there and he told them they could use his barn, which they did.[24]

On May 25 Maj. Gen. Erasmus D. Keyes, commander of the IV Corps, and his staff arrived at Laurel Hill and asked to use it as a headquarters to which Savage agreed. Keyes left on May 27 and that same day Brig. Gen. Samuel P. Heintzelman, commander of the III Corps, arrived and established his headquarters there. Up to this time Savage's buildings and crops had suffered very little damage and the Federal troops were generally civil, though he was occasionally called a "damned rebel and secesh" by some of the soldiers. After the first day of the battle of Fair Oaks, on May 31, Savage said, "Their wounded came pouring in like an avalanche." That was when things started to go downhill for Savage. He wrote later:

> They took almost entire possession of my dwelling, and when I appealed to the Adj. Gen'l for protection, he replied to me that "he had no protection to give, nor did I deserve any," "that I was a damned secessionist, and had been instructed in bringing about this state of things, and my head ought to be cut off, and the sooner I got away, the better."[25]

That night the destruction of Savage's property commenced in earnest. According to Savage:

> They forced nearly every lock on the place and stole very nearly all my stores, together with crockery and innumerable articles of furniture, forced my corncribs and took all the corn, all long forage, ground and cut all my oats and wheat and hay, burned my enclosures of every description, destroyed my fruit trees, took the boards from my buildings for every use they could apply them, broke up and destroyed my farming implements, stole two horses, about 80 hogs, some sheep and cattle, and appeared to try how much they could damage me.[26]

Things were getting so rough that on June 2, George Savage sent his three daughters and their female tutor to stay with a neighbor. The next day was no better so his wife left also. On June 12 George Savage became ill and went to a hospital in Richmond. He returned to Laurel Hill on the 16th to try to save what he could of his property, but that evening he was arrested and taken to McClellan's headquarters where he was kept overnight without being told what he was charged with. The next morning George Savage was told that he was going to be taken to Fort Monroe that afternoon. He told the officers that his wife was sick and being taken to Fort Monroe might kill her. Savage wrote later, "Feeling profoundly convinced that to be taken up under these circumstances would kill my wife. I told the officers that, although feeling that my allegiance was due to the Southern Confederacy, that I would take their oath, which I did, however, without kissing the Book." After taking the oath of allegiance George Savage was allowed to go back to his farm.[27]

At this time the Savage farm was also being used as a subsistence and ammunition depot. Food, supplies and ammunition were brought by rail from White House Landing and stockpiled at Savage's Station and from there taken by wagon to the various Corps areas.[28]

On June 16 McClellan's medical director, Surgeon Charles S. Tripler, ordered the establishment of a general hospital at Savage's Station. This large hospital would consolidate all the patients currently in the various division hospitals. After the patients were stabilized at Savage's Station they could be taken by rail to White House Landing and put aboard hospital ships for transport north. By June 22 the new hospital had received 600 patients. After the battles of Gaines Mill on June 28, the hospital received another 1,500 patients and casualties were still pouring in. The hospital was so overwhelmed that many of the men had no shelter and were laying outside exposed to the elements. The last load of patients was sent to the hospital ships at White House Landing on June 29. The next day Brig. Gen. "Jeb" Stuart and his Confederate cavalry took possession of the landing.[29]

The hospital at Savage's Station where between 2,500 and 3,000 Union soldiers were left to the mercy of the Confederates as the Army of the Potomac retreated to the James River (Library of Congress).

4. The Battle of Savage's Station

Top: The last load of sick and wounded soldiers to leave the hospital at Savage's Station for White House landing. *Bottom:* Rail cars near McClellan's headquarters at Savage's Station (both photographs Library of Congress).

When Franklin and Smith arrived at Savage's Station to find out where Smith's supports were they found only Brig. Gen. Thomas F. Meagher's Irish Brigade and the 15th Massachusetts Infantry that had been sent to the station to destroy the supplies and equipment that had to be abandoned. Franklin quickly sent word to Sumner explaining the situation and suggested that Smith's division should continue on to Savage's Station

Union supply vessels at anchor at White House Landing (Library of Congress).

as it was a good fighting position and thought that Sumner ought to relocate there also. Sumner soon replied to Franklin stating that he was presently engaged with the enemy, but as soon as things quieted down he would join Franklin with his II Corps. Soon after Franklin had sent his note to Sumner, Heintzelman rode into the station where Franklin told him what he had done. Heintzelman agreed with Franklin's actions and said that he would bring his III Corps to the station also. With that done Franklin ordered Smith to march his division to Savage's Station where it arrived at about noon and took a position in the woods near the Williamsburg Road.[30]

After the Vermont Brigade left Dr. Trent's house, Co. E of the 5th Vermont was bringing up the rear and watching for Confederates. Before long the Vermonters spotted a group of mounted men following them. The suspicious group was just far enough away that they could not be identified as Union or Confederate cavalrymen and therefore a close watch was kept on them. What the men in Company E did not realize was that

4. The Battle of Savage's Station

without permission Pvt. Mandus W. Hill, a 19-year-old farmer from Arlington, Vt., had left the ranks and gone back to the group of men. The unidentified men were in fact rebels and they captured Hill. He was held in a prisoner of war camp in Richmond until exchanged at Aiken's Landing on August 5 and returned to his company where he deserted the following November.[31]

As Sumner's and Heintzelman's units were retreating down the railroad track, military supplies and equipment at Savage's Station that could not be moved were being destroyed. After Sumner arrived, which was around 2 p.m., he put more men to the task of destroying the supplies. This brought the destruction to a fevered pitch.[32]

Chaplain John J. Marks of the 63rd Pennsylvania Infantry was visiting the hospital at Savage's Station and later recalled:

> About noon the work of destruction commenced, and no language can paint the spectacle. Hundreds of barrels of flour and rice, sugar and molasses, salt, and coffee, were consigned to the flames; and great heaps of these precious articles in a few moments lay scorching and smoldering. A long line of boxes of crackers, fifteen feet high, were likewise thrown into the mass; and the workmen seemed to have a savage and fiendish joy in consigning to the flames what a few days afterwards they would have given thousands to obtain. The scene was altogether unearthly and demoniac. The men, blackened with smoke and cinders, were hurling into the fire boxes of goods, tents, fragments of broken cars, and barrels of whisky and turpentine; and then would be hurled into the burning mass boxes of ammunition, and explosion followed explosion, throwing up fragments of shells into the heavens, and the flames mounted above the tops of the loftiest trees.[33]

One unnamed Vermonter's letter printed in the *Burlington Free Press* recorded the sights he observed while Smith's division was resting at Savage's Station:

> Marching some ten miles, we reached by circuitous route, the railroad at Savage Station. Here large details of men were destroying property of all kinds, burning commissary stores, breaking guns, blowing railroad track and finally loading an engine and twenty cars with powder, the fuse was lighted and engine started off full speed towards White House. The train had gone about two miles, when the explosion occurred; it was grand and terrific beyond description. An immense column of thick smoke, seemingly miles in extent, ascended upward toward the sky red and lurid with the intense heat of a southern sun.[34]

After the II Corps' arrival at the station Sumner stationed Brig. Gen. John Sedgwick's division on the farm road that connected the Williamsburg Road and Savage's Station. Sedgwick's three brigades, Col. Alfred Sully's first brigade, Brig. Gen. William W. Burns' second brigade and Brig. Gen. Napoleon J.T. Dana's third brigade were strung out on the western side of the ravine west of the farm road and north of the Williamsburg Road. Richardson's division was stationed on the north side of the railroad tracks where it was not directly involved in the ensuing battle. Heintzelman's III Corps also arrived at Savage's Station at about 2 p.m. and Heintzelman put his men in the woods along the Williamsburg Road. Then, on his own, Heintzelman decided to leave the area. He included his rational for this decision in his after-action report:

> The whole open space near Savage's was crowded with troops—more than I supposed could be brought in action judiciously. An aide from the commanding general had in the morning reported to me to point out a road across the White Oak Swamp starting from the left of General Kearny's position and leading by Brackett's Ford. General Kearny, having also reconnoitered it, sent a portion of his division and his artillery by this road. Feeling it to be impossible for all the troops to retire by the roads leading by Savage Station, I ordered the whole of my corps to take this road, with the exception of Osborn's and Bramhall's batteries. These, at General Smith's request, I directed to report to him, as all his batteries had already retired.

Unfortunately, Heintzelman failed to inform General Sumner, leaving Sumner thinking that his left flank was covered.[35]

Near 3 p.m. Baldy Smith ordered his division to prepare to march to White Oak Swamp. The men slowly got to their feet and strapped on their knapsacks. It was a typical Virginia summer day, hot and humid. As soon as the division was formed it departed Savage's Station with the troops shuffling along raising clouds of dust on the Williamsburg Road.[36]

Shortly before 4 p.m. Generals Sedgwick and Franklin rode over to the Savage's Station hospital to visit some of their wounded friends. As they returned they decided to visit Heintzelman's headquarters which they figured was in the woods across the Williamsburg Road. As they rode over the open field, they saw a group of men come out of the woods near the Williamsburg Road, but some distance from the place where they expected to find Heintzelman. Franklin thought they were Union troops but General Sedgwick looked at them more closely, stopped, and exclaimed: "Why, those men are rebels!" The two generals "then turned back in as dignified a manner as the circumstances would permit." That was when a Confederate artillery piece started lobbing shell at them. A second piece soon joined the first, and they kept up the fire until they were finally silenced by several Union batteries. Franklin wrote later, "This ludicrous incident prevented what might have been a disastrous surprise for our whole force." A few minutes later one of Sumner's signalmen reported the approach of Confederate infantry and the presence of the railroad gun. To protect the gun crew the Land Merrimac halted in a cut of the railroad over which ran the Dry Bridge, and started shelling the Federal troops in the open field at Savage's Station. The time was about 5 p.m. and the battle was on. As soon as the fighting broke out, General Sumner dispatched an orderly to tell Baldy Smith to return with his division with all possible speed.[37]

Magruder's units had come down the railroad in generally the same formation as they had been in the battle at Orchard Station with Brig. Gen. David R. Jones' division on the far left. Magruder's division was between Jones' division and the railroad with Brig. Gen. Howell Cobb's brigade forward and Brig. Gen. Richard Griffith's brigade in the rear of Cobb as the reserve. Griffith's brigade was now commanded by Col. William Barksdale in the wake of Griffith's mortal wounding. McLaws' division was on the south side of the railroad track with Brig. Gen. Joseph B. Kershaw's brigade stretching from the railroad track to the Williamsburg Road. Brig. Gen. Paul J. Semmes' brigade completed the Confederate battle line with its left flank on the Williamsburg Road and running into the woods where Heintzelman's III Corps should have been. Magruder established his headquarters on the Dry Bridge that crossed over the railroad where he had a good view of the battlefield.[38]

The main part of the fighting for the Confederates at Savage's Station would fall on Kershaw's and Semmes' brigades. Kershaw put his 2nd South Carolina on his left with the 2nd's left flank on the railroad. The 3rd South Carolina was in the center and the 7th South Carolina was on the 3rd's left with its left flank on the Williamsburg Road. The 8th South Carolina was behind the other regiments as the reserve. These were the troops that Franklin and Sedgwick had seen.[39]

Franklin quickly rode to Sumner's headquarters to inform him of the situation and get instructions. This was when Sumner discovered that Heintzelman had left without informing him. Sumner ordered two regiments of General Burns' brigade to attack the Confederates in the woods near the Williamsburg Road. These were Kershaw's men and they were spoiling for a fight. Burns chose the 72nd and 106th Pennsylvania. The right of the 72nd was touching the railroad and the left of the 106th was on the Williamsburg Road. As Burns was getting his two regiments in line a scout informed him that more rebels were in the woods on the left of the Williamsburg road. The troops Burns saw were from Semmes' brigade. Burns asked Sumner for reinforcements and Sumner sent the 1st Minnesota. Burns had just enough time to get the 1st Minnesota across the Williamsburg Road before the rebels attacked.[40]

Captain Delaware B. "Del" Kemper brought his four small six-pounder guns of the Alexandria (Va.) Light Artillery down the Williamsburg Road. Reaching a small hill just south of the Williamsburg Road, Kemper unlimbered his pieces and went into action. It was not, however, a good position because the view of the Federals was obscured. So as the cannoneers rammed and fired Kemper went off in search of a better vantage point. He found soon an opening on the edge of some woods. From there, recalled Sgt. Patrick Gorman, Kemper "could see the Yankee batteries better than we could and he directed our fire by signs." But Federal artillery near Savage's Station had more guns and better ammunition and soon focused their fire on Kemper. The Alexandrians withstood the fire for about five minutes, then as Kemper later wrote, "the superior character and number of the enemy's pieces compelled me to withdraw...."[41]

At almost the same time Kershaw discovered Burns' line of battle he received an order from Magruder to attack. Kershaw advanced his skirmish line forward and soon ran into Burns' troops and artillery fire. The South Carolinians moved through the woods to the edge of the field. Burns found that he still did not have enough troops and a gap developed between the 106th and 72nd Pennsylvania. Burns described what happened next in his after-action report:

> These dispositions were in progress when the enemy attacked most furiously with infantry, he having been playing with artillery upon me during the whole movement across the field, which was answered by General Sumner's batteries. The battle raged along the whole line, but concentrated gradually toward my two weak points, the center and the Williamsburg road. I urged more regiments, which were promptly sent me. Before these arrived, however, the enemy made a rush on the center, wounded me [in the face, but he remained in command] and killed the captain of the left company of Baxter's (Captain McGonigle), forced through to the fence, and flaunted their flag across the rails, broke the line for a moment, but the brave men rallied and drove them back.[42]

The fight then moved toward the Williamsburg Road where another gap had developed in Burns' line between the 106th Pennsylvania and the 1st Minnesota. Thankfully, the 88th New York came across the field at the double-quick cheering. Burns threw them into the gap on the road where the enemy opened artillery and rifle fire on them, but the New Yorkers never faltered and finally drove the rebels back. The 82nd New York appeared on the field and Burns sent it to the gap in the center. While Burns was getting his line shored up Smith's division appeared.[43]

Smith's division had slogged along about two miles toward White Oak Swamp when the men heard the thundering of artillery back at the station. Not long after hearing the artillery a mounted orderly that Sumner had sent caught up with Smith and relayed Sumner's order to bring his command back to the station to secure the Union left flank.[44]

Smith had his division do an about face and start back to the station with Hancock's brigade in the lead with Brooks' and then Davidson's brigades following it. Part of the time the men were forced to double-quick despite the heat. Just before reaching the point where they were to meet the enemy, Sumner ordered Smith to send one brigade forward,

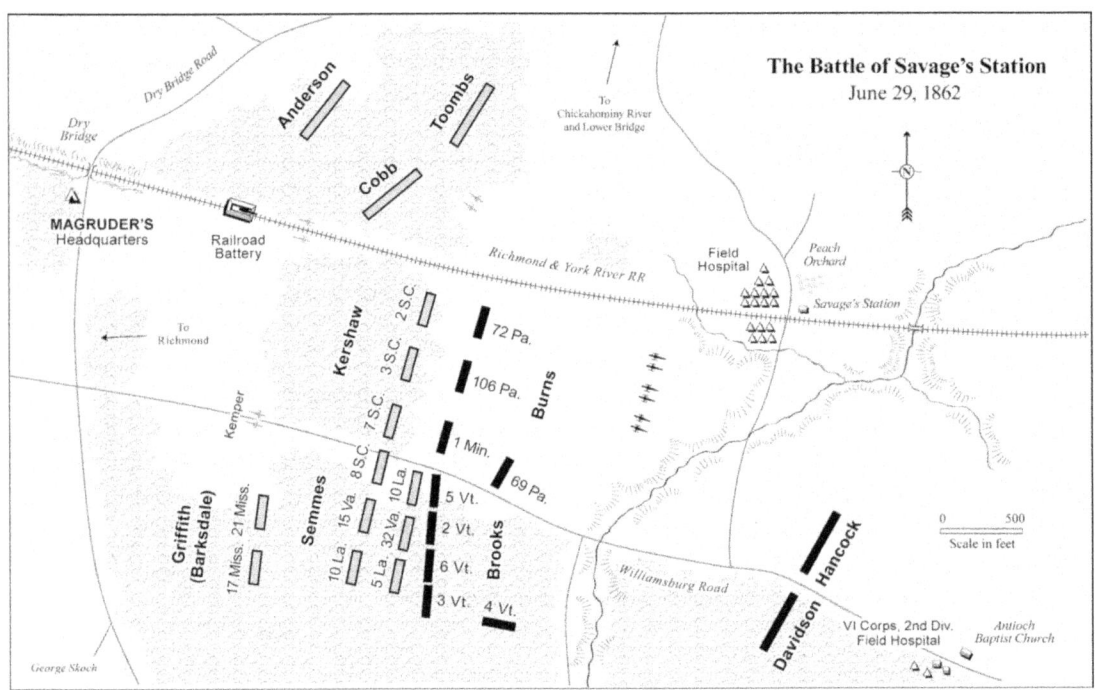

Battle of Savage's Station, June 29, 1862.

one to the right and kept a third in reserve. In compliance with this order Smith sent Brooks' brigade forward, sent Hancock's brigade to the right to support Richardson's division, where they were not engaged, and left Davidson's brigade in reserve. At the same time General Franklin's medical director, Dr. Joseph B. Brown, established a field hospital in a vacant house and blacksmith shop across the Williamsburg Road from the Antioch Baptist Church located about a half a mile from where the Green Mountain Boys would be engaged.[45]

Brooks' orders were to advance into the woods on the left of the Williamsburg Road, opposite Brig. Gen. William W. Burn's brigade, and to push back the enemy who was swarming into the woods in front and threatening to envelop Burns' left flank. General Brooks formed his command with a line of battle composed of the 5th Vermont on the right, commanded by Lieut. Col. Lewis A. Grant since Col. Smalley was absent on sick leave, and the 6th Vermont on the left. The 2nd Vermont was in column formation behind the 5th Vermont as support. The 3rd Vermont was in column formation behind the 6th Vermont as its support. The 4th Vermont was sent off to the left to secure the left flank and was held in reserve and saw no action. Brooks ordered the 2nd Vermont's Col. Whiting to send two companies forward as skirmishers. Whiting chose companies A and K, under the command of the 2nd Vermont's Major James H. Walbridge.[46]

The skirmish line pushed forward through the woods stumbling through thick scrub brush and vines and soon came to a clearing about a mile and a half from where they started. That was when the rebels opened up on them. As Pvt. Daniel F. Cooledge of Co. A wrote in his diary, "we were received by a very hot fire." It was now near 7 p.m. and the thick woods were starting to get dark.[47]

As soon as the enemy rifle and artillery fire began Co. A started taking casualties.

4. The Battle of Savage's Station

Pvt. Thomas Morrisey, a 27-year-old Irish immigrant from Bennington, Vt., was hit in the head by a rebel bullet. Although the bullet did not break the skin, he received a serious contusion. After reaching the safety of the James River several days later Morrisey was sent north to a U.S. army general hospital where he would spend the rest of his time in the army until he received a disability discharge in March of 1863 for "vertigo and occasional derangement."[48]

Private James H. Shippee a Halifax, Vt., native was hit by a rebel minie ball in the left groin. As the bullet passed through the 25-year-old laborer's thigh it grazed his femur, but fortunately did not fracture it. His buddy, Pvt. Williams H. Sears, helped him to the VI Corps, 2nd division, field hospital. Shippee was captured the next day and was not paroled until August 3. Like Morrisey, Shippee spent the rest of his time in the service in the hospital. He was given a disability discharge from the army on November 27, 1862.[49]

Private Benjamin S. Barnard, a 30-year-old farmer from Peru, Vt., was taken down by a shell fragment that sliced through his left calf muscle. He was left in the VI Corp, 2nd division, field hospital and captured the next day. After being paroled Barnard was sent to the U.S. Army General Hospital at Broad and Cherry Streets in Philadelphia, Penn. When his wound healed he was left with a scar three inches long and one-inch wide on his left calf and "muscular rigidity" that left him with a bad limp. He was given a disability discharge from the army on November 7, 1862, and returned home to his wife and two children.[50]

Twenty-one-year old Pvt. Daniel F. Cooledge from Plymouth, Vt., was wounded in the leg. He was hit in the back of his right thigh by a rebel minie ball that ripped through his thigh and exited out the front. Thankfully for Cooledge the bullet missed his femur, but did injury to nerves and tendons that would trouble him the rest of his life. His wound was extremely painful and he was unable to walk. After the battle five of his comrades carried him as far as the VI Corps, 2nd division, field hospital where they had to leave him before resuming their march to the James River.[51]

At six feet and one inch tall, Pvt. Daniel M. Priest made an excellent target and one of the rebels took advantage of it. Priest, a 24-year-old farmer from Plymouth, Vt., was hit in the left arm about four inches above his wrist

Major James H. Walbridge of the 2nd Vermont. Walbridge was promoted to colonel on February 9, 1863, and elevated to command of the 2nd Vermont. He resigned from the army on April 1, 1864, in ill health (U.S. Army Heritage and Education Center).

fracturing his radius and injuring nerves, tendons, and muscles. He would keep his arm, but his hand was left partially paralyzed.[52]

Although Co. K did not lose as many men as Co. A, the two they did lose were killed outright. They were Corp. Truman H. Hunter, a 23-year-old carpenter from Goshen Co., N.Y., and Pvt. Calvin Clair, a 19-year-old farmer from Shoreham, Vt.[53]

After making initial contact with the enemy Maj. Walbridge led the skirmishers to the left and around to the rear of the brigade. During the rest of the battle the skirmishers served as a rear guard to keep shirkers from sneaking off.[54]

Although this was the first battle the Vermont Brigade fought as a whole, the evening shadows and the thick woods caused the regiments to drift apart and consequently the battle was fought as four separate actions. Because of this the author will cover each regiment separately as it became engaged.

After the skirmish line had proceeded several hundred yards the four regiments of the Vermont Brigade started forward. Soon after entering the woods the 5th Vermont marched straight over the 20th New York from General Davidson's brigade. The New Yorkers had been ordered in earlier, but had halted in the woods and refused to advance. This regiment had joined Smith's division only several weeks before. Its men were mostly recruited in the saloons and beer gardens of New York City. They made a fine appearance on parade, but proved to be poor fighters. This was their first experience under fire, and they had thrown themselves on the ground and refused to move. Company I's Sgt. Lucius Bigelow, still angered by the New Yorkers, wrote years later, "I remember as if it was yesterday the way we tramped over that line of cringing men, cursing them soundly for their cowardice." After stepping over, and on, the New Yorkers the 5th Vermont reformed its lines and marched on.[55]

The 5th Vermont neared the open field where the skirmishers were moving off to the left and immediately started receiving enemy fire. That was when Pvt. Joseph Clair started falling back. This was the first time he had been in direct combat and his nerve failed him. During the first hail of bullets Clair shouted, "By God I can't stand that," and took off for the rear. Sergeant Merrill T. Sampson yelled at Clair to get back into line. Then Sampson turned to attend to some other men that were falling back and when he turned back around again Clair was gone. Sampson would not see Clair again for nine months.[56]

As the 5th Vermont broke into the cleared field it was fired on by 7th South Carolina 200 yards directly in their front where the South Carolinians were ensconced in a gorge. The only time the Vermonters could see them was when they stood up to fire. The Vermonters were also taking fire from Capt. Del Kemper's battery to their right.[57]

With orders to push the rebels back Lt. Col. Grant ordered a bayonet charge. As the men fixed bayonets and straightened up their lines Pvt. Ira A. Nicholson in Co. G, tripped on a vine and fell down. In the process of falling down he somehow wound up with two inguinal [intestinal] hernias, one on each side of his lower abdomen. Ignoring the pain, he picked himself up and got back into his place in the formation. Then, with a yell the 5th Vermont charged forward at the double-quick.[58]

As soon as the Green Mountain Boys started running across the open field men began to fall. Nineteen-year-old Second Lt. Brownson M. Barber in Co. K was knocked down by a minie ball that hit his left leg. He would suffer from his wound until he died on July 20 in a prisoner of war camp in Richmond.[59]

Pvt. Nelson K. Holt of Co. H from Brandon, Vt., was knocked down by a shot in the head. Luckily for him it was a glancing blow about two inches above his left ear. Even so, the bullet cut open his scalp and left a permanent indentation in his skull. After the wound healed he suffered partial memory loss. He would eventually be transferred to the Invalid Corps.[60]

After tripping over a vine and getting a double hernia, Pvt. Ira Nicholson's troubles were not over. During the charge Nelson was shot in the left hip. The ball hit him on the outside of his hip joint and exited out his left buttock near his anus. After the battle Nicholson was taken to the VI Corps, 2nd division, field hospital and captured the next day. After being paroled he spent six months in the Brooklyn College U.S. Army General Hospital in New York City where he was given a disability discharge for chronic diarrhea on December 24, 1862.[61]

Second Lieutenant Brownson M. Barber of Co. H, 5th Vermont. Barber was killed at the Battle of Savage's Station on June 29, 1862 (Vermont Historical Society).

As soon as the 5th Vermont got closer Del Kemper ordered his gunners to switch to canister rounds and the Alexandrian's fire ripped through the Federal ranks. The 8th South Carolina soon arrived to support Kemper, and the fighting grew more fierce in front of the battery. According to one of Kemper's gunners, "The Yankees were now very close to us, and it looked like the battery would be taken in a short time." The men held to their pieces, however, and poured canister into the Federals at a range of 200 yards.[62]

Lieutenant Colonel Grant mentioned in his after-action report that when the regiment got within 40 to 50 yards of the gorge, "the rebel force protected there broke and ran in nearly every direction." The rebels were pushed out of the gorge but, the 5th Vermont had sustained a terrible number of casualties to accomplish it. Although the battle had barely started, the number of casualties would only get worse. Additionally, the 8th South Carolina was beyond the gorge that had been vacated by the 7th South Carolina. Here Grant halted his regiment and the companies sought out whatever protection was available which consisted of a scattering of trees on its left. Protection for its center and right consisted of a few trees and a slight swale in the ground to the front.[63]

It was here that the 5th Vermont came under sustained rifle fire from the left and right as well canister from Kemper's guns. As Lt. Col. Grant remembered the fire was, "with deadly effect." The boys in the 5th Vermont started dropping like flies. One unnamed 5th Vermont officer wrote in a letter to the editor of Montpelier's *The Green Mountain Daily Freeman*, "Here most of our men fell fighting like heroes. Some fired away their sixty rounds of cartridges, and took more from their dead and wounded comrades."[64]

The 5th Vermont was now south and to the rear the 7th South Carolina, which had reformed and was north of the Williamsburg Road mixing it up with Burns' regiments.

With the 7th South Carolina out of the way, the 5th Vermont now was facing the 10th Georgia of Semmes' brigade that had just been sent forward. Semmes' brigade was arrayed with the 10th Georgia on the left. The 32nd Virginia was on the 10th Georgia's right and the 5th Louisiana was on the 32nd Virginia's right. The 15th Virginia and the 10th Louisiana were behind the front three regiments in reserve. The 5th Vermont was now caught in a deadly cross-fire between the 10th Georgia and the 8th South Carolina.[65]

The volume of fire directed at the 5th Vermont was horrific. Within 20 minutes every other man in the regiment was either dead or wounded and casualties continued to mount. The Vermonters fired at such a rapid rate that their rifles became heated and fouled with powder residue rendering them useless and forcing them to take those of their fallen comrades.[66]

The Belden brothers, Shelden and Phineas, were standing shoulder to shoulder in company B firing as fast as they could when Shelden was hit in the right arm. The rebel minie ball struck him a few inches below the shoulder joint and shattered his humerus and then took out part of his shoulder blade. After the battle Phineas took his brother to the VI Corps, 2nd division, field hospital. On July 2 Shelden's right arm was amputated at the shoulder joint along with a portion of his right shoulder blade by the 5th Vermont's surgeon, William P. Russell, one of the doctors who had been detailed to remain at the VI Corps hospital. After the operation Shelden developed lung fever which left him with a dry hacking cough. Corporal Shelden Belden was paroled at City Point, Va., on July 25.[67]

Private James P. Elmer in Co. H had knelt and put his elbow on his knee to steady his rifle when a minie ball tore through his right hip. The 23-year-old farmer from Addison, Vt., was left at the VI Corps, 2nd division, field hospital after the battle. He never returned to his company.[68]

Company C's Sgt. Miner E. Fish, a 22-year-old farmer from Sheldon, Vt., was struck in the left arm three inches above his left elbow. Fish would return to his company and be promoted to second lieutenant before being wounded again in the battle of the Wilderness in May of 1864.[69]

After Sgt. Fish was wounded another Co. C man, Pvt. Thomas H. Fortune, a laborer from St. Albans, Vt., was hit twice by rebel minie balls, once in the left arm and once in the left hip. Fortune would survive his wounds, but his soldiering days were over.[70]

Private Robert Johnson, a 29-year-old immigrant from London, England, in Co. C was shot in the upper right arm. The bullet shattered the humerus causing him to be left at the VI Corps, 2nd division, field hospital. A surgeon finally got around to seeing Johnson on July 3 and determined that his arm could not be saved and amputated it. Johnson left the army with a disability discharge on April 14, 1863.[71]

Private Squire A. Marvin in Co. C received a nasty wound when he was hit in the groin by a minie ball. The bullet first hit his scrotum then went into his left groin, traveled upward and lodged near his spine. Not only was Pvt. Marvin lucky enough not to be paralyzed, he was somehow able to stay with his company on the march to the James River. He was discharged from the army on October 4 with the minie ball still embedded in his back.[72]

Company D's commander, Capt. Reuben C. Benton, a lawyer from Johnson, Vt., was slightly wounded in the arm. Although suffering from malaria he remained with his command.[73]

Company D soldier, Pvt. Jason O. French, from Cambridge, Vt., and his comrade,

4. The Battle of Savage's Station

Top, left: **Private James P. Elmer, Co. H, 5th Vermont.** Elmer was shot in the right hip during the Battle of Savage's Station on June 29, 1862, and was captured by the Confederates (U.S. Army Heritage and Education Center). *Top, right:* **Sergeant Miner E. Fish, Co. C, 5th Vermont.** Fish was wounded in the arm and ear in the Battle of Savage's Station on June 29, 1862 (Tim Cooper collection). *Right:* **Captain Reuben C. Benton, commander of Co. D, 5th Vermont,** was slightly wounded in the arm at the Battle of Savage's Station June 29, 1862 (Francis Guber collection).

Pvt. William Hinkson of Worcester, Vt., were standing side by side on the front line firing their rifles when each went down on one knee to reload. In the process of reloading, French was hit by a rebel minie ball in the right shoulder. As Hinkson was in the process of putting the cap on his rifle French fell over knocking Hinkson's rifle aside and splattering Hinkson with blood. The ball had entered French's shoulder from the front and went through his body taking part of the shoulder blade with it as it exited out his back about seven inches lower than where it had entered and about three inches from his spine. He was knocked unconscious and as he lay motionless and bleeding profusely Hinkson assumed he was dead. After the battle Pvt. Thomas Long, another of French's comrades, wanted to take several men to retrieve French's body, but Capt. Benton refused. French, however, was not dead and would survive his wound. It would not be his last.[74]

The Marcy brothers, privates Edward and Ephraim from Craftsbury, Vt., in Co. D were both victims of the heavy Confederate fire. Ephraim was hit on the top of his head by either a bullet or a canister ball. The missile fractured his skull and left a diagonal groove across the top of his head. He was also knocked unconscious for about an hour. After the battle he was taken to the VI Corps, 2nd division, field hospital where his wound, which was bleeding profusely, was dressed. Edward suffered a gunshot wound and was also left at the field hospital with his brother and both were taken captive the next day. Ephraim Marcy was paroled on July 19, but Edward, too badly wounded to be paroled, died of his wounds in Richmond on July 24.[75]

Company D's Pvt. Edgar Bullard received a gruesome wound. A rebel minie ball hit the outside of his right thigh about three inches above his knee. It passed through his thigh ripping out pieces of muscle, tendon, nerves, and bone. Then it went through his left thigh doing the same damage as it had in his right one. Incredibly, despite the pain, loss of blood, and no dressings on his wounds, Bullard was somehow able to march with comrades to Harrison's Landing on the James River where he was sent north to an army hospital. By the middle of September of 1863 his wounds had healed and Bullard returned to his unit. He was mustered out of the army at the expiration of his service on September 15, 1864.[76]

Private Ammon S. McGee in Co. D, took a painful and debilitating hit in his right leg just below the knee by a canister ball. The ball tore his leg open and broke both bones. Unable to continue on to Harrison's Landing with his company he was left at the VI Corps, 2nd division, field hospital.[77]

Company F's Corp. Friend A. Brainard received two wounds during the battle. First, he was hit in the left arm near the shoulder by a rebel minie ball that passed through his arm shattering the humerus. No sooner had Brainard been shot than a Confederate shell fragment cut off a large tree limb above him which fell striking his head and knocking him unconscious. He laid on the field unconscious all night and was captured by the Confederates the next morning. He was taken to the VI Corps, 2nd division, field hospital where he was treated.[78]

Company G's Captain Benjamin R. Jenne, a 29-year-old school principal, was cheering his men on when a Confederate minie ball took off most of his right thumb. Then a shell fragment struck his penis leaving a stricture (narrowing of the urethra) after it healed. He was taken to the VI Corps, 2nd division, field hospital and captured the next day. After he was paroled and his wounds healed Jenne returned to his company and was promoted to major and became the Vermont Brigade's chief of staff.[79]

As Del Kemper's cannons blasted canister rounds at the Vermonters, one of the cast iron balls hit Pvt. Henry Harrison Wilder of the 5th Vermont's Co. F in the chest. Sergeant Merrill T. Samson wrote to Wilder's mother several days after the battle describing the particulars of her son's death:

> Henry had been engaged but a few moments, had fired about 5 or 6 times at the enemy when a grape shot from a cannon that was immediately in the road in front of us struck him in the breast about 4 inches below the throat or top of the breast bone, passing through his cross belt that passes over the left shoulder & across the breast under the right arm. Harrison fell to the ground with the words Oh dear. As soon as he fell he spoke to John McCormic (a fellow from Bridport that stood by his side) & asked for a drink of water. He gave it to him & after Harrison had drinked he then said oh tell Merrill to come here I want to see once more & they called to me but on account of the great confusion & noise of musketry I did not hear him call. In a short time he asked for water again. They gave it him as many times as he asked for it. He seemed to be in considerable pain yet took or rather <u>bore</u> his fate

Left: Captain Benjamin R. Jenne, Co. G, 5th Vermont. His right thumb was shot off and he was hit in the penis by a shell fragment during the Battle of Savage's Station on June 29, 1862. After the battle he was captured by the Confederates (Vermont Historical Society). *Right*: Private Henry Harrison Wilder, Co. F, 5th Vermont. Wilder was killed by a canister ball at the Battle of Savage's Station on June 29, 1862 (University of Vermont).

like a true & noble Soldier. While lying on the ground he turned over 2 or 3 times & then died seeming very easy. He was not heard to say any thing but to ask for water & exclaim oh dear as he fell & desired me to come to him as he wanted to see me once more & the last words he uttered were give it to them boys. After he was shot he lived about 15 minutes was in his right mind all of the time but was not heard to say any thing about home.[80]

Second Lt. Olney A. Comstock of Co. I was killed by two rebel minie balls through his head. He was described in George G. Benedict's *Vermont in the Civil War* as, "an unusually athletic man, a vigorous wrestler, and a stout and brave soldier. He fell in the courageous and active discharge of his duty." Today Comstock's remains lie in an unmarked grave in the Seven Pines National Cemetery in Sandston near Richmond, Va. He left behind an elderly mother and a disabled father.[81]

Private Francis D. Hammond, Co. D, from Pawlet, Vt., was wounded in the right thigh. He was helped along by his comrades after the battle on the march to the James River thereby avoiding capture by the rebels. Because of stiffness in his right hip joint after his wound healed Hammond was given a disability discharge from the army on December 3, 1862, in Cumberland, Md.[82]

Company H's Captain, Charles W. Seagar, a 24-year-old mason from Brandon, Vt., was hit almost simultaneously by two rebel minie balls. One minie ball hit him in the front of his right arm several inches below his shoulder joint, traveled inward and upward

Left: Second Lieutenant Olney A. Comstock, Co. I, 5th Vermont. Olney was killed by two minie balls to the head at the Battle of Savage's Station on June 29, 1862 (Vermont Historical Society). *Right:* Private Francis D. Hammond, Co. D, 5th Vermont Infantry Regiment. Hammond was shot in the right thigh during the Battle of Savage's Station on June 29, 1862. He survived his wound and lived until 1903 (Charles F. Walter).

and lodged in the muscle under his shoulder blade. The other ball struck him in his right cheek and traveled rearward between the skin and cheekbone and lodged in his neck muscles. Somehow he was able to travel with his company and made it to Harrison's Landing where he was sent to the hospital at Camp Parole in Annapolis, Md., where the bullet in his neck was surgically removed.[83]

The Stedman brothers, Francis, age 21, and Irwin, age 18, in Co. H were two unlucky soldiers. Both brothers were seriously wounded in the battle. A minie ball hit Francis on the inside of his left ankle. The ball exited through the other side of his ankle taking part of his Achilles tendon with it. Irwin was hit in the left buttock by a minie ball. The bullet went in missing the pelvic bone and lodged in his scrotum. The Stedman's were too badly wounded to accompany their regiment on the retreat after the battle and both were left at the VI Corps, 2nd division, field hospital where they were captured the next day. After being paroled they were taken to Hammond U.S. Army General Hospital at Lookout Point, Md. Soon after arriving at the hospital Irwin had the bullet that was lodged in his scrotum surgically removed through his perineum. After recuperating from his wound

Francis' leg was so stiff he could no longer serve in the field and was transferred to the Invalid Corps.[84]

Company E, the Equinox Guards, from Manchester, Vt., suffered more casualties at Savage's Station than any other company in the 5th Vermont. Company E went into the battle with three commissioned officers and 56 men. It came out with only seven men unharmed. But the story of Company E's Cummings boys from Manchester, Vt., is about as tragic as any in the Civil War. Peter and Louisa Cummings had five sons and a nephew in the battle of Savage's Station and only one returned home alive. Thankfully, Peter and Louisa had passed on before the war, Peter in 1859 and Louisa in 1860, respectively, and were spared the heartache of what happened to their sons and nephew.[85]

Henry A. Cummings, the first son of Peter and Louisa Cummings was shot in the right thigh. The minie ball hit him in the front of his thigh about two inches below his crotch cutting muscles, tendons, and splintering his femur as it bored through his leg and exited out the back. He was left at the VI Corps, 2nd division, field hospital after the battle as his regiment continued on toward White Oak Swamp and was captured the next day. He was paroled on July 25 and was sent to an army hospital in Washington, D.C., where he was given a disability discharge on January 15, 1863, and sent home. The second Cummings son, Hiram P. Cummings, was severely wounded and died on July 7. Edmund M. Cummings, the third Cummings son, was mortally wounded and died that night. The fourth Cummings son, William E. Cummings, was also mortally wounded and died on July 2. The fifth and final son, Silas A. Cummings, was mortally wounded and died on July 4. The Cummings brothers' cousin, William Henry Harrison Cummings, was severely wounded in the right thigh. After the battle William was taken to the VI Corps, 2nd division, field hospital where his leg was amputated. He was captured with the other patients the next day and was paroled on July 17. He was taken to an army hospital in Baltimore, Md., where he died from his wound on August 2, 1862.[86]

Co. E's First Lt. William H.H. Peck, received a ghastly wound in the face. A rebel minie ball hit him under his right cheek bone and ploughed rearward and downward coming to rest just behind and below his left ear. As the 5th Vermont was making its way to the James River after the battle Captain Charles P. Dudley remembered finding Lieutenant Peck on the Williamsburg Road between the battlefield and the VI Corps, 2nd division, field hospital. Dudley stopped to talk to Peck and the lieutenant pleaded, "Captain isn't you gonna take me along." Dudley replied, "we cannot, there is no way to do it." Dudley had to leave his friend expecting to never see him again. But not long

First Lieutenant William H.H. Peck, Co. E, 5th Vermont. Peck was wounded in the face at the Battle of Savage's Station on June 29, 1862 (Vermont Historical Society).

afterward Peck got up and followed all night the moving crowd of soldiers to the river. Without anything to eat for two days he finally found his company and was put on board one of the steamers.[87]

Private John R. Wilkins, a 19-year-old farm laborer from Pawlett, Vt., in Co. E had to be the luckiest man in the 5th Vermont. During his four years of service he was wounded no less than 13 times and lived to tell about it. Wilkins was slightly wounded the first time on April 16, 1862, at Lee's Mill. At the battle of Savage's Station he was wounded three times. The first wound was a gunshot wound in the right leg. This ball was never removed. Next, he was hit in his left side. This ball which had lodged between two of his broken ribs was later extracted. Lastly, he was shot through the upper left arm with the ball exiting through his shoulder blade. He was either able to march with his company, or was lucky enough to be one of the wounded to be transported in the regiment's wagons to Harrison's Landing. He would be wounded nine more times during his term of service.[88]

Another unfortunate Company E soldier to be downed by a rebel minie ball was 23-year-old Corp. Willard K. Bennett from Manchester, Vt. Corporal Henry Stiles of the 2nd Vermont's Co. A wrote the following letter to Willard's mother telling her of her son's death and how it happened:

> I write you today because I promised Willard I would do so, you have no doubt heared of the sad fate of Co. E at the battle of Savage Station Sunday evening June 29. My co. was deployed as skirmishers and were scattered somewhat. We were on the left of the fight but towards the close of the fight I passed to the right to find my Regt. pausing a moment amid a shower of bullets, I hearded some one speak and I knew it was Willard voice. I asked him if he was hurt and he said he was fatally wounded in the center of the bowels. I then went up to him to help him from the field but he wished me to leave him for he said it is of no use—I cannot live. I urged him to try to get away to the hospital. He finally concluded to try. I helped him to his feet and leaning upon me he walked a short distance and said he could go no further. The order then came for the brigade to form a new line. He then said he would try and go back of the line which I assisted him to do and then went for a stretcher but could not find one. I procured a piece of canvas and with the help of three others, carried him some distance when we met men with a stretcher. We laid him on it. He was then carried to the hospital. As soon as he was placed on the stretcher I went to assist in carrying others from the field. I did not see him again. I understand the surgeon could do nothing for him. The ball did not pass thru him. I promised I would write—his great care seemed to be for his mother. He did not wish to live for himself but for his mother. Said he "Oh what will my poor mother do, what will my poor mother do." The hospitals are now in the hands of the rebels. When we hear from them we can learn of Willard's fate. I do not think it possible that he could live but a short time but perhaps he is alive. Co. E of the 5th suffered the most of any Company in the brigade. I had three ... mates but they are all gone. I am the only one left of four who were always together. We sympathize deeply with you in your affliction but can only look to God, hoping and trusting that all may be well.

Willard Bennett was in fact dead leaving another grieving mother back in Vermont.[89]

As the battle raged Second Lt. Samuel Sumner, Jr., of Co. D was mortally wounded. Captain John R. Lewis, commander of the 5th Vermont's Co. I, wrote Sumner's father about the circumstances of his son's death:

> After we arrived on the battle field I noticed that he seemed as little fatigued as excited as any one that I noticed, as Capt. Benton was acting field officer [and in command of the left wing of the 5th Vermont] Lt. Sumner was in command of the Co. The conformation of the ground was such that our line just as we arrived at our most advanced position had become crowded, and the right of my Co. and the left of Co. D had become intermixed, this brought us nearer together & in passing back and forth along the line I met him several times. Just in front of his Co. was a slight elevation in the

ground and by causing the men to load and fire lying & kneeling they were considerably protected. The duties of the officers here consisted in keeping the men up into line and preventing those in the rear from firing while lying down so as [not] to endanger their comrades in front, and also in cheering on the men to a rapid & effective fire.

While engaged in opening some extra cartridges for my men I had kneeled down so as to be protected by the rise in the ground. While thus engaged I noticed that Lt. Sumner was kneeling near me. Just then I heard the order from some source not to fire into the point of woods on our right for our friends were there. I heard Lt. Sumner repeat this order, but turning to me remarked that they were firing on us from that point and we both decided that a heavy cross fire was cutting down our men and that it came from that point. We both immediately directed our men to return the fire in that quarter—Immediately almost Lieut. Sumner still kneeling rec. his death wound. He gave a slight groan, or said oh! and reeling to the left fell over on his side facing me and so near that I did not have to move a foot to reach him, his face lay in the dust so I took hold of him and turned him on his back—spoke to him and tried to get an answer. He appeared not to breath and I thought that he was dead but about a minute later he heaved a deep sigh and I think was dead. I did not see his sword & could not see his left hand as he lay, but noticed that his pistol case had brought round in front and as he lay his right hand was on it. I also noticed that his blanket was rolled and still over his shoulder. I saw no wound nor blood about his person, but looked for none and supposed that he must have been shot through the heart.

Second Lieutenant Samuel Sumner, Co. D, 5th Vermont. Sumner was mortally wounded at the Battle of Savage's Station on June 29, 1862 (Vermont Historical Society).

When we were ordered to fall back at the close of the engagement and supposed that of course we should return to take care of the killed & wounded, but it seems that it could not be and we immediately commenced a march that had no halt until morning. Many of the wounded were helped or got off the field to a temporary hospital half a mile in the rear. Here they were left with Dr. Russell and another Surg. I am in hopes that the Dr. with some of the less severely wounded visit the battle ground in the morning so that perhaps that he might secure any valuables that he had on his person and also see he was respectfully buried and the place marked."[90]

Warren Dutton recalled years later a conversation between Lt. Col. Lewis Grant and Capt. Charles Dudley. "Before the fight closed, the Col. coming along said to the Capt.—'Why are your men not firing? Why did you stop their firing?' It was quite dark then, and the men were lying behind trees, some thirty of them. 'Colonel,' said the Captain, 'I guess those men can't fire anymore.' The Col. went up to them thro the shower of shot and found them all killed or wounded. He walked quietly away."[91]

When darkness finally came the firing ceased and the 5th Vermont held its ground. The regiment had gone into the battle with 400 men. Its loss in killed and wounded was

206, most of whom fell in the first half hour. At the battle of Savage's Station the 5th Vermont earned the dubious distinction of losing more men in a single battle than any other Vermont regiment in the Civil War.[92]

The 6th Vermont started forward with the Fifth, but as it moved through the thick woods it bore more to the left widening a gap between the two regiments. One Confederate regiment took advantage of this mistake and in the twilight charged into the gap and fired off a volley into the 6th Vermont before retreating. Continuing to move forward the 6th Vermont ran into a hornet's nest of lead and cast-iron balls and started taking causalities.[93]

A rebel minie ball gouged out a furrow one and one-half inches wide and four inches long on the inside of Pvt. Edwin M. Carlisle's thigh. Even though the 19-year-old farmer from Plymouth, Vt., in the 6th Vermont's Co. E had lost a lot of blood he was able to stay with his company during the retreat and made it safely to the James River.[94]

Corporal Alexander W. Davis, a 20-year-old blacksmith from Hardwick, Vt., in Co. D was shot in the left foot. After the battle, although in extreme pain, he hobbled along with the other wounded men toward White Oak Swamp. Davis had made about three miles by the next morning when he and number of other wounded and sick Union soldiers were swept up by Confederate cavalry and taken back to Savage's Station.[95]

While keeping his men in line Second Lt. George E. Wood of Co. B was wounded in the right shoulder. After the bullet penetrated his flesh it turned and traveled 13-inches down his arm and lodged on the inside of his elbow joint. Unable to march with his unit when the Vermont Brigade left for the James River after the battle, Wood was left at the VI Corps, 2nd division, field hospital and captured. After being paroled he was sent to a Union army hospital where the bullet was removed from his arm. After his wound had healed he was unable to withstand the rigors required of an infantry officer in the field and was assigned as the chief of the ambulance corps of the VI Corps' second division on November 21, 1862.[96]

Thirty-eight-year-old Pvt. James R. Murray in Co. G from Duxbury, Vt., was shot through both thighs by the same minie ball, fracturing the femur in one of them. Unable to march, he was left at the VI Corps, 2nd division, field hospital after the battle. Murray's leg with the fractured femur was amputated on July 4 and he died that night from complications from the operation. He was buried behind the field hospital. He left a wife and two children.[97]

Being the company color bearer in the Civil War was a very dangerous job as it made a soldier an extremely visible target. Corporal Guy C. Martin from Swanton, Vt., was Company K's color bearer that night in the dark woods and paid the price for it. He was wounded by a shell fragment in the left thigh. He was left at the VI Corps, 2nd division, field hospital after the battle and was captured the next day. Martin was paroled several weeks later and arrived at the Long Island College Hospital in Brooklyn, N.Y., on July 14, 1862. He was so weak from his wound, which by that time was infected with gangrene, that all he could utter was his name and the word "Vermont." He died of his wound on July 17.[98]

Private Abial H. Patch from Braintree, Vt., was the tallest man in Company H standing six-feet and five-inches tall. Unfortunately, his height made him an obvious target. A rebel brought him down with a shot in his left arm near his shoulder. Although painful the bullet missed the humerus, enabling him to move out with his company after the battle. He spent the rest of his time in the army convalescing in hospitals until he was given a disability discharge for his wound and heart disease on December 28, 1862.[99]

Already suffering from a rupture in his scrotum that he got lifting a log earlier in the month, Pvt. John Scott, a 37-year-old immigrant from Edinburgh, Scotland, in Co. K was wounded in his left thigh near the hip joint. Unable to march he was left at the VI Corps, 2nd division, field hospital. Two weeks later the hospital at Savage's Station was closed and all the patients were transported to Richmond. Unlike most of the patients Scott was taken to a military hospital instead of a prisoner of war camp. There a rebel surgeon treated the wound in his hip. Because Scott's left testicle was so badly swollen the doctor opened Scott's scrotum and cut his spermatic cord in an attempt to alleviate the swelling and pain. Scott was paroled on July 17 and sent to a military hospital in Alexandria, Va., where he was given a disability discharge on November 29, 1862. Although he survived his wound, problems with his scrotum would ruin his life.[100]

Total darkness finally brought a halt to hostilities and the 6th Vermont held its position in the woods until the Vermont Brigade was withdrawn.[101]

As the gap between the 5th and 6th Vermont started to widen, Colonel Whiting saw what had happened and wanted to fill the gap. Unfortunately, the 2nd Vermont was still in column formation. Instead of stopping and forming his regiment in line of battle, he screamed over the din, "Charge bayonets!" There was no such maneuver from a column formation in the tactics books, and in the confusion, the regiment froze. Whiting admitted later that he was, "at wits end." Out of shear desperation he could think of nothing else to do but to order his men to cheer which they did with a vengeance. This broke the impasse, and they were quickly deployed in line of battle and charged forward to plug the hole. Colonel Whiting admitted later, "That command to cheer I lay up as the best act performed by me during my service. Only soldiers can estimate what a cheer may accomplish when matters seem to be on the balance."[102]

As the 2nd Vermont got nearer the enemy, it quickly began taking casualties. Pvt. Charles C. Dodge of Co. F took multiple hits. One bullet pierced his neck just behind his right ear, as another one almost simultaneously grazed his head behind his left ear. Pvt. Elijah S. Brown, also of Co. F, helped Dodge to the VI Corps, 2nd division, field hospital. Later Brown wrote of the casualties in his company, "Charles Dodge is one of them & he is probably dead for when I left him he could not speak the ball passed through his neck he was bleeding to death & fast & the Dr. said he would not live for an hour & then I left him for the enemy was close on to me...." Although weakened from the loss of blood, Dodge dragged himself into a ravine where he saw water trickling from a wooden spout that a local farmer had stuck into a spring. He let the water run over his head to cool his wounds. After being captured Dodge was placed in Libby Prison in Richmond and was paroled on September 13. He was transferred to the Invalid Corps on January 15, 1863, and was discharged from the service June 20, 1864. His wound left his mouth partially paralyzed causing a speech impediment.[103]

Not long after Private Dodge was hit, Captain Randall, commander of Co. F, saw another one of his men receive a wound. Pvt. Henry L. Harris was hit almost simultaneously in his left side and right hand but was able to keep on firing. A few minutes later another bullet hit him in the right arm finally taking him down. He had received a nasty wound in the upper arm just below the shoulder. The arm was amputated the next day. He was imprisoned in Richmond until paroled on September 13, 1862, and served in the Invalid Corps until he was discharged June 20, 1864.[104]

Another one of Captain Randall's men that was wounded was Pvt. Harlan P. Stoddard of Waitsfield, Vt. He was hit by a bullet that entered the left side of his pelvis fracturing the pelvic bone, passed through the rectum and finally exited through his left buttock.

Stoddard was left writhing on the ground in the darkness. He was taken as a prisoner of war the next day and paroled on July 25. He spent the next year in the hospital and was given a disability discharge from the army in August of 1863.[105]

Shot in the left thigh, Pvt. Watson Cheney in Co. K from Franklin, Vt., was left at the VI Corps, 2nd division, field hospital. In addition to his wound he was also suffering from chronic diarrhea. Watson would survive incarceration in a prisoner of war camp and be exchanged only to die in a Union army hospital.[106]

Private William H. Clark of Co. E took a buck and ball round in the front of his thighs. His left thigh was hit by the round ball, and one of the buckshot hit near his right groin. For some reason neither round could be removed by the surgeons in either the Confederate hospital where he was taken after he was captured, or the Federal general hospital in Philadelphia where he was admitted after he was paroled on August 6. He would have to use a cane for the rest of his life. The shot that wounded Clark came from one of the three regiments of Semmes' brigade that was using smooth-bore muskets with buck and ball ammunition consisting of a round lead ball and three buckshot. In his after-action report, Semmes stated, "Much of the time the enemy were engaged at a distance of not above 40 yards. Their heavy comparative loss doubtless resulted mainly from the greater efficiency of our smooth-bore muskets with buck and ball at short range, the superior steadiness of our men, and the precision of their fire."[107]

Company B's 19-year-old Pvt. Seth N. Eastman from Topsham, Vt., was wounded in the right thigh by a buck and ball round from a rebel smooth-bore musket. He was very lucky that the bullet did not hit his femur, but unlucky in that the ball and the buckshot could never be removed. When the Vermonters pulled back after the battle to resume their march toward the James River several of Eastman's comrades, Privates Franklin Bixby and William Bagley, tried to help him along, but he was so weak from the loss of blood they left him at the VI Corps, 2nd division, field hospital. What Eastman saw there amazed and shocked him:

> There were many wounded men here, some much more seriously wounded than I. One man that I knew had both of his legs broken, another had one of his broken. I was comforted to a certain extent thinking I was much better than they. No tongue can describe, no pen can portray the scenes that I saw in and around that blacksmith shop that night. Men were slowly bleeding to death without any help or sympathy. Some were praying, others were cursing and swearing, many were thirsty and begged for water in vain, others called for their friends and relatives and cries for help could be heard in all directions. I could not sleep from pain, thirst and thinking what the morrow would bring. In the morning, many of the wounded were dead having bled to death in some cases. I saw several men stone dead sitting up against a stone or a tree, many more were almost dead with no one to wait on them. This was the only time I saw the rear of our army after a retreat during the whole war.[108]

When the war broke out Pvt. Vernon D. Rood was studying to become a lawyer at the New Hampton Institute in Fairfax, Vt. At age 19 he dropped out of school and enlisted as a private in Co. H, 2nd Vermont, on May 16, 1861. Now fighting in the twilight in the dark woods he was wounded in the right leg. A rebel minie ball hit in the front of his thigh about five inches below his crotch and drilled clear through. It missed the femur, but damaged nerves in his leg that would trouble him the rest of his life.[109]

Williamstown, Vt., native Pvt. John E. Clough in Co. D had the top part of the middle finger of his left hand shot off at the first joint. After reaching Harrison's Landing several days later the rest of his injured finger was amputated.[110]

Private Orville E. Moore, a native of Tunbridge, Vt., in Co. E, was hit by a buck and ball round. The three buckshot merely cut his clothing, but the round ball hit him in the right groin. After the battle Moore's comrades left him at the VI Corps, 2nd division, field hospital.[111]

The 3rd Vermont started forward with the rest of the brigade just to the rear of the 6th Vermont, but while moving through the dark woods, it lost sight of the other Vermont regiments. Without realizing it, the 3rd Vermont had veered too far to the left, totally losing the protection of the regiment in front. As it advanced, and still in column formation, it came under artillery fire that thankfully damaged more trees than men. When Lieutenant Colonel Wheelock Veazey, acting commander of the 3rd Vermont, Col. Hyde being absent due to illness, realized his predicament, he put his regiment in line of battle and continued to press forward.[112]

Private John E. Clough, Co. D, 2nd Vermont. Clough had the top portion of the middle finger of his left hand shot off at the Battle of Savage's Station on June 29, 1862 (Mark Hersey).

As the 3rd Vermont was moving cautiously through the woods, Brig. Gen. Semmes was moving the 5th Louisiana to the Confederate right, straight into the path of the 3rd Vermont. When about 40 yards apart, Semmes could hear troops moving through the underbrush in the darkness in front of him, but he could not tell if it was friend or foe. He halted the 5th Louisiana and ordered Pvt. John Maddox of Co. K, to go forward and challenge the unit in front of them. Maddox cautiously moved forward and yelled out, "Who are you?" The answer out of the darkness was, "Friends." Maddox then asked, What regiment?" Private Charles B. Dubois of the 3rd Vermont's Co. G recalled what happened next:

> Some fool in Co. C answered back "The Third Vermont." Co. C was the extreme left company of the regiment and next in line to ours. And immediately this answer was given they opened fire on us, not fifteen yards away. Company C received the volley endways and came tumbling over us in great confusion. Several of our men were hit, among them Capt. Corbin wounded and Lieutenant Ramsey killed. We did not return the fire, as it was so dark and so much confusion prevailed it would be difficult to distinguish friend from foe. The enemy retired after receiving a few shots from some of the men of Company C.[113]

Company C's commander, David T. Corbin, a 29-year old lawyer from Wells River, Vt., was wounded in the hand and jaw. He was carried to the VI Corps, 2nd division, field hospital where he was captured the next day. He was paroled on July 17 and sent to a hospital in Alexandria, Va. After his wounds healed he was unable to perform field duty and resigned his commission on November 11, 1862.[114]

Thirty-one-year-old Second Lt. John W. Ramsey from Newbury, Vt., in Co. C was shot dead and left on the field.[115]

Left: Captain David T. Corbin, Co. C, 3rd Vermont. Corbin was shot in the hand and jaw at the Battle of Savage's Station on June 29, 1862. As a result of his wounds he resigned from the army the following November. *Right:* Second Lieutenant John W. Ramsey, Co. C, 3rd Vermont, was killed at the Battle of Savage's Station on June 29, 1862 (both photographs Vermont Historical Society).

Company C's first sergeant, Alonzo C. Armington, a 23-year-old shoemaker from Waterford, Vt., was wounded in the left leg. He was struck by a musket ball in the leg near his hip. He was taken to the VI Corps, 2nd division, field hospital and some time the same night his wounded leg was amputated. Unfortunately, he did not survive the amputation. The next day a group of captured Union prisoners of war were marching past the field hospital where they were halted and ordered to bury the bodies. They did so in the field a few rods to the rear of the house and blacksmith shop. One of the prisoners, First Sgt. Miles K. Stone, from the 3rd Vermont's Co. I, got the opportunity to help bury his friend Alonzo Armington.[116]

Corporal George W. Bonett was one of the luckier wounded soldiers in Company C. One 5th Louisiana soldier fired a buck and ball round at Bonett. The round ball went between Bonett's legs but the buck shot had spread enough that all three hit him. Two hit him in the right thigh and the third one hit him in the left thigh. While the wounds were very painful Bonett was able to keep up with his company after the battle and safely made it to Harrison's Landing.[117]

Captain Thomas Nelson, Jr., the commander of Co. I was shot in the left foot. The bullet took off most of his big toe and mangled the two toes next to it. Even though his boot was dripping blood he stayed in command of his company. After the battle Nelson's three injured toes were amputated.[118]

Private Moses A. Parker, a Concord, Vt., native in Co. C, was also wounded in the foot. He was struck by a rebel minie ball that imbedded itself in his left foot. Unable to march with his wounded foot he was left at the VI Corps, 2nd division, field hospital where he was captured the next day. After being paroled Private Parker was sent to Hammond U.S. Army General Hospital at Point Lookout, Md., where on September 27, 1862, he was given a disability discharge from the army due to lameness from his wound.[119]

A rebel minie ball hit Company I's Pvt. Rosson O. Sanders, a farmer from Lunenburg, Vt., in his right leg half-way between his knee and ankle. The bullet shattered when it hit his tibia enlarging the wound. Sanders was left at the VI Corps, 2nd division, field hospital when the Vermont Brigade continued on toward the James River after the battle and was captured. After Sanders was paroled on July 22 he was sent to the Satterlee U.S. Army General Hospital in West Philadelphia, Penn., where he was given a disability discharge on December 5, 1862. The next day he enlisted in Troop M, 1st U.S. Cavalry Regiment.[120]

Private Josephus W. Voodry of Fairfield, Vt., was one of the few Company G soldiers to be wounded. He was hit in the right knee by a rebel minie ball about three-quarters of an inch from the outer edge of his knee cap lodging in the knee joint. Because of the darkness Voodry was not found. During the night he crawled three quarters of a mile on his hands and his one good knee to the VI Corps, 2nd division, field hospital where he was captured the day after the battle. The minie ball was cut out of his knee four days later. Voodry was paroled on July 22 and was sent to the Satterlee U.S. Army General Hospital in West Philadelphia, Penn., where he was given a disability discharge on August 3, 1862.[121]

After the firing stopped the 3rd Vermont halted in place until ordered to fall back an hour later.[122]

As an aside the author has always wondered why John Maddox, a lowly private in 5th Louisiana, was mentioned by name in Brigadier General Semmes' after-action report. The two most likely reasons are that Semmes knew of Maddox because he was a brave, devil-may-care soldier that was always chosen for dangerous assignments or he was a well-known trouble maker that Semmes did not mind sacrificing. Research on Maddox provides additional insight and the second scenario seems the most likely.

John Maddox, a 37-year-old Irish immigrant, from New Orleans enlisted in Co. K of the 5th Louisiana Infantry Regiment on May 7, 1861. During the winter of 1861–1862 the 5th Louisiana was encamped with a number of other regiments at Young's Mill. At approximately 11 p.m. on December 29, 1861, Maddox and Privates Richard Murray and Martin Henahan, both of Co. K, were playing cards in Murray's hut when an argument broke out between Maddox and Murray. As the argument escalated Maddox whipped out a large pocket knife and stabbed Murray in his left side between the ninth and tenth ribs nearly killing him. Maddox then grabbed Murray's and Henahan's money off the table and ran back to his hut. Minutes later Company K's commander, with revolver in hand, escorted Maddox to the guardhouse.[123]

Maddox was brought before a court-martial board on January 8, 1862, and charged with "stabbing with intent to kill" and "theft." He was found guilty and was sentenced to four months hard labor while wearing a 12-pound ball on a three-foot chain affixed to his ankle. He served his time from March through June 1862. He was released in time to join his regiment for the battle of Savage's Station.[124]

Private John Maddox was shot through his left knee joint on July 2, 1863, at the battle of Gettysburg and had his left leg amputated several inches above his knee joint. He spent the rest of the war in army hospitals.[125]

John Maddox's propensity for using a knife would be demonstrated two more times after the war. Maddox stabbed a John Rogers in the chest on Notre Dame Street in New Orleans on February 18, 1868. Rogers died several hours later. During Maddox's trial a reporter from the *Times-Picayune* described Maddox as "a man of middle age, dark hair and eyes, and his appearance is rough, weather beaten, and rugged." The results of the trial are unknown. If he was sentenced to prison it was a short sentence because on February 4, 1871, Maddox struck again. This time he stabbed a Tom McCuin in the chest in New Orleans near the Mississippi River. Fortunately, this time the wound was not fatal. After this incident John Maddox seems to fade into history.[126]

After the firing had subsided and darkness set in, General Brooks and Major Walbridge were rounding up troops on the left of the brigade when they heard rustling in the bushes in the darkness. Walbridge called out, "What troops are those?" Someone off in the darkness replied, "Who are you?" Walbridge called out again, "What regiment is that?" The reply was, "You tell!" Then out of the night Walbridge and Brooks heard the order, "Ready!" They did not wait for "Aim! Fire!" and wheeled their horses around for a quick getaway. The expected spray of bullets followed in a split second. Walbridge, who was by now laying forward on his horse's neck to make as small a target as possible, escaped without a scratch. Brooks was not as lucky and was hit on the underside of his right thigh a few inches up from the back of his knee, but did not give up command. He wrote his father that the wound "was just enough to call a wound but not enough to amount to anything." Brooks was probably downplaying the severity of his wound so as not to worry his father. Private Elisha S. Brown of the 2nd Vermont's Co. F recalled seeing Brooks after he was wounded and wrote, "Gen wounded in the knee, but he did not leave us in the fight to get out the [illegible] way we could but stayed with his men & his horse & Sadle was covered with Blood."[127]

By 9 p.m. it was pitch dark and both the Confederate and Federal commanders were afraid to maneuver their troops any more for fear of firing into their own units. The Confederates fell back as the Vermonters gathered up their wounded as best they could in the dark and dropped them off at the VI Corps, 2nd division, field hospital. Their dead, unfortunately, had to be left lying on the field. To add more misery to the situation at a little after 9 p.m. a fierce thunder storm erupted.[128]

Not long after the firing ceased the VI Corps medical director came by the VI Corps, 2nd division, field hospital and told Dr. William P. Russell, the 5th Vermont's surgeon, Dr. William J. Sawin, the 2nd Vermont's assistant surgeon, and Dr. William W. Potter, the 57th New York's surgeon, that they would have to remain behind with the wounded when Smith's division moved out. To assist the surgeons about a dozen enlisted men from the Vermont Brigade were detailed to remain at the hospital.[129]

The final tally of casualties for the Vermont Brigade in this action was 358. The 2nd Vermont lost five men killed and 43 wounded, three mortally. The 3rd Vermont had six men killed and 43 wounded. The 4th Vermont, while not participating in the battle, left five men sick in the hospital. The 5th Vermont, of course, had the highest casualty rate with 45 killed and 158 wounded, 27 mortally, and three missing. The 6th Vermont had 15 men killed, 51 wounded, six mortally, and nine missing. Total casualties for the battle of Savage's Station were 919 Union soldiers to 444 Confederates. Combined with casualties at Orchard Station the casualties for the day were 1,038 for the Union and 473 for the Confederates.[130]

About a half an hour after the shooting ceased, Franklin suggested to General Sumner

Left: Assistant Surgeon William Sawin, 2nd Vermont. Dr. Sawin was detailed to remain at the VI Corps field hospital after the Battle of Savage's Station and was captured by the rebels (U.S. Army Heritage and Education Center). *Right:* Surgeon Willian P. Russell, 5th Vermont. Dr. Russell was detailed to remain at the VI Corps field hospital after the Battle of Savage's Station and was captured by the rebels (Vermont Historical Society).

that if he had no objection Franklin would carry out McClellan's orders and get Smith's division on the road to White Oak Swamp Bridge. Sumner angrily answered, "No, General, you shall not go, nor will I go—I never leave a victorious field. Why! if I had twenty thousand more men, I would crush this rebellion." Franklin handed Sumner a copy of McClellan's order that all troops must cross White Oak Swamp that night. A candle was found and lit so Sumner could read the order. After reading the order Sumner barked, "General McClellan did not know the circumstances when he wrote that note. He did not know that we would fight a battle and gain a victory." By this time Franklin recalled later, "I was at my wit's end. I knew that General McClellan's arrangements did anticipate a fight exactly like that just over, and that unless the whole force was

Right: Private Emery L. Smith, Co. G, 6th Vermont Infantry Regiment. Smith was one of the Vermonters left at the VI Corps field hospital as a nurse. After the war he was elected as the first mayor of Barre, Vt. (Vermont Historical Society).

on the other side of the swamp by the next morning, his movement might be seriously delayed."[131]

At this point Baldy Smith asked Franklin to introduce Smith's aide de camp, Lieutenant Mathew Barry, to General Sumner. After the introduction Lieutenant Barry told Sumner that he had seen General McClellan only a short time before, that McClellan knew there had been a fight, and fully expected that all of the troops would cross White Oak Swamp that night. Finally convinced, Sumner turned to his staff and exclaimed, "Gentlemen, you hear the orders; we have nothing to do but to obey." With that the impasse was broken.[132]

Shortly after 10 p.m. Smith had his division pulled together and was on the road in a pouring rain slogging toward the James River some 20 miles off in the darkness. The men were tired to death and with heavy hearts having to leave behind their dead and wounded brothers, cousins, neighbors, and childhood friends.[133]

Tragically, when the II Corps and Smith's division departed Savage's Station they left nearly 3,000 wounded and sick soldiers at the hospital at the station and the field hospitals in the surrounding area.

After the battle of Savage's Station the Confederate railroad battery lay dormant. In June of 1863 a turntable was built at White House so the battery could be turned and aimed. In this manner it could fire on any vessels coming up the Pamunkey River. The battery was called into action again on June 4, 1864, as Grant's army neared Richmond. Lt. Barry and his artillerymen at Drury's Bluff were again ordered to man the mobile gun. The battery was pushed down the track to Bottom's Bridge where it remained until June 14, but was never used. The battery seems to have remained in the Richmond area until the siege of Petersburg where it may have been taken in the summer of 1864 although there is no written evidence.[134]

Whether or not George Savage stayed on his farm during battle of June 29 is not recorded, but on July 4 he and another Henrico County man were arrested by Confederate authorities for having taken the oath of allegiance to the United States and were charged with disloyalty. The charges against both men were dropped after they renounced the oath to the United States and reaffirmed their allegiance to the Confederate cause.[135]

Not long after the Federal troops left Savage's Station Mary Savage wrote her brother about what was left of the farm:

> No doubt you think it strange that I have not written to you since getting out of the Yankee lines; the fact is we have been in so much trouble that I have not had the heart to write and did not feel as if I could collect my thoughts sufficiently to do anything, I can with truth say, I have seen more trouble and suffered more agony of mind in the last two months than I have ever suffered in all my life before.
>
> I could not begin to give you a description of the utter desolation of our once happy farm. Mr. Savage had not had for years such prospect of fine crops. His crops were all grazed and destroyed. Our garden is ruined; you could not tell we ever had a garden. Hospital tents are pitched all over it. My furniture was stolen and broken. Even my crockery that was packed away in an outer store room was destroyed. They broke open both my store rooms in the yard and swept them of their entire contents. Had the army remained much longer quartered upon us, we should have been obliged to draw rations from them, for they took everything from us, with the exception of a little broom. There was nothing left for them to do but burn the house. I have no doubt they would have done it on their retreat, but for its being a hospital. All who have seen the place say they would not recognize it, but for the house. The out buildings are more or less destroyed. From the low grounds up through our entire farm they have burnt every fence, and the enclosure around the yard and garden. We have not a gate on the place. The fine large gates as you enter our farm are also burned.[136]

Once the Confederate forces took control of the hospital at Savage's Station and moved the patients to Richmond on July 13, Savage was able to start repairing some of the damage to his property and got back to farming. Life, however, did not get better for him. On August 15 his wife, Mary, died and was buried in Hollywood Cemetery in Richmond. Then, on November 17, 1862, his house was accidentally destroyed by a fire. After his house was destroyed George Savage rented a house in Richmond between Cary and Canal streets.[137]

George Savage tried to sell his farm in August of 1863, but it never sold. The fact that it had been occupied and nearly destroyed by Union troops along with the fear that the Yankees might come back, probably made it seem like a bad investment. George Savage apparently returned to his farm at some point as he died in Henrico County on September 30, 1867, at the age of 56. He was buried in Hollywood Cemetery beside his wife Mary. His farm was put up for auction in 1870.[138]

5

The Ambush at White Oak Swamp

As Smith's division left Savage's Station on the Williamsburg Road it was slowed by mud and miles of wagons, ambulances, and artillery units. Even though it was pitch black and still raining, the road, in many places, was lit up by hundreds of camp fires burning along the roadside where stragglers, wounded men, and teamsters were making coffee. The roads were so clogged the troops on foot took to marching in the woods beside the road. All night long the procession continued at a snail's pace.[1]

Private William E. Daniels, a shoemaker turned soldier from Middlebury, Vt., in the 5th Vermont's Co. B, was trying to keep up with his comrades, but weakened by diarrhea, he fell out by the roadside. Unable to see him in the darkness an artillery caisson ran over him severely injuring the small of his back, left hip, and right shoulder. A few minutes later Pvt. Frank Cunningham, one of Daniels' childhood friends from Middlebury also in Co. B, found Daniels' seemingly lifeless body in the darkness by the side of the road. Realizing his friend was alive he asked him where he was hurt. Daniels, barely able to speak, replied, "across the back." Cunningham thought Daniels' back was broken. About that time an ambulance came by and a surgeon told Cunningham to put Daniels aboard. With the help of another soldier Cunningham put Daniels in the ambulance. Daniels never returned to his company.[2]

Another 5th Vermont soldier, Corp. Amos A. Wright, in Co. A was also suffering from severe diarrhea. After struggling for several miles to keep up with his company he could go no further and laid down in the woods by the roadside. Private Alexander W. Davis, Co. D, 6th Vermont, who had been shot in the left foot was determined not to be captured and hobbled along with other wounded men toward White Oak Swamp. Davis had made about three miles by the next morning when he, Corporal Wright and numerous other wounded and sick Union soldiers were swept up by Confederate cavalry and taken back to the hospital at Savage's Station. On July 13 the hospital at Savage's Station was closed and the men were taken to prison camps in Richmond. Wright and Davis both ended up in the infamous prisoner of war camp on Belle Isle, a 54-acre island in the middle of the James River.[3]

Sometime after midnight the rain finally stopped making life a little easier for the Green Mountain Boys, but they were still tired, hungry, and thirsty. Captain George W. Quimby in Co. D, 4th Vermont, wrote from Harrison's Landing on July 12, 1862, of the brutal march, "But the fatiguing march of that night to get through the White Oak Swamp and to destroy the bridge before the Rebels could prevent it. It was awful—tired—worn out and thirsty—with no decent water to be had for love or money—I heard men offer money and I would have given 25 cents for a drink of good water." Pvt. Charles B. Dubois, Co. G, 3rd Vermont still remembered the thirst years later when he included it in his memoirs:

> Water was exceedingly scarce. Our canteens were empty. We were very thirsty, and would accept anything that was wet. We finally came to a mud puddle through which the teams of the entire army had passed and it was the only water available at that time, although filthy and liberally tainted with droppings of the animals, we ventured to help ourselves to it. One swallow was enough to sicken a dog, and we concluded to go dry until we could find something better which we did when we crossed the stream at day light. We had marched continually without a wink of sleep, and very little rest.[4]

Smith's division reached the White Oak Swamp Bridge at about 3 a.m. The men's steps quickened a little as they crossed the bridge knowing that they were finally safe. With Baldy Smith standing by the bridge cheering them on as they crossed their spirits were lifted even higher. After his division had crossed the bridge, Smith had his units march up the hill opposite the swamp until they reached a plateau about 50 feet above the swamp on the east side of the road, facing north, to hold the crossing. Davidson's brigade's left flank was placed on the road with Brooks' Vermont Brigade to its right, followed by Hancock's brigade. At this time Smith was in command of all the units at White Oak Swamp Bridge which included his division, Brig. Gen. Israel B. Richardson's division of the II Corps and Brig. Gen. Henry M. Naglee's brigade of Peck's division of the IV Corps that had been guarding Bottom's Bridge. Naglee's brigade was placed on the west side of the road opposite Davidson's brigade. Richardson's division left Savage's Station at 1 a.m. on June 30, serving as the rear guard for the army. In his after-action report General Richardson, a Fairfax, Vt., native, wrote:

Corporal Amos A. Wright, Co. A, 5th Vermont. Wright was captured by the rebels after he fell out of the ranks on the march to the James River (U.S. Army Heritage and Education Center).

> After marching until nearly daybreak in the morning, on coming up to the bridge I found the mass of stragglers from other parts of the army wedged in so as to be unable to move. I impressed them with the necessity of crossing as rapidly as possible or the enemy would be upon us and the rear of the army cut off. By the greatest exertions of myself and staff I succeeded in getting this mass over by sunrise and my own division, and the bridge was broken up and burned by about 10:00 a.m.[5]

After Richardson's division arrived Baldy Smith placed it on the west side of the road between Naglee's brigade and White Oak Swamp. Capt. Rufus D. Pettit's Battery B of the 1st New York light Artillery and Capt. Romeyn. B. Ayres' battery F of the 5th U.S. Artillery were positioned between Richardson's division and the swamp. Capt. Thaddeus P. Mott's 3rd New York Artillery was positioned on the east side of the road in front of Smith's division. Smith's order from McClellan was to hold the crossing at all costs until relived by an order from him.[6]

The last organized Federal unit to cross White Oak Swamp Bridge before it was burned was Capt. George W. Hazzard's batteries A and C of the 4th U.S. Artillery. Hazzard's batteries had inadvertently been left behind in the vicinity of Savage's Station when the other Federal units pulled out for White Oak Swamp. Exhausted from fighting the past several day's Hazzard and his artillerymen slept through the heavy down pour of rain that night. Somehow Hazzard had not received word to move out. The next morning the artillerymen were awakened by drums and bugles from the Confederate camps near them. Hazzard quickly ordered his men to quietly limber their guns and move out. Hazzard and two of his guns remained behind to cover the withdrawal. When the rest of his guns had proceeded down the Williamsburg road a short distance, Hazzard had the remaining two guns limbered and followed. For the first mile the horses were kept at a walk, then they broke into a trot and reached White Oak Swamp Bridge without incident. After crossing the bridge Hazzard's batteries were positioned on the west side of the road a short distance upstream from the bridge site in front of Richardson's division.[7]

The Vermonters were halted about a quarter of a mile above the bridge and east of the road in an open field bordered in the rear by a stand of pines. Here they stacked arms and everyone, officers and men, sank to the ground totally exhausted from the fight at Savage's Station and the night's march. Most of them immediately went to sleep while a few took the opportunity to get some water and eat whatever was left in their haversacks.[8]

According to the 2nd Vermont's Private Wilbur Fisk, "After crossing the creek at White Oak Swamp on a small eminence well calculated for defense, we threw down our blankets and assumed a horizontal position without stopping to calculate our proximity to the enemy or our chances of being awakened by a compliment of shells."[9]

Generals Franklin and Smith established their headquarters in the yard of a wood frame house near Smith's division. The house was owned by a man named James H. Britton. Writing years later General Franklin related a conversation he had with Mr. Britton that morning:

> In the house which has been described as about the middle of the left clearing lived an old man with a young wife and a child about two years old. He came to me about 10 o'clock and asked if I thought there would be a fight there that day. I told him that there certainly would be. He then asked when I thought it would begin. I thought in about half an hour. "Then," said he, "I will have time to take my wife and child to my brother who lives about half a mile down the swamp, and get back before it begins." "Yes," said I, "but why come back at all?" "Why," said he, "if I don't your men will take all my chickens and ducks."[10]

In addition to the infantry and artillery units covering the hill on the south side of the swamp, there were also hundreds of wagons, ambulances, and pack mules.[11]

At about 10:30 that morning Franklin joined McClellan at Glendale some two miles from White Oak Swamp Bridge where McClellan had summoned his corps commanders for a meeting to lay out their defensive positions for the day. Glendale was not

5. The Ambush at White Oak Swamp

This photograph shows why it was difficult to cross the White Oak Swamp anywhere other than the several bridges that existed. It was, and still is, a tangled mass of swampy water, mud, vines and brush (Library of Congress).

a town, but rather an intersection of the Charles City, Long Bridge, and Willis Church Roads.[12]

Back at the VI Corps field hospital the morning of Monday, June 30, revealed the human destruction sustained in the battle the previous night. Pvt. Lucius D. Savage of the 2nd Vermont's Co. F, who had been shot in the back of his right knee, noted in his diary:

> Sleep was entirely out of the question as some of our men were terribly wounded and in their agony or oblivion would groan and yell at all times during the night.
> Monday morning June 30th at daylight I determined to resume my journey towards the James

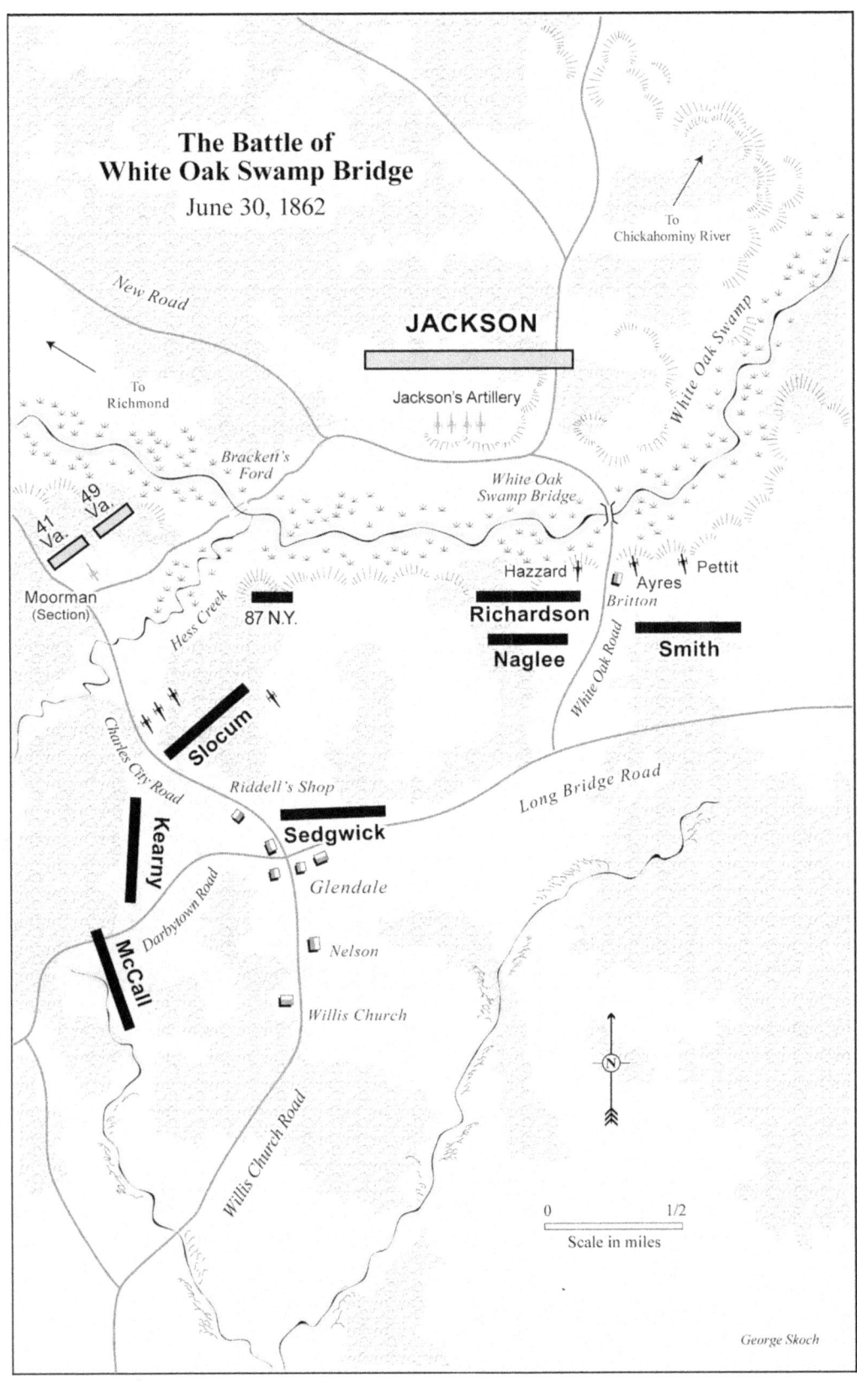

River. I rolled my blankets up, placed them on my knapsack, but upon attempting to arise I found that I could not raise my wounded leg from the floor an instant. So I unrolled my blankets and laid down again, realizing for the first time that I was left with hundreds of others to be taken prisoners. As I looked out the door upon attempting to get up I saw the rear guard of our troops passing in the direction of White Oak Swamp. I aroused some of our boys who were not wounded and told them I reckoned this was their time to leave if they did not want to be taken prisoners. And all but one (a Dutchman in a NY Reg't.) availed themselves of the opportunity and went along with our troops. About 8 o'clock a.m. the Confederates made their appearance, first indicated by a line of skirmishers emerging from the woods through which we charged the night before, followed by "Stonewall" Jackson and staff who rode past and halted upon a little eminence near the house where I lay. [They] took out their glasses and examined the country in the direction of White Oak Swamp.

During Monday I was carried on a stretcher (by some of our men who had remained to care for the wounded) back to another house nearer the battlefield of the previous night, where there was a larger number of our men left that were wounded. A day or two after my arrival here I was somewhat startled after having had some conversation with some of the nurses to hear someone ask if that was L.D. Savage. And upon looking in the direction of the nurse I saw E.W. Loomis with one arm gone. He had been lying under the porch of the house as it had been raining and had just emerged from his den. And standing there with a old dirty Army blanket thrown over his shoulder, I could not think from his appearance it was anyone I had ever seen, but I recognized his voice upon asking who it was. We were outdoors during our stay at this place and it rained most of the time. My wound was quite painful. My foot and leg were much discolored and I feared it was mortifying. I called the attention of Dr. Bromley of a Michigan Reg't. to it and he examined it carefully and said that the blood circulated a little. [He] told me that the ball in passing through my leg had bruised the main artery, but did not sever it, which caused the stopping of the circulation. After a few days this discoloring disappeared and my leg resumed its natural color.[13]

Pvt. Daniel F. Cooledge in the 2nd Vermont's Co. A recorded his miserable experience at the field hospital in his diary:

We lay out last night. It rained some. My leg pained me so that I could not sleep much. Our troops all moved off last night except a rear guard. The advance of the enemy came up at about noon and was soon passing by in a continual stream which was kept up until near night. Jackson's forces passed here today. Firing can be heard in the advance. There are about sixty or seventy of us in and around this house. It is intensely hot here in the sun. What a hard lot it is to be surrounded by so many helpless men some of them suffering everything but death. One poor fellow died at my left hand this afternoon.[14]

Dr. William W. Potter, one of the three doctors left at the VI Corps 2nd division field hospital, told of his experience on June 30 the day after the battle:

Sometime during the forenoon, about 10 o'clock I should think, the head of General D.H. Hill's division halted in front of the hospital, and from him a pass was obtained which authorized me to visit the battlefield of the evening before, for the purpose of ascertaining if any of the wounded had been overlooked. This I did in the afternoon accompanied by one of the guards, and met on the field a Confederate ambulance squad in charge of a sergeant, already engaged in the same duty. A few wounded were found in the woods on the left, and I also counted about seventy Union dead, most of which lay in the opening through which the Williamsburg Road passes out into the open [where the 5th Vermont lost so many men].[15]

On Tuesday July 1, the VI Corps field hospital was closed and the wounded men were consolidated with the other patients at the hospital at Savage's Station. On July 13 the Savage's Station hospital was closed and the patients and doctors were transported to Richmond on railroad flat cars and incarcerated in prisoner of war camps.[16]

In 1866 the Federal government, through pressure from Clara Barton and others, initiated a program to reinter the remains of Union soldiers that were scattered across the south by the tens of thousands in government cemeteries. In Henrico County sites for four national cemeteries were selected. One of the four sites was on the Williamsburg Road in what is now the town of Sandston. This cemetery, named the Seven Pines National Cemetery, would be the final resting place for the remains from the battlefields of Fair Oaks/Seven Pines and the surrounding area of French's Field/King's School House, Fair Oaks Station, and Savage's Station, including the men buried at the VI Corps field hospital, and the surrounding fields and woods. The cemetery originally consisted of 1.3-acres, but two more small parcels were added in 1874 and 1875 increasing its size to 1.9-acres. Tragically, of the 1,356 Federal remains reinterred in this cemetery 1,202 remain unknown.[17]

On the afternoon of Monday, June 30, things were about to heat up at the White Oak Swamp Bridge. While the Union troops were sleeping and resting, General Stonewall Jackson's command arrived on the hill on the north side of White Oak Swamp opposite General Smith and his troops. As quietly as possible a road was cut through the woods and approximately 30 pieces of artillery were brought forward and aimed at boys in blue across the valley. At about 2 p.m. everything was ready on the Confederate side of the valley. Lanyards were pulled and the cannons belched forth a fury of shot and shell that fell into the ranks of the unsuspecting Yankees.[18]

After Baldy Smith had positioned his troops he wrote later that he:

> ... looked over the ground, made my disposition of the division, and then threw myself on the ground and tried to get some sleep. I had, however, been too long without it or was too anxious, and giving it up as a failure I thought to refresh myself with a cold bath. Taking matters very leisurely and being about half dressed I was surprised by the most terrific roar of cannons and crashing of projectiles. Opening the door of the little outhouse, where I was, I saw a great number of pieces had been quietly placed on the opposite bank, and that they were throwing an immense quantity of iron—in fact the air seemed literally full of it. Trying to get hold of my Negro groom, I found he had taken my best horse in the direction of safety, and I saw no more of him or horse for two days. An English servant with me at the time the guns opened was very cool and went and saddled another horse, and brought [it] to me during which time I had finished dressing, and began to take an inventory of losses.[19]

Some of the rounds burst when they struck the ground while others burst in the air over the Yankee's heads. Solid cannon balls were also in the mix and would go bouncing along after they hit the ground destroying anything in their path. Men, who only split seconds before, had been sound asleep, sprang to their feet. In addition to being scared out of their wits, they were totally disoriented and ran in every direction for cover. Officers were wandering about in the smoke and dust looking for their commands. Private Kirk Rand of the 2nd Vermont's Co. C related his experience during the shelling:

> as we were tired most of us were asleep when the first thing we know we were greeted with a shower of shell, grape and every other missile that is used in cannons. it was awful of all the cannonading I ever saw or heard that beat the whole and to add to the scene Mott's battery which was in front of us catched it so hard that they had to cut their horses loose and leave some of their pieces and their horses and officers horses. [Horses] that had broke loose came tearing through our ranks knocking some of us over and scattering in every direction. we were more afraid of the horses than we were the shells.[20]

The 20th New York that the Green Mountain Boys had marched over at Savage's Station embarrassed themselves again in this bombardment as General Smith related in his autobiography:

Brigadier General Smith's favorite horse and his groom. The groom took off with the horse before Smith could mount it when the Confederates shelled the Union position at White Oak Swamp on June 30, 1862 (Vermont Historical Society).

One of my regiments, the 20th New York Volunteers, had scattered like chaff. On getting some staff officers after them we managed to collect six hundred, but four hundred only returned when driven back by hunger two days afterwards.[21]

Private Charles Dubois in the 3rd Vermont's Co. G was about scared to death when the shells started exploding as he wrote later in his memoirs:

I jumped to my feet, grabed the first gun on the stack that I could lay my hand on, the greatest confusion prevailed, it was every man for himself. We did not stop to dress on the right general guide or on the colors. I jumped the fence that skirted the open field in a single bound, passed through a strip of woods and came out into another clearing filled with men and artillery. Shells were bursting amongst this vast heard of teams, unutterable confusion prevailed. I became mixed up in this tangle and lost my regiment and saw no more of it that day.

As I passed near a four horse team, the driver of which was making desperate efforts to get his team out of a mixup, a shot came over, passed very near me, struck a right-wheel horse, cutting off both of his fore legs, unhorsing the driver who picked himself up and without stopping to argue the question, made good time for a less exposed position, leaving the team in a badly mixed up condition. I did not stop to repair damages, as I had important business of my own to attend to, viz: to find a more congenial atmosphere further on as shot and shell were flying thick and fast and I was very anxious to get out of their reach, and did not propose to leave any stone unturned that would delay the accomplishment of this object. Under any other circumstances I should doubtless have gone with the regiment over the fence and took refuse with them in the pine woods nearby, but being so suddenly disturbed from my slumbers, and not a little bewildered and somewhat panick stricken, I took in my haste a different direction from the main body of the regiment. I became lost, and after the firing had ceased or at least after I had gotten out of range of the shot and shell I became myself again. The most important question was, where was my regiment. I supposed that it had been scattered to the four winds of the earth like myself and I knew not where to look for it so I decided to keep right on down the road which most likely would lead me to the James River.[22]

Not long after the Confederate bombardment commenced Stonewall Jackson saw some of the Union units on the other side of the swamp moving up the hill to get away from the shelling and thought they might be retreating. Thinking there might be a way to get across the swamp he had Col. Thomas T. Munford's 2nd Virginia Cavalry ride down to the bridge site to see if they could get across there. Munford and his men rode down to the bridge and stopped. To Munford crossing looked almost impossible. Stonewall rode up behind him and told him to try crossing. Munford and some of his men went thrashing across the muddy swamp and actually made it to the opposite side with Jackson and General D.H. Hill right behind them. Jackson told Munford to charge the Federal guns up the hill. Obeying orders, Munford and his cavalrymen charged toward the enemy only to be stopped by intense rifle fire. They swerved left and rode downstream and crossed back over the swamp. Seeing that the Union force was larger than they thought, Jackson and D.H. Hill wheeled about and struggled back over the swamp. That was the only attempt Jackson made on June 30 to cross White Oak Swamp.[23]

General Franklin was on his way back to White Oak Swamp Bridge from his meeting with McClellan and the other Corps commanders when he heard the start of the Confederate bombardment. Franklin remembered later, "I had gone but a short distance when a bombardment commenced in the direction of the bridge, the severity of which I had never heard equaled in the field. The wood through which I was riding seemed torn to pieces with round shot and exploding shells. But the danger was really greater from falling branches than from the shot, which did small damage."[24]

After the bombardment started the Vermonters collected fairly quickly in the pines behind the field where they had been asleep. The coolness with which some of their officers, like the Second Vermont's assistant surgeon Carpenter who rode back and forth in the crowd, calmed the men down. Within several minutes General Brooks rode slowly among them on his iron-gray horse and the regiments fell into formation amid cheers for their general. Brooks then threw a skirmish line forward, just beyond the tree line, and waited for what might come next. "Our division having rallied from what bid fair to panic, we held our ground," remembered the 2nd Vermont's Captain John Tyler.[25]

As soon as the rebel artillery opened up Captain Ayres ordered his and Mott's batteries into position to open at once in reply. This unequal contest continued only a short time when Mott's battery was shot up and thrown into confusion and soon became useless. At that time General Smith ordered all the batteries engaged to be withdrawn across the field. Ayres' battery was drawn off to the right and rear, so as to be in position on the left of Smith's division and the right of Richardson's. The order came at an opportune time as the woods on the right flank of the position would very soon be full of enemy sharpshooters. Captain George Hazzard's guns of companies A and C of the 4th U.S. Artillery were on the west side of the road and were screened from the rebel's view by trees, but the rebel artillerymen fired at the smoke from Hazzard's guns with some success. In his new position Ayres' guns joined Hazzard's and they pounded the Confederates and, of course, the Confederates did likewise. The artillery duel continued until darkness brought it to a close. During the afternoon Captain Hazzard was hit in the leg by a shell fragment shattering the bone. He died on August 14 in an army hospital in Baltimore, Md., from complications of his wound.[26]

During the shelling James H. Britton's house was riddled with shells. One of the first shells to hit the house took off one of Mr. Britton's legs and he bled to death. General Franklin said that the poor old man, "had sacrificed himself for his poultry."[27]

Near 4 p.m. Jackson sent several units upstream to see if they could find a crossing. Several of Franklin's units saw the movement and reported it to Franklin who asked Sumner for support. Sumner sent Brig. Gen. Napoleon J.T. Dana's and Col. Alfred Sully's brigades of Sedgwick's division. There was no further rebel movement after Dana and Sully arrived and at 5 p.m. they were sent back to Sumner.[28]

The artillery duel went on sporadically all day until finally ceasing at nightfall. Considering the amount of iron the Confederates threw across the swamp, the casualties in the Vermont Brigade were fairly light. Corporal John Carmody, a 29-year-old Irish immigrant from Springfield, Vt., and one of General Smith's enlisted orderlies, lost the hearing in his right ear from the concussion of a bursting shell. Private Phineas Belden, a store clerk from Benson, Vt., in the 5th Vermont's Co. B had a shell burst behind him. The concussion from the explosion injured his spine and fragments from the shell perforated the back of his legs. Fortunately, he was placed in the back of a baggage wagon and made it safely to Harrison's Landing. Because of the results of his wounds Belden's soldiering days were over and he was given a disability discharge from the army on May 14, 1863. Twenty-one-year-old Private James Laden from Bennington, Vt., in Co. A, 4th Vermont, was hit by a piece of shrapnel that struck him on the inside of his lower left leg and passed clean through shattering his tibia. Like Belden, Laden was placed in a baggage wagon for the rest of the trip to Harrison's Landing. The acting sergeant major of the 6th Vermont, Dexter E. Boyden, was wounded in the head by a shell fragment. Unable to march with his regiment he was left at the bridge where he was captured by the rebels and taken back to the hospital at Savage's Station. He was paroled on August 5, 1862. Boyden would recover from his wound and live a very colorful life.[29]

In addition to the artillery bombardment the rebel sharpshooters were also firing at the mass of blue-clad troops. George S. Flanders, a 24-year-old farmer from Cavendish, Vt., in Co. C, 4th Vermont, was shot in the right hand. The bullet went through his hand breaking several bones and severing tendons. On the march to the James River Flanders fell out of the ranks and was left by the roadside where he was captured by the rebels. After he was paroled he was sent to the U.S. Army general hospital at Annapolis, Md. Sometime later Flanders was transferred to the hospital at the Convalescent Camp in Alexandria, Va. After his wound healed he could no longer bend the fingers on his right hand rendering him unable to fire a rifle and he was given a disability discharge from the army on February 9, 1863.[30]

While the artillery duel was taking place at White Oak Swamp Bridge, the other part of Lee's plan to cut McClellan's line of march in half at Glendale Crossroads was taking place. One of the main roads leading to this important junction was defended by Slocum's division of Franklin's VI Corps. Huger's division was moving down the Charles City road toward the crossroads, but spent most of the day chopping through abatis that Slocum had erected in front of his position. Porter's V Corps had already taken possession of Malvern Hill so the best Lee could hope for was to sever McClellan's line at Glendale and gobble up the Federal units strung out from Glendale and White Oak Swamp Bridge then turn his attention to Porter. Lee positioned Maj. Gen. Theophilus H. Holmes' division of 6,000 unseasoned troops between the back side of Malvern Hill and the James River, but Porter's artillery kept them from moving up Malvern Hill. Magruder's division was moving toward Glendale on the Darbytown Road and Longstreet's division was on its way to Glendale on the Long Bridge Road.[31]

Magruder was ordered to send reinforcements to Holmes and would not take part in the days action. Poor staff work prevented Lee's seven divisions from making a coordinated effort to stop McClellan's movements. In the meantime Glendale was reinforced by the divisions of Sedgwick, Kearny, McCall, and Hooker. Lee, however, ordered Longstreet and A.P. Hill to attack at Glendale even though this would not get under way until 4:40 p.m. and there was little chance of success. The battle lasted until dark with the Union holding their position allowing the rest of the army to safely make its way to Malvern Hill. In this short, but fierce battle McClellan lost 2,853 men killed and wounded to Lee's 3,615. This battle is also known as the battle of Frayser's Farm.[32]

Smith's division resumed its march to the James River at about 11 p.m. when he drew his division out quietly from its lines. By having officers shout false orders, the Confederates were fooled into thinking that the division was still in place. In this march Smith moved by a comparatively unused road, two miles south of Willis Church Road over which the main portion of the army moved. This road had been reconnoitered by a member of General Smith's staff the previous day and found to be useable. "The discovery of this road," says General Franklin, "made the concentration of the troops at Malvern Hill a completed maneuver by noon of the 1st of July, and was due to the fertile brain of General Smith, who ordered the exploration." General D.H. Hill wrote later, "That night Franklin glided silently by Longstreet and A.P. Hill. He had to pass within easy range of their artillery; but they did not know he was there." Although almost most tired to death Smith's troops pushed on through the night until soon after daylight Tuesday morning when they reached the James River at Turkey Bend.[33]

In leaving White Oak Swamp Bridge General Smith and his staff were almost left to be captured by the enemy as he related years later:

> Arrangements were made for the order of march—a battery was left to fire occasionally to indicate we were still on the ground, and I laid down to get some sleep, giving orders to my staff to call me in an hour. My aides were as myself and we slept for some hours and finally I awoke to find everything gone, and we were far behind, and in danger of being picked up by the enemy's advance. We did not loiter along the road till we had caught up. Having found by an examination made by Captain West of my staff a new road which would be unoccupied by other troops, we had sent word to Heintzelman next on our left that he must look out for his rear as we would not be behind him, we had a clear march.[34]

At daylight Smith's division halted in a field near Turkey Creek where the James River was close enough that the men could see the masts of the Federal gunboats off in the distance. Everyone was absolutely exhausted. General Smith wrote of the march in his autobiography, "There is no agony I have ever experienced to compare with that of an intense desire to sleep on horseback. Accustomed to falling asleep and continually waking the seconds of sleep were filled with the most horrible nightmares in addition to intense physical pain. That march is burned into my memory."[35]

Breakfast and sleep, however, would have to wait. Responding to the threat of the rebels closing in on Malvern Hill, Smith's division was ordered to backtrack a short distance and deploy in line of battle in some woods facing Western Run on the right of the army. It remained deployed all day, but the enemy never appeared in its front.[36]

On July 1 Lee made his final attempt to destroy McClellan's retreating army at Malvern Hill. General Porter had taken advantage of this natural defensive position and had his units in place by about 9 a.m. on June 30. He also had time to post 250 pieces of artillery to cover every enemy approach. The area between his defensive line and Long Bridge Road was one vast kill zone. This battle would be one of Lee's worst mistakes of the war. Lee had inadequate maps and he had not reconnoitered the area. He also ignored a warning by a member of D.H. Hill's staff, who was familiar with the area, that the hill could be made almost impregnable. Despite all of that Lee was determined to attack and destroy the Army of the Potomac.[37]

For this attack Stonewall Jackson was to continue his advance from the north and to approach Malvern Hill along Willis Church Road. His command included his own division as well as those of Whiting, Ewell, and D.H. Hill. Magruder who was behind Jackson was to follow the same road and form on Jackson's right. Longstreet and A.P. Hill were to be in reserve. Lee planned to mass his artillery to support the Confederate infantry attack.[38]

Jackson's command reached Western Run, a formidable swamp barrier, and halted to reconnoiter the enemy defenses covering his approach. Magruder was misinformed by local guides and took the Long Bridge Road southwest and marched away from the battlefield to an obscure country lane his guides assured him was Willis Church Road.[39]

At approximately 1 p.m. as the Confederates were trying to get their artillery in position the Union artillery opened up on them. By 2:30 p.m. it was apparent to Lee that his guns were not going to succeed in giving his infantry the necessary support and within an hour all but a few of the rebel guns were silenced.[40]

After mistakenly being informed that the Federals were retreating Lee ordered Magruder, who had finally found his way back to the battlefield, to attack. Magruder's intended attack with 15,000 men disintegrated into an advance of only a third of his men and without artillery support he was repulsed with heavy losses.[41]

When D.H. Hill heard Magruder's advance start he misconstrued it as being the signal prescribed for the general assault and he led a suicidal attack along Willis Church Road. Brigadier General Ambrose R. Wright and Brig. Gen. William Mahone on the Confederate right also advanced. Colonel John B. Gordon led some of Brig. Gen. Robert E. Rodes' regiments to within 200 yards of the Union guns only have them torn apart. Brigadier General Roswell S. Ripley's brigade was shot to pieces as it advanced across open ground in the face of the Federal artillery. Several other rebel brigades were sent reeling back. In the end Lee's attack at Malvern Hill was a total disaster. General D.H. Hill said later, "It was not war—it was murder." The casualties at Malvern Hill were staggering with McClellan losing 3,214 men killed, wounded, and missing. Lee's loss was even greater with total of 5,355 casualties.[42]

At 2 a.m., July 2, just as the rain started to pour, Smith's division was on the move again toward the James River. The road immediately turned into a sea of sticky mud. As the Vermont Brigade was slipping and sliding along, Pvt. Edwin A. Cummings, Company G's fifer in the 4th Vermont, who was suffering from chronic hepatitis, was so weak that he collapsed by the roadside and was captured by the Confederates the next day. He was paroled on August 3 and sent to Hammond U.S. Army General Hospital at Point Lookout, Md., where he was given a disability discharge on November 1, 1862. Unlike Cummings,

Corp. Eri S. Gunnison in the 2nd Vermont's Co. F was keeping up with his comrades until, unseen in the darkness, he was trampled by a troop of Union cavalry severely injuring his back. He was found the next day and brought to Harrison's landing where he was put aboard ship and sent to Hammond U.S. Army General Hospital at Fort Lookout, Md. Sometime later he was transferred to Satterlee U.S. Army General Hospital, West Philadelphia, Penn. He was returned to duty March 4, 1863. Still suffering from his injuries, Corporal Gunnison was not able to perform field duties and on October 5, 1863, he was transferred to Co. F, 6th Regiment of the Invalid Corps.[43]

With the end near, the men were throwing away everything that would impede their flight. The roadside was littered with thousands of rifles, knapsacks, and other types of military equipment. In the middle of the road were dead and dying mules and horses along with abandoned wagons mired down in the morass of mud. Physically exhausted and sick soldiers fell out by the hundreds only to be picked up later by the Confederates and imprisoned. In the morning's darkness and the miserable downpour, Smith's men slogged on through the mud until a little after noon, when they finally reached the safety of Harrison's Landing.[44]

The 3rd Vermont's Lt. Col. Wheelock G. Veazey described this march later stating:

> No person can give any conception of the wake of a retreating army after such a campaign in such a country. It simply beggared description. Stragglers sick and dying, arms of every description, stores of all kinds, abandoned wagons, broken down horses and mules, mud so deep that no bottom could be reached. All these at every step; and then add the sickening feeling of defeat and retreat, and the momentary expectation of a rear attack, and no help within reach. Weary, hungry, exhausted, sick, what torment could be added, except the loss of honor? Such was our dreary march as a rear guard to Harrison's Landing.[45]

In his autobiography General Smith told a humorous story about himself as he reached Harrison's Landing:

> On reaching Harrison's Landing I came to a steep path down to a valley. The soil was of clay and the heavy rain had made it very slippery. The descent was so steep that I dismounted to lead my horse down. I had no sooner touched the crest that my feet went out from under me,—the bridle was pulled out of my hand and I ploughed a hollow track clear to the bottom, an excess of mud falling over my legs in cataracts. On reaching the bottom I looked up and saw my dejected horse with head down and a picture woe. I could not get back to him and was in a quandary, when fortunately a soldier, probably a straggler, appeared and led my horse to me,—when I mounted I had pounds of extra mud for him to carry.[46]

At Harrison's Landing, the majority of the army was clustered on what was actually Berkeley Plantation. For some reason, over the years, the area had become named for the landing on the James River in front of the house. Berkeley, built in 1725, was the historic home of Virginia's Harrison family, which had produced Benjamin Harrison, a signer of the Declaration of Independence, and William Henry Harrison, ninth president of the United States. It was also the site of the first official Thanksgiving service in 1619. In the Harrison's fields along the river, which measured roughly four miles by one mile, McClellan had squeezed in 90,000 soldiers, 288 artillery pieces, 3,000 wagon and ambulances, 27,000 horses and mules, and 2,500 head of cattle.[47]

In no time the soldiers had stomped the soggy fields into a sea of impassable semi-liquid paste. After the divisions had been guided into their positions the men sank exhausted to the ground. Those that still had them, put up their tents, using the wheat in the fields as flooring. Those without tents just pulled their rubber blankets over them and slept the sleep of the dead. The 4th Vermont was sent out that night for picket duty in front of the division. The rain continued through most of the night and by morning the men who had set up tents now had wet canvas in their faces as the ground was too saturated to hold their tent pegs.[48]

While the exhausted Yankees had been sleeping, Jeb Stuart, whose cavalry had been shadowing the retreating Yankees, set up his artillery on Evelynton Heights across Herring Creek from Berkeley Plantation, near Westover Church. Evelynton Heights was about 20 feet higher than the fields around Berkeley and provided an excellent field of fire. A little after 8 a.m., Stuart let loose several rounds that fell into the sleeping Yankees' camp causing quite a stir, but doing little damage. McClellan ordered Smith to take his division up to the heights and chase off the rebels, which was done in no time. To stabilize the situation, Smith asked McClellan to send up Slocum's division reuniting the VI Corps. As soon as the rebels were gone Smith set his men to digging fortifications. Smith's men would continue digging for the next six weeks.[49]

McClellan immediately dispersed his divisions for better defense of the area. Smith's division was moved to the area surrounding Westover Church, on the Edmund Ruffin farm, called Evelynton. The entire army was then set to work, day and night, digging an entrenchment that would eventually surround the entire army from Herring Creek to Kimages Creek. Edmund Ruffin was an ardent and fire-eating secessionist who was supposed to have been given the honor of firing the first shot at Fort Sumter. When the south lost the war, Ruffin wrapped himself in a Confederate flag and shot himself in the head with a rifle.[50]

Westover Church was established in 1613. The structure around which Smith's division camped was built in 1737. The quaint little church had been attended over the years by presidents Washington, Jefferson, William Henry Harrison, and Tyler. As with most property in Virginia, including churches, the Vermonters paid little respect. The 2nd Vermont's Lieutenant Chester K. Leach wrote his wife, "The Co.s are making ovens with the brick from the wall around the church to bake bread, but how long they will have the benefit of them is more than I can tell." Several weeks later he wrote, "The boys are feeling quite well now, on account of having soft bread to eat, which each Co. makes themselves and good bread it is too. Butter is to be had too." To this day the wall around the church has not been replaced.[51]

The inevitable accidents that happen in army camps started just days after the Vermont Brigade arrived at Harrison's Landing. Drum Major John Wheeler had survived the Seven Days without a scratch only to accidentally shoot himself in the foot while cleaning his pistol several days after reaching Harrison's Landing. After he was treated in his regimental hospital he was sent to the Judiciary Square U.S. Army General Hospital in Washington, D.C. Orville D. Cobleigh, a private from Waterford, Vt., in Co. G, 4th Vermont, also safely survived the Seven Days and the march to Harrison's Landing without injury. Then, on July 8, he was cleaning his rifle, which he thought was unloaded, and accidently shot himself in the left hand. The ball crushed some of the metacarpal bones and tore tendons as it passed through. Pieces of bone worked their way out of the wound for several years after the accident. He was evacuated to the Philadelphia Episcopal U.S. Army General Hospital in Philadelphia, Penn., where he was given a disability discharge from the army on October 26, 1862.[52]

On the 4th of July Smith's division assembled and was reviewed by McClellan. On July 8 the entire Army of the Potomac was reviewed by President Lincoln. It was nearly

Westover Church as it appears today. Westover Church was established in 1613 (Sarah J. Zeller).

dark before the President reached the Vermont Brigade which had been waiting for him for hours. Although hot and tired, and probably more than a little annoyed, the men had spirit enough to give him three cheers and a tiger roar.[53]

During the review on July 4 a lone drummer boy, 12-year-old Willie Johnston from St. Johnsbury, Vt., in Co. D, 3rd Vermont, drummed for the review. Although he was only 5 feet tall, Willie was the only drummer in the second division that had retained his drum during the retreat to the James River. Others, to include grown men, had thrown theirs away. When the secretary of war, Edwin M. Stanton, heard this story he recommended Willie for the Medal of Honor for "Gallantry in the Seven Days fighting and the Peninsula Campaign." The medal was presented to Willie on September 16, 1863, personally by the secretary of war. Willie Johnston is the youngest recipient of the Medal of Honor.[54]

Whether sour grapes, or the truth, Charles B. Dubois in the 3rd Vermont's Co. G had a different opinion of little Willie Johnston and his heroic deeds and said so in his memoires:

> Right here I wish to correct a wrong impression which has gotten into print in different publications in the State of Vermont in regard to the "Drummer Boy" of Company D of our regiment, Willie Johnston, by name.... The facts in this case so far as I have ever been able to learn them from personal observation and from statements from comrades acquainted with the facts are these. Willie was a little boy, a pet with the boys, and a sort of a mascot for the regiment. He could drum just a little. I have my doubts as to his ever being mustered into the United States service. He was cared for by Mrs. Harman, the hospital nurse and on long marches rode on the teams, and he and his drum were carried through the seven days campaign on the teams, and the statement of his drum being the only one brought to Harrison's Landing is most absurd and does a great injustice to other drummers who

brought their drums through the struggle of the seven days. But his case is only parallel with hundreds of other "Youngest Soldiers" and Drummer Boys I've read of in many writings on the war of the rebellion.[55]

The day after the review by the president was a scorcher, and a number of the Vermonters went down to Herring Creek, behind Westover Church, for a swim. A group from the 2nd Vermont's Co. E was led by Sgt. George E. Allen. The boys stripped down and jumped in. Allen swam across the creek, which was about 120 to 150 feet wide, and was returning when he was seized by stomach cramps and sank. He clawed his way to the surface and yelled for help, but the man nearest him was a weak swimmer and was afraid to attempt to rescue him. Allen sank again, surfaced one more time, and then went down for good. Several men ran back to camp to get help, but by the time a rescue party arrived it was too late. Due to the swiftness and depth of the water they could not recover his body.[56]

The next morning a number of the boys from Co. E went back to the creek and finally found Allen's body floating face down on the surface. His body was brought to camp and Allen was buried the next day just south of the church overlooking the creek where he had drowned.[57]

While the men themselves had a pretty good idea as to who had been killed, wounded, and captured during the battles of the past month, that was not the case for the families back home. Newspaper battle reports were often incorrect and so were the casualty lists. An example of the anxiety born by loved ones in Vermont involves Major Charles H. Joyce of the 2nd Vermont.

During the last two weeks of July, Major Joyce received word from Vermont that his wife had received an erroneous telegram informing her that he had been killed at the battle of Savage's Station. His wife apparently took the news very badly and even though she soon found out the information was a mistake, she was still quite distraught. Joyce submitted a request for a leave of absence on August 3, stating, "Leave of absence for twenty days is hereby respectfully requested to enable me to return to Vermont to visit my family who are quite ill, caused by a false telegram to them that I was killed in the fight at Savage's Station, & also to recruit my own health, which is such as to render me unfit for duty." Even though his request went all the way up the chain of command to the assistant secretary of war, Joyce did not get his leave of absence. Rather than resign to go home, he contented himself with corresponding with his wife by mail.[58]

At the evening dress parade on July 20 Privates William Flanders and Henry G. Hunter, both of Co. B, 2nd Vermont, were drummed out of camp. They had been sentenced by court-martial earlier for refusing to fall in with the regiment to meet the enemy on June 1. Two members of the 2nd Vermont's Co. A, Private Nelson C. Bradford, a native of Fitchburg, Mass., who had enlisted in Bennington, Vt., and 24-year-old Pvt. Jerome Draper, from Shaftsbury, Vt., were sentenced to be drummed out of camp. They had been convicted of going AWOL on May 31 and missing the same movement that Flanders and Hunter missed. Bradford did, in fact, get drummed out with the two men from Company B, but Private Draper deserted rather than face the humiliation. He was arrested at home on January 21, 1864, and charged with desertion.[59]

Maj. Gen. Henry W. Halleck, the new chief of staff of the army, came to Harrison's Landing on July 25 to consult with McClellan. McClellan wanted to cross the James and assault the yet unfortified city of Petersburg, a valuable Confederate railroad hub. Halleck was dead set against the idea and insisted that McClellan move up the north bank of the James River and attack Richmond. By the time Halleck left, McClellan was under the impression Halleck was going to send reinforcements so the army continued to sit along the banks of the James River until the reinforcements arrived.[60]

The four weeks without enemy action at Harrison's Landing was interrupted in the wee hours of the morning on August 1. On the opposite side of the James River from Harrison's Landing was Coggin's Point jutting out into the river. Here the width of the river was reduced to a mere 1,000 yards. During the last couple days of July the Confederates had silently, and without detection, positioned 43 pieces of artillery there and aimed them at the Federal fleet and the camps at Harrison's Landing. At 1 a.m. on August 1 they unleashed their guns. Lieutenant Leach described what happened:

> Thursday night about one o'clock we were somewhat broke of our slumbers by heavy artillery fire from the Rebs on the side of the river the boats in the river. For awhile they had it all their own way, but after a while the gunboats and artillery on this side commenced returning the compliments, when the matter was soon ended. We being to the front and farther from the river were not reached although some shots came well towards us.[61]

The bombardment only lasted about a half an hour and Union losses were light with 10 men killed and 15 wounded. By August 3 McClellan had sufficient forces across the river to secure the point and preclude any further surprise attacks.[62]

The Virginia heat, bad food, and the labor the men were performing daily at Harrison's Landing were wearing them down as August rolled around. This irritation was evident in a letter written to the editor of the *Watchman and State Journal* in Montpelier, Vt., by an unidentified soldier on the 6th Vermont on August 1:

> Our food consists of the three simple kinds of army rations, viz: hard bread, saltpeter beef and greesy coffee. When I do take up a paper and read that "the Quartermaster General has decided to furnish the army with vegetables fresh from the Northern market," it makes me wish he would. We acknowledge the receipt of some potatoes once, and then we were so *diseased* for vegetables that we "ate them skins and all!" While we are waiting for reinforcements it does seem to me that we might be made more comfortable.—Still I am willing to bide my time in hope that the future will bring forth something to increase our comfort and ambition. It is a dull routine during this excessive hot weather, to go on picket guard once in four days and shoveling and chopping wood the other three, with the squalid food we receive.[63]

While McClellan's army had been campaigning on the Peninsula, the Federal government created a new army on June 26, 1862. Although named the Army of Virginia, it was more a collection of units than a real army. Its mission was to protect Washington and the Shenandoah Valley and to move east of the Blue Ridge Mountains to draw Confederate troops away from Richmond. It consisted of three corps with a strength of about 47,000 men and was commanded by Maj. Gen. John Pope.[64]

Robert E. Lee was now in a very tenuous position. The Army of the Potomac lay on the outskirts of Richmond. Burnside's army of 7,500 men was at Newport News, Va. Burnside was something of a wild card with the ability to march up the Peninsula to reinforce McClellan or move up the south side of the James and attack Petersburg. Lastly, Pope could drive south to link-up with McClellan.[65]

Lee watched and waited. Then on July 12, Pope left Washington. Knowing he could not wait and withstand an attack from the combined forces of McClellan and Pope, Lee sent Jackson with two divisions to intercept Pope. The two forces clashed at Cedar Mountain on August 9. Pope's men were driving the Confederates back until Maj. Gen. Ambrose P. Hill's division delivered a crushing counterattack and the Union forces fell back.[66]

In late July, General McClellan cautiously made one foray out of his fortifications with 17,000 men to try to push toward Richmond. The expedition met stiff resistance at Malvern Hill and McClellan pulled his troops back. That was his last action of the Peninsula Campaign. Several days later McClellan started moving his army to Northern Virginia to reinforce General Pope.[67]

Smith's division, again rear guard for the army, did not leave Harrison's Landing until August 16 several days after the move began. The Vermont Brigade left camp about 4 o'clock on Saturday afternoon, marched five or six miles and halted for the night at Charles City Court House. Part of the delay was the 25-mile long wagon train that preceded the VI Corps. Colonel Whiting stated, "It was forty-five hours after the first train passed, till our brigade, next to the last, passed out."[68]

Twelve miles were made on August 17 bringing Smith's division to the Chickahominy River where they crossed a 2,000-foot pontoon bridge spanning the river and camped for the night. On Tuesday, August 19, the division reached Williamsburg, passing by the College of William and Mary and the old Virginia Capitol. Smith's division camped that night near the spot where they had witnessed the battle of Williamsburg.[69]

The march down the Peninsula continued for two more days with camps at Yorktown, Big Bethel, and finally Hampton on August 22 where the Vermont Brigade remained until the next day.[70]

On Sunday morning, August 23, the Vermont Brigade, along with the rest of the VI Corps, marched out of Hampton to Fort Monroe where they boarded steamers and sailed up the Chesapeake Bay to the Potomac River, leaving the Peninsula in its wake.[71]

The Vermont Brigade would go on to participate in every battle of the Army of the Potomac and more:

Second Bull Run, Va., August 29–September 1, 1862
Crampton's Gap, Md., September 14, 1862
Antietam, Md., September 17, 1862
First Fredericksburg, Va., December 13, 1862
Marye's Heights, Va., May 3, 1863
Salem Heights, Va., May 4, 1863
Gettysburg, Penn., July 1–3, 1863
Funkstown, Md., July 10, 1863
Rappahannock Station, Va., November 7, 1863
Wilderness, Va., May 5–10, 1864
Spotsylvania, Va., May 10–18, 1864
Cold Harbor, Va., June 1–12, 1864
Petersburg, Va., June 18, 1864
Charlestown, W. Va., August 21, 1864
Reams' Station, Va., June 29, 1864
Ft. Stevens, Md., July 11, 1864
Opequan, Va., September 13, 1864
Winchester, Va., September 19, 1864
Fisher's Hill, Va., September 21–22, 1864
Cedar Creek, Va., October 19, 1864
Petersburg, Va., March 25–27, 1865
Petersburg, Va., April 2, 1865
Sailor's Creek, Va., April 6, 1865

In these battles the Vermont Brigade would continue to distinguish itself, but at a price. The five original regiments of the Vermont Brigade entered the service with 4,747 officers and men. During the war the State of Vermont would add 4,070 replacements for a total of 8,817 that served in the brigade. Of this number, 578 men were killed in action and 395 died of wounds received in battle for a total of 973. Seven hundred and seventy-four men died of disease and 135 died in Confederate prisoner of war camps. The total number of wounded was 2,328. The reputation of the Vermont Brigade is something that all Vermonters can be proud of forever.[72]

6

The Aftermath

This chapter gives the reader an insight into the realities of war by covering the aftermath of the Seven Days and how those seven days had a profound effect on the Vermont soldiers and their families for the rest of their lives. After the ghastly sights they saw during the Seven Days the unwounded Vermonter's letters were devoid of the enthusiasm for the war that they had in the spring of 1862. They were no longer so sure of the outcome of the war. Those that had been wounded were starting the period of recuperation which for some would take years, if they fully recovered at all. The following are the stories of 29 Vermonters that were wounded and of the families of the men that were killed.

Vermont Brigade Staff
William Thomas Harbaugh Brooks

William Thomas Harbaugh Brooks, the son of DeLarma and Lila (Harbaugh) Brooks, was born on January 28, 1821, in Lisbon, Ohio. He obtained an appointment to West Point at the age of 16 and graduated in 1841, 46th in a class of 52. He was commissioned as a second lieutenant in the 3rd U.S. Infantry Regiment on July 1, 1841. He served in the Seminole War and on the western frontier from 1843 to 1845. In 1845 and 1846 he was in the military occupation of Texas. He fought in the Mexican War with the 3rd U.S. Infantry where he won brevet promotions to captain and major. While in Mexico Brooks suffered from bladder problems which an army surgeon attributed to drinking alkaline water and from exposure. He served as the acting adjutant general of Maj. Gen. David E. Twigg's division from 1847 to 1848, and as Twiggs' aide de camp 1848 to 1851. Following frontier duty in New Mexico from 1852 to 1858 Brooks served in Texas from 1860 to 1861 and in garrison duty at Ft. Hamilton, N.Y., in late 1861. While in New Mexico in 1852 Brooks had great difficulty urinating. After an examination an army surgeon found that Brooks had a stricture in his urethra. The doctor was able to perform a minor operation to clear a part of the stricture, but recommended that Brooks get a leave of absence and go east for an operation, which he apparently did.

William T.H. Brooks married Almeria "Alma" B. Drake on August 5, 1857, in Marion, Ind. William and Alma had three children: John Crafts Wright, born on July 14, 1862; Mary Ruth born on May 2, 1865, and William DeLarma born on June 22, 1867. Alma was the daughter of Brig. Gen. James Perry and Priscilla Holmes (Buell) Drake. James P. Drake had served in the Blackhawk War and the Mexican War and had been active in the Indiana militia achieving the rank of brigadier general and was a very wealthy land speculator.

Brooks was promoted to brigadier general of U.S. Volunteers on September 28, 1861, and given command of the Vermont Brigade on October 3. He was chosen not only for his leadership abilities, but because he was of Vermont lineage, his father having been born in Montpelier. General Brooks was wounded in the leg during the battle of Savage's Station on June 29, 1862, by a bullet that hit him on the back of his thigh a few inches up from the back of his knee, but did not give up command. He wrote his father that that the wound "was just enough to call a wound but not enough to amount to anything." He was wounded again later that fall at the battle of Antietam. On the afternoon of that battle Brooks had his men lying down in a cornfield awaiting orders while bullets and artillery shells flew overhead. Brooks himself was up walking around when a rebel sharpshooter shot him in the mouth knocking out two teeth. One of his aides ran to him and asked if he was badly hurt. "No," he replied spitting out a molar, "had a tooth pulled." Although in serious pain he did not leave his command for medical attention until after dark.

Brooks was given command of the 1st division of the VI Corps in October of 1862. He was promoted to major general on June 10, 1863, and put in command of the Department of the Monongahela headquartered in Pittsburgh. During this assignment he was demoted to brigadier general. This demotion was probably caused by Brooks' being involved with other VI Corps commanders attempting to get Maj. Gen. Ambrose Burnside removed from command after the defeat at Fredericksburg in December of 1862. In April of 1864 he was again in division command. Although Brooks had a number of leaves of absence from the army for medical attention, he continued to suffer from his blocked urethra off and on throughout the war. By the summer of 1864 the pain was intolerable and he resigned from the army on July 14. After the war William and Alma Brooks moved to Huntsville, Ala., where Alma's family, siding with the south, had moved. There General Brooks farmed. William Brooks died of cystitis on July 19, 1870, and was buried in Huntsville's Maple Hill Cemetery. After his death Alma received a veteran's widow's pension.

Alma D. Brooks married J. Murray Robertson on December 28, 1874, in Madison, Ala. J. Murray Robertson died on November 2, 1910. After Robertson's death Alma's veteran's widow's pension was reinstated. She died at the home of her niece in Chattanooga, Tenn., on September 4, 1921. She was buried beside General Brooks in Maple Hill Cemetery.[1]

Daniel Franklin Cooledge
Co. A, 2nd Vermont Infantry Regiment

Daniel Franklin Cooledge, the son of Daniel Waterman and Lydia (Davison) Cooledge, was born in Plymouth, Vt., on December 3, 1839. The Cooledges moved to Ludlow, Vt., when Daniel was 15 years old. At the outbreak of the Civil War Cooledge dropped out of Ludlow's Black River Academy and enlisted in Co. A, 2nd Vermont Infantry Regiment, on October 16, 1861. During the battle of Savage's Station on June 29, 1862, Cooledge was wounded in the leg. He was hit in the back of his right thigh by a rebel minie ball that tore through his thigh and exited out the front. Thankfully for Cooledge the bullet missed his femur, but did injure nerves that would trouble him the rest of his life. His wound was extremely painful and he was unable to walk. After the battle five of his comrades carried him as far as the VI Corps field hospital where they had to leave him before resuming their march to the James River. Because of lack of shelter Cooledge laid out in the open with other wounded men that night. To make matters worse it began raining on the unsheltered men and there were not enough doctors to tend to all of the wounded men.

Cooledge noted in his diary the next day that there was very little sleep for him and the rest of the men laying in the rain without anyone to tend to their wounds. He also noted that some men were "suffering everything but death." On July 2 Cooledge found space in a crowded tent and was able to get out of the rain. His only food that day was two or three pieces of hardtack and some coffee. It was a wonder he could even eat at all with the sight outside his tent where he could see "limbs and arms of poor fellows strewn about as though it was a slaughter house." On July 5 he wrote, "I endured as much pain last night as ever in my life and it seemed so with all for groans and curses could be heard on every side." On July 1 the VI Corps field hospital was closed and all the patients were transferred to the hospital at Savage's Station.

Cooledge remained at the hospital at Savage's Station until it was closed on July 13 and most of the patients were transported to Richmond by train. Unfortunately, the train was loaded to capacity before Cooledge and a number of other patients could get aboard and they were left at Savage's Station until the next day when they were transported to Richmond and placed in prisoner of war camps. Cooledge was incarcerated in the infamous Libby Prison. While there he did not receive any medical attention and food was scarce and of poor quality, usually watery soup. Bread they had to buy with their own money. Fortunately, Cooledge's stay was short and he was exchanged on July 22. He and other prisoners were taken by rail to City Point downriver from Richmond and loaded aboard ship. They arrived at Fort Monroe in Hampton, Va., the next evening. On July 24 Cooledge was sent to Satterlee U.S. Army General Hospital in West Philadelphia, Penn., where he was admitted two days later.

On August 27 Cooledge's mother arrived at the Satterlee General Hospital determined to take her son home. The key to getting a disability discharge for Cooledge was getting a copy of his descriptive list from his company. A descriptive list was the document in the Civil War used to prove one's identify. It contained information such as height, color of hair and eyes, place of birth, etc. Daniel had requested his descriptive from his company commander on July 28, but it had not arrived despite his repeated requests. By September 4 Mrs. Cooledge could not stand the wait anymore and went to Annapolis, Md., to see the district commander, Brig. Gen. William R. Montgomery, to try to speed up the delivery of her son's descriptive list, but to no avail. Finally, on September 13 Daniel's descriptive list arrived at the hospital and the administrative process to discharge him from of the army began. Daniel was given a disability discharge from the army on September 17 and two days later he and his mother were on a train heading north. They arrived back home in Ludlow on September 23.

After visiting all his friends and relatives, Daniel decided to return to Black River Academy and prepare for college. At first he was quite enthusiastic, but after a week he started getting bored. His year in the army had given him experiences that the other students could not comprehend and he probably suffered from what we now know as post-traumatic stress disorder which effected his ability to concentrate. He struggled through the winter term before quitting.

On March 19, 1863, Daniel filed for and received a government disability pension of $4 a month. A short time later he decided to become a physician. He studied under

Dr. William Chapin in Ludlow, attended lectures at the University of Vermont and graduated from the Bellevue Hospital Medical School of the University of New York in 1867. In 1868 Daniel bought Dr. Chapin's practice. While he was in medical school Daniel married Viola Alice Marsh on September 4, 1866, in Plymouth, Vt. After his graduation from medical school they made their home in Ludlow where they lived the rest of their lives. Between 1868 and 1885 Daniel and Viola had two sons and three daughters.

In 1870 Dr. Cooledge bought half interest in a drugstore in Ludlow and two years later became its sole proprietor. Viola assisted him in the drugstore and became Vermont's first registered female pharmacist. The drugstore evolved into a small general store, but as Dr. Cooledge was socially conservative his store did not sell alcoholic beverages or tobacco products. He also did not sell books "of a pernicious or immoral character." In addition to his drugstore and medical practice, Dr. Cooledge became an examiner for the U.S. Pension Bureau in 1885, a practice which he continued for four years.

Daniel Cooledge was an active member of his community. He was heavily involved in the Florence Memorial Library, a deacon in the Congregational Church, a trustee of the Black River Academy, and was for many years commander of Ludlow's Grand Army of the Republic Oliver O. Howard Post No. 33.

Daniel and Viola's seemingly idyllic life was not without tragedy. In 1899 their youngest son, Leon D. Cooledge, was visiting his brother Bernard who was a millinery salesman in Chicago. While there Leon followed in his father's footsteps and enlisted in the army that August. He was assigned to Co. M, 37th U.S. Volunteer Infantry. It was at the height of the Spanish American War and Leon was sent to the Philippine Islands. He died of typhoid fever in the town of Santa Cruz on the island of Luzon on July 31, 1900. Young Cooledge's body was returned to Ludlow a little over two months later where he was buried in Ludlow's Pleasant View Cemetery on October 5.

As he grew older Dr. Cooledge's wound and the infirmities of old age were having a serious effect on him and by 1906 his overall health declined. In 1909 Viola wrote the U.S. Pension Bureau:

> The enclosed applicant Daniel F. Cooledge, was for quite a number of years examining surgeon here at Ludlow, Vt. and saw much of trying to get as large a pension as possible. He has, perhaps, been over conscientious in applying himself. He has a pension of $4.00 per month and later it was increased to $6.00 then at $12.00 at the proper age for it. All his life since 1862 he has suffered from severe aches in head, back of neck & spine and was at one time treated for spinal difficulty by a New York specialist as well as for heart trouble. He is now unable to use his wounded leg (right one) to walk and has not been dressed for five weeks or more. Has been able to do scarcely anything for nearly three years. His signature compared with his former writing will show you how he can use his right hand and arm, can partially feed himself when at his best.

Although the 1910 U.S. Census lists Daniel's occupation as a physician one can only wonder if he was really able to attend to patients. The same census indicates that Viola was running the drugstore. Daniel F. Cooledge died in Ludlow on September 17, 1911, at age 71, of arteriosclerosis and was buried in Pleasant View Cemetery. After Daniel's death Viola applied for and received a $36-a-month veteran's widow's pension. She continued to manage the drugstore until her death on June 6, 1934, at age 87, of myocardial degeneration. She was buried in Pleasant View Cemetery beside Daniel, her two sons and two of her three daughters.[2]

Harvey King Goodwin
Co. E, 2nd Vermont Infantry Regiment

Harvey King Goodwin, the son of James and Dolly (King) Goodwin, was born in Tunbridge, Vt., on September 7, 1823. He married Martha Stowell in Windsor, Vt., on March 17, 1845. Martha died in 1852. Harvey then married Sarah Jane Johnson, on April 2, 1853, in St. Johnsbury Center, Vt. They had three children, two of whom lived to maturity, Sarah Adelia Goodwin and Harvey Sheridan Goodwin. Harvey was 12 years Sarah's senior. Harvey had always been considered eccentric by the people of Tunbridge. He owned a farm of a little over 100 acres where he made the majority of his living, but he also was a part time preacher, poet, penmanship teacher, and portrait painter. Several years prior to the Civil War Harvey was a member of the Tunbridge Militia. After the outbreak of the war Harvey enlisted in Co. E, 2nd Vermont Infantry Regiment, as a drummer on May 15, 1862. It did not take long for Harvey's eccentricity to become evident to everyone in his company. When the regiment was mustered into service in Burlington on June 20, 1862, Harvey initially refused to take the oath but was finally persuaded do so by his comrades.

The 2nd Vermont arrived in Washington, D.C., on June 26, 1861. The following month on July 21 the regiment fought in the first battle of Bull Run. On August 11 Harvey wrote home to his friend and neighbor, George Cowdery:

> I suppose you have heard all about the Battle of Bull Run in which we were engaged. That was a dreadful day. I was in that Battle and saw the whole fight. No one who has ever been in a battle can tell or realize its horrors. The field was strued with the dead and dying. Horses lay piled upon the field with their dead riders beneath them. I saw men with arms shot off, with legs broken, with wounds of every description. The roar of the cannon and groans of the dying was to horrible for description.

A month after the Union defeat at Bull Run, on August 14, Goodwin accidentally shot off the end of his right forefinger while cleaning his pistol. He was given a 30-day furlough four days later to go home to Tunbridge to heal up. After returning to his company Goodwin again displayed his bizarre behavior. Henry R. Hayward, who had been Goodwin's first sergeant, stated, "He would sit for some time with his head between his hands and his elbows on his knees. At those times you could hardly get a word out of him. He would not make any conservation with you at all. Did not do it every day, but often." But worst of all was Goodwin's refusal to beat the army's drum calls. He wanted to use his own. It finally got to the point his drum was taken away from him and he was given a fife to play.

As the Vermont Brigade was on the march from Gouldin's farm to Savage's Station on June 29, 1862, Harvey Goodwin fell out of the ranks and sat down against a tree and refused to go any further. First Sergeant Hayward said to Goodwin, "Harvey, you will be taken in five minutes if you don't move." But Goodwin would not budge. He just shook his head no and said he did not care. With that Hayward moved on and that was the last he ever saw of him. Goodwin died in a prisoner of war camp in Richmond on July 7.

On February 12, 1863, Sarah Goodwin filed for and received a veteran's widow's pension of $8 a month. Not long after Harvey's death Sarah and her two children moved back to her hometown of Lancaster, N.H., where she married Francis B. Pellett on May 3, 1874. In marrying Pellet Sarah gave up her veteran's widow's pension. Francis Pellett's first wife, Sallie Griggs, had died on October 31, 1870, in Abington, Conn., leaving him with eight children. After their marriage Sarah and Francis lived in his house in Abington. Francis B. Pellett died on April 30, 1898, and was buried in the Abington Cemetery. Sarah reapplied for her widow's pension on January 17, 1906, and it was reinstated. Sarah died in 1925 in Pomfret, Conn., at age 89, and was buried in the Abington Cemetery beside Francis.

One of Harvey's children from his first marriage, Henry King Goodwin who was born on December 14, 1847, also served in the Civil War. Henry enlisted in the 2nd Massachusetts Heavy Artillery on November 21, 1863, at age 16. His company was captured in Plymouth, N.C., in April of 1864 and Henry and the other men were sent to the Andersonville Prison Camp in Georgia. Henry survived his incarceration and was released in 1865. After the war Henry became a harness maker in Lawrence, Mass., and on March 18, 1870, he married Martha A. Bragg. Henry and Martha were divorced in late November 1875. A week or so after his divorce Henry married Eldora L. Waggone in Lawrence, Mass., on December 4, 1875. Not long after his second marriage Henry became a telegrapher and became very interested in electrical communication. In 1879 he went into a telephone business with a man named Gardner. This endeavor lasted about a year and Henry enrolled in the Massachusetts Institute of Technology. He remained in school for a year and then went to work for an Albert D. Swan in the Molecular Telephone Company. On August 27, 1885, thinking that Albert Swan had cheated him out of a patent on a telephone switchboard he had invented, Henry walked into Swan's office and shot him in the back of the head with a pistol and killed him. After he shot Swan Henry turned himself into the police. Henry went to trial that fall. His lead defense attorney was none less than Benjamin F. Butler, the infamous Union Civil War major general. Citing the eccentricity of the Goodwin family members and Henry's time in the Andersonville prison, Butler tried using insanity as a defense. The jury did not buy the insanity defense and Henry was sentenced to prison for life in the Charlestown, Mass., State Prison. While in prison Henry was an exemplary prisoner and installed and operated the prison telephone system. Henry's wife lobbied for years to have him pardoned and in 1905 he was paroled with the proviso that he leave Massachusetts and never return. By the time he was released his wife had died. Henry was offered a job with a mining company in Nevada and went west a few days after he was released. On his second day in Nevada he was thrown from a wagon and was severely injured leaving his left side paralyzed. Henry spent the rest of his life in veteran's homes in California where he died on March 20, 1920. He was buried in the Los Angeles National Cemetery.[3]

Harlan Page Stoddard
Co. F, 2nd Vermont Infantry Regiment

Harlan Page Stoddard, the eldest son of William Tell and Mary (Porter) Stoddard, was born on February 17, 1837, in Waitsfield, Vt., where his father operated a tannery. He enlisted as a private in Co. F, 2nd Vermont Infantry Regiment, on March 7, 1861. Before being mustered into service in June he married Electa J. Sabins on May 19. At the battle of Savage's Station on June 29, 1862, Stoddard received a ghastly wound in the pelvis from a rebel minie ball. The bullet entered just to the left of his penis, fractured his pubic arch, went through his colon, and came out a little to the left of the anus and through his left buttock. He was taken to the VI Corps field hospital where he was captured the next day with the rest of the patients. He was soon taken to Richmond and admitted to hospital number 4 (also known as the Baptist Institute Hospital) on 10th Street. He was paroled at City Point, Va., on July 25, 1862. After his release Stoddard was transferred to the Broad and Cherry Streets U.S. Army General Hospital in Philadelphia, Penn. When he was well enough he was transferred to the Baxter U.S. Army General Hospital in Burlington, Vt., where his doctor, Acting Assistant Surgeon Samuel W. Thayer, wrote that Stoddard, "passed feces through both openings for several weeks." Stoddard remained in the hospital for a year before he was well enough to be given a disability discharge on July 30, 1863. The next month he applied for and received a government disability pension of $8-a-month.

After being discharged from the army Stoddard returned to Waitsfield and went back to farming. Harlan and Electa had two children, Ida, born on November 22, 1863, and Thompson William born on October 14, 1871. Electa died on April 23, 1872, at the age of 31. On June 16, 1872, Harlan married Carrie S. Spaulding, in Waitsfield and they had two children. Harlan continued to farm although his health slowed him down. On September 4, 1873, a pension medical examiner in Montpelier made a report on Harlan's condition, stating, "A discharge from the wound over the pubic bone is now uncomfortable and disagreeable. There is quite a growth at the entrance wound. The ball entered through the left pubis and made its exit through the buttock of the same side. There is an artificial anus, and the disability continues total." Carrie Stoddard died of liver cancer on September 30, 1903, at age 52. After Carrie's death Harlan married Laura E. (Sterling) Prosser on February 1, 1906. Despite his wound and other disabilities Harlan Stoddard lived until April 8, 1920, when he died of heart disease at age 83 at the Vermont State Hospital (also known as the Vermont State Asylum for the Insane) in Waterbury. He was buried in the Waitsfield Village Cemetery beside his first and second wives. Laura Stoddard died on December 26, 1921.

Tell Stoddard had three other sons that served in the Civil War only one of which survived. Horace B. Stoddard served in Co. F of the 2nd Vermont with Harlan. He was shot in the head and killed in the battle of the Wilderness on May 5, 1864. Lathrop Thompson Stoddard served in two different regiments. He enlisted as a private at age 18 in Co. B, 13th Vermont and was slightly wounded at the battle of Gettysburg on July 3, 1863, while serving as color bearer. He was mustered out of service on July 21. He enlisted in Co. C of the 17th Vermont on January 2, 1864, and was selected as a corporal. He was gravely wounded at the battle of the Crater on July 30, 1864, at Petersburg, Va. He was captured and died as a prisoner of war on August 4. William H. Stoddard enlisted in Co. H, 6th Vermont, in late 1863 and served until the end of the war, although he spent most of his time in the hospital with typhoid fever.[4]

George W. Bonett
Cos. A &C, 3rd Vermont Infantry Regiment

George W. Bonett, the son of Luther and Fanny (Carr) Bonett, was born in Waterford, Vt., on November 7, 1842. At the age of 18 he went to St. Johnsbury and served a three year apprenticeship with Luke Buzzell as an iron founder. He enlisted in Co. C, 3rd Vermont Infantry Regiment, in St. Johnsbury on June 1, 1861, and was promoted to corporal on June 1, 1862. Bonett was wounded on June 29, 1862, at the battle of Savage's Station. During the battle the 3rd Vermont was exchanging fire with the 5th Louisiana Infantry which was using old smooth-bore muskets that fired buck and ball ammunition. One Louisiana soldier got George Bonett in his sights and fired. The round ball went between Bonett's legs but the buck shot had spread enough that all three hit him. Two hit him in the front of his right thigh and one hit him in the front of his left thigh. While the wounds were painful Bonett was able to keep up with his company after the battle and safely made it to Harrison's Landing.

Corporal Bonett was promoted to sergeant in Co. C on November 1, 1862, and reenlisted on December 21, 1863. He was promoted to first lieutenant in Co. A of the 3rd Vermont on June 26, 1864. Bonett was wounded for a second time on September 19, 1864, at the battle of Winchester, Va. He was hit in the left leg several inches below his knee by a piece of shell producing a slight wound. On October 18, 1864, Lieutenant Bonett was promoted to captain of Co. A. During the final breakthrough at Petersburg, Va., on April 2, 1865, Captain Bonett was serving on the Vermont Brigade staff. In the performance of his duties, he and two aides captured a company of rebel soldiers. For this act Bonett was cited for gallantry and given a brevet promotion to major. After Lee's surrender at Appomattox Courthouse on April 9, 1865, the VI Corps was sent to Danville, Va., to keep the rebels from reforming their government there. While in Danville Captain Bonett and his company were on picket duty along the River Dan and Bonett received his third and final wound of the war. A rebel sniper shot Bonett in his forehead. Thankfully, the bullet had expended its energy by the time it reached Bonnett and did not penetrate his skull. It did, however, lay his scalp open for several inches starting just above his hair line and landed him in the regimental hospital for three weeks. Captain Bonett was mustered out of service with his regiment on July 11, 1865.

After returning home from the war George Bonett married Nancy Jane Morris on September 4, 1865, and they settled in St. Johnsbury where George worked for the E. and T. Fairbanks Scale Co. as a moulder. George remained with the Fairbanks Co. for 10 years. He then rented an old unused iron foundry and went into business for himself, eventually employing 10 to 15 men. In 1884 he sold his business to the Acme Iron Works. By 1887 George's wartime wounds were catching up with him. His legs ached and he frequently had headaches from his head wound. On June 22 of that year he applied for and received a government disability pension. Starting to slow down, Bonnett opened a grocery store that he operated for several years. After his stint in the grocery business he returned to the Fairbanks Co. and finished out his career. George W. Bonett died on Sunday, January 19, 1908. Nancy J. Bonett died on February 15, 1919. At the time of her death she was receiving a $25-a-month veteran's widow's pension.[5]

John Carmody
Co. A, 3rd Vermont Infantry Regiment

John Carmody, the son of Michael and Margaret (Leyden) Carmody, was born in Liscannor, County Clare, Ireland, probably on March 21, 1833. The Carmodys and their two sons, John and Thomas, arrived in Boston in May of 1848. After spending time in Massachusetts, Connecticut, and New Hampshire (during which time Michael apparently died), John and Thomas moved to Springfield, Vt., sometime around 1852. On April 2,

1854, John married Mary Corbett in Bellows Falls, Vt. They were married by a traveling priest named Father Zeph Druon, of Rutland, who traveled a circuit through southern Vermont because there were very few Catholic churches in the state at that time. Later that year, in December, John became a naturalized citizen.

John Carmody was working as a spinner in the Holmes, Whitmore & Co. woolen mill in Springfield up until 1860 when the mill burned. After that he farmed until the outbreak of the Civil War when he enlisted in Co. A, 3rd Vermont Infantry Regiment, on May 7, 1861, and was mustered into service on July 16. In September 1861, Carmody was detailed as a mail agent and mounted orderly for Col. William F. Smith. Shortly after being detailed as an orderly, Carmody's horse fell on him injuring his left knee. After recovering from his injury, but still unable to mount a horse, Carmody was detailed as the Second division's (Smith's division) mail agent after Colonel Smith had been promoted to brigadier general. When Smith's division became part of the newly formed VI Corps on May 18, 1862, Carmody also performed mail agent duties for the VI Corps, which he did for the rest of his enlistment. On June 30, 1862, at White Oak Swamp Carmody lost the hearing in his right ear from the concussion from a bursting shell. On September 3, 1863, Carmody was riding in a train's mail car when it left the track in Warrenton, Va. He was thrown out, hitting his left knee on a tree stump. In addition to reinjuring his left knee, he was badly bruised and suffered a concussion. After this injury he was sent to the VI Corps hospital for three weeks. He was supposed to be sent to a hospital in Washington, D.C., but the chief quartermaster of the VI Corps asked him if he would stay promising that he could ride in the mail wagon since he was unable to stand very well. Carmody's knee did not heal for six weeks and remained painful and stiff the rest of his life. John Carmody was mustered out of service on July 27, 1864, and returned to Springfield, Vt.

After returning home Carmody tried working in the woolen mills again, but because of pain in his injured left leg from having to stand all day, he could only work for several weeks before he would be forced to quit. In the winter of 1864–1865 Carmody returned to Virginia where he was a shoe clerk for a sutler (a mobile PX for the soldiers) for about six weeks before returning to Springfield. John and Mary Carmody divorced in May of 1872 with John being charged with "intolerable severity." John remained in Springfield until 1874 when he moved to Charlestown, N.H., and opened a saloon and restaurant. In May of 1876 Carmody left for California where he did odd jobs until returning to Springfield, Vt., in the fall of 1877. In January 1878 John applied for and received a government disability pension for rheumatism. The following month he again opened a saloon and restaurant which he operated until May of 1879 when state authorities found that he did not have a license to operate the business. Unable to pay the fine he was incarcerated in the Vermont House of Correction in Rutland. After a year in prison Carmody was released and returned to Springfield in May of 1880. A month later he again moved across the Connecticut River to Charlestown, N.H., where he went to work in a rag shop. In 1881 he worked in a woolen mill in Bellows Falls, Vt., and filed a new pension application, this time for his knee. In 1883 he opened a small grocery store in Rockingham, Vt. In 1886 he was unemployed and living in Charlestown, N.H., when he was awarded a pension for partial disability due to his knee injury. In 1888 he had a saloon and restaurant in Charlestown, N.H., and was awarded a pension for total disability. From 1888 to 1890 he did odd jobs before entering the New Hampshire Soldiers' Home in Tilton, N.H. John Carmody died of heart failure at age 59 on July 6, 1892, and was buried in Saint Catherine's Cemetery in Charlestown, N.H.[6]

James Laden
Co. A, 4th Vermont Infantry Regiment

James Laden was born in Bennington, Vt., in September 1840. The 21-year-old farmer enlisted as a private in Co. A, 4th Vermont Infantry Regiment, on August 22, 1862. At the battle of Dam No. 1 on April 16, 1862, in Newport News, Va., Laden was hit by a bullet that took off the end of his left thumb and cut open the underside of his left forefinger. After being treated by his regimental surgeon he was given a 60-day furlough to go to home to recuperate. He rejoined his regiment on June 26 at Gouldin's farm on the outskirts of Richmond. Laden survived the fights at Gouldin's farm and Savage's Station, but he was not so lucky at White Oak Swamp Bridge on June 30. During the barrage by General Stonewall Jackson's artillery Laden was hit by a piece of shrapnel that struck him on the inside of his lower left leg and passed clean through. On its way through the shell fragment shattered his tibia. He was placed in a baggage wagon for the rest of the trip to Harrison's Landing. Once at the landing Laden was put aboard a ship and taken to Camden Street U.S. Army General Hospital in Baltimore, Md. The doctor there thought he may have to amputate the leg because it was so swollen and blue, but it soon improved. Slivers of bone would work their way out during the healing process. When the wound healed he was left with a two-inch-diameter scar at the entrance of the wound and a one-inch scar at the exit. Laden was given a disability discharge from the army on March 21, 1863. In May of 1863 he applied for and received a government disability pension.

With his leg seemingly much better James Laden, enlisted in Co. F, 17th Vermont Infantry Regiment on October 3, 1863, giving up his disability pension. After 10 months of service his leg wound had developed a chronic ulcer and he was admitted to Baxter U.S. Army General Hospital in Burlington, Vt., on July 22, 1864, where a piece of bone was taken out of the wound. He was sent back to his unit in the winter of 1864, but the wound broke open again and Laden was given another disability discharge on January 4, 1865. James Laden enlisted in the regular army in late 1865 and was assigned to Co. H, 13th U.S. Infantry Regiment. The 13th U.S. Infantry was designated as the 22nd U.S. Infantry Regiment September 21, 1866, and sent to the Dakota Territory where its mission was to keep the white settlers from stealing land from the Indian reservations and to keep gold prospectors out of the Black Hills.

Laden apparently liked the Native American way of life because after he was mustered out of the army on November 17, 1868, he settled in with the Lakota Indians on the Spotted Tail Agency in Nebraska and lived off his government disability pension that had been reinstated. The Spotted Tail Agency was moved to the Rose Bud River in South Dakota in 1878 where that year Laden married a full blooded Native American woman named Mary. They soon had a daughter who they named Lucy. Mary died in 1878 and what became of Lucy is unknown. James Laden married Elizabeth "Eliza" Schmidt, who was half Native American, on July 27, 1887, on the Rose Bud Indian Reservation. Between 1887 and 1903 James and Eliza had six children.

By 1914 James Laden was receiving a disability pension of $24 a month, but time and his wound had taken their toll on him and he applied for a pension increase. In his application for the increase Laden stated that he had been wounded by a sword or bayonet, he was not sure which, at the battle of Dam No. 1 and that he had also sustained a flesh wound on the underside of his right wrist. [The wound to his thumb and forefinger had to have been caused by a minie ball as the 4th Vermont never got close enough to the rebels for him to have been wounded by either a sword or a bayonet.] He was also suffering from the wound in his left leg and from arthritis in his left shoulder and neck. The U.S. Pension Bureau sent an investigator to the Rose Bud Reservation, near what is today Berkley, S.D., to interview Laden and some of the people that had supplied affidavits on his behalf. The investigator interviewed David Galineaux and his wife, Louis Menard and Thin Elk. All indicated that Laden had a good reputation, although in his younger days he had been a hard drinker. Thin Elk told the investigator that he ought to be paid for his interview, but the investigator explained that was not the way it worked. When Laden was interviewed he acknowledged that his correct name was James Laden, but on the reservation he was known as Kelly Laden. Why he was called Kelly could not be explained by Laden or anyone else interviewed. Also, his last name was sometimes spelled Layton and other times Leighton. The investigator also learned that Laden had an Indian name that translated to "Bad Language" because of his constant use of profanity. He admitted to the investigator that he had not been wounded in the right wrist in the army and that he had sustained the wound in an effort to punch a man standing behind the glass panel in the door of a saloon from which he had been ejected. The investigator also noted that Laden's memory was very bad and that details of his military service were sketchy at best. Laden did receive a small pension increase.

On February 18, 1919, Eliza filed for a divorce from James for cruelty. How long he might have mistreated her is unknown, but in March of 1918 he drew a gun on Eliza and threatened to shoot her and another time threatened her with a straight razor. Finally, she had enough and left him to live with relatives. A short time later she returned home to retrieve some of her belongings and James threatened to hit her with a poker. After Eliza left him, James was unable to care for himself and he moved in with his daughter, Mabel Brown, in Wood, S.D., where he died on April 6, 1919. He was buried in Trinity Cemetery in Mission, S.D. After James' death Eliza applied for and received a veteran's widow's pension.[7]

George W. Gibson
Co. C, 4th Vermont Infantry Regiment

George W. Gibson, the son of Israel and Sarah (Barry) Gibson, was born in Petersham, Mass., in 1841. Although a small man measuring only five feet, four and one-half inches tall, he did not let his small stature keep him from joining the army when the Civil War broke out. He enlisted in Co. C, 4th Vermont Infantry Regiment, on August 22, 1861. He listed his residence on his enlistment papers as Charlestown, N.H., but he enlisted in Cavendish, Vt. During the battle of Gouldin's Farm on June 27, 1862, Gibson was shot in the face. A rebel minie ball struck him in his left cheek shattering his jaw bone. The ball then traveled down his neck near the windpipe and jugular vein exiting over the top of his left shoulder blade. Miraculously, he lost no teeth. In its path of destruction the ball damaged some of the nerves in his left shoulder causing partial paralysis of his left arm. After being treated at Gouldin's Farm Gibson was taken to the hospital at Savage's Station where he was captured on June 30. On July 13 he was imprisoned in Richmond. After being paroled on July 22, Gibson was admitted to the McKim's Mansion U.S. Army General Hospital in Baltimore, Md., on July 25, 1862, where eight small fragments of the bone were removed from beneath his jaw muscle. On September 19, 1862, he was transferred to the West's Buildings U.S. Army General Hospital in Baltimore where he was given a disability discharge from the army on October 9.

By the next winter Gibson had regained sufficient use of his left arm to re-enter the army. He enlisted in Co. G, 9th New Hampshire Infantry Regiment, on December 10, 1863. He joined his regiment in January in Kentucky where it was guarding a major railroad. The 9th New Hampshire was ordered to Virginia in the spring of 1864 to become part of General Grant's move to Richmond. Gibson weathered the terrible battles of the Wilderness, Spotsylvania, Cold Harbor and the start of the Siege of Petersburg in the summer of 1864. His luck finally ran out in the battle of Poplar Springs Church on the outskirts of Petersburg on September 30. On that day the fighting was taking place on the Pegram farm and George Gibson was shot in the left leg. A rebel minie ball tore through his leg from front to back near the knee joint fracturing his knee cap on its way through. Because he could not walk Gibson was left on the battlefield. One of Gibson's comrades, Corp. J. Frank Foster, had been captured with a number of other men of the 9th New Hampshire and were being herded to the rear. Foster saw Gibson lying on the ground and broke ranks to give him aid. For some reason the rebels left him alone. Foster remained with Gibson and was recaptured when the Union wounded were rounded up two days later. The wounded, and the few men that had remained behind to care for them, were transported by ambulance to a hospital in Petersburg. The next day the men and their nurses were put on rail flatcars and taken to Richmond. As they crossed the James River in Richmond they could see the infamous prisoner of war camp on Belle Isle and feared that was their destination, but they were pleasantly surprised when they were taken to a hospital. On October 8, 1864, George Gibson, Frank Foster, and a number of other men were paroled. Gibson was taken to St. John's College U.S. Army General Hospital in Annapolis, Md., where he was given a disability discharge from the army on May 22, 1865.

After the war George married Elvira E. Basford in St. Albans, Vt., on December 9, 1865. After they married George and Elvira resided in Holyoke, Mass. According to the 1880 U.S. Census George and Elvira separated sometime between 1870 and 1880. In 1880 George was still in Holyoke, but living in a boarding house and Elvira was living in a boarding house in Keene, N.H., and working as a dress maker. George and Elvira Gibson were divorced on November 15, 1885.

George next married Elizabeth S. (Parker) Knight. Elizabeth had previously been married to Andrew J. Knight who was a veteran of the 37th Massachusetts Infantry Regiment, but he died of typhoid fever on July 25, 1881, in Holyoke. After their marriage George and Elizabeth lived in Tyringham, Mass., where George worked as a shoemaker. As the years went by the effects of George's wounds and old age were taking their toll and he was unable to perform manual labor. His government disability pension was increased, but it was barely enough to sustain him and Elizabeth. George Gibson died of a heart attack on April 5, 1909, in Tyringham and was buried in the Forestdale Cemetery in Holyoke. After George's death Elizabeth applied for a veteran's widow's pension on April 22. Her pension was approved and it was her main support until she died of a heart attack in Tyringham on March 28, 1915. She was buried beside George in the Forestdale Cemetery.[8]

John P. Bedell
Co. D, 5th Vermont Infantry Regiment

There is one external pile tumor ¾ in. in diameter and 1¼ in. long. Two pile tabs. There are three internal tumors measuring from ¾ to 1 inch in diameter plainly seen and a mass of tissue congested and inflamed farther internal which cannot be plainly outlined on account of the intense pain caused by speculum [a medical tool for investigating body orifices]. Blood and pus followed the removal of the instrument. The claimant never has a normal movement of the bowels. He suffers daily and continuously from this condition. Has diarrhea as often as once in ten days, lasting from three to five days at a time, causing him to keep from exercise and often confining him to bed. There is intense inflammation and many points of ulceration of the mucus membrane as far internally as can be seen. This condition alone would prevent any man of a younger age from doing any manual labor whatsoever.

That was how a U.S. Pension Bureau medical examiner described one of John P. Bedell's ailments in an examination conducted in 1910. Unfortunately, that was only one of his problems.

John P. Bedell, the son of Daniel C. and Huldah (Carter) Bedell, was born on April 30, 1838, in Woodbury, Vt. He had little education and was not able to read or write. Bedell enlisted in Co. D, 5th Vermont Infantry Regiment, on August 19, 1861. At that time he was a robust young man of 25, though rather small in stature measuring only five feet and five inches tall. Although he was small one of his uncles described him as a, "cast iron man." Bedell was wounded in the battle of Savage's Station on June 29, 1862, where a rebel minie ball tore through his upper right arm. Fortunately, the bullet missed the bone, but destroyed considerable muscle and other tissue. He was however, able to stay up with his comrades on the march to the James River thereby avoiding being captured at the hospital at Savage's Station.

After reaching Harrison's Landing, Bedell was put aboard ship and sent to the South Street U.S. Army General Hospital in Philadelphia, Penn., where he remained for about two months before being sent to the Convalescent Camp Hospital in Alexandria, Va. About the time he left South Street Hospital he started suffering from chronic diarrhea. Because of the diarrhea Bedell remained in Alexandria until winter before being sent to the Governor Smith U.S. Army General Hospital in Brattleboro, Vt. He was returned to his regiment in late summer of 1863. Although he had lost some range of motion of his arm due to his wound, he was allowed to reenlist on December 15, 1863.

John Bedell campaigned with his regiment until his diarrhea became so bad that he was sent to the Lovell U.S. Army General Hospital in Portsmouth Grove, R.I., and from there to Sloan U.S. Army General Hospital in Montpelier, Vt. He was returned to his regiment in early spring and was honorably discharged on June 29, 1865, exactly three years to the day after being wounded at Savage's Station.

After returning to Vermont John moved in with his uncle, William H. Bedell, in Elmore. By that time he was bedridden with diarrhea, relieving himself 12 to 20 times in a 24-hour period. His hemorrhoids bled so profusely that his uncle called the local doctor whose treatments gave John some relief and the diarrhea became less severe, but never disappeared. It was more than a year after his return home that John was able to do any manual labor. In December 1865 John applied for and received a government disability pension of $8 a month for partial loss of the use of his wounded right arm, chronic diarrhea, hemorrhoids, rheumatism (arthritis), and varicose veins in his right leg.

For a number of years John Bedell somehow managed to work as a farm hand, in spite of his diarrhea. He married Mina "Minnie" Conley in Hyde Park, Vt., on May 30, 1875, but the marriage was short lived as Minnie died several years after their marriage. As time went by John was unable to do any type of manual labor and by 1900 he was totally dependent on his government disability pension of $14 a month for his livelihood. After a medical examination in 1910 for a pension increase, John's health had deteriorated to the point that his pension was raised to $30 a month. In addition to his chronic diarrhea and hemorrhoids, the varicose veins in his right leg made it almost impossible for him to walk and the arthritis in his back and neck limited his ability to turn his head. Due to these ailments he required almost 24-hour a day attention. John Bedell finally succumbed to chronic diarrhea on July 28, 1916, in Morrisville, Vt., and was buried there in Pleasant View Cemetery. By the time he died his pension had been raised to $50 a month.[9]

The Cummings Boys
Co. E, 5th Vermont Infantry Regiment

The story of the Cummings boys is about as tragic as any in the Civil War. Peter and Louisa (Gleason) Cummings of Manchester, Vt., had five sons and a nephew in the war and only one returned home alive. All were causalities in the battle of Savage's Station on June 29, 1862. Thankfully, Peter and Louisa had passed on before the war, Peter in 1859 and Louisa in 1860, and were spared the heartache of what happened to their sons and nephew.

Henry A. Cummings, the first son of Peter and Louisa Cummings, was born in Manchester, Vt., in 1822. He married Mary Jane Ellison in Townsend, Vt., on September 23, 1850, and they had six children. Henry enlisted in Co. E, 5th Vermont Infantry Regiment, on August 26, 1861. During the battle of Savage's Station Henry was shot in the right thigh. The minie ball hit him in the front of his thigh about two inches below his crotch cutting muscles, tendons, and splintering his femur as it bored through his leg and exited out the back. He was left at the VI Corps field hospital after the battle as his regiment continued on toward White Oak Swamp. He was captured the next day by rebel troops. The VI Corps field hospital was closed on July 1 and the patients were transferred to the hospital at Savage's Station. On July 13 the hospital at Savage's Station was closed and the staff and patients were transported by train to Richmond and placed in prisoner of war camps. Henry was paroled at City Point on July 25 and taken down the James River to Hampton where he was admitted to the Chesapeake U.S. Army General Hospital on July 27. The next day he was sent to a hospital in Washington, D.C. Henry remained in the hospital until he was given a disability discharge on January 15, 1863, and sent home.

Henry's leg never did completely heal and between his discharge from the army and 1871 his wound opened several times as pieces of bone worked their way out. In December of 1863 he applied for and received a government disability pension at the rate of $8 a month, which was eventually was raised to $12. In 1873 his leg would often swell and make him quite lame. The leg pained him when he sat down and he could only walk with help. Henry tried to carry on with farming, but his wound finally brought that to a halt and his sons had to take over. Henry Cummings died of stroke on March 11, 1885. The attending physician noted on the death certificate that his wound had caused the stroke. He was buried in Manchester's Factory Point Cemetery. After Henry's death Mary received a veteran's widow's pension until her death on October 14, 1925, at the home of one of her sons in Bennington, Vt.

Twenty-six year-old Hiram P. Cummings, the second Cummings son, enlisted in Co. E, 5th Vermont, on August 28, 1861. He stood six feet tall and was a well-muscled lumberman. Hiram was a good soldier and on June 26, 1862, he was promoted to corporal. Three days later he was severely wounded at the battle of Savage's Station and died of his wound on July 7.

Edmund M. Cummings, the third Cummings son, was born in 1839 in Manchester. He married Melissa J. Eaton on April 24, 1861. Edmund left his farm and followed his brothers when he enlisted in Co. E, 5th Vermont, on February 22, 1862. He joined his company at Gouldin's Farm outside of Richmond, Va., on June 15. Fourteen days later at the battle of Savage's Station Edmund was mortally wounded and died the same day.

On November 14, 1862, Melissa applied for and received a veteran's widow's pension of $8 a month. In 1866 she was living with her grandfather and in 1880 she was living with her parents John and Susan Eaton. Melissa died of bowel cancer in Manchester on May 30, 1891, at age 47. She never remarried and was childless.

William E. Cummings, the fourth Cummings' son, was born in Genesee, N.Y., in 1835, but grew up in Winhall, Vt. He married Caroline J. Johnson in Manchester on May 14, 1861. William was 26 years old and Caroline was 17. William and Caroline's life together was cut short when William enlisted as a private in Co. E, 5th Vermont, on August 26, 1861, and left for war. William was wounded at the battle of Savage's Station and died two days later on July 2.

After William's death Caroline applied for and received an $8-a-month veteran's widow's pension. She gave up her widow's pension when she married David Hon sometime prior to 1872. David Hon was a veteran who had served in Co. E, 9th Vermont Infantry Regiment. David left Caroline in September of 1872 and they later divorced. On April 22, 1874, Caroline was arrested for stealing a cloak from the family for whom she worked as a maid and was taken to jail. About an hour after being placed in a cell Caroline was discovered trying to hang herself with her shawl. The next day she tried to kill herself again by drinking a bottle of iodine. Although found unconscious she survived. The punishment for the larceny seems to be lost to time. Caroline next married Amos Johnson on September 17, 1874, in Peru, Vt. She was 30 years old and Amos was 21. Caroline Johnson died on February 26, 1882, in Londonderry, Vt., of tuberculosis at age 36. She was still married to Amos at the time of her death.

Silas Asabel Cummings, Peter and Louisa Cummings' fifth and final son, enlisted in Co. E, on August 20, 1861. Prior to enlisting he worked with his brother Henry as a lumberman. Silas was wounded in the battle of Savage's Station and died on the 4th of July.

Hiram, Edmund, William, and Silas Cummings were all buried on the Savage farm. In 1866 the U.S. government had the bodies in the area of Savage's Station reinterred in the Seven Pines National Cemetery, in what is today Sandston, Va. The majority of the reinterred remains were unidentified. Such was the fate of the Cummings brothers.

The Cummings brothers' cousin William Henry Harrison Cummings enlisted in Co. E, 5th Vermont, on August 26, 1861. Like the rest of the Cummings boys, William H.H. Cummings was wounded in the battle of Savage's Station. He was severely wounded in the right thigh. After the battle William was taken to the VI Corps field hospital where his leg was amputated. He was captured with the other patients the next day. William was paroled on July 17 at Haxall's Landing and taken to Baltimore where he was admitted to the Camden Street U.S. Army General Hospital on July 21. William H.H. Cummings died from his wound on August 2, 1862. He was buried on August 3 in the Loudon Park National Cemetery in Baltimore in section A, site 1480.[10]

Jason Olds French
Co. D, 5th Vermont Infantry Regiment

Jason Olds French, the fourth child of Mark and Mary Lyon French, was born June 28, 1839, in Cambridge, Vt. He enlisted in Co. D, 5th Vermont Infantry Regiment, on August 13, 1861. During the battle of Savage's Station, on June 29, 1862, Company D was on the front line firing at the enemy. French and his comrade, Pvt. William Hinkson of Worcester, Vt., had fired their rifles and each went down on one knee to reload. In the process of reloading, French was hit by a rebel minie ball in the right shoulder. As Hinkson was in the process of putting the cap on his rifle French fell over knocking Hinkson's rifle aside and splattering him with blood. The ball had entered French's shoulder from the front and went through his body taking part of the shoulder blade with it as it exited out his back about seven inches lower than where it had entered and about three inches from his spine. He was knocked unconscious and as he lay motionless and bleeding profusely Hinkson assumed he was dead. After the battle Pvt. Thomas Long, another of French's comrades, wanted to take several men to retrieve French's body, but Company D's commander, Capt. Reuben C. Benton, refused his request. French, however, was not dead and was captured by Stonewall Jackson's troops the next day. He was taken to the field hospital at Savage's Station. On July 13 the hospital and the patients and doctors were taken to Richmond and placed in prisoner of war camps. While a prisoner, Pvt. Ephraim B. Marcy, also of Company D who had been wounded and captured along with French, tended to French's wound. Both French and Marcy were paroled on July 19. After being paroled French was evacuated to the hospital at Camp Parole at Annapolis, Md., where he remained until given a disability discharge from the army on November 17, 1862. French returned home to Johnson, Vt., where he continued to recuperate from his wound.

After his wound was completely healed French enlisted in Co. C, 17th Vermont Infantry Regiment, on February 24, 1864, the last infantry regiment raised in Vermont. At the battle of Cold Harbor, on June 3, 1864, French was shot in the chest. He was hit four inches below and one inch to the side of his right nipple between the eighth and ninth ribs. The bullet traveled downward as it plunged through his body clipping his lung, liver, and intestines before exiting through his back. From the field he was taken to the IX Corps Hospital. On June 7 he was admitted to the Emory U.S. Army General Hospital in Washington, D.C., where he was suffering from the loss of blood as well as internal injuries. He was pale, his lips were blue, his extremities were cold and he was short of breath. He also had a distended abdomen, was nauseous and would occasionally vomit. French was in such bad shape that his condition was entered as a case study in the Surgeon General's *Medical and Surgical History of the War of the Rebellion* that was published after the war. He was given brandy and beef tea and warm towels were placed on his arms and legs until his body temperature was raised. Over the next several days French fought to stay alive while the doctors worked hard to save him. They fed him wine whey, beef tea, and chicken broth for nourishment while they gave him turpentine enemas. Yet his abdomen remained distended and tender and his wound oozed. He also appeared jaundiced. By June 11 the tenderness in his abdomen had abated and he had a normal body temperature. He was given a generous diet of milk with Dover's powder [a mixture of ipecac and opium] at bedtime. He made steady, but slow progress, and by June 15 he had a good appetite and his bowels were regular. Between June 20 and June 25 French had a setback. His wound started discharging large amounts of pus and blood clots. In place of the Dover's powder he was given tincture of the sesquichloride of iron and by July 2 the discharges from his wound subsided and his improvement continued. On August 19 French was well enough to be transferred to Governor Smith U.S. Army General Hospital in Brattleboro, Vt. On November 22, 1864, he was transferred to the Veteran Reserve Corps in Indianapolis, Ind., where he did light duty. He was discharged from the service on July 21, 1865, and returned home to Johnson.

On July 3, 1881, Jason French married Elizabeth "Lizzie" Miller Potter, in Swanton, Vt. Jason and Lizzie settled in Cambridge where Jason farmed. Lizzie gave birth to a son on November 22, 1883, who they named Philip Sheridan French. Tragically, Lizzie died seven days later on November 29 of blood poisoning. Jason never remarried and sometime after Lizzie died he moved back to Johnson where he continued to farm and was a member of the Old Brigade Grand Army of the Republic Post No. 47.

As time went by French's wounds took their toll. In 1895 he was barely able to move his right arm and had constant pain in his right side where the bullet had gone through him. He was often bedridden. Although he had been receiving a government disability pension over the years it had never been enough to hire someone to take care of him and he had to rely on relatives to do such things as dressing and undressing. By 1910 French was totally disabled and unable to take care of himself and required assistance "preparing his food, attending to the calls of nature, preparing his medicines and general wants." Jason O. French died on April 21, 1913, of a heart attack and was buried beside his wife in Johnson's Lamoile View Cemetery.[11]

Francis Dennison Hammond
Co. I, 5th Vermont Infantry Regiment

Francis Dennison Hammond, the son of Daniel F. and Deborah (Hall) Hammond, was born in South Granville, N.Y., on August 4, 1837. When the Civil War broke out Francis was farming in Pawlet, Vt., where he enlisted in Co. I, 5th Vermont Infantry Regiment, on February 24, 1862. He married Harriet Elizabeth Chapin on April 9, 1862, three days before he was mustered into service. Harriet was the daughter of Samuel and Mary (Chittenden) Hammond and was born on July 28, 1843, in South Granville, N.Y. During the battle of Savage's Station Francis was wounded in the right thigh. He was helped along by his comrades after the battle on the march to the James River and thereby avoided capture by the rebels. Because of stiffness in his right hip joint caused by his wound Hammond was given a disability discharge from the army on December 3, 1862, in Cumberland, Md.

After being discharged from the army, Francis returned to Pawlet where he and Harriet farmed and had two sons, George William born on September 2, 1864, and Fred Samuel born on August 24, 1867. After farming in Vermont for several years Francis and Harriet settled in their hometown of Granville, N.Y., where their third and final child,

Francis Nahum, was born on February 11, 1871. Harriet died on September 10, 1891, and was buried in Granville's Elmwood Cemetery. On November 6, 1895, Francis married Ella Spencer in Middle Granville, N.Y. Ella was very involved in the women's suffrage movement in upstate New York. Francis died on December 9, 1903, and was buried in Elmwood Cemetery beside his first wife. In August 1904 Ella applied for and received a veteran's widow's pension. She died in Granville, N.Y., in 1910.

Robert Johnson
Co. C, 5th Vermont Infantry Regiment

Robert Johnson was born in London, England, in 1835. Whether he immigrated to Canada, or came straight to America is unknown, but he enlisted in Co. C, 5th Vermont Infantry Regiment, in Duxbury, Vt., on August 21, 1861. At the time of his enlistment he was 28 years old, stood five- feet and five-inches tall, had gray eyes, and dark hair and was working as a laborer. At the battle of Savage's Station Johnson was shot in the upper right arm. The bullet shattered the humerus and he had to be left at the VI Corps field hospital when the Vermont Brigade moved on toward the James River after the battle. Johnson was captured along with the rest of the hospital staff and patients the next day. The VI Corps field hospital was closed on July 1 and the patients were transferred to the hospital at Savage's Station. A surgeon finally got around to seeing Johnson on July 3 and determined that his arm could not be saved and amputated it. On July 13 Johnson was moved by rail from Savage's Station to a prisoner of war camp in Richmond where he remained until he was paroled at City Point on July 25. After being paroled Private Johnson was sent to the Satterlee U.S. Army General Hospital in Philadelphia, Penn. Sometime later he was transferred to the U.S. Army General Hospital in West Philadelphia. He remained there until given a disability discharge from the army on April 14, 1863. On May 7, 1863, Johnson filed for and received a government disability pension for his wound. After 1863 little is known about Robert Johnson. A Robert Johnson appears in the 1870 U.S. Census living in Fairfield, Vt. His age is recorded as 40, his place of birth England, and he was a farmer. His wife's first name was Delia and she was 32 years old. This may be the same person. A Robert Johnson died of a stroke at the county farm in Boscawen, N.H., on March 25, 1891. He was 58 years old and was born in England. He was buried in the Woodlawn Cemetery in Penacook, N.H. Much later a U.S. Pension Bureau examiner stated that Robert Johnson who served in Co. C, 5th Vermont, died in 1891 in New Hampshire, so this must the correct person.

Now fast forward to October 16, 1918. This is the date that Mary Ann McGlynn filed for a veteran's widow's pension. Mary Ann McGlynn was the daughter of John and Mary (Cole) Tarpey and was born in Doncaster, England, on January 13, 1852. Mary Ann's father died when she was eight years old and she and her mother immigrated to America where they settled in Bennington, Vt. In her teenage years Mary Ann used to go to New York City where she would visit her mother's half-sister. There she met Philip McGlynn, her mother's half-sister's step son. Mary Ann married Philip McGlynn on May 23, 1876. Philip ran a scrap metal business as well as a livery stable and became quite well off. When Philip died on March 14, 1904, he left Mary Ann financially very comfortable. Unfortunately, she made several bad investments and lost most of her money. After her finical downturn Mary Ann moved in with her daughter, Anna E. Gardiner, and her husband in Caldwell, N.J. Three years after Mary Ann moved in Anna's husband died and Anna, her two children and Mary Ann moved to Jamaica on Long Island where Anna taught school. On January 6, 1917, Anna's seven year old son died and in her grief she made her mother's life unbearable and a week after the boy's death Mary Ann moved to Bennington, Vt., to live with her spinster cousin.

A little over a year after moving to Bennington, Mary Ann McGlynn was penniless and her cousin was desperately ill in the hospital. That was when she decided to apply for a veteran's widow's pension. During their marriage Philip McGlynn had told Mary Ann that he had enlisted in Co. C, 5th Vermont Infantry Regiment, under the name Robert Johnson. He said he had changed his name because he was underage and was afraid that his father would find out that he had enlisted and would have the army kick him out. Mary Ann walked to the nearby Vermont Soldiers' Home and looked up Robert Johnson in Peck's *Revised Roster of Vermont Volunteers in the War of the Rebellion*. There on page 155 was listed Robert Johnson. Thinking that was her husband Mary Ann used the data to file for her pension.

After almost two years of gathering more information for the U.S. Pension Bureau, a Bureau examiner interviewed Mary Ann McGlynn on January 26, 1920. During the interview the examiner told her that the real Robert Johnson had lost his right arm in the army and had died in New Hampshire in 1891. The examiner told MaryAnn that a Thomas Johnson had served in Co. K of the 5th Vermont and that might have been her husband. Because Philip McGlynn's true identity could not be confirmed Mary Ann did not get a pension. She died of tuberculosis in Bennington on June 20, 1923, at age 71.

On March 3, 1863, Congress passed the Enrollment Act that allowed the Federal government to draft men into service. In this act Congress embedded a provision that allowed a man who was drafted to hire a substitute to take his place. This led to two types of unscrupulous men — bounty brokers and bounty jumpers. Bounty brokers were the agents who recruited men for substitutes. Those that were money-hungry and wanted to make a quick buck would recruit men that were either unfit for military service or men that were unsavory characters. The latter led to bounty jumpers, who were men that would sign on as substitutes but desert as soon as they could after they were paid their bounty. Many would repeat this process time and time again from state to state. Philip McGlynn was one of the latter. He enlisted in Windsor, Vt., on August 12, 1864, as a substitute for Hugh G. Miller, a wealthy farmer from Ryegate, Vt. For enlisting as a substitute he got $300 from Miller, plus a $100 bounty from the U.S. government. After he was mustered into service, McGlynn was sent south with a group of other recruits. On September 6, 1864, while in Alexandria, Va., McGlynn slipped away from his group and put on civilian clothes. He walked around Alexandria for a few hours taking in the sights and then headed down the railroad tracks for Washington, D.C. At the Potomac River he was turned back by a military guard. Upon returning to downtown Alexandria McGlynn was caught and incarcerated in the Prince Street Military Prison. He was charged with desertion and brought before a court-martial on December 18, 1862. During the trial he admitted that he had enlisted under the name Robert Johnson so he could desert and enlist again and get another bounty. McGlynn was found guilty and was sentenced to lose all pay due him up to that date and to forfeit $10 of his pay for the next 24 months. He finally reached his company at Patrick Station in Dinwiddie Co., Va., on January 8, 1865. From his compiled military service record it appears that McGlynn became a good soldier and was honorably discharged on August 12, 1864. He probably told his wife he went by the name Robert Johnson to hide the fact that he had been court-martialed. One part of Philip McGlynn's story was correct, he was underage when he enlisted in 1864. On his enlistment paper he claimed his age as 25. According to his death certificate he was only 16 at the time.[12]

Edward H. Marcy and Ephraim B. Marcy
Co. D, 5th Vermont Infantry Regiment

The Marcy brothers, Edward H. and Ephraim B., the sons of Marvin R. and Vilana (Tallman) Marcy, were born in Craftsbury, Vt., Edward in 1840 and Ephraim in 1842. The Marcy's had moved to Craftsbury from Boston about 1840 where Marvin farmed. Not long after settling in Craftsbury Marvin was stricken with neuralgia and a general debility. Because their father became partially disabled Edward and Ephraim had to work on the farm as soon as they were strong enough. On August 25, 1860, Ephraim married Abby M. Mason in Craftsbury and they moved in with his parents. Edward enlisted in Co. D, 5th Vermont Infantry Regiment, on August 19, 1861. Ephraim followed his older brother three days later. The Marcy brothers' enlistment in the army left their parents short of two men to help run the farm. In an effort to make up for his loss, Edward allotted his $7-a-month state pay to his parents.

During the battle of Savage's Station on June 29, 1862, both Edward and Ephraim Marcy were wounded. Ephraim was hit on the top of his head by either a bullet or a shell fragment. The missile fractured his skull and left a diagonal groove across the top of his head, which knocked him unconscious for about an hour. After the battle he was taken to the VI Corps field hospital where his wound, which was bleeding profusely, was dressed by the 5th Vermont's assistant surgeon Henry C. Shaw. Edward suffered a gunshot wound and was also left at the in the hospital with his brother. The hospital staff and patients were captured the next day. On July 1 the VI Corps field hospital was closed and the patients were transferred to the hospital at Savage's Station. When the hospital at Savage's Station was closed on July 13 the patients and staff were taken to Richmond by rail and placed in prisoner of war camps. Ephraim Marcy was paroled on July 19, 1862, at City Point. Edward was too badly wounded to be paroled and was left in Richmond where died of his wounds on July 24. After he was paroled Ephraim was sent to the general hospital at Fort Monroe where he remained for about three weeks. He was then sent to the general hospital at Camp Parole in Annapolis, Md., until he returned to his unit on December 15, 1862. Although at times he could only perform light duty Ephraim was a good soldier and was promoted to corporal on March 1, 1863. He served out his three-year obligation and was mustered out of service on September 15, 1864.

For a year or so after Edward's death Marvin and Vilana Marcy were able to live off of Edward's back pay. When that ran out in October 1865 Vilana filed for a government dependent mother's pension which she received at the rate of $8 a month starting at Edward's date of death. Marvin R. Marcy died on October 14, 1871, and was buried in Craftsbury Common Cemetery. Vilana died of old age at age 81 on January 15, 1896, and was buried beside her husband. By the time of her death her pension had been raised to $12 a month.

After his discharge from the army, Ephraim Marcy returned to his wife Abby in Craftsbury. Between 1870 and 1879 they had five children, four of whom lived to adulthood.

Although Ephraim suffered some from his wound while in the army, it was after his discharge that it grew worse. The wound would cause intense pain on the right side of his head and in his right eye. Sometimes it would cause pain on the entire right side of his body. In the severe cases he would be bedridden for several days to several weeks. To run the farm he would have to hire help, thus cutting into his profits. In 1871 Ephraim filed for a government disability pension which was awarded at only $2 a month. By 1878 he physically could not farm any longer and he learned the sash and blind trade which was less physically demanding. By 1883 Ephraim's condition was worse and he requested another examination by the U.S. Pension Bureau for a possible increase in his pension. In an affidavit to the Bureau Ephraim wrote that he was suffering attacks of dizziness and sometimes staggered and had to cling to something for support. Sometimes when walking he had a tendency to walk to the right and he staggered as though he was intoxicated. Occasionally he experienced difficulty in conversation finding the right word and would sometimes use the wrong one. Periodically he would experience a feeling of pressure in his head as though he was wearing a tight crown and at such times everything would look dark and he would feel faint. He also suffered from panic attacks that were ushered in by a feeling of distress and faintness in the pit of his stomach, sometimes to the degree that he would vomit. The same thing would occasionally happen during his sleep and he would wake up sweating profusely. Finally, within the last few years he had developed a bad cough and was coughing up blood. Because of these symptoms his pension was increased to $14 a month.

Abby Marcy died on April 4, 1906, and was buried in Craftsbury Branch Cemetery. Not long after her death Ephraim moved to Kalispell, Mont., hoping that the clean air would help cure his cough. His health, however, continued to decline and he was admitted to the Montana Soldiers' Home in Columbia Falls where he died of Parkinson's disease on September 25, 1916. His body was taken was taken back to Craftsbury, Vt., where he was buried beside Abby.[13]

Dr. William Pierson Russell
Staff, 5th Vermont Infantry Regiment

William Pierson Russell, the son of Isaac Newton and Martha (Pierson) Russell, was born in Charlotte, Vt., on January 6, 1810. On September 9, 1834, Dr. Russell married Lydia Bass in Middlebury. Dr. Russell was commissioned as the surgeon of the 5th Vermont Infantry Regiment, on August 15, 1861, at age 51.

Before leaving Vermont Dr. Russell contracted a severe case of diarrhea which continued to plague him in the field. On September 19 he was given a 25-day leave of absence to return home to recuperate leaving the health of the regiment in the hands of Assistant Surgeon Henry C. Shaw of Waitsfield, Vt. In Dr. Russell's absence someone in the command reported to the governor of Vermont that Dr. Russell was an alcoholic. Consequently, Governor Fairbanks wrote the following letter to the secretary of war:

Sept. 24th 1861

The Hon. Simon Cameron
Secy. of War
Sir,

> Under the provisions of the laws of Vermont, and in accordance with General Order 25 of your department, I appointed Wm. P. Russell, M.D. as Surgeon of the 5th Regiment Vermont Vols., he having passed the required examination by the medical board appointed by me.
>
> Since commissioning Dr. Russell, information entirely reliable, has been communicated to me that he is a confirmed inebriator. That he is frequently intoxicated, and during much of this time is wholly disqualified for the duties.
>
> A proper regard for the health and security of the regiment induces me to request, very respectfully, that you will refuse to approve of his appointment, and order his discharge.
>
> I have the honor to be
> Your obt. Servt. Erastus Fairbanks

In Dr. Russell's compiled military service record there is a general order dated September 30, 1861, discharging him from the service, but the order must have been revoked as there is a letter from the division surgeon dated December 12, 1861, stating:

> Enclosed please find Dr. Russell's letter containing statement by what authority his acting as Surgeon of the 5th Vt. Regt. I would add that Dr. Russell has been acting effectively as Surgeon of the Regiment since November 5th [The date Russell returned to the regiment from his leave of absence].

That statement seemed to close the controversy as Dr. Russell continued to be the surgeon for the regiment.

After the battle of Savage's Station on June 29, 1862, Dr. Russell and Dr. William J. Sawin, assistant surgeon of the 2nd Vermont, were detailed to remain with the wounded Vermont soldiers at the VI Corps field hospital that had been established in a house and blacksmith shop about a mile from Savage's Station. The next day doctors Russell and Sawin, along with their patients were captured by General Stonewall Jackson's troops. Jackson ordered the Vermonter's hospital consolidated with the one at Savage's Station the next day and the patients moved to the hospital at Savage's Station. Doctor Russell remained at Savage's Station until Confederate authorities ordered the hospital there to be closed on July 13 and all the doctors and patients were put aboard flat cars and transported to Richmond. The train arrived about 2 p.m., but for some reason the Federal soldiers were kept on the flat cars all night without food or blankets. At 3 a.m. the next morning the prisoners of war were ordered off the train cars and marched to Libby prison. Dr. Russell remained in Libby Prison until he was paroled on July 17 at Haxall's Landing several miles downriver from Richmond. After he was exchanged he was taken a few more miles further down river and reunited with his regiment at Harrison's Landing.

Although back with his regiment, Dr. Russell was too sick to carry out his duties. When the Vermont Brigade left Harrison's Landing in mid-August for Fort Monroe Dr. Russell was too sick to ride his horse and had to make the trip in an ambulance. From Fort Monroe the Vermont Brigade was taken to Alexandria where it marched toward Centerville. Dr. Russell was in no condition for field duty and was left in Alexandria to care for the 5th Vermont's assistant surgeon, Henry C. Shaw, who was suffering from typhoid fever. Dr. Shaw died on September 7, 1862. By this time Dr. Russell had also contracted typhoid fever and after Shaw's death he was sent to a hospital in Washington, D.C. Six days after arriving Dr. Russell was given a 25-day leave of absence to return to Vermont to recuperate. Near the expiration of his leave of absence Dr. Russell visited Samuel W. Thayer, the surgeon general of Vermont, who extended his leave of absence 20 more days, but with Russell in Vermont and the 5th Vermont's assistant surgeon dead, Dr. Russell was given a disability discharge from the army on October 11, 1862, and a new surgeon and assistant surgeon were recruited for the 5th Vermont.

After his discharge from the army Dr. Russell's health was in a terrible state. His attending physician wrote that Russell, "was much emaciated, his skin of a coppery yellowish hue, indicating a grave disturbance of the gastric and hepatic functions. He remained in this condition for a long time suffering from excessive diarrhea and extreme debility." After a year of recuperation Russell regained most of his health and was able to resume his practice. Then in April of 1864 he had a series of mini-strokes and in May the next year he had a major stroke that left his left side paralyzed. Immediately following the stroke he was unable to move or speak, but he gradually regained his speech and some motion. Unable to walk without assistance he had to give up his practice. In June of 1869 he applied for and received a government disability pension. Dr. Russell did not live long after receiving his pension dying on June 4, 1872, at age 62. He was buried in Middlebury's West Cemetery.

After Dr. Russell's death Lydia Russell applied for a veteran's widow's pension. During the process of gathering affidavits in support of her pension Dr. Russell's drinking became an issue again. Lydia's uncle, Dr. Zacheus Bass, looked the special examiner of the Pension Bureau square in the eyes and said, "I told him he was not entitled to a pension when he was trying to get it. I told him he never had an honest hair in his head, if he had, it was pulled out before I knew him. He used to drink like the devil." Dr. Charles L. Allen wrote:

> I resided in Middlebury and practiced by the side of Dr. Russell, that we were on good terms socially, and that I know that he habitually used intoxicating drinks, often to excess. In January 1862 I visited Camp Griffin, remaining several days, and saw the Dr. frequently, and know that he used them freely at that time. In September 1862 I attended him professionally in Washington, D.C. At that time he was alarmingly prostrated by gastritis, which I then attributed (as I do now) to his excessive use of alcoholic drink.

A number of Dr. Russell's fellow officers supplied affidavits that were less accusatory than those of Bass' and Allen's. While they all said that Dr. Russell would occasionally have a drink it never interfered with the performance of his duties. Whether or not Dr. Russell drank to excess or not Lydia was awarded her pension. Why the issue of Dr. Russell's drinking never surfaced in his pension application remains a mystery. Lydia Russell died of cancer on August 30, 1888, at age 74 and was buried beside her husband. The Middlebury Grand Army of the Republic post No. 89 was named after William P. Russell.[14]

Jonathan Stedman
Co. H, 5th Vermont Infantry Regiment

Francis Cullen Stedman
Co. H, 5th Vermont Infantry Regiment

Irwin Wisewell Stedman
Co. H, 5th Vermont Infantry Regiment

The stories of the Stedmans have to be told as one since Jonathan Stedman was the father of Francis and Irwin and all three of them served in Co. H of the 5th Vermont Infantry Regiment together.

Jonathan Stedman, the son of Orison and Deborah (Jones) Stedman, was born in Benson, Vt., on November 19, 1816. According to the 1840 U.S. Census Jonathan was married and farming in Orwell, Vt. He had married Mary L. Wisewell who was an Orwell native. The exact date of their marriage remains unknown, but in 1840 U.S. Census they had no children so the approximate date of their marriage was probably 1838 or 1839. At the time the census was taken Mary was pregnant with their first child. Mary gave birth on December 10, 1840, to Francis Cullen Stedman. Their next child, Irwin Wisewell Stedman, was born on March 4, 1844. Their third and final child, Moses Stedman, was born in August of 1849. Sometime prior to the birth of Moses the Stedmans moved to Rutland, Vt., where Moses was born and where Jonathan started a shoemaking business.

When they completed school Francis worked as a farm laborer and Irwin worked as an apprentice shoemaker with his father. After the Confederates fired on Fort Sumter the Stedman brothers resisted enlisting in the army, but on August 30, 1861, 18-year-old Irwin could not resist the temptation any longer and enlisted in Co. H, 5th Vermont Infantry Regiment. Twenty-year-old Francis followed his younger brother and enlisted in Co. H of the 5th Vermont on September 3. Jonathan enlisted in Co. H of the 5th Vermont the next day. Jonathan's enlisting is somewhat surprising since he was 44 years old and had a successful shoemaking business. One can only wonder if he enlisted to look out for his sons.

At the battle of Savage's Station on June 29, 1862, both of the Stedman brothers were seriously wounded. A minie ball hit Francis on the inside of his left ankle near the bone and exited through the other side taking part of the Achilles tendon with it. Irwin was hit in the left buttock by a minie ball. The bullet entered near, but missed the pelvic bone and lodged in his scrotum. The Stedman's were too badly wounded to accompany their regiment on the retreat after the battle and were left at the VI Corps field hospital where they were captured the next day. The VI Corps field hospital closed on July 1 and the patients were moved to the hospital at Savage's Station. On July 13 the hospital at Savage's Station also closed permanently requiring the patients and staff to be transported by rail to Richmond and placed in prisoner of war camps. After spending a month incarcerated in Richmond the brothers were paroled at City Point below Richmond on August 3. From City Point they were taken to Hammond U.S. Army General Hospital at Lookout Point, Md. Soon after arriving at the hospital Irwin had the bullet that was lodged in his scrotum surgically removed through his perineum. After recuperating from his wound his leg was so stiff Irwin could no longer serve in the field and was transferred to Co. D, 9th Regiment of the Invalid Corps where he served until was discharged from the army on September 15, 1864.

After Francis recuperated from his wound he was sent back to his regiment. On September 25, 1863, he was detailed as an ambulance driver. This might have been instigated by his father who had been detailed as an ambulance driver on August 8, 1862. If Jonathan thought being an ambulance driver would keep Francis safe he was wrong. Francis was wounded again on June 3, 1864, at the battle of Cold Harbor, on the outskirts of Richmond, Va. This time he was hit by a shell fragment on his right side just below the shoulder blade. After being treated in the field he was sent to the Lincoln U.S. Army General Hospital in Washington, D.C. After his wound healed the doctors decided he was no longer fit for active duty and transferred him to 171 Co., 2nd Battalion of the Veteran Reserve Corps and he was sent to the Baxter U.S. Army General Hospital in Burlington, Vt., for light duty until he was discharged on July 17, 1865.

6. The Aftermath

For some reason Jonathan Stedman was discharged from the army by War Department special order no. 383 dated November 4, 1864. The paperwork took a while to reach his regiment, but he was finally discharged on November 14, 1864. Jonathan returned home to Mary and restarted his shoemaking business. Jonathan died at age 64 of tuberculosis on July 22, 1881, and was buried in Orwell's Mountain View Cemetery. After Jonathan's death Mary applied for and received a government veteran's widow's pension until she died at age 80 of asthma on April 6, 1898. She was buried beside her husband.

After his discharge Francis Stedman returned home to Orwell where he married Elvira Skeels on January 14, 1864. They had one child, Mary Olive, born on September 20, 1866. Elvira died on May 26, 1871, of tuberculosis. Six months later Francis married Henrietta "Etta" Angelica Tabor on November 9. Francis and Etta's' first child, Mary, died of a fever on March 14, 1873, at age six. On July 4, 1875, Francis and Etta had their second and final child, Ida May, born on July 4, 1875. Francis suffered from his war wound as he got older. His left foot would swell and ache. His right side ached where he had been struck by the shell fragment. All of these ailments were exacerbated by his work as a farm hand. By 1895 Francis had to slow down so he applied for and received a government disability pension to supplement his reduced income. Francis died of arteriosclerosis on October 8, 1917, and was buried in Mountain View Cemetery in Orwell. After Francis' death Etta received a veteran's widow's pension. Etta died on January 2, 1936, of heart disease.

Irwin Stedman married Miamma L. Fuller on May 12, 1865, in West Rutland, Vt. Over the next 17 years they had five children: Eva A. born on August 29, 1866; Mary S. born on June 8, 1872; Cora A. born on June 3, 1877; Moses A. born on March 2, 1880, and Earl F. born on January 11, 1882. In September 1875 Irwin filed for and later received a small government disability pension for the effects of his wound. According to the 1880 U.S. Census Irwin and Miamma were living in Orwell with Irwin's father and Irwin was working with his father as a shoemaker.

During the afternoon of Monday, September 2, 1895, Irwin was at the home of his son-in-law, Charles M. Cooke, in Orwell. Charles Cooke had married Irwin's daughter Mary in 1892. Cooke was away that afternoon and Irwin went out into the pasture to round up some horses to make up a team to pull a carriage. What Irwin did not know was that one of the horses was very dangerous and had previously cornered several people in the stall and attacked them. Unknowingly, Irwin took this horse into a stall and was immediately cornered and kicked in the head. The horse kicked with such ferocity that its hind legs got caught on top of the divider between the stalls. Irwin was found lying unconscious in the stall by a family member and the local doctor was summoned. The only thing that had saved Irwin's life was the horse's getting caught on the stall divider. When the doctor arrived a half hour later he found Irwin laying unconscious with his face covered with blood from a cut on the left side of his head that ran from his eye to his ear from the horse's shoe. The doctor later stated the wound "was a deep gash and a depression in the skull that you could lay a finger in." The cut was stitched up and hot water bottles were put on his arms and legs in an attempt to revive him, but Irwin remained unconscious for a week. For a while after regaining consciousness he appeared dazed and had trouble remembering the names of friends and family. The injury also adversely effected his eyesight causing him to see double, but a special pair of glasses helped his vision a little.

Over the years Irwin's dazed condition improved somewhat, but his old war wound troubled him more and more. He also suffered from arthritis, nephritis and had problems with headaches from the incident with the horse. The 1900 U.S. Census indicated he was trying to make a living as a day laborer, but his age and ailments made that almost impossible. Due to his disabilities his government disability pension was increased several times over the years and by the 1920s he was receiving $50 a month.

Miamma died on March 12, 1919, and was buried in Orwell's Mountain View Cemetery. Irwin died on February 9, 1923, of chronic nephritis and was buried beside his wife.[15]

Noah C. Thompson
Co. B, 5th Vermont Infantry Regiment

David R. Thompson
Co. B, 5th Vermont Infantry Regiment

Noah C. Thompson and David R. Thompson, the sons of Alden and Matilda (Heath) Thompson, were raised for most of their childhoods in village of Lincoln, Vt. Just before 1860 the Thompsons moved five miles west to the town of Bristol. There on August 20, 1861, at the age of 18, Noah enlisted in Co. B, 5th Vermont Infantry Regiment. His older brother David followed Noah by enlisting in the same company 18 days later on September 7. During the battle of Savage's Station Noah was severely wounded in the right thigh. David had to leave his brother at the VI Corps field hospital as the Vermont Brigade continued its march to the James River after the battle. Noah, along with the rest of the staff and patients at the VI Corps field hospital, was captured by the rebels the next day. On July 1 all of the patients at the VI Corps field hospital were transferred to the hospital at Savage's Station. On July 13 the hospital at Savage's Station was closed and the staff and patients were transported to Richmond by rail and placed in prisoner of war camps. On July 25 Noah was paroled at City Point and sent to the U.S. Army General Hospital in Chester, Penn., where he was admitted on July 29. He deserted on October 2 and went home to Vermont where he married Victoria L. Orcutt in Bristol on October 5, 1862. He surrendered himself to the army under a presidential proclamation of amnesty for deserters and served out the rest of his time in Co. I, 1st Battalion of the Invalid Corps beginning on August 1, 1863, until he was mustered out of service on July 1, 1865.

Noah's life after his military service spiraled downward. Several years after their marriage, Noah suspected Victoria of having an affair with a horse dealer and local Bristol ruffian by the name of John A. Ring. It wasn't long before Noah confronted Ring and a fight ensued in which Noah gave Ring a severe thrashing. On Saturday evening, April 15, 1871, the two men went at it again. While a group of men were hanging out in front of the Bristol Hotel, the hotel's hostler told Ring, who had been drinking, that he could not whip any man in the group. Noah Thompson, who was one of the on lookers stepped forward and said, "Perhaps you can whip me." Ring said to Thompson, "Keep away from me, I don't want anything to do with you" and backed toward his team that was standing nearby. At the same time he put his hand in his pocket and took out a single bladed pocketknife. Thompson said, "I know you are armed, if you was not I would knock you." Ring replied, "Come down here and I will make a hole through you." Thompson said he guessed he had a right to walk around anywhere chose to, and walked to within six or eight feet of Ring. That was when Ring lunged at Thompson and stabbed him in the neck. The two men then grabbed hold of each other and fell to the ground. By the time Thompson got the knife away from Ring he had been stabbed eight or 10 times. The first slash by Ring was the fatal wound severing Thompson's jugular vein. Thompson was picked up and laid on the front steps of Dr. Haseltine's drug store where he gasped two or three times and died. His last words were, "I have got the knife." Noah Thompson was buried in Bristol's Greenwood Cemetery and Victoria was left with a young son.

Ring was arrested on the spot, but soon broke away and made a run for it before being recaptured and placed in irons. He came to trial during the December term of the Addison County Court and was convicted of murder. He was sentenced on January 13, 1872, to serve 11 years in the state penitentiary. In 1878 several people in Bristol petitioned the governor to pardon Ring. It seems the judge who tried the case was of the opinion that Thompson had been the aggressor and that Ring's sentence should have been as light as the law would allow. The pardon was also recommended by nine of the jurors that convicted Ring. On September 27, 1878, the governor pardoned John Ring.

After Noah's death, Victoria Thompson had an affair with a man named John H. Barnum. Some people at the time claimed the affair started before Noah's death. Barnum, a wealthy retired grocer, was married with children ranging from adulthood to age seven. Apparently Victoria and Barnum were not very discrete as the affair was the talk of the town. Barnum did not help matters by telling people that he had fathered Victoria's child before Noah's death. Finally, by July 1876 a number of the men in the town had had enough and cornered Barnum in Victoria's house one evening. Several of the men were sent to get tar and feathers to teach Barnum a lesson, but while they were gone Barnum paid off the men guarding him and made his escape. Several nights later a charge of powder was put under Victoria's house and ignited. The explosion knocked out several windows and did damage to one side of the house. Fortunately, Victoria was not home at the time. That was the last straw for Victoria and John Barnum and they ran off together to parts unknown. After Victoria and John Barnum left Bristol a column appeared in the Montpelier *Argus and Patriot*, stating, "Victoria victimized him. Separated him from his lawful family, and no doubt the curses of Satan will follow her." After John Barnum deserted his wife Julia, she filed for and received a divorce. Some years later John Barnum returned to Bristol where he died of kidney disease on June 8, 1899, and was buried in Greenwood Cemetery. Julia died the next year and was buried beside her ex-husband. Whether they lived together after his return to Bristol is not known. Victoria Thompson's fate remains a mystery.[16]

Liking the military life David R. Thompson reenlisted on December 15, 1863, and two months later he was promoted to corporal. During David's time in the army he had been in many battles, but had always escaped injury. On May 10, 1864, Col. Emory Upton, with 12 handpicked regiments, including the 5th Vermont, made a charge on the salient at Spotsylvania Court House. During this charge David's luck ran out. He was hit by a rebel minie ball in the upper left arm fracturing the humerus as it passed through. After being treated at the front he was eventually sent to Baxter U.S. Army General Hospital in Burlington, Vt. After his arm healed he could no longer perform field duty and was transferred to 171 Co., 2nd Battalion of the Invalid Corps. He served at the Baxter General Hospital until he was mustered out of service on February 24, 1865.

Other than he applied for and received a $4-a-month government disability pension, exactly what happened to David R. Thompson after his discharge from the army remains somewhat of a mystery. He does not reappear until he marries Alma Jane Heath in La Crosse, Wis., on May 22, 1886. Alma had previously been married to Frank B. Ross and had two sons. It appears that Alma and Frank Ross had divorced and Alma went back to her maiden name. She was also a native Vermonter from Starksboro. After their wedding they moved to Chicago, Ill. In 1894 Alma moved back to Vermont taking her daughter and all of the family furniture and household goods. According to David, Alma left without any cause or justification. In the spring of 1898 Alma returned to Chicago and moved back in with David. In March of 1899 David got a job with the Joplin Lead and Zinc Company in Joplin, Mo. Alma stayed in Chicago and David promised to send her $20 or $25 a month. Alma moved back to Vermont for the final time in April 1900. David left Joplin, Mo., in 1901 and moved back to La Crosse, Wis., where he remained for several months before being admitted to the Wisconsin Soldiers' Home in King, Wis., where he remained until the spring of 1903. After leaving the Soldier's Home David moved to Clarence, Iowa, where with the financial help of his brother Daniel, he started a restaurant. In May of 1905 Alma filed for half of David's disability pension, which by then was $12, claiming he had deserted her. That is when the charges and counter-charges began. David contended he had not deserted Alma and that he had supported her as he had agreed to until he left his job in Joplin and then sent her money whenever he could. The fight ended when David died on November 10, 1907, in Milwaukee, Wis. At that time Alma got all of David's pension. By the time she died in January 1937, she was receiving $30 a month.[17]

Wilson Daniel Wright
Co. B, 5th Vermont Infantry Regiment

Wilson Daniel Wright, the son of Reuben R. and Maria (Smith) Wright, was born in Cornwall, Vt., on July 1, 1838. When the Civil War broke out in the spring of 1861 the 23-year-old farmer enlisted in Co. I, 1st Vermont Infantry Regiment, on May 2 and was selected as a corporal. The 1st Vermont was formed in response to President Lincoln' call for 75,000 troops to be activated for three months to put down the rebellion, surely enough time to get the job done. Wright's three-month service in the 1st Vermont was uneventful. His regiment served in Hampton and Newport News, Va. The 1st Vermont was only in one battle, the battle of Big Bethel on June 10, and Wright's company was not involved. He was mustered out with his regiment on August 15. Wright apparently liked military life and a little over a month later he reenlisted in Co. B, 5th Vermont Infantry Regiment. Because of his prior military experience, Wright was chosen as the first lieutenant of his company.

Wright's military career was going well until the battle of Savage's Station on June 29, 1862, when he was wounded. While standing in line of battle to repulse a rebel charge he was hit by a minie ball in his upper left thigh about eight inches below his crotch. The ball passed through his leg and exited out through his left buttock. Unable to continue on with his company he was left at the VI Corps field hospital and was captured the next day. On July 1 the VI Corps field hospital was closed and the patients were transferred to the hospital at Savage's Station. On July 13 the hospital at Savage's Station was closed and the staff and patients were loaded onto flat cars and taken by train to Richmond. Because he was an officer, Wright was incarcerated in the infamous Libby Prison. Luckily for him he was quartered with the 5th Vermont's surgeon, Dr. William P. Russell, who was able to care for his wound. Wright was paroled on July 17 at Haxall's Landing on the James River below Richmond. He spent the next several months in army hospitals until his leg healed. After the wound healed Wright had very limited motion in his left leg and he was given a disability discharge from the army on October 2, 1862.

After his discharge from the army Wright returned home to Middlebury where he married Emily Mary Dyer in Rutland on December 4, 1862. Emily was a woman with a past. Her first marriage in 1857 was to a man named Chauncey A. Barnes and they lived in Berlin, Ohio. They were only married a few years before they divorced. On December 31, 1860, Emily M. (Dyer) Barnes married Hiram B. Keyser in Rutland, Vt. They had only been married a little over a year when Hiram's wife found out her husband had remarried without divorcing her. She confronted Hiram and Emily and vowed to make trouble. Emily wanted no part of the Keyser's problems and quickly filed for divorce. Emily's marriage to Hiram B. Kyser was annulled on the February 2, 1863, in the February term of the Vermont Supreme Court in Rutland, Vt. Additionally, Emily was awarded all of the property that she and Hiram had collected during their marriage. While living in Middlebury Wilson worked as a hostler. In July of 1863 he filed for and received a government disability pension of $4 a month for the wound in his left hip. In 1867 Wilson and Emily left Vermont and moved to St. Paul, Minn. There they bought a house and some land and they built a stable and went into the livery business. Not long after establishing the livery business Wilson started a real estate business. In March of 1875 Wilson and Emily adopted a seven year old girl named Helen. With the family rounded out and Wilson's business interests prospering the Wright's seemed to be living the American dream. But their idyllic life was just a façade. Behind closed doors terrible things were happening. It all came to light when Wilson sued Emily for divorce in 1900.

Because of his businesses Wilson had to travel a lot and when he was home he quite often worked until after midnight. While he was away Emily entertained men, usually young ones, in her house. In a 1903 affidavit Emily's daughter, Helen, testified:

> I remember one time when I was 13 or 14 years old that one William Hunt came into our house and went into the parlor and laid down on the divan and Mrs. Wright was in another room. All of a sudden Hunt jumped up and came out to her and said he had been dreaming of monkeys, at the same time he took hold of himself in a very improper way, and Mrs. Wright told me to go to bed which I did. My room was near Mrs. Wright's and after I went to bed I heard them go to bed and I heard them laughing and talking when I went to sleep. I awoke once during the night and heard them talking then. When I got up the next morning Mrs. Wright called me and as I came through the dining room the portieres to her bedroom were not tightly closed and I saw Mr. Hunt in bed with her. Mrs. Wright sent me out for oyster crackers and when I came back Mr. Hunt was standing in her bedroom door only partly dressed. He had on no coat or vest and was fastening his suspenders. The table was set with pure white linen, the best china, glasses and silverware and oyster stew for breakfast. At another time I supposed her to be sick in bed; she wore nightgowns all open down the front. I had just come into the house one afternoon and she was already to go to bed. I heard a step on the porch and looking out saw that it was Mr. Hunt. I told her to hurry and cover herself up and instead of that she stood in the doorway in plain sight of Mr. Hunt with her nightgown open from neck to the floor exposing her nude form. My aunt, Mrs. Lusetta W. Austin, and I both saw it. I have seen Mrs. Wright show her legs many times to Hunt and other men. At one time Hunt roomed at our house and I took coffee in to him in the morning and Mrs. Wright was sitting on the edge of his bed with her hands underneath the bedclothes. I have seen Mrs. Wright sit in Mr. Hunt's lap and embrace him and put her hands on his privates many times and I have known Hunt to be in Mrs. Wright's bedroom a great many times with her. Hunts relations with Mrs. Wright continued for a long time until he married and went away.

Lusetta W. Austin, Wilson's sister, had lived in one of Wilson's rental homes in St. Paul near the Wilson's home for 14 years starting in 1888. Lusetta was totally deaf and could not attest to what was said in Emily's house, but what she saw corroborated Helen's affidavit.

Helen and Lusetta also testified that when drunk Emily would verbally and physically fight with Wilson. She would curse at him, pull his beard and strike him with his cane.

Wilson Wright also was not without fault. At one o'clock in the morning in November of 1884 Emily caught Wilson having sex with her niece, Carrie Davis. He was sitting in a chair with Carrie sitting astride his lap. This caused quite an uproar in the family. Carrie's husband sued her for divorce for adultery, but because he continued to live with her after the incident the court ruled that he had condoned the offense and denied him the divorce.

As Wilson and Emily had acquired property over the years it had for some unexplained reason had been put in Emily's name. In October 1892 Emily signed an agreement that she would sign over all the property to Wilson and in exchange he would support her the rest of her life, but he reneged on the deal and gave her nothing. Emily was too old and infirm to support herself and had to be taken in by an Episcopal home for elderly women on Seventh Street in St. Paul.

Wilson finally got what he wanted when the Vermont Orange County Court awarded him a divorce from Emily on June 6, 1903, for her intolerable severity and adultery. In the meantime Emily had been trying to get half of Wilson's government disability pension, but after the divorce the U.S. Pension Bureau ruled that she was ineligible because she was no longer his wife.

Wilson D. Wright died on March 27, 1932, of cerebral anemia at age 93. He was buried in the Los Angeles National Cemetery. What happened to Emily is unknown.[18]

Seth N. Eastman
Co. B, 6th Vermont Infantry Regiment

Seth N. Eastman, the son of Bernard S. and Harriett (Weed) Eastman, was born in Topsham, Vt., on August 4, 1843. When the Civil War broke out he was a student in the Newbury Seminary in Newbury, Vt., and he enlisted as a private, in Co. B, 6th Vermont Infantry Regiment, on September 26, 1861, at age 17. In December Eastman contracted typhoid fever. He spent about two months in the regimental hospital at Camp Griffin and then was transported to a hospital in Philadelphia. He did not return to his company until the spring of 1862. His company commander wrote later, "when returned to the company he was hard of hearing and I noticed he with difficulty understood the order and that I had to speak loud and plain to make him understand conservation and he continued to be hard of hearing while I knew him in the service after that time." Eastman's hearing would only get worse with time.

At the battle of Savage's Station on June 29, 1862, Eastman was wounded in the right thigh by a buck and ball round from a rebel smooth bore musket. He was very lucky that the bullet did not hit his femur, but unlucky that the ball and buckshot could never be removed. When the Vermonters pulled back after the battle to resume their march toward the James River several of Eastman's comrades, Privates Franklin Bixby and William Bagley, tried to help him along. But weakening from the loss of blood they left him at the VI Corps field hospital. What Eastman experienced there amazed and shocked him:

6. The Aftermath

There were many wounded men here, some much more seriously wounded than I. One man that I knew had both of his legs broken, another had one of his broken. I was comforted to a certain extent thinking I was much better than they. No tongue can describe, no pen can portray the scenes that I saw in and around that blacksmith shop that night. Men were slowly bleeding to death without any help or sympathy. Some were praying, others were cursing and swearing, many were thirsty and begged for water in vain, others called for their friends and relatives and cries for help could be heard in all directions. I could not sleep from pain, thirst and thinking what the morrow would bring. In the morning, many of the wounded were dead having bled to death in some cases. I saw several men stone dead sitting up against a stone or a tree, many more were almost dead with no one to wait on them. This was the only time I saw the rear of our army after a retreat during the whole war.

After their defeat at Malvern Hill on July 1, the bulk of the Confederate army pulled back closer to Richmond passing by Savage's Station. Eastman continued:

After their army and their wounded had gotten safely by, they turned their attention to their wounded prisoners of which I was one. Up to this time, we had no care or attention and had lain in our bloody clothes for 5 or 6 days and our wounds had become maggoty and the helpless ones were in horrible condition. The rebel physicians used turpentine on a feather to drive the maggots out of the wounds, a little would work very effectively out of any kind of wound. My wound was maggoty and one application of the turpentine drove all the maggots out. I was careful to keep them out after that because I could help myself and had no broken bones. I could walk on a crutch with difficulty and all such were gathered and loaded on flat cars and taken to Richmond and put in Libby Prison or into tobacco warehouses that stood near the prison.

I stayed in the yard of the prison the first night of my stay as the guest of the Southern Confederacy. We had something to eat there. I don't remember exactly what but it was no better than corn bread and water. After this I was confined in a large tobacco warehouse for a week and then was sent to Belle Island which was a sand bar in the James River. No attention was ever paid to my wound except to drive the maggots out, it was very hard to keep them out however as I was very filthy and dirty and had nothing to help myself with. There were about 6000 prisoners on this island of six acres and it was very difficult for me in my weakened condition to hobble to the river for baths, consequently I was not very clean, but I was young and soon the wound began to heal and in about 6 weeks it was all healed up with the ball still in there. No surgeon ever tried to extract it and it is still in there now as this is written. The wound did not trouble much if I laid still so that I had to take my chances with the other 6000. There was very little to eat and no water to drink except that out of the river. I stayed in this prison until October 13 when I was chosen and paroled not to serve against the Southern Confederacy until such time I had been properly exchanged which happened a few weeks later when I was given a musket and cartridge box and ordered to take my place in Co. B 6th Vt. Regiment of Volunteers and do duty as usual. I am unable at this time to give the exact date of my return to duty but it was sometime in Nov. 1862. I was glad to get back to my place in the ranks again as I was sick and tired of being a paroled prisoner with nothing to do. They would not give me a furlough to go home as I expected. They thought I would not come back again and they were probably right too.

Eastman served honorably with his company and was promoted to corporal on December 29, 1863. He was mustered out of service at the expiration of his enlistment on October 28, 1864, without being wounded again. This was an amazing feat considering he went through some of the bloodiest fighting of the war in such battles at first and second Fredericksburg, the Wilderness, Spotsylvania, and Cold Harbor.

After returning to Vermont Eastman studied medicine under Dr. George K. Bayley for two years and then under Dr. George K. Plumley for a year. He graduated in January 1869. He also studied medicine at the Eclectic Medical College of Pennsylvania and Dartmouth Medical College and received degrees from both institutions. Seth Eastman married Evalona Darling, the daughter of Jonathan R. and Sarah M. (Taisey) Darling, on June 25, 1875, in Ryegate, Vt. They settled in Groton, Vt., in 1868 where they remained for the rest of their lives. Seth and Evalona had two sons: Cyrus D. born on October 2, 1877, and Bernard S. born on June 20, 1880. For many years, in addition to his practice in the Groton area, Dr. Eastman was also a member of the U.S. Board of Examiners for the U.S. Pension Bureau for veterans applying for government disability pensions.

On June 18, 1877, Dr. Eastman applied for a government disability pension for his loss of hearing and pain from his leg wound, both of which were getting worse. He was successful in his application and received a $12-a-month pension. In 1886 his leg wound was troubling him more. There was a prickly sensation in the bottom of his right foot, a loss of sensation in his leg, and he had difficulty walking. He also could not lie on his right side as it caused him pain and numbness in his right leg and hip. By 1890 Eastman was almost totally deaf as explained by his father-in-law, Jonathan R. Darling, in a statement to the U.S. Pension Bureau, "[That Eastman] Is now quite deaf and frequently does not hear when spoken to unless given special attention does not hear common elevation of the voice. When spoken to frequently inquires what was said." By 1892 his pension had been increased to $20 a month and in 1918 to $30 a month.

Dr. Eastman's son Cyrus graduated from the Montpelier Seminary in 1896 and appeared to have a bright career ahead of him until soon after graduation he contracted tuberculosis. After spending several months in sanatoriums in Colorado and New Mexico he died on February 2, 1900, and was buried in the Eastman family plot in Groton's Old Village Cemetery. Evalona also died of tuberculosis on June 16, 1903, at age 49, and was buried in the Old Village Cemetery. Dr. Seth Eastman died on April 13, 1914, of heart disease and was buried beside his wife.[19]

John Scott
Co. K, 6th Vermont Infantry Regiment

John Scott was born in Edinburgh, Scotland, in October of 1807. When he emigrated to the United States and how he got to Vermont is unknown. He married Lydia J. Marsh in 1838 and they had one child, Jonathan Sidney Scott, who was born on October 18, 1843, in Vermont. What happened to Lydia remains a mystery. John married again in early 1850. This time he married Lydia J. Gabree. From 1855 to March of 1862 they had four children. In 1850 John and Lydia were living in Georgia, Vt. John enlisted as a private in Co. K, 6th Vermont Infantry Regiment, on February 1, 1862, in Burlington. In early June of 1862 the Vermont Brigade was stationed on the east side of the Chickahominy River and was engaged in building corduroy roads. On June 5 Private John Scott lifted a log that caused a strain in his scrotum causing his testicles to swell. He was put on light duty for several days and then put back to work. On June 29, 1862, at the battle of Savage's Station Scott was wounded in his left thigh near the hip joint. Unable to march he was left at the VI Corps field hospital and the next day Scott, along with the rest of the hospital staff and patients, was captured by the rebels. The VI Corps field hospital was closed on July 1 and all the patients were transferred to the hospital at Savage's Station. The hospital at Savage's Station was closed on July 13 and all the patients were transported to Richmond. Unlike most of the patients Scott was taken to a military hospital instead of a prisoner of war camp. There a rebel surgeon treated the wound in his hip. Because Scott's left testicle was so badly swollen the doctor opened Scott's scrotum and cut its spermatic cord in an attempt to alleviate the swelling and pain. Scott was paroled on July 17, 1862, at Haxall's Landing a few miles below Richmond. After being paroled he was sent to an army hospital in Alexandria, Va., where he was given a disability discharge on November 29, 1862.

After his discharge from the army John returned home to Georgia where he worked as a farm laborer when his physical ailments would allow it. In February of 1863 John filed for and received an $8-a-month government disability pension. Even though he was still having trouble with his testicles he managed to father four more children between 1863 and 1873. Sometime between 1860 and 1870 John and Lydia moved their family to Milton, Vt. By 1869 John's physical condition was no better. His limp was getting worse and his left testicle was still greatly swollen and the incision in his scrotum would break open from time to time and release pus. Because of this he was unable to work most of the time and relied on his disability pension. In September of 1880 John requested a re-examination for a pension increase. In the results of the examination the doctor noted that for a number of years John's scrotum had to be opened about every two months to release the pus and that John was always in quite a bit of pain. He also noted that John was unable to work and was being taken care of by the town. The doctor wrote that he felt the only cure was castration which was not done. John's pension was increased to $12 a month. About 1890 John was re-examined again and his condition had deteriorated even more. His scrotum was still having to be opened to drain on a regular basis. Using Vermont sugar makers' parlance the doctor wrote that when John's scrotum became too painful, "he has it tapped and drawn off." John still could not work and was still being taken care of by the town. The doctor also noted, "There is no prospect of its ever being any better." Lydia J. Scott died on November 2, 1900, and was buried in Georgia Plains Cemetery. That same year John was so feeble that he could not even feed himself. He died of heart disease at age 86 on January 27, 1904, at the house of one of his daughters in South Hero, Vt. He was buried in Georgia Plains Cemetery beside Lydia. When he died he was receiving a $24-a-month disability pension.

John Scott's first son, and only child with Lydia Marsh, Jonathan S. Scott enlisted in the 3rd Vermont Light Artillery on December 23, 1864. Before he could be mustered into service he was transferred to Co. B, 17th Vermont Infantry Regiment, which was having recruiting problems. Not wanting to be in the infantry Jonathan deserted on January 11, 1865. After deserting Jonathan seems to have intentionally disappeared. In today's records he does not reappear until the 1910 U.S. Censes as John S. Scott living in Chicago, Ill. He was working as a carpenter and his wife, Eliza, was operating a boardinghouse. Jonathan died in Chicago on December 20, 1914. Eliza died on August 9, 1930. Both Jonathan and Eliza are buried in the Mt. Pleasant Cemetery in Lodi, Wis.[20]

Chapter Notes

Chapter 1

1. *Caledonian (St. Johnsbury, Vt.),* February 16, 1866; Mark M. Boatner, III, *The Civil War Dictionary* (New York: Vintage Civil War Library, 1991), 537.
2. George G. Benedict, *Vermont in the Civil War,* 2 vols. (Burlington, Vt.: The Free Press Association, 1886 and 1888), 17, all references are to vol. 1 unless otherwise noted; Charles E. Heller and William A. Stofft, *America's First Battles, 1776–1965* (Lawrence: University Press of Kansas, 1986), 82.
3. Benedict, *Vermont in the Civil War,* 18, 24.
4. *Ibid.,* 32–61.
5. *Ibid.,* 26–27, 62–63.
6. *Ibid.,* 63.
7. Benedict, *Vermont in the Civil War,* 63–64; Theodore S. Peck, *Revised Roster of Vermont Volunteers and Lists of Vermonters Who Served in the Army and Navy of the United States During the War of the Rebellion, 1861–66* (Montpelier, Vt.: Watchman Co., 1892), 30; http://vermontcivilwar.org/get.php?input=6361; Western Historical Company, *History of the St. County, Michigan, containing an account of its settlement, growth, development and resources* (Chicago: A.T. Andreas & Co., 1883), 684; http://trees.ancestry.com/tree/4641417/person/24020884226; *Kalamazoo (Mich.) Gazette,* February 24, 1914; Henry Whiting's compiled military service record, Records of the Adjutant General's Office, 1780–1917, Record Group 94, National Archives and Records Administration Building, Washington, DC., hereinafter cited as the individuals name and compiled military service record; Paul G. Zeller, *The Second Vermont Volunteer Infantry Regiment, 1861–1865* (Jefferson, N.C.: McFarland, 2002), 37–38, 44, 106, 120; Chester K. Leach, Civil War letters, Special Collections, Bailey/Howe Library, University of Vermont, Burlington, Vt.; Ulysses S. Grant. *Personal Memoirs of Ulysses S. Grant.* New York: Charles L. Webster & Company, 1886. Reprinted by Konecky and Konecky, Old Say Brook, Conn., 1992, 37.
8. Benedict, *Vermont in the Civil War,* 64; George J. Stannard's compiled military service record, Peck, *Revised Roster,* 30, 344; Hiram Carlton, *Genealogical and Family History* of the *State of Vermont.* 2 vols. (New York: The Lewis Publishing Co., 1903), vol. 1, 150–151; Abby Maria Hemenway, *The Vermont Historical Gazetteer: a magazine, embracing a history of each town, civil, ecclesiastical, biographical and military,* vol. 2 (Burlington, Vt.: Tuttle Co., 1923) 385–387.
9. Benedict, *Vermont in the Civil War,* 65–69.
10. *Ibid.,* 76–83.
11. *Ibid.,* 88–89.
12. Benedict, *Vermont in the Civil War,* 128–130; Peck, *Revised Roster,* 70; Hinckley, Erik S., and Tom Ledoux, comps. and eds. *They Went to War,* comp. and ed., *They Went to War: A Biographical Register of the Green Mountain State in the Civil War* (Bloomington, Ind.: Trafford Publishing, 2010), 126; *The Pottsville (Penn.) Republican,* October 5, 1918; Ezra J. Warner, *Generals in Blue: Lives of the Union Commanders* (Baton Rouge: Louisiana State University Press, 1964), 462–463; Boatner, *The Civil War Dictionary,* 775–776.
13. Benedict, *Vermont in the Civil War,* 130–131; Herbert M. Schiller, ed, *Autobiography of Major General William F. Smith 1861–1864* (Dayton, Ohio: Morningside House Inc., 1990), 29–30.
14. Benedict, *Vermont in the Civil War,* 129.
15. Peck, *Revised Roster,* 90, 92; Jesse Adams, Civil War letters, Cavendish Historical Society, Cavendish, Vt.
16. Benedict, *Vermont in the Civil War,* 127; *Orleans Independent Standard (Irasburg, Vt.),* July 26, 1861; *Lamoille Newsdealer (Hyde Park, Vt.),* July 26, 1861; *Bennington (Vt.) Free Press,* July 26, 1861; John Terrill's complied military service record.
17. Benedict, *Vermont in the Civil War,* 129–131; Peck, *Revised Roster,* 67; Schiller, *Autobiography,* 30; *The Pottsville (Penn.) Republican,* October 5, 1918; John E. Balzer, ed., *Buck's Book: A View of the 3rd Vermont Infantry Regiment* (Bolingbrook, Ill.: Balzer & Associates, 1993), 9.
18. Benedict, *Vermont in the Civil War,* 132, Peck, *Revised Roster,* 104; William Scott's compiled military service record; Howard Coffin, *Full Duty: Vermonters in the Civil War* (Woodstock, Vt.: The Countryman Press, 1993), 86–87.
19. Benedict, *Vermont in the Civil War,* 132, Coffin, *Full Duty,* 87; William Scott's compiled military service record.
20. Benedict, *Vermont in the Civil War,* 133–134; Coffin, *Full Duty,* 88–89; William Scott's compiled military service record.
21. Benedict, *Vermont in the Civil War,* 156–159; Boatner, *The Civil War Dictionary,* 482; Peck, *Revised Roster,* 749; Hinckley and Ledoux, *They Went to War,* 212.
22. Benedict, *Vermont in the Civil War,* 30, 158; Peck, *Revised Roster,* 10, 108; Henry N. Worthen's compiled military service record; William Alba Ellis, *Norwich University, Her History, Her Graduates, Her Roll of Honor* (Concord, N.H.: Rumford Press, 1898), 370–371.
23. Benedict, *Vermont in the Civil War,* 181; Hinckley and Ledoux, *They Went to War,* 205.
24. George S. Maharay, *Vermont Hero: Major General Lewis A. Grant* (New York: iUniverse, Inc., 2006), 1–2.
25. Warner, *Generals in Blue,* 290–292; Ethan S. Rafuse, *McClellan's War: The Failure of Moderation in the Struggle for the Union* (Bloomington: Indiana University Press, 2005), 118.
26. Benedict, *Vermont in the Civil War,* 91–92; *Daily Free Press (Burlington, Vt.),* September 20, 1861; Janet B. Hewett et al., eds., *Supplement to the Official Records,* Part

II—Record of Events, Vol. 69, Serial No. 81, 80 vols. Wilmington, N.C.: Broadfoot Publishing Company, 1998, 240; *The Daily Green Mountain Freeman (Montpelier, Vt.)*, September 21, 1862; Hazzard Stevens, *The Life of Isaac Ingalls Stevens*, 2 vols. (Boston: Houghton, Mifflin, 1900), 2, 327; Benedict, *Vermont in the Civil War*, 90–92; Zeller, *The Second Vermont*, 44; Alan D. Gaff, *On Many a Bloody Field: Four Years in the Iron Brigade* (Bloomington: Indiana University Press, 1996), 54; Rafuse, *McClellan's War*, 132–133.

27. *Official Records*, vol. 5, 168–169, 172; Stevens, *The Life of Isaac Ingalls Stevens*, vol. 2, 329.

28. *Official Records*, vol. 5, 168–169, 172; Stevens, *The Life of Isaac Ingalls Stevens*, vol. 2, 329.

29. *Official Records*, vol. 5, 169.

30. *Ibid.*, 169, 179.

31. Robert J. Driver, *1st Virginia Cavalry* (Lynchburg, Va.: H.E. Howard, 1991), 19; *Official Records*, vol. 5, 83.

32. Driver, *1st Virginia Cavalry*, 19; *Official Records*, vol. 5, 83; William Miller Owen, *In camp and Battle with the Washington Artillery of New Orleans* (Boston: Ticknor & Co., 1885), 54–55; David F. Riggs, *13th Virginia Infantry* (Lynchburg, Va.: H.E. Howard, Inc., 1988), 7.

33. *Official Records*, series I, vol. 5, 169–170, 177; Stevens, *The Life of Isaac Ingalls Stevens*, vol. 2, 330.

34. *Official Records*, series I, vol. 5, 169–170, Stevens, *The Life of Isaac Ingalls Stevens*, 330.

35. John Hamilton's compiled military service record, Records of the Adjutant General's Office, 1780–1917, Record Group 94, National Archives Building, Washington, DC.

36. *Official Records*, series I, vol. 5, 173; Gaff, *On Many a Bloody Field*, 55; Riggs, *13th Virginia Infantry*, 8; Hiram Antibus' compiled military service record.

37. *Official Records*, series 1, vol. 5, 173; Asbury Inlow's compiled military service and government disability pension records.

38. Benedict, *Vermont in the Civil War*, 134–135; *Official Records*, series I, vol. 5, 177; Peck, *Revised Roster*, 80; Evelyn H. Farnham's government disability pension record; Record Group 94, Records of the Adjutant General, National Archives and Records Administration, Washington, D.C., 3rd Vermont Volunteer Infantry Regiment Descriptive, Letter, and Order Book.

39. Todd, *Seventy-Ninth Highlander*, 77; *Official Records*, series I, vol. 5, 175; James H. Van Riper's compiled military service record

40. Benedict, *Vermont in the Civil War*, 134; Moses A. Parker, Civil War letter, Parker Family Papers, Special Collections, Bailey/Howe Library, University of Vermont, Burlington, Vermont; Moses A. Parker's compiled military service record.

41. Benedict, *Vermont in the Civil War*, 134–135; *Official Records*, series I, vol. 5, 177; Peck, *Revised Roster*, 79–83; Susan C. Meserve's pension record; *Burlington Free Press*, September 20, 1861; Doc 575, Evelyn H. Farnham letters, Johnson Family Papers, Vermont Historical Society, Barre, Vt.; Works Progress Administration grave index, Vermont Historical Society, Barre, Vt.

42. Silas R. Coburn and George A. Gordon, *Genealogy of the Descendants of Edward Colburn/Coburn* (Lowell, Mass.: Courier-Citizen Company Press, 1913), 232; Peck, *Revised Roster*, 81, 761; Stephen Crane, "A Taste for Figures," *Vermont Life*, vol. 8 (Fall 1953); Benedict, *Vermont in the Civil War*, 135.

43. Peck, *Revised Roster*, 80–82; Oscar D. Eastman's compiled military service record; Alonzo C. Armington's compiled military service record; Newell A. Kingsbury's compiled military service record; *Aurora of the Valley (Newbury, Vt.)*, September 21, 1861.

44. *Official Records*, series I, vol. 5, 177.

45. *Ibid.*, series I, vol. 5, 171, 178–179.

46. *Ibid.*, series I, vol. 5, 168, 178.

47. Stevens, *The Life of Isaac Ingalls Stevens*, vol. 2, 332.

48. Benedict, *Vermont in the Civil War*, 235–236; Schiller, *Autobiography*, 30; Bruce Catton, *The Army of the Potomac: Mr. Lincoln's Army* (Garden City, N.Y.: Doubleday & Company, Inc., 1952), 61–64.

49. Benedict, *Vermont in the Civil War*, 236; Warner, *Generals in Blue*, 47.

50. Benedict, *Vermont in the Civil War*, 235; Schiller, *Autobiography*, 30.

51. Benedict, *Vermont in the Civil War*, vol. 1, 73 131–132, vol. 2, 414; Peck, *Revised Roster*, 70; Wheelock G. Veazey's compiled military service record; Prentiss C. Dodge, comp., *Encyclopedia Vermont Biography* (Burlington, Vt.: Ullery Publishing Company, 1912), 8; Jacob G. Ullery, comp., *Men of Vermont: An Illustrated Biographical History of Vermonters and Sons of Vermont* (Brattleboro, Vt.: Transcript Publishing Company, 1894), part 2, 408.

52. Benedict, *Vermont in the Civil War*, 96; Hewitt, *Supplement to the Official Records*, 240.

53. Benedict, *Vermont in the Civil War*, 158–160, 180–183; Peck, *Revised Roster*, 67–68, 142.

54. Benedict, *Vermont in the Civil War*, 14; Peck, *Revised Roster*, 181; Nathan S. Lord, Jr.'s compiled military service record; Hinkley and Ledoux, *They Went to War*, 148; http://www.civilwarindex.com/armyin/officers/7th_in_infantry_officers.pdf.

55. Benedict, *Vermont in the Civil War*, vol. 1, 128, 209, vol. 2, 402; Peck, *Revised Roster*, 70, 181; Hinckley and Ledoux, *They Went to War*, 148.

56. Benedict, *Vermont in the Civil War*, 208–210; Peck, *Revised Roster*, 177, 181; Hinckley and Ledoux, *They Went to War*, 48–49.

57. Benedict, *Vermont in the Civil War*, 237–238; Zeller, *The Second Vermont*, 52.

58. Benedict, *Vermont in the Civil War*, 237–240; *Official Records*, vol. 5, 92; *Green Mountain Freeman (Montpelier, Vt.)*, December 6, 1861; Zeller, *The Second Vermont*, 52.

59. Benedict, *Vermont in the Civil War*, 236–240; *Official Records*, vol. 5,108, 713; Zeller, *The Second Vermont*, 53.

Chapter 2

1. Benedict, *Vermont in the Civil War*, 241; Frank J. Welcher, *The Union Army, 1861–1865, Operation and Operations*, vol. 1 (Bloomington: Indiana University Press, 1989), 795–796, all references are to vol. 1; Alexander S. Webb, *The Peninsula-McClellan's Campaign of 1862* (New York: Scribner's, 1881), 22, 26; Rafuse, *McClellan's War*, 132.

2. Welcher, *The Union Army*, 796; Webb, *The Peninsula*, 18–24; John V. Quarstein, *Hampton and Newport News in the Civil War: War Comes to the Peninsula* (Lynchburg, Va.: H.E. Howard, Inc., 1998), 80.

3. Benedict, *Vermont in the Civil War*, 241; Welcher, *The Union Army*, 251; Webb, *The Peninsula*, 32.

4. Benedict, *Vermont in the Civil War*, 241–242; Welcher, *The Union Army*, 796; Webb, *The Peninsula*, 24–28, 32.

5. Welcher, *The Union Army*, 796; Webb, *The Peninsula*, 27–32; Brian K. Burton, *Extraordinary Circumstances: The Seven Days Battles* (Bloomington: Indiana University Press, 2001), 7.

6. Benedict, *Vermont in the Civil War*, 243–244; Quarstein, *Hampton and Newport News*, 22, 26. In 1621 an enterprising Englishman who had settled in Ireland, joined with a friend, Captain William Newce, to bring over an advance party of fifty Irishmen and a small herd of cattle to Virginia, which they sold to the Virginia Company at a good profit. With their profits they established

a plantation at the tip of the Virginia Peninsula that they called "New Port Newce" (Newport News), Bernard Bailyn, *The Barbarous Years: The Peopling of British North America: The Conflict of Civilizations, 1600–1675* (New York: Vintage Books, 2013), 83.

7. Benedict, *Vermont in the Civil War*, 244–245; *Watchman (Montpelier, Vt.)*, May 23, 1862.

8. Benedict, *Vermont in the Civil War*, 244–245; George T. Stevens, *Three Years in the Sixth Corps*, 2nd ed. (New York: D. Van Nostrand, Publisher, 1870), 31; Hewett, Suderow and Trudeau, *Supplement to the Official Records*, 241; *Watchman (Montpelier, Vt.)*, May 23, 1862.

9. Welcher, *The Union Army*, 797; *Official Records*, vol. XI, part 1, 5–6; Zeller, *The Second Vermont*, 60.

10. Welcher, *The Union Army*, 797; *Official Records*, vol. XI, part1, 6–8; Zeller, *The Second Vermont*, 61.

11. *Official Records*, vol. III, 865; Paul D. Casdorph, *Prince John Magruder: His Life and Campaigns* (New York: John Wiley & Sons, Inc., 1996), 117, 119; Quarstein, *Hampton and Newport News*, 31.

12. Casdorph, *Prince John*, 5; Ezra J. Warner, *Generals in Gray: Lives of the Confederate Commanders* (Baton Rouge: Louisiana State University Press, 1959), 207–208; Boatner, *The Civil War Dictionary*, 501; Quarstein, *Hampton and Newport News*, 31.

13. *Official Records*, vol. II, 38; John V. Quarstein, *Big Bethel: The First Battle* (Charleston, S.C. and London: The History Press, 2011), 38.

14. Benedict, *Vermont in the Civil War*, 247–248; Webb, *The Peninsula*, 48–50; *Official Records*, vol. XI. Part 1, 317–318, 359; English Combatant, *Battle-Fields of the South, from Bull Run to Fredericksburg: with Sketches of Confederate Commanders, and Gossip of the Camps* (reprint, Time-Life Books, Inc., 1984), 167; Steven W. Sears, *To the Gates of Richmond: The Peninsula Campaign* (New York: Ticknor & Fields, 1992), 37–38.

15. *Official Records*, vol. XI, part 1, 9; Webb, *The Peninsula*, 44; Thomas W. Hyde, *Following the Greek Cross or Memories of the Sixth Army Corps* (Columbia: University of South Carolina Press, 2005. First published 1894 by Houghton Mifflin), 40.

16. Benedict, *Vermont in the Civil War*, 245; *Green Mountain Freeman (Montpelier, Vt.)*, April 29, 1862; *Official Records*, vol. XI, part 1, 300, 358; Hewett, Suderow and Trudeau, *Supplement to the Official Records*, 242; Webb, *The Peninsula*, 44; Hyde, *Following the Greek Cross*, 40; *Watchman (Montpelier, Vt.)*, May 23, 1862; Zeller, *The Second Vermont*, 61.

17. Webb, *The Peninsula*, 47–48; Hyde, *Following the Greek Cross*, 40.

18. Benedict, *Vermont in the Civil War*, 246; *Official Records*, vol. XI, part1, 300, 358; David W. Blight, ed., *When This Cruel War Is Over: The Civil War Letters of Charles Harvey Brewster* (Amherst: University of Massachusetts Press, 1992), 109; Joseph K. Newell, *"Ours," Annals of the Tenth Regiment: Massachusetts Volunteers in the Rebellion* (Springfield, Mass.: C.A. Nichols & Co., 1875), 80; Robert H. Rhodes, *All for the Union: A Historical Record of the 2nd Rhode Island Volunteer Infantry in the War of the Great Rebellion as told by the Diary of Elisha Hunt Rhodes* (New York: Orion Books, 1991), 62; Zeller, *The Second Vermont*, 61.

19. Benedict, *Vermont in the Civil War*, 246; *Official Records*, vol. XI, part 1, 300, 358; Hewett, Suderow and Trudeau, *Supplement to the Official Records*, 242; Peck, 166; Peter Brady's compiled military service record; "Vermont, Vital Records, 1760–1954," database with images, *FamilySearch* (https://familysearch.org/ark:/61903/1:1:XFNV-DHM, accessed 2 November 2015), Peter Brady, 05 Jul 1864, Death; State Capitol Building, Montpelier; FHL microfilm 27,486; *St. Albans (Vt.) Messenger*, April 24, 1862.

20. Benedict, *Vermont in the Civil War*, 245; *(Montpelier, Vt.) Green Mountain Freeman*, April 29, 1862; *Official Records*, vol. XI, 300, 358; Rhodes, *All for the Union*, 62; Hyde, *Following the Greek Cross*, 40; Hewett, Suderow and Trudeau, *Supplement to the Official Records*, 242; Zeller, *The Second Vermont*, 61.

21. Benedict, *Vermont in the Civil War*, 246–247; *Official Records*, vol. XI, part 1, 258; Hewett, Suderow and Trudeau, *Supplement to the Official Records*, 242; Stevens, *Three Years in the Sixth Corps*, 34; Erasmus D. Keyes, *Fifty Years Observation of Men and Events—Civil and Military* (New York: Charles Scribner's Sons, 1885), 441–442; *Watchman (Montpelier, Vt.)*, May 23, 1862.

22. John Michael Priest, editor-in-chief, *One Surgeon's Private War: Doctor William Potter of the 57th New York* (Shippensburg, Penn.: White Mane Publishing Company, Inc., 1996), 19; William P. Russell's compiled military service record.

23. Benedict, *Vermont in the Civil War*, 247; *Green Mountain Freeman (Montpelier, Vt.)*, April 29, 1862; *Official Records*, vol. XI, part 1, 358–359; William T.H. Brooks, Civil War letters, U.S. Army Heritage and Education Center, U.S. Army War College, Carlisle, Penn.

24. *Official Records*, vol. XI, part 1, 358; Stevens, *Three Years in the Sixth Corps*, 34, 36; Hyde, *Following the Greek Cross*, 41; W.T.H. Brooks' letters; Zeller, *The Second Vermont*, 62.

25. Benedict, *Vermont in the Civil War*, 246–248; Keyes, *Fifty Years Observation*, 442; Zeller, *The Second Vermont*, 62.

26. Webb, *The Peninsula*, 45–47.

27. Benedict, *Vermont in the Civil War*, 248; *Green Mountain Freeman (Montpelier, Vt.)*, April 29, 1862; Stevens, *Three Years in the Sixth Corps*, 37; Charles M. Hapgood diary, 1862, University of Vermont Bailey/Howe Library Special Collections, Burlington, Vt.; Zeller, *The Second Vermont*, 63

28. *Official Records*, vol. XI, part 2, 10; Sears, *To the Gates of Richmond*, 39; Webb, *The Peninsula*, 58; Hyde, *Following the Greek Cross*, 44; Boatner, *The Civil War Dictionary*, 740; Zeller, *The Second Vermont*, 63.

29. Benedict, *Vermont in the Civil War*, 248; Stevens, *Three Years in the Sixth Corps*, 38; Zeller, *The Second Vermont*, 63.

30. Benedict, *Vermont in the Civil War*, 248–249; Charles M. Hapgood diary; Lucius D. Savage, A Diary with Recollections of Prison and Hospital, Vermont Historical Society, Barre, Vt.; *Watchman (Montpelier, Vt.)*, May 23, 1862.

31. Benedict, *Vermont in the Civil War*, 247–248; Webb, *The Peninsula*, 48–50; *Official Records*, vol. XI, part 2, 317–318, 359; English Combatant, *Battle-Fields of the South*, 167; Sears, *To the Gates of Richmond*, 37–38, Douglas Southall Freeman, *R.E. Lee: A Biography*, vol. 2 (New York: Charles Scribner's Sons, 1936), 18, all references are to vol. 2 unless otherwise noted; Zeller, *The Second, Vermont*, 62–63.

32. Schiller, *Autobiography*, 34; Zeller, *The Second Vermont*, 63.

33. Benedict, *Vermont in the Civil War*, 248–249; Stevens, *Three Years in the Sixth Corps*, 38; Charles M. Hapgood diary; Chester K. Leach letters; Hewett, Suderow and Trudeau, *Supplement to the Official Records*, 242; Zeller, *The Second Vermont*, 63.

34. Welcher, *The Union Army*, 198–199; Zeller, *The Second Vermont*, 63–64.

35. Chester K. Leach letters; Charles M. Hapgood diary; Zeller, *The Second Vermont*, 64.

36. Webb, *The Peninsula*, 63; Benedict, *Vermont in the Civil War*, 250; *Official Records*, vol. XI, part 2, 416–418; Zeller, *The Second Vermont*, 64.

37. Webb, *The Peninsula*, 64; Benedict, *Vermont in the Civil War*, 249–250; *Official Records*, vol. XI, part 2, 418; Quarstein, *Hampton and Newport News*, 132–133; http://search.ancestry.com/cgi-bin/sse.dll?indiv=1&db=1860usfedcenancestry&gss=angs-d&new=1&rank=1&msT=1&gsfn=john+t.&gsfn_x=0&gsln=garrow&gsln_x=0&msrpn_ftp=warwick+county%2c+va&_83004003-n_xcl=f&MSAV=1&uidh=cd1&pcat=35&fh=0&h=34149394&recoff=&ml_rpos=1; Zeller, *The Second Vermont*, 64.

38. *Official Records*, vol. XI, part 2, 372; Benedict, *Vermont in the Civil War*, 251; *(Burlington, Vt.) Daily Free Press*, April, 28, 1862; Lucius Savage diary; Zeller, *The Second Vermont*, 64–65.

39. Benedict, *Vermont in the Civil War*, 250; *Official Records*, vol. XI, part 2, 364.

40. Benedict, *Vermont in the Civil War*, 251.

41. Benedict, *Vermont in the Civil War*, 251; Peck, *Revised Roster*, 109.

42. Benedict, *Vermont in the Civil War*, 251–252; *Official Records*, vol. XI, part 2, 319, 372, 417; Zeller, *The Second Vermont*, 65.

43. Benedict, *Vermont in the Civil War*, 251–252.

44. Benedict, *Vermont in the Civil War*, 252; Peck, *Revised Roster*, 156, 159; Charles P. Dudley's compiled military service record; Charles C. Spaulding's compiled military service record.

45. Benedict, *Vermont in the Civil War*, 252.

46. Benedict, *Vermont in the Civil War*, 253; *Official Records*, vol. XI, part 2, 372; Zeller, *The Second Vermont*, 65.

47. *Official Records*, vol. XI, part 2, 419, 421; Zeller, *The Second Vermont*, 65.

48. Benedict, *Vermont in the Civil War*, 252–253.

49. *Official Records*, vol. VI, part 2, 372; Benedict, *Vermont in the Civil War*, 253; Schiller, *Autobiography*, 35; Zeller, *The Second Vermont*, 65.

50. Benedict, *Vermont in the Civil War*, 254.

51. Benedict, *Vermont in the Civil War*, 101; Peck, *Revised Roster*, 51; William Fuller's compiled military service record.

52. Benedict, *Vermont in the Civil War*, 254–256; Peck, *Revised Roster*, 84; Alonzo Hutchinson's compiled military service record; Balzer, *Buck' Book*, 28.

53. Benedict, *Vermont in the Civil War*, 254–255.

54. Benedict, *Vermont in the Civil War*, 255; Peck, *Revised Roster*, 84; Alonzo Hutchinson's compiled military service record; Jeremiah Bishop's compiled military service record; "Vermont Vital Records, 1760–1954," database with images, *FamilySearch* (https://familysearch.org/ark:/61903/1:1:XFSL-GW7: 5 November 2017), Alanson Jerome Bishop and Mary Ann Jondro, 10 Jan 1874, Marriage; State Capitol Building, Montpelier; FHL microfilm 540,060; Balzer, *Buck's Book*, 28.

55. Benedict, *Vermont in the Civil War*, 255.

56. Benedict, *Vermont in the Civil War*, 257; Peck, *Revised Roster*, 70, 89; Samuel E. Pingree's compiled military service record; Edward A. Chandler's compiled military service record.

57. Benedict, *Vermont in the Civil War*, 255; Peck, *Revised Roster*, 87; George Q. French's compiled military service record; Albert C. Eisenberg "The 3rd Vermont has Won a Name": Corporal George Q. French's Account of the Battle of Lee's Mills, Virginia. *Vermont History*, Fall 1981, Vol. 49, No, 4, 226–227.

58. *Official Records*, vol. XI, part 2, 375; Benedict, *Vermont in the Civil War*, 256–258; Balzer, *Buck's Book*, 30; Zeller, *The Second Vermont*, 66.

59. Benedict, *Vermont in the Civil War*, 263; Peck, *Revised Roster*, 76, 84, 85, 87, 89, 92, 102; Emerson E. Whitcomb's compiled military service record; *(Montpelier) Vermont Watchman*, April 25, 1862; Wesley Davis' compiled military service record; Jason D. Niles compiled military service record; Hiram C. Holmes' compiled military service record; Charles Turner's compiled military service record; Charles H. Page's compiled military service record; Richard H. Rowell's compiled military service record.

60. Benedict, *Vermont in the Civil War*, 256; Balzer, *Buck's Book*, 30.

61. Benedict, *Vermont in the Civil War*, 257; Balzer, *Buck's Book*, 30.

62. Balzer, *Buck's Book*, 30.

63. Rosenblatt, *Hard Marching*, 20–21; Peck, *Revised Roster*, 88; John Roe's compiled military service record.

64. Benedict, *Vermont in the Civil War*, 261–262; William Scott's compiled military service record.

65. Benedict, *Vermont in the Civil War*, 262–263; Peck, *Revised Roster*, 87; James Fletcher's compiled military service record; *Rutland (Vt.) Weekly Herald*, April 24, 1862.

66. Benedict, *Vermont in the Civil War*, 263; Peck, *Revised Roster*, 87; Robert J. Titterson, *Julian Scott: Artist of the Civil War and Native America* (Jefferson, N.C.: McFarland, 1997), 32–33; Julian Scott's compiled military service record; Ephraim Brown's compiled military service record; John Backum's compiled military service record.

67. Peck, *Revised Roster*, 741; Julian Scott's compiled military service record; W.F. Beyer and O.F. Keydel, eds., *Deeds of Valor: How America's Heroes Won the Medal of Honor*, vol. 2 (Detroit, Mich.: The Perrien-Keydel Company, 1903), 21–22.

68. Benedict, *Vermont in the Civil War*, 212, 259.

69. Benedict, *Vermont in the Civil War*, 162–163, 259–264; *Green Mountain Freeman (Montpelier, Vt.)*, May 6, 1862; Peck, *Revised Roster*, 116, 118, 136, 137; David J. Dibble's compiled military service record; Stephen B. Niles' compiled military service record; Franklin N. Grimes' compiled military service record; Henry B. Atherson's compiled military service record; Zeller, *The Second Vermont*, 66–67.

70. Benedict, *Vermont in the Civil War*, 213; Peck, *Revised Roster*, 198; Edwin F. Reynolds' compiled military service record.

71. Benedict, *Vermont in the Civil War*, 260–261; Peck, *Revised Roster*, 193, 204; David B. Davenport's compiled military service record; Charles F. Bailey's compiled military service record.

72. Peck, *Revised Roster*, 191; Luther Graves' compiled military service record; Nathan Graves' compiled military service record.

73. Peck, *Revised Roster*, 190, 191, 200; Dana C. Ayers' compiled military service record; Elisha M. Goddard's compiled military service record; Henry White's compiled military service record.

74. Benedict, *Vermont in the Civil War*, 263–264; Ruluf L. Bellows' compiled military service record; Edward A. Holton's compiled military service record.

75. Benedict, *Vermont in the Civil War*, 212–213.

76. Benedict, *Vermont in the Civil War*, 263; Peck, *Revised Roster*, 204; David B. Davenport's compiled military service record; Henry D. Davenport's compiled military service record.

77. Benedict, *Vermont in the Civil War*, 264.

78. *Green Mountain Freeman (Montpelier, Vt.)*, May 6, 1862.

79. *Official Records*, vol. XI, part 2, 450; Chester K. Leach letters; Rhodes, *All for the Union*, 63; *Daily Free Press (Burlington, Vt.)*, April 28, 1862; Zeller, *The Second Vermont*, 67–68.

80. Francis D. Hammond, Civil War letter, in the possession of Charles F. Walker.

81. Welcher, *The Union Army*, 797–798; Sears, *To the Gates of Richmond*, 46; Freeman, *R.E. Lee: A Biography*, vol. 2, 19–23.

82. Benedict, *Vermont in the Civil War*, 267–268; Charles M. Hapgood diary; Chester K. Leach letters.
83. Balzer, *Buck's Book*, 32; Chester K. Leach letters; *Green Mountain Freeman (Montpelier, Vt.)*, May 6, 1862; Blight, *When This Cruel War Is Over*, 116; Zeller, *The Second Vermont*, 68.
84. Balzer, *Buck's Book*, 32.
85. Benedict, *Vermont in the Civil War*, 268; Sears, *To the Gates of Richmond*, 61; Jeffery D. Wert, *General James Longstreet: The Confederacy's Most Controversial Soldier—A Biography* (New York: Simon & Shuster, 1994), 103; Zeller, *The Second Vermont*, 69.
86. *Green Mountain Freeman (Montpelier, Vt.)*, May 27, 1862; Zeller, *The Second Vermont*, 69–70.
87. Stevens, *Three Years in the Sixth Corps*, 47; Welcher, *The Union Army*, 801; *Official Records*, vol. XI, part 3, 140; Hewett, Suderow and Trudeau, *Supplement to the Official Records*, 242; Hyde, *Following the Greek Cross*, 48; Zeller, *The Second Vermont*, 70.
88. Benedict, *Vermont in the Civil War*, 269; Welcher, *The Union Army*, 801; Zeller, *The Second Vermont*, 70.
89. Sears, *To the Gates of Richmond*, 68, 70; Benedict, *Vermont in the Civil War*, 269; Earl C. Hastings, Jr., and David Hastings. *A Pitiless Rain: The Battle of Williamsburg, 1862* (Shippensburg, Pa: White Mane Publishing Company, 1997), 55–56; Zeller, *The Second Vermont*, 70–71.
90. Benedict, *Vermont in the Civil War*, 270; *Green Mountain Freeman (Montpelier, Vt.)*, May 27, 1862; Charles M. Hapgood diary; Webb, *The Peninsula Campaign*, 73; Zeller, *The Second Vermont*, 71.
91. Benedict, *Vermont in the Civil War*, 271; Sears, *To the Gates of Richmond*, 73–74; *Green Mountain Freeman (Montpelier, Vt.)*, 27 May 1862; Zeller, *The Second Vermont*, 71.
92. Benedict, *Vermont in the Civil War*, 270; Boatner, *The Civil War Dictionary*, 929; Sears, *To the Gates of Richmond*, 73; Welcher, *The Union Army*, 801; Webb, *The Peninsula*, 73–74; Hastings, *A Pitiless Rain*, 63–66, 71; Zeller, *The Second Vermont*, 71.
93. Benedict, *Vermont in the Civil War*, 271; Sears, *To the Gates of Richmond*, 73–74; Webb, *The Peninsula*, 77; Schiller, *Autobiography*, 36; Zeller, *The Second Vermont*, 71.
94. Benedict, *Vermont in the Civil War*, 272; Sears, *To the Gates of Richmond*, 74; Webb, *The Peninsula*, 78; Zeller, *The Second Vermont*, 71.
95. Benedict, *Vermont in the Civil War*, 272; Schiller, *Autobiography*, 37, Zeller, *The Second Vermont*, 71.
96. Benedict, *Vermont in the Civil War*, 272; Zeller, *The Second Vermont*, 71.
97. Benedict, *Vermont in the Civil War*, 273; Schiller, *Autobiography*, 37; Zeller, *The Second Vermont*, 71.
98. Benedict, *Vermont in the Civil War*, 274; Sears, *To the Gates of Richmond*, 76–77; Zeller, *The Second Vermont*, 71.
99. Benedict, *Vermont in the Civil War*, 273; Sears, *To the Gates of Richmond*, 81; Welcher, *The Union Army*, 802; Hastings, *A Pitiless Rain*, 105; Zeller, *The Second Vermont*, 71.
100. *Green Mountain Freeman (Montpelier, Vt.)*, May 27, 1862; Sears, *To the Gates of Richmond*, 83; Zeller, *The Second Vermont*, 71.
101. Sears, *To the Gates of Richmond*, 82; Webb, *The Peninsula Campaign*, 81; Zeller, *The Second Vermont*, 71–72.
102. Benedict, *Vermont in the Civil War*, 274; Sears, *To the Gates of Richmond*, 82; Webb, *The Peninsula*, 81; Lucius Savage diary; Zeller, *The Second Vermont*, 72.
103. Chester K. Leach letters; Zeller, *The Second Vermont*, 72.

Chapter 3

1. Benedict, *Vermont in the Civil War*, 275; Stevens, *Three Years in the Sixth Corps*, 58; *Daily Free Press (Burlington, Vt.)*, May 20, 1862; Webb, *The Peninsula*, 83; Lucius Savage diary; Malcolm Hart Harris, comp., *Old New Kent County: Some Account of the Planters, Plantations and Places in New Kent County*, vol. 1 (Baltimore, Md.: Clearfield, Co., 2006), 155–156; Zeller, *The Second Vermont*, 73.
2. Sears, *To the Gates of Richmond*, 107–108; *Official Records*, vol. XI, part 2, 23, *Green Mountain Freeman (Montpelier, Vt.)*, June 3, 1862; Chester K. Leach letters; *Daily Free Press (Burlington, Vt.)*, May 20, 1862; Lucius Savage diary; Zeller, *The Second Vermont*, 73.
3. *Green Mountain Freeman (Montpelier, Vt.)*, June 3, 1862.
4. Benedict, *Vermont in the Civil War*, 275; Chester K. Leach letters; Charles M. Hapgood diary; *Green Mountain Freeman (Montpelier, Vt.)*, June 3, 1862; Stevens, *Three Years in the Sixth Corps*, 58.
5. Benedict, *Vermont in the Civil War*, 275; *Official Records*, vol. XI, part 3, 24; Stevens, *Three Years in the Sixth Corps*, 60.
6. Stevens, *Three Years in the Sixth Corps*, 60; *Green Mountain Freeman (Montpelier, Vt.)*, June 3, 1862; Kirk Rand, Civil War letters, Sallie Joy White Collection, Schlesinger Library, Radcliffe College, Cambridge, Mass.; Lucius Savage diary; Zeller, *The Second Vermont*, 73.
7. James Hagemann, *The Heritage of Virginia: The Story of Place Names in the Old Dominion* (West Chester, Pa.: Whitford Press, 1988), 266–267; Boatner, *The Civil War Dictionary*, 477–478.
8. Wheelock Graves Veazey papers, 1853–1939, Vermont Historical Society, Barre, Vt.
9. Sears, *To the Gates of Richmond*, 104.
10. Sears, *To the Gates of Richmond*, 104; Burton, *Extraordinary Circumstances*, 9; Zeller, *The Second Vermont*, 74.
11. Benedict, *Vermont in the Civil War*, 277; Welcher, *The Union Army*, 804–806; Webb, *The Peninsula*, 84; Zeller, *The Second Vermont*, 74.
12. Boatner, *The Civil War Dictionary*, 303–304; Warner, *Generals in Blue*, 159–160.
13. Benedict, *Vermont in the Civil War*, 276–278; Stevens, *Three Years in the Sixth Corps*, 65–66; Schiller, *Autobiography*, 39; Sears, *To the Gates of Richmond*, 110; Lucius Savage diary; Daniel F. Cooledge Civil War Diary 1862, Vermont Historical Society, Barre, Vt.; Zeller, *The Second Vermont*, 75.
14. Schiller, *Autobiography*, 39.
15. Welcher, *The Union Army*, 807; Stevens, *Three Years in the Sixth Corps*, 66; Zeller, *The Second Vermont*, 75.
16. Benedict, *Vermont in the Civil War*, 277; Stevens, *Three Years in the Sixth Corps*, 65–66.
17. *Green Mountain Freeman (Montpelier, Vt.)*, June 3, 1862.
18. Benedict, *Vermont in the Civil War*, 187; Wheelock Graves Veazey papers.
19. Benedict, *Vermont in the Civil War*, 163; Peck, *Revised Roster*, 114; Augustus D. Ayling, *Revised Roster of Soldiers and Sailors of New Hampshire in the War of the Rebellion* (Concord, N.H.: I.C. Evans, Public Printer, 1895), 23, 1085; http://vermontcivilwar.org/get.php?input=6388; *Gallipolis (Ohio) Journal*, June 5, 1862; Charles Whitwell's compiled military service record; http://www.civilwararchive.com/Unreghst/unnhtr3.htm#1stinf; *Registers of Deaths of Volunteers, compiled 1861–1865*. ARC ID: 656639. Records of the Adjutant General's Office, 1780's–1917. Record Group 94. National Archives at Washington, D.C.; "England and Wales Census, 1841," database with

images, *FamilySearch*; https://familysearch.org/ark:/61903/1:1:MQRP-DY6, accessed 29 December 2015, Charles Whitwell in household of Francis Whitwell, St Alkmond, Shropshire, England; from "1841 England, Scotland and Wales census," database and images, *findmypast*; "England Births and Christenings, 1538–1975," database, *FamilySearch* https://familysearch.org/ark:/61903/1:1:JQT3-PT5, accessed 29 December 2015, Charles Whitwell, 24 Mar 1829; citing, reference; FHL microfilm 503,525, 510,675; https://www.shropshiretourism.co.uk/attractiondetails.php?estid=7377; Carlton Young, *Voices from the Attic: The Williamstown Boys in the Civil War*. (Syracuse, Ind.: William James Morris, Inc., 2015), 50.

20. Burton, *Extraordinary Circumstances*, 14; Stevens, *Three Years in the Sixth Corps*, 67; Zeller, *The Second Vermont*, 75–76.

21. Benedict, *Vermont in the Civil War*, 102; Peck, *Revised Roster*, 30; Zeller, *The Second Vermont*, 76.

22. Benedict, *Vermont in the Civil War*, 187; Wheelock Graves Veazey papers; Orlando B. Reynolds compiled military service record; Peck, *Revised Roster*, 150.

23. Benedict, *Vermont in the Civil War*, 279–280; Stevens, *Three Years in the Sixth Corps*, 112; Sears, *To the Gates of Richmond*, 138; Boatner, *The Civil War Dictionary*, 273; Freeman, *R.E. Lee*, 77; Webb, *The Peninsula*, 115; Welcher, *The Union Army*, 809–812.

24. Benedict, *Vermont in the Civil War*, 280; Webb, *The Peninsula*, 117.

25. Benedict, *Vermont in the Civil War*, 280; Lucius Savage diary.

26. Benedict, *Vermont in the Civil War*, 282; Quincy F. Thurston's compiled military service record; William Writ Henry family papers, 1846–1915, Vermont Historical Society, Barre, Vt.; Peck, *Revised Roster*, 46.

27. Benedict, *Vermont in the Civil War*, 282; Louis H. Manarin, *Henrico County Field of Honor*, vol. 1. (Richmond, Va.: Printed by the Carter Printing Company, 2004), 86, all references are to vol. 1 unless otherwise noted; Stevens, *Three Years in the Sixth Corps*, 115.

28. Manarin, *Henrico County Field of Honor*, 97, vol. 2, 861; Burton, *Extraordinary Circumstances*, 145.

29. *Green Mountain Freeman (Montpelier, Vt.)*, July 1, 1862.

30. Manarin, *Henrico County Field of Honor*, 103–104; Clifford Dowdey, *The Seven Days: The Emergence of Robert E. Lee* (New York: The Fairfax Press, 1978), 170–171; Zeller, *The Second Vermont*, 81.

31. Burton, *Extraordinary Circumstances*, 25–26; Shiller, *Autobiography*, 39.

32. Cooledge diary.

33. Benedict, *Vermont in the Civil War*, 281.

34. Smiley Bancroft papers, 1840–1885, Vermont Historical Society, Barre, Vt.

35. Benedict, *Vermont in the Civil War*, 281.

36. Manarin, *Henrico County Field of Honor*, 86; David W. Judd, *The Story of the Thirty-Third N.Y.S. Vols.* (Rochester, N.Y.: Benton and Andrews, 1864), 118.

37. Boatner, *The Civil War Dictionary*, 816; Burton, *Extraordinary Circumstances*, 18–22; Freeman, *R.E. Lee*, 97–101; Manarin, *Henrico County Field of Honor*, 98–99.

38. Freeman, *R.E. Lee*, 104–105; Frances H. Kennedy, ed., *The Civil War Battlefield Guide* (Boston: Houghton Mifflin Company, 1990), 58–60; Dowdey, *The Seven Days*, 152.

39. Freeman, *R.E. Lee*, 104–105; *The Civil War Battlefield Guide*, 58–60.

40. Freeman, *R.E. Lee*, 111.

41. Ibid., 112.

42. Ibid., 112.

43. Peck, *Revised Roster*, 132; http://vermontcivilwar.org/get.php?input=5725; http://trees.ancestry.com/tree/26548416/person/13911761857; Silas H. Stone's compiled military service. Silas H. Stone's government disability pension record, Records of the Office of the Secretary of the Interior, Record Group 48, National Archives and records Administration Building, Washington, DC., hereinafter cited as the individual's name and government disability pension record.

44. David J. Dameron, *Benning's Brigade*, vol. 2 (Westminster, Md.: Heritage Books, 2004–2005), 11; William T. Fluker's compiled military service record; Jesse M. Hackney's compiled military service record; John McCluskey's compiled military service record; John Tilley's compiled military service record.

45. Cooledge diary.

46. George H. Randall Papers, University of Vermont Bailey/Howe Library Special Collections, Burlington, Vt.

47. Benedict, *Vermont in the Civil War*, 282; Peck, *Revised Roster*, 123; Eleazer Wells Bartholomew' compiled military service; Civil War Letters of Ransom W. Towle and Thomas N. Flanders, 1861–1865, Vermont Historical Society, Barre, Vt.; Burton, *Extraordinary Circumstances*, 27.

48. 3rd Vermont Infantry Regiment, Regimental Order Book, Record Group 94, Records of the Adjutant General's Office, 1790s–1917, National Archives and Records Administration, Washington, D.C.

49. Benedict, *Vermont in the Civil War*, 283; Shiller, *Autobiography*, 40–41; Burton, *Extraordinary Circumstances*, 41–42.

50. Cooledge diary.

51. Benedict, *Vermont in the Civil War*, 282; Manarin, *Henrico County Field of Honor*, 105–119; Boatner, *The Civil War Dictionary*, 603–604.

52. Freeman, *R.E. Lee*, 118; Burton, *Extraordinary Circumstances*, 51.

53. Benedict, *Vermont in the Civil War*, 282; Freeman, *R.E. Lee*, 122–130; Boatner, *The Civil War Dictionary*, 540–541; Kennedy, *The Civil War Battlefield Guide*, 60.

54. Benedict, *Vermont in the Civil War*, 281; Freeman, *R.E. Lee*, 122–130; Boatner, *The Civil War Dictionary*, 540–541; Kennedy, *The Civil War Battlefield Guide*, 60.

55. Sears, *To the Gates of Richmond*, 213–214.

56. Benedict, *Vermont in the Civil War*, 282–283.

57. Benedict, *Vermont in the Civil War*, 283; Burton, *Extraordinary Circumstances*, 80–81.

58. Benedict, *Vermont in the Civil War*, 283; Shiller, *Autobiography*, 40–41; Burton, *Extraordinary Circumstances*, 41–43; *Official Records*, vol. 11, part 1, 139–140, part 2, 466–467; *The Daily Green Mountain Freeman (Montpelier, Vt.)*, July 24, 1862; Manarin, *Henrico County Field of Honor*, 120–121; Rosenblatt, *Hard Marching*, 37.

59. Boatner, *The Civil War Dictionary*, 321; Kennedy, *The Civil War Battlefield Guide*, 62–64; Welcher, *The Union Army*, 818–819.

60. Boatner, *The Civil War Dictionary*, 321; Kennedy, *The Civil War Battlefield Guide*, 64; Welcher, *The Union Army*, 818–819.

61. Boatner, *The Civil War Dictionary*, 321; Kennedy, *The Civil War Battlefield Guide*, 64–65; Welcher, *The Union Army*, 818–819.

62. Benedict, *Vermont in the Civil War*, 284; *Official Records*, vol. XI, part 2, 660–661; 746–747; Evander M. Law, "The Fight for Richmond in 1862," *The Southern Bivouac*, vol. VI, January 1887–May 1887, 717.

63. Benedict, *Vermont in the Civil War*, 286; Manarin, *Henrico County Field of Honor*, 122; Burton, *Extraordinary Circumstances*, 145; *Official Records*, vol. XI, part 2, 466–467.

64. Benedict, *Vermont in the Civil War*, 283–284; *Official Records*, vol. XI, part 2, 462–463; Burton, *Extraordinary Circumstances*, 142.

65. Benedict, *Vermont in the Civil War*, 283–284; *Official Records*, vol. XI, part 2, 269; Burton, *Extraordinary Circumstances*, 142; Manarin, *Henrico County Field of Honor*, 124.
66. Peck, *Revised Roster*, 169; http://vermontcivilwar.org/get.php?input=21634; Andrew Laffie's compiled military service record; Mary Laffie's dependent mother's pension record; *(Montpelier) Vermont Watchman and State Journal*, July 18, 1862.
67. Peck, *Revised Roster*, 147; http://vermontcivilwar.org/get.php?input=4471; George H. Parker's compiled military service and government disability pension records.
68. Peck, *Revised Roster*, 62; http://vermontcivilwar.org/index/namesearch.php; Samuel A. Shattuck's compiled military service record.
69. http://www.vermontcivilwar.org/units/6/kimball/62/0712.php; http://www.vermontcivilwar.org/get.php?input=2688.
70. Robert U. Johnson, and Clarence C. Buel, eds. *Battles and Leaders of the Civil War. Being for the most part contributions by Union and Confederate officers*. vol. 2, New York: Century Co., 1887–1888), 367; *Official Records*, vol. XI, part 2, 467.
71. Manarin, *Henrico County Field of Honor*, 126; *Official Records*, vol. XI, part 2, 689; Law, "The Fight for Richmond in 1862," 717.
72. Benedict, *Vermont in the Civil War*, 285; Manarin, *Henrico County Field of Honor*, 127–128; *Official Records*, vol. XI, part 2, 467, 478; *The Burlington (Vt.) Free Press*, July 4, 1862.
73. Manarin, *Henrico County Field of Honor*, 126–127; *Official Records*, vol. XI, part 2, 740, 743; Evander M. Law, "The Fight for Richmond in 1862," 717.
74. Manarin, *Henrico County Field of Honor*, 127; *Official Records*, vol. XI, part 2, 695, 689–690.
75. *Official Records*, vol. XI, part 2, 743.
76. Manarin, *Henrico County Field of Honor*, 129; William H. Andrews, *Footprints of a Regiment: A Recollection of the 1st Georgia Regulars, 1861–1865, annotated and with an Introduction by Richard M. McMurray* (Atlanta, Ga.: Longstreet Press, 1992), 42.
77. Manarin, *Henrico County Field of Honor*, 129; *Official Records*, vol. XI, part 2, 690; Law, "The Fight for Richmond in 1862," 717.
78. Manarin, *Henrico County Field of Honor*, 130; Burton, *Extraordinary Circumstances*, 144.
79. Manarin, *Henrico County Field of Honor*, 130–131.
80. *Official Records*, vol. XI, part 2, 471.
81. Manarin, *Henrico County Field of Honor*, 130; *The National Tribune* (Washington, D.C.), October 22, 1881; William B. Edwards, *Civil War Guns* (Harrisburg, Penn.: The Stackpole Company, 1962), 229–231; Francis A. Lord, *Civil War Collector's Encyclopedia* (New York: Castle Books, 1965), 159; Benedict, *Vermont in the Civil War*, 285; *Official Records*, vol. XI, part 2, 475, 478.
82. *Lewiston (Penn.) True Democrat*, July 30, 1862.
83. Manarin, *Henrico County Field of Honor*, 130–131; *Official Records*, vol. XI, part 2, 701; William M. McIntosh's compiled military service record; Law, "The Fight for Richmond in 1862," 717; Scott C. Patchan, "The Battle of Garnett's Farm," *Civil War*, Issue 51, June 1995, 65.
84. *The Burlington (Vt.) Free Press*, July 4, 1862.
85. Peck, *Revised Roster*, 184, 201, 203; Benedict, *Vermont in the Civil War*, 286; *Official Records*, vol. XI, part 2, 480; http://vermontcivilwar.org/get.php?input=3443; Oscar G. Kelsey's compiled military service record; *(Montpelier) Vermont Watchman & State Journal*, August 1, 1862; Susan M. Kelsey's Civil War widow's pension record; George A. Shonio's compiled military service and government disability pension records; http://vermontcivilwar.org/get.php?input=12084; James Clark's compiled military service record; *Caledonian (St. Johnbury, Vt.)*, July 25, 1862; *Green Mountain Freeman (Montpelier, Vt.)*, July 23, 1862; John J. Duffy, Samuel B. Hand and Ralph H. Orth, eds. *The Vermont Encyclopedia* (Hanover, N.H.: University Press of New England, 2003), 187; http://www.lincolnvermont.org/about/index.html; Works Progress Administration Vermont Veterans' gravestone inscriptions card file, Vermont Historical Society, Barre, Vt.; Casper Honorus Dean letter, Vermont in the Civil War, http://vermontcivilwar.org/index.php.
86. Benedict, *Vermont in the Civil War*, 286; *Official Records*, vol. XI, part 2, 480; Manarin, *Henrico County Field of Honor*, 131.
87. Harlan P. Paige Papers, University of Vermont Bailey/Howe Library Special Collections, Burlington, Vt.
88. Peck, *Revised Roster*, 111, 118; http://www.vermontcivilwar.org/get.php?input=17553; George W. Gibson's compiled military service and government disability pension records; U.S. Surgeon General's office, *The Medical and Surgical History of the War of the Rebellion (1861–65)* (Washington: Government Printing office, 1870–1888), part 1, vol. 2, Chap. 2, sec. 2, 365; *Springfield (Mass.) Republican*, April 9, 1909; http://vermontcivilwar.org/get.php?input=5047; *St. Albans (Vt.) Daily Messenger*, January 29, 1906; Frederick C. Rogers' compiled military service and government disability pension records.
89. Ted Tunnell, ed. *Carpetbagger from Vermont: The Autobiography of Marshall Harvey Twitchell* (Baton Rouge: Louisiana State University Press, 1989), 39; Peck, *Revised Roster*, 111, 118, 135, 138; Leonard A. Stearns' compiled military service record; http://vermontcivilwar.org/get.php?input=5047; *St. Albans (Vt.) Daily Messenger*, January 29, 1906; Frederick C. Rogers' compiled military service and government disability pension records; George W. Gibson's compiled military service and government disability pension records; Elizabeth S. Gibson's veteran's widow's pension record; U.S. Surgeon General's office, *The Medical and Surgical History of the War of the Rebellion (1861–65)*, part 1, vol. 2, Chap. 2, sec. 2, 365.
90. Manarin, *Henrico County Field of Honor*, 131; *Official Records*, vol. XI, part 2, 702, 704; Patchan, "The Battle of Garnett's Farm, 65."
91. Benedict, *Vermont in the Civil War*, 286.
92. Benedict, *Vermont in the Civil War*, 287; Manarin, *Henrico County Field of Honor*, 131–132.
93. Benedict, *Vermont in the Civil War*, 287–288; Schiller, *Autobiography*, 42; Manarin, *Henrico County Field of Honor*, 152; Burton, *Extraordinary Circumstances*, 169; Schiller, *Autobiography*, 42; Johnson and Buel, *Battles and Leaders of the Civil War*, 367.
94. *(Green Mountain Freeman Montpelier, Vt.)*, July 15, 1862; Manarin, *Henrico County Field of Honor*, 134.
95. Burton, *Extraordinary Circumstances*, 168; *Official Records*, vol. XI, part 2, 690.
96. David W. Judd, *The Story of the Thirty-Third N.Y.S. Volunteers or Two Years Campaigning in Virginia and Maryland* (Rochester, N.Y.: Benton & Andrews, 29 Buffalo Street, 1864), 127; *Official Records*, vol. XI, part 2, 473; Law, "The Fight for Richmond in 1862," 717–718; Burton, *Extraordinary Circumstances*, 171.
97. Casper H. Dean letter.
98. Benedict, *Vermont in the Civil War*, 287–288; Shiller, *Autobiography*, 42; Chester K. Leach letters; Charles M. Hapgood diary; Lucius Savage diary; Dorothy Sutherland Melville, *Tyler-Browns of Brattleboro* (Jericho, N.Y.: Exposition Press, Inc., 1973), 81; Zeller, *The Second Vermont*, 80.
99. Peck, *Revised Roster*, 42; http://vermontcivilwar.org/get.php?input=25352; Frank C. Paddleford's compiled military service record; Mary R. Cabot, *Annals of Brattleboro Vermont, 1681–1895*, vol. 2 (Brattleboro, Vt.: Press of

E.L. Hildreth & Co., 1922), 775, 779; Melville, *Tyler-Browns of Brattleboro*, 81; Zeller, *Second Vermont*, 80.

100. Benedict, *Vermont in the Civil War*, 288.

101. Judd, *The Story of the Thirty-Third*, 127–128.

102. *Official Records*, vol. XI, part 2, 690; Manarin, *Henrico County Field of Honor*, 135; Burton, *Extraordinary Circumstances*, 170; Dowdey, *The Seven Days*, 265.

103. Manarin, *Henrico County Field of Honor*, 136; *Official Records*, vol. XI, part 2, 473; Burton, *Extraordinary Circumstances*, 171.

104. Manarin, *Henrico County Field of Honor*, 137; Judd, *The Story of the Thirty-Third*, 128–129.

105. *Official Records*, vol. XI, part 2, 704–705.

106. *Official Records*, vol. XI, part 2, 690; 705, 711; Warren Wilkinson and Steven E. Woodworth, *A Scythe of Fire: A Civil War Story of the Eighth Georgia Infantry Regiment* (New York: William Morrow, An Imprint of HarperCollins Publishers, 2002), 143; Manarin, *Henrico County Field of Honor*, 137–139; Frederick D. Bidwell, *History of the Forty-Ninth New York Volunteers* (Albany, N.Y.: J.B. Lyon Company, Printers, 1916), 13.

107. Manarin, *Henrico County Field of Honor*, 139; Judd, *The Story of the Thirty-Third*, 130; Burton, *Extraordinary Circumstances*, 172.

108. Dowdey, *The Seven Days*, 254–254; Manarin, *Henrico County Field of Honor*, 145–147; Welcher, *The Union Army*, 821.

109. Dowdey, *The Seven Days*, 251.

Chapter 4

1. Benedict, *Vermont in the Civil War*, 289; Manarin, *Henrico County Field of Honor*, 155; Burton, *Extraordinary Circumstances*, 185; *Official Records*, vol. XI, part 2, 463–464.

2. *The Daily Dispatch (Richmond, Va.)*, September 18, 1862; email from D.W. Kerns, Jr., and Robert E.L. Krick, July, 11, 2012, Richmond National Battlefield Park, Richmond, Va.; County of Henrico, *Inventory of Early Architecture and Historic Sites* (County of Henrico, Va., 1976), 71.

3. Peck, *Revised Roster*, 47; http://vermontcivilwar.org/get.php?input=2501; http://trees.ancestry.com/tree/60030596/person/42053085951; http://www.findagrave.com/cgi-bin/fg.cgi?page=gr&GSln=goodwin&GSfn=henry&GSmn=k.&GSbyrel=all&GSdy=1920&GSdyrel=in&GSst=6&GScntry=4&GSob=n&GRid=3711943&df=all&; Harvey K. Goodwin's compiled military service record; Sarah J. Goodwin's veteran's widow's pension record.

4. Benedict, *Vermont in the Civil War*, 289; Burton, *Extraordinary Circumstances*, 185–186; Manarin, *Henrico County Field of Honor*, 172; *Official Records*, vol. XI, part 2, 463.

5. Benedict, *Vermont in the Civil War*, 290; Manarin, *Henrico County Field of Honor*, 172; *Official Records*, vol. XI, part 2, 463.

6. Manarin, *Henrico County Field of Honor*, 134; Burton, *Extraordinary Circumstances*, 179–180; Hagemann, *The Heritage of Virginia*, 20–21, 114–115.

7. Burton, *Extraordinary Circumstances*, 180; *Official Records*, vol. XI, part 2, 662.

8. Dowdey, *The Seven Days*, 257–262; Manarin, *Henrico County Field of Honor*, 134, 159; Burton, *Extraordinary Circumstances*, 180; Sears, *To the Gates of Richmond*, 260–261.

9. *Official Records*, vol. XI, part 2, 662; Dowdey, *The Seven Days*, 167; Manarin, *Henrico County Field of Honor*, 159; Burton, *Extraordinary Circumstances*, 184.

10. Welcher, *The Union Army*, 822; Manarin, *Henrico County Field of Honor*, 150.

11. *Official Records*, vol. XI, part 2, 662–663; Manarin, *Henrico County Field of Honor*, 159–160.

12. *Official Records*, vol. XI, part 2, 663.

13. *Official Records*, vol. XI, part 3, 575–576.

14. John V. Quarstein, *The Battle of the Ironclads* (Charleston, S.C.: Arcadia Publishing, 2005), 28; David H. Schneider, *Civil War Times*, "Lee's Armored Car," February 2011, vol. XLX, no. 1, 56–58; Joseph L. Brent, *Mobilizable Fortifications, and their Controlling Influence in War* (Boston and New York: Houghton, Mifflin and Company, 1885), 57–58; *Richmond (Va.) Examiner*, July 8, 1862; *Official Records*, vol. XI, part 3, 610, 615; *Official Records*, vol. XXXVI, part 3, 725–726.

15. John W.H. Porter, *A Record of Events in Norfolk County, Virginia, from April 19th, 1861, to May 10th, 1862, with a History of the Soldiers and Sailors of Norfolk County, Norfolk City and Portsmouth, who Served in the Confederate States Army or Navy* (Portsmouth, Va.: W.A. Fiske, Printer and Bookbinder, 1892), 296; http://search.ancestry.com/cgi-bin/sse.dll?db=pubmembertrees&gss=sfs28_ms_db&new=1&rank=1&msT=1&gsfn=james%20e.&gsln=barry&msbdm=4&msbdy=1814&msbpn_ftp=Georgia%2C%20USA&msbpn=13&msbpn_PInfo=5-%7C0%7C1652393%7C0%7C2%7C3245%7C13%7C0%7C0%7C0%7C0%7C&msddd=25&msddm=1&msddy=1903&msdpn_ftp=Norfolk%2C%20Independent%20Cities%2C%20Virginia%2C%20USA&msdpn=24283&msdpn_PInfo=8-%7C0%7C1652393%7C0%7C2%7C3245%7C49%7C0%7C24255%7C24283%7C0%7C&MSAV=0&uidh=cd.

16. Porter, *Record of Events in Norfolk*, 296.

17. Porter, *Record of Events in Norfolk*, 297; Quarstein, *The Battle of the Ironclads*, 132.

18. Porter, *Record of Events in Norfolk*, 297.

19. *Richmond (Va.) Examiner*, July 8, 1862; Charles F. Bryan, Jr., and Nelson D. Lankford, eds., *Eye of the Storm: A Civil War Odyssey: written and illustrated by Robert Knox Sneden* (New York: Free Press, 2000), 76.

20. *Official Records*, vol. XI, part 2, 663,691; Manarin, *Henrico County Field of Honor*, 166; Burton, *Extraordinary Circumstances*, 186–190; *American Citizen (Canton, Miss.)*, July 4, 1862; *Confederate Veteran*, vol. IX, 1901, 20.

21. *Official Records*, vol. XI, part 2, 663; Sears, *To the Gates of Richmond*, 267–268; Manarin, *Henrico County Field of Honor*, 166–167; Burton, *Extraordinary Circumstances*, 192–193; Boatner, *The Civil War Dictionary*, 732.

22. Louis H. Manarin and Charles H. Peple, *The History of Henrico County* (The County of Henrico, Virginia, 2011), 238; http://www.csa-railroads.com/Richmond_and_York_River.htm; "Virginia, Deaths and Burials, 1853–1912," index, *FamilySearch* (https://familysearch.org/ark:/61903/1:1:XR7Q-MVJ, accessed 28 May 2015), Geo. M. Savage, 30 Sep 1867; citing Henrico County, Virginia, reference p 181 e 22; FHL microfilm 2,056,983.

23. Charles Lewis Slattery, *Felix Reville Brunot, 1820–1898, A Civilian in the War for the Union, President of the First Board of Indian Commissioners* (New York: Longmans, Green, Co., 1901), 63; *The Daily Dispatch (Richmond, Va.)*, February 2, 1852, August 27, 1863; *Richmond (Va.) Whig*, October 21, 1870; http://www.csa-railroads.com/Richmond_and_York_River.htm; Bryan and Lankford, *Eye of the Storm*, 71–72.

24. Manarin, *Henrico County Field of Honor*, 8; Louis H. Manarin and Clifford Dowdey, *The History of Henrico County* (Charlottesville: University Press of Virginia, 1984), 259.

25. Manarin and Dowdey, *The History of Henrico County*, 259.

26. Ibid., 260.

27. Ibid., 260.

28. *Official Records*, vol. XI, part 1, 156, 169.

29. Slattery, *Felix Reville Brunot*, 61–64; John Swineburne, *Reports on the Peninsula Campaign, Surgical Experience, & etc.* (Albany, N.Y.: Steam Press of C. Van

Benthuysen, 1863), 4–6; John Priest, *One Surgeon's Private War*, 35; *Official Records*, vol. XI, part 1, 189–191.
  30. Johnson and Buel, *Battles and Leaders*, 370; *Official Records*, vol. XI, part 2, 464.
  31. Peck, *Revised Roster*, 161; http://vermontcivilwar.org/get.php?input=19449; *Manchester (Vt.) Journal*, July 15, 1862; Mandus W. Hill's compiled military service record.
  32. Benedict, *Vermont in the Civil War*, 289; Manarin, *Henrico County Field of Honor*, 170.
  33. James J. Marks, *The Peninsular Campaign in Virginia; or, Incidents and Scenes on the Battle-fields and in Richmond* (Philadelphia, Penn.: J.B. Lippincott & Co., 1864), 245.
  34. *The Burlington (Vt.) Free Press*, 4 July, 1862.
  35. Benedict, *Vermont in the Civil War*, 290; *Official Records*, vol. XI, part 2, 90, Schiller, *Autobiography*, 43; Manarin, *Henrico County Field of Honor*, 175.
  36. Benedict, *Vermont in the Civil War*, 291–293; Schiller, *Autobiography*, 43; *Official Records*, Vol. IX, part 2, 464; *The Burlington (Vt.) Free Press*, July 4, 1862; Zeller *The Second Vermont*, 80.
  37. Johnson and Buel, *Battles and Leaders*, 371–372; Burton, *Extraordinary Circumstances*, 212–214; Manarin, *Henrico County Field of Honor*, 175–177; Welcher, *The Union Army*, 823; Benedict, *Vermont in the Civil War*, 291.
  38. Benedict, *Vermont in the Civil War*, 292–293; Johnson and Buel, *Battles and Leaders*, 371–372; Burton, *Extraordinary Circumstances*, 212–214; Manarin, *Henrico County Field of Honor*, 175–177.
  39. Manarin; *Henrico County Field of Honor*, 175; *Official Records*, Vol. IX, part 2, 721.
  40. Burton, *Extraordinary Circumstances*, 214; Manarin, *Henrico County Field of Honor*, 177; *Official Records*, Vol. IX, part 2, 91.
  41. Michael J. Andrus, *The Brooke, Fauquier, Loudon and Alexandria Artillery* (Lynchburg, Va.: H.E. Howard, 1990), 1–2, 12–13; https://www.findagrave.com/cgi-bin/fg.cgi?page=gr&GRid=38793806; Burton, *Extraordinary Circumstances*, 214; *Official Records*, Vol. IX, part 2, 732.
  42. *Official Records*, Vol. IX, part 2, 91; Manarin; *Henrico County Field of Honor*, 179–181.
  43. *Official Records*, Vol. IX, part 2, 91.
  44. Benedict, *Vermont in the Civil War*, 291–293; Schiller, *Autobiography*, 43; *Official Records*, Vol. IX, part 2, 464; Zeller, *The Second Vermont*, 80–81.
  45. Benedict, *Vermont in the Civil War*, 292; Priest, *One Surgeon's War*, 35; *Democrat & Chronicle (Rochester, N.Y.)*, October 22, 1891.
  46. Benedict, *Vermont in the Civil War*, 292; *The Burlington (Vt.) Free Press*, July 4, 18, 1862; *Official Records*, vol. XI, part 2, 477; Zeller, *The Second Vermont*, 81.
  47. Benedict, *Vermont in the Civil War*, 294–295; *Official Records*, vol. XI, part 2, 477–478; Daniel F. Cooledge Civil War Diary, 1862.
  48. Peck, *Revised Roster*, 35; http://www.vermontcivilwar.org/get.php?input=24403; Thomas Morrisey's compiled military service record.
  49. Peck, *Revised Roster*, 36, 454; http://vermontcivilwar.org/get.php?input=28791; James H. Shippee's compiled military service and government disability pension records; http://trees.ancestry.com/tree/70528123/person/36221750957.
  50. Peck, *Revised Roster*, 34; http://www.vermontcivilwar.org/get.php?input=8669; Benjamin S. Barnard's compiled military service and government disability pension records.
  51. Peck, *Revised Roster*, 34; http://www.vermontcivilwar.org/get.php?input=12737; Daniel F. Cooledge's compiled military service and government disability pension records; Cooledge diary.

  52. Peck, *Revised Roster*, 34–36; http://www.vermontcivilwar.org/get.php?input=26705; Daniel M. Priest's compiled military service and government disability pension records; Zeller, *The Second Vermont*, 82.
  53. Peck, *Revised Roster*, 64; Truman Hunter's compiled military service record; Calvin Clair's compiled military service record.
  54. Benedict, *Vermont in the Civil War*, 293; *Official Records*, vol. XI, part 2, 477–478; Cooledge diary; Zeller, *The Second Vermont*, 82.
  55. Benedict, *Vermont in the Civil War*, 295.
  56. Peck, *Revised Roster*, 23, 163; http://vermontcivilwar.org/get.php?input=11990; Joseph Clair's compiled military service and government disability pension records.
  57. Benedict, *Vermont in the Civil War*, 295.
  58. Benedict, *Vermont in the Civil War*, 295; Peck, *Revised Roster*, 167; http://vermontcivilwar.org/get.php?input=24923; Ira A. Nicholson's compiled military service and government disability pension records; *Official Records*, vol. XI, part 2, 476, 478–479; Manarin, *Henrico County Field of Honor*, 184.
  59. Peck, *Revised Roster*, 173; http://vermontcivilwar.org/get.php?input=274; Brownson M. Barber's compiled military service record; *Argus and Patriot (Montpelier, Vt.)*, January 14, 1885; *The Vermont (Montpelier) Watchman and State Journal*, August 1, 1862; Works Progress Administration Vermont veterans' gravestone inscriptions card file, Vermont Historical Society, Barre, Vt.
  60. Peck, *Revised Roster*, 169; http://vermontcivilwar.org/get.php?input=19728; Nelson K. Holt's compiled military service and government disability pension records.
  61. Peck, *Revised Roster*, 167; http://vermontcivilwar.org/get.php?input=24923; Ira A. Nicholson's compiled military service and government disability pension records.
  62. Andrus, *Brooke, Fauquier, Loudon and Alexandria Artillery*, 13; Boatner, *The Civil War Dictionary*, 119.
  63. Benedict, *Vermont in the Civil War*, 295–296; *Official Records*, vol. XI, part 2, 479; Manarin, *Henrico County Field of Honor*, 184; Peck, *Revised Roster*, 167; http://vermontcivilwar.org/get.php?input=24923; Ira A. Nicholson's compiled military service and government disability pension records.
  64. *Official Records*, vol. XI, part 2, 479; *The Green Mountain Daily Freeman (Montpelier, Vt.)*, July 30, 1862.
  65. Manarin; *Henrico County Field of Honor*, 185; *Official Records*, vol. XI, part 2, 720–721, 741.
  66. Benedict, *Vermont in the Civil War*, 296.
  67. Peck, *Revised Roster*, 151; http://vermontcivilwar.org/get.php?input=9121; *The Vermont (Montpelier) Watchman and State Journal*, August 1, 1862; U.S. Surgeon General's Office, *Medical and Surgical History*, part 2, vol. 2, chap. 9, sec. 3, p. 638; Frederick Sheldon Belden's compiled military service and government disability pension records.
  68. Peck, *Revised Roster*, 168; http://vermontcivilwar.org/get.php?input=16082; James P. Elmer's compiled military service and government disability pension records.
  69. Peck, *Revised Roster*, 153, 156; http://vermontcivilwar.org/get.php?input=16594; Miner E. Fish's compiled military service and government disability pension records.
  70. Peck, *Revised Roster*, 154; http://www.vermontcivilwar.org/get.php?input=16940; Thomas H. Fortune's compiled military service and government disability pension records.
  71. Peck, *Revised Roster*, 155, 174, http://vermontcivilwar.org/get.php?input=20752; Robert Johnson's compiled military service record; U.S. Surgeon General's office, *The Medical and Surgical History of the War of the Rebellion (1861–65)* (Washington: Government Printing office, 1870–1888), part 2, vol. 2, Chap. 9, sec. 4, 756.
  72. Peck, *Revised Roster*, 155; http://vermontcivilwar.

org/get.php?input=23152; Squire A. Marvin's compiled military service and government disability pension records.

73. Peck, *Revised Roster*, 156; http://vermontcivilwar.org/get.php?input=468; Reuben C. Benton's compiled military service and government disability pension records.

74. Peck, *Revised Roster*, 157, 582; Jason O. French's compiled service and pension records; http://www.vermontcivilwar.org/get.php?input=17137; U.S. Surgeon General's Office, *Medical and Surgical History*, part 2, vol. 2, Chap. 6, sec. 3, 144.

75. Peck, *Revised Roster*, 158; http://vermontcivilwar.org/get.php?input=22917; Edward H. Marcy's compiled military service record; Ephraim B. Marcy's compiled military service and government disability pension records.

76. Peck, *Revised Roster*, 157; http://vermontcivilwar.org/get.php?input=10691;Edgar Bullard's compiled military service and government disability pension records.

77. Peck, *Revised Roster*, 158; http://vermontcivilwar.org/get.php?input=23505; Ammon S. McGee's compiled military service and government disability pension records.

78. Peck, *Revised Roster*, 163; http://www.vermontcivilwar.org/get.php?input=661; Friend A. Brainard's compiled military service and government disability pension records.

79. Peck, *Revised Roster*, 165; http://vermontcivilwar.org/get.php?input=3302; Benjamin R. Jenne's compiled military service and government disability pension records.

80. Peck, *Revised Roster*, 163; http://vermontcivilwar.org/get.php?input=6397; Henry Harrison Wilder Papers, University of Vermont, Bailey/Howe Library Special Collections, Burlington, Vt.; Henry H. Wilder's compiled military service record.

81. Peck, *Revised Roster*, 23, 150; http://vermontcivilwar.org/index.php; ancestry.com; Benedict, *Vermont in the Civil War*, 182, 188; Olney A. Comstock's compiled military service record; *The Green Mountain Freeman (Montpelier, Vt.)*, 11 July, 1862.

82. Peck, *Revised Roster*, 171; http://vermontcivilwar.org/get.php?input=18686; Francis D. Hammond's compiled military service record.

83. Peck, *Revised Roster*, 20, 167; http://vermontcivilwar.org/get.php?input=5235; Charles W. Seagar's compiled military service and government disability pension records.

84. Peck, *Revised Roster*, 169; http://www.vermontcivilwar.org/get.php?input=29839; Francis C. Stedman's compiled military service and government disability pension records; http://www.vermontcivilwar.org/get.php?input=29840; Irvin W. Stedman's compiled military service and government disability pension records.

85. Benedict, *Vermont in the Civil War*, 297.

86. Peck, *Revised Roster*, 160, 361; Brian L. Knight, *No Braver Deeds: The Story of the Equinox Guards* (Friends of Hildene, Inc., Manchester, Vt., 2004), 31, 161, 194, 213; http://vermontcivilwar.org/get.php?input=13139; Henry A. Cummings' compiled military service and government disability pension records; http://vermontcivilwar.org/get.php?input=13143; Hiram P. Cummings' compiled military service record; Edmund M. Cummings's compiled military service record; http://www.vermontcivilwar.org/get.php?input=13155; http://www.vermontcivilwar.org/get.php?input=13160; William E. Cummings' compiled military service record; Silas A. Cummings' compiled military service record; http://vermontcivilwar.org/get.php?input=13160; William H.H. Cummings compiled military service record.

87. Peck, *Revised Roster*, 21, 159, 170, 733; http://vermontcivilwar.org/get.php?input=4556; *St. Albans (Vt.) Messenger*, July 17, 1862; William H.H. Peck's compiled military service and government disability pension records; Knight, *No Braver Deeds*, 195–196.

88. Peck, *Revised Roster*, 162; Benedict, *Vermont in the Civil War*, 185; http://vermontcivilwar.org/get.php?input=32582; John R. Wilkins' compiled military service and government disability pension record.

89. Peck, *Revised Roster*, 31; Knight, *No Braver Deeds*, 29–30; http://www.vermontcivilwar.org/get.php?input=455; Willard K. Bennett's compiled military service record.

90. Fitch Family Papers, John R. Lewis to Samuel Sumner, Sr., dated July 1862, University of Vermont Bailey/Howe Library Special Collections, Burlington, Vt.

91. Knight, *No Braver Deeds*, 189.

92. Benedict, *Vermont in the Civil War*, 297.

93. *Ibid.*, 298.

94. Peck, *Revised Roster*, 17, 196; http://vermontcivilwar.org/get.php?input=11308; Edwin M. Carlisle's compiled military service and government disability pension records.

95. Peck, *Revised Roster*, 193, 718; http://www.vermontcivilwar.org/get.php?input=1637; Alexander W. Davis' compiled military service and government disability pension records.

96. Peck, *Revised Roster*, 16, 183, 186, http://vermontcivilwar.org/get.php?input=33091; George E. Wood's compiled military service and government disability pension records.

97. Peck, *Revised Roster*, 203; http://vermontcivilwar.org/get.php?input=24680; James R. Murray's compiled military service record; Susan L. Murray's veteran's widow's pension record.

98. Peck, *Revised Roster*, 210; http://www.vermontcivilwar.org/get.php?input=23066; Jeffrey D. Marshall, *A War of the People, Vermont Civil War Letters* (Hanover, N.H.: University Press of New England, 1999), 92; Guy C. Martin's complied military service record.

99. Peck, *Revised Roster*, 206; http://vermontcivilwar.org/get.php?input=25706; Abial H. Patch's compiled military and government disability pension records.

100. Peck, *Revised Roster*, 212; http://www.vermontcivilwar.org/get.php?input=28384 580; John Scott's compiled military service and government disability pension records.

101. Benedict, *Vermont in the Civil War*, 298.

102. Benedict, *Vermont in the Civil War*, 298–299.

103. Peck, *Revised Roster*, 51; http://www.vermontcivilwar.org/get.php?input=13988; Charles C. Dodge's compiled military service and government disability pension records; Elijah S. Brown letters; Zeller, *The Second Vermont*, 83.

104. Peck, *Revised Roster*, 51; http://www.vermontcivilwar.org/get.php?input=18851; Henry L. Harris' compiled military service and government disability pension record; Zeller, *The Second Vermont*, 83.

105. Peck, *Revised Roster*, 52; Harlan P. Stoddard's compiled military service and government disability pension records; Zeller, *The Second Vermont*, 83.

106. Peck, *Revised Roster*, 211, 397; http://vermontcivilwar.org/get.php?input=11882; Watson Cheney's compiled military service record.

107. Peck, *Revised Roster*, 47; *Official Records*, Vol. XI, part 2, 721; William H. Clark's compiled military service and government disability pension records; Zeller, *The Second Vermont*, 83.

108. Peck, *Revised Roster*, 187; http://www.vermontcivilwar.org/get.php?input=15894; Some of the Recollections of S.N. Eastman, M.D., Vermont Historical Society, Barre, Vt.; Seth N. Eastman's compiled military service and government disability pension records.

109. Peck, *Revised Roster*, 59; http://vermontcivilwar.org/get.php?input=27733;Vernon D. Rood's compiled military service and government disability pension records; Zeller, *The Second Vermont*, 83.

110. Peck, *Revised Roster*, 54; http://www.vermontcivilwar.org/get.php?input=12268; John E. Clough's compiled military service and government disability pension records.
111. Peck, *Revised Roster*, 48; http://vermontcivilwar.org/get.php?input=24261; Orville E. Moore's compiled military service and government disability pension records; "Massachusetts, Deaths, 1841–1915," index and images, *FamilySearch* (https://familysearch.org/pal:/MM9.1.1/N43T-PTB, accessed 28 Jul 2014), Sarah A Moore, 13 Nov 1911; citing Boston, Massachusetts, 92, State Archives, Boston; FHL microfilm 2393945; "Massachusetts, Deaths, 1841–1915," index and images, *FamilySearch* (https://familysearch.org/pal:/MM9.1.1/N7F8-4JQ, accessed 28 Jul 2014), Orville E. Moore, 17 Jan 1900; citing Boston, Massachusetts, v 507 p. 31, State Archives, Boston; FHL microfilm 1843729; http://en.wikipedia.org/wiki/Victor_Moore.
112. Benedict, *Vermont in the Civil War*, 299; Zeller, *The Second Vermont*, 83.
113. Benedict, *Vermont in the Civil War*, 299–301; Peck, *Revised Roster*, 94; Charles B. Dubois, Memoir of his Civil War Experiences, June 1861–July 1864, Vermont Historical Society, Barre, Vt.
114. Peck, *Revised Roster*, 79; http://vermontcivilwar.org/get.php?input=1430; David T. Corbin's compiled military service record.
115. Peck, *Revised Roster*, 79; http://www.vermontcivilwar.org/get.php?input=4837; John W. Ramsey's compiled military service record.
116. Peck, *Revised Roster*, 80; Alonzo C. Armington's compiled military service record; Albert G. Chadwick, comp., *Soldiers' Record of the Town of St. Johnsbury, Vermont, in the War of the Rebellion, 1861–5.* (St. Johnsbury, Vt.: C.M. Stone & Co, Book and Job Printers, Caledonian Office, 1883), 169–170; Ellery Bicknell Crane, *Historic Homes and Institutions and Genealogical and Personal Memoirs of Worcester County Massachusetts with a History of the Worcester Society of Antiquity*, vol. 2. (New York: The Lewis Publishing Company, 1907), 373–375.
117. Peck, *Revised Roster*, 73; http://vermontcivilwar.org/get.php?input=606; George W. Bonett's compiled military service and government disability pension records.
118. Peck, *Revised Roster*, 70, 98; http://vermontcivilwar.org/get.php?input=4268; George A. MacDonald, ed., "The Bloody Seven Days' Battles," *Vermont Quarterly: A Magazine of History*, vol. XV, no. 4, October 1947, 232; Thomas Nelson's compiled military service and government disability pension records.
119. Peck, *Revised Roster*, 82, 622; Moses Parker's compiled military service record; Benedict, *Vermont in the Civil War*, 134; Moses A. Parker, Civil War letter, Parker Family Papers, Special Collections, Bailey/Howe Library, University of Vermont, Burlington, Vt.
120. Peck, *Revised Roster*, 101; Rosson O. Sander's compiled military service and government disability pension records.
121. Peck, *Revised Roster*, 101; http://www.vermontcivilwar.org/get.php?input=28155; Rosson O. Sander's compiled military service and government disability pension records.
122. Benedict, *Vermont in the Civil War*, 299.
123. John Maddox's compiled military service record.
124. *Ibid.*
125. *Ibid.*
126. *New Orleans (La.) Commercial Bulletin*, February 19, 1868; *Times-Picayune (News Orleans, La.)*, February 19, 1868, February 5, 1871.
127. Benedict, *Vermont in the Civil War*, 300; Elijah S. Brown letter, Vermont Historical Society, Barre, Vt.; *Burlington (Vt.) Free Press*, July 18, 1862; Zeller, *The Second Vermont*, 84.
128. *Official Records*, vol. XI, part 2, 87–717; Stevens, *Three Years in the Sixth Corps*, 103.
129. Benedict, *Vermont in the Civil War*, 303; Priest, *One Surgeon's Private War*, 35–36; *Burlington (Vt.) Free Press*, July 18, 1862.
130. Benedict, *Vermont in the Civil War*, 300; *Official Records*, vol. XI, part 2, 374; Zeller, *The Second Vermont*, 85.
131. Shiller, *Autobiography*, 44; Johnson and Buel, *Battles and Leaders*, 372.
132. Shiller, *Autobiography*, 45; Johnson and Buel, *Battles and Leaders*, 372.
133. Benedict, *Vermont in the Civil War*, 303; *Official Records*, vol. 11, part 2, 464; Charles M. Hapgood diary.
134. http://www.csa-railroads.com/Essays/Orignial%20Docs/OR/OR%20Series%201,%20Vol.%2036,%20Part%203,%20Page%20875.htm; *Official Records*, series 1, vol. 36, part 3, 725–726, 875; Manarin, *Field of Honor*, vol. 2, 399; "David H. Schneider, "Lee's Armored Car," 56–57.
135. Manarin and Dowdey, *The History of Henrico County*, 258–259.
136. *Richmond (Va.) Daily Whig*, October 9, 1862.
137. Manarin and Dowdey, *The History of Henrico County*, 259; http://www.findagrave.com/cgi-bin/fg.cgi?page=gr&GSln=savage&GSfn=mary&GSmn=e.&GSbyrel=all&GSdy=1862&GSdyrel=in&GSst=48&GScntry=4&GSob=n&GRid=93885598&df=all&; *Richmond Whig*, November 18, 1862; *Richmond (Va.) Daily Whig*, November 25, 1862.
138. "Virginia, Deaths and Burials, 1853–1912," index, *FamilySearch* (https://familysearch.org/ark:/61903/1:1:XR7Q-MVJ, accessed 28 May 2015), Geo. M. Savage, 30 Sep 1867; citing Henrico County, Virginia, reference p. 181 e 22; FHL microfilm 2,056,983; http://www.findagrave.com/cgi-bin/fg.cgi?page=gr&GSln=savage&GSfn=george&GSmn=morton&GSbyrel=all&GSdy=1867&GSdyrel=in&GSst=48&GScntry=4&GSob=n&GRid=93885595&df=all&; *Richmond (Va.) Whig*, October 21, 1870.

Chapter 5

1. Benedict, *Vermont in the Civil War*, 303; Dubois Memoir; Zeller, *The Second Vermont*, 88.
2. Peck, *Revised Roster*, 151, http://vermontcivilwar.org/get.php?input=13417; William E. Daniels' compiled military service and government disability service records.
3. Peck, *Revised Roster*, 147, 193, 718; http://www.vermontcivilwar.org/get.php?input=6573; Amos A. Wright's compiled military service and government disability pension records; http://vermontcivilwar.org/index.php; Alexander W. Davis' compiled military service and government disability pension records.
4. Dubois Memoir.
5. Welcher, *The Union Army*, 824–825; Manarin, *Henrico County Field of Honor*, 214–215; *Official Records*, vol. XI, part 2, 55; Warner, *Generals in Blue*, 402.
6. Welcher, *The Union Army*, 824–825; Burton, *Extraordinary Circumstances*, 235–236; *Official Records*, vol. XI, part 2, 55.
7. Manarin, *Henrico County Field of Honor*, 189; Burton, *Extraordinary Circumstances*, 230, 252.
8. Benedict, *Vermont in the Civil War*, 304; Welcher, *The Union Army*, 824; Zeller, *The Second Vermont*, 85.
9. Rosenblatt, *Hard Marching*, 39.
10. Johnson and Buel, *Battles and Leaders*, vol. 2, 378.
11. Benedict, *Vermont in the Civil War*, 304; Dubois Memoir.
12. Burton, *Extraordinary Circumstances*, 292; Dowdey, *The Seven Days*, 283–284.
13. Lucius Savage Diary.
14. Cooledge Diary.

15. Priest, *One Surgeon's Private War*, 36–37.
16. Priest, *One Surgeon's Private War*, 37; Cooledge Diary.
17. https://www.cem.va.gov/cems/nchp/sevenpines.asp; Drew Gilpin Faust, *This Republic of Suffering: Death and the American Civil War* (New York: Alfred A. Knopf, 2008), 235–236; Manarin, *Henrico County Field of Honor*, vol. 2, 858.
18. Benedict, *Vermont in the Civil War*, 304–305; Zeller, *The Second Vermont*, 85.
19. Schiller, *Autobiography*, 45–46.
20. Benedict, *Vermont in the Civil War*, 304–305; Stevens, *Three Years in the Sixth Corps*, 104; Kirk Rand letters; Zeller, *The Second Vermont*, 85.
21. Shiller, *Autobiography*, 46.
22. Dubois Memoir.
23. Dowdey, *The Seven Days*, 310–311; Burton, *Extraordinary Circumstances*, 254–255.
24. Johnson and Buel, *Battles and Leaders*, vol. 2, 376–377.
25. Benedict, *Vermont in the Civil War*, 305–306; (Burlington, Vt.) *Daily Free Press*, 2 August 1862; Melville, *Tyler-Browns of Brattleboro*, 82; Zeller, *The Second Vermont*, 86.
26. *Official Records*, vol. XI, part 2, 465–466; *New York Tribune*, December 9, 1862; Manarin, *Henrico County Field of Honor*, 215–219; Burton, *Extraordinary Circumstances*, 255.
27. Benedict, *Vermont in the Civil War*, 305; Shiller, *Autobiography*, 46; Manarin, *Henrico County Field of Honor*, 217; Johnson and Buel, *Battles and Leaders*, vol. 2, 378.
28. Johnson and Buel, *Battles and Leaders*, vol. 2, 377.
29. Benedict, *Vermont in the Civil War*, 307; Shiller, *Autobiography*, 46; Peck, *Revised Roster*, 19, 74, 113, 151, 201, 588; John Carmody's compiled military service and government disability pension records; Phineas Belden's compiled military service record; http://vermontcivilwar.org/get.php?input=10006; Dexter E. Boyden's compiled military service record http://www.vermontcivilwar.org/get.php?input=21619; James Laden's compiled military service and government disability pension records.
30. Peck, *Revised Roster*, 118; http://vermontcivilwar.org/get.php?input=16736; George S. Flanders' compiled military service and government disability pension records.
31. Burton, *Extraordinary Circumstances*, 180; *Official Records*, vol. XI, part 2, 662; Boatner, *The Civil War Dictionary*, 914–915.
32. Boatner, *The Civil War Dictionary*, 914–915
33. Benedict, *Vermont in the Civil War*, 307–308.
34. Shiller, *Autobiography*, 46–47.
35. Benedict, *Vermont in the Civil War*, 308; (Montpelier, Vt.) *Green Mountain Freeman*, 29 July 1862; Schiller, *Autobiography*, 47; *Official Records*, vol. XI, part 2, 464.
36. Benedict, *Vermont in the Civil War*, 308; (Montpelier, Vt.) *Green Mountain Freeman*, July 29, 1862; *Official Records*, vol. XI, part 2, 464; Welcher, *The Union Army*, 829, Zeller, *The Second Vermont*, 86.
37. Boatner, *The Civil War Dictionary*, 504.
38. *Ibid.*, 504.
39. *Ibid.*, 504.
40. *Ibid.*, 506.
41. *Ibid.*, 506.
42. *Ibid.*, 506–507.
43. Benedict, *Vermont in the Civil War*, 309–310; (Montpelier, Vt.) *Green Mountain Freeman*, July 29, 1862; *Official Records*, vol. XI, part 2, 72; Peck, *Revised Roster*, 50, 129; http://www.vermontcivilwar.org/get.php?input=1535; Edwin A. Cummings' compiled military service record; http://vermontcivilwar.org/get.php?input=2661; Eri S. Gunnison's compiled military service and government disability pension records; Zeller, *The Second Vermont*, 86.
44. Benedict, *Vermont in the Civil War*, 309–310; (Montpelier, Vt.) *Green Mountain Freeman*, July 29, 1862; Schiller, *Autobiography*, 49; Sears, *To the Gates of Richmond*, 338; *Official Records*, vol. XI, part 2, 72, 464; Zeller, *The Second Vermont*, 86.
45. Benedict, *Vermont in the Civil War*, 310.
46. Schiller, *Autobiography*, 48.
47. Sears, *To the Gates of Richmond*, 338–339; Hagemann, *Heritage of Virginia*, 114–115; Paul Wilstach, *Tidewater Virginia* (New York: Tudor Publishing Co., 1945), 141; D. Gardiner Tyler, *A History Pictorial Review of Charles City County, Virginia* (Expert Graphics, 1990), 58; Zeller, *The Second Vermont*, 86.
48. Benedict, *Vermont in the Civil War*, 311; Johnson and Buel, *Battles and Leaders*, vol. 2, 427; Zeller, *The Second Vermont*, 86.
49. Benedict, *Vermont in the Civil War*, 311; Schiller, *Autobiography*, 49; Johnson and Buel, *Battles and Leaders*, vol. 2, 427–428; *Official Records*, vol. XI, part 2, 464; Zeller, *The Second Vermont*, 87.
50. Benedict, *Vermont in the Civil War*, 311; Johnson and Buel, *Battles and Leaders*, vol. 2, 428; Chester K. Leach letters; Boatner, *The Civil War Dictionary*, 712; Zeller, *The Second Vermont*. 87.
51. Hagemann, *Heritage of Virginia*, 264; Chester K. Leach letters; Zeller, *The Second Vermont*, 87.
52. John Wheeler's compiled military service record; Daniel D. Cobleigh's compiled military service record.
53. Benedict, *Vermont in the Civil War*, 311; Zeller, *The Second Vermont*, 88.
54. Peck, *Revised Roster*, 85, 741; Robert G. Poirier, *They Could Not Have Done Better: Thomas O. Seaver and the 3rd Vermont Infantry in the War for the Union* (Newport, Vt.: Vermont Civil War Enterprises, 2005), 57.
55. Dubois Memoir.
56. Chester K. Leach letters; Charles C. Morey diaries; Peck, *Revised Roster*, 47; George E. Allen's compiled military service record; Zeller, *The Second Vermont*, 88.
57. *Ibid.*
58. Charles H. Joyce's compiled military service record; (Montpelier, Vt.) *Green Mountain Freeman*, 11 July, 1862; Zeller, *The Second Vermont*, 89.
59. Peck, *Revised Roster*, 34, 37; William Flanders' compiled military service record; Henry G. Hunter's compiled military service record; Nelson C. Bradford's compiled military service record; Jerome Draper's compiled military service record; *The Manchester (Vt.) Journal*, July 29, 1862.
60. Alfred H. Guernsey and Henry M. Alden, *Harper's Pictorial History of the Civil War* (New York: The Fairfax Press, 1866), 380; Sears, *To the Gates of Richmond*, 351–354; Catton, *Mr. Lincoln's Army*, 155–156.
61. Gurensey and Alden, *Harper's Pictorial History of the Civil War*, 380; *Official Records*, vol. XI, part 2, 74; Chester K. Leach letters; Zeller, *The Second Vermont*, 90.
62. Gurensey and Alden, *Harper's Pictorial History of the Civil War*, 380; *Official Records*, vol. XI, part 2, 74; Zeller, *The Second Vermont*, 90.
63. *Montpelier (Vt.) Watchman and State Journal*, August 8, 1862.
64. Catton, *Mr. Lincoln's Army*, 28; Sears, *To the Gates of Richmond*, 349–350; Boatner, *The Civil War Dictionary*, 101, 658–659; Johnson and Buel, *Battles and Leaders*, vol. 2, 458.
65. Sears, *To the Gates of Richmond*, 349–350; Boatner, *The Civil War Dictionary*, 108; Douglas S. Freeman, *R.E. Lee: A Biography* (New York: Charles Scribner's Sons, 1936), vol. 2, 257–258.
66. Boatner, *The Civil War Dictionary*, 102; Johnson

and Buel, *Battles and Leaders*, vol. 2, 459; Freeman, *R.E. Lee*, vol. 2, 261–266, 271–272; Sears, *To the Gates of Richmond*, p. 350.

67. Sears, *To the Gates of Richmond*, 354–355; *Official Records*, vol. XI, part 2, 77–78; Gurensey and Alden, *Harper's Pictorial History of the Civil War*, 380; Catton, *Mr. Lincoln's Army*, 156.

68. Benedict, *Vermont in the Civil War*, 312; Chester K. Leach letters; Zeller, *The Second Vermont*, 91.

69. Ibid.

70. Ibid.

71. Benedict, *Vermont in the Civil War*, 313.

72. Ibid., 617.

Chapter 6

1. Benedict, *Vermont in the Civil War*, 332–333, 236, 329; Warner, *Generals in Blue*, 47; Alabama, County Marriages, 1809–1950, index and images, *FamilySearch* (https://familysearch.org/pal:/MM9.1.1/VZVZ-S3Z, accessed 29 May 2014), J Murray Robertson and Alma D Brooks, 29 Dec 1874; *Montgomery (Ala.) Advertiser*, September 5, 1921; http://genforum.genealogy.com/al/madison/messages/1221.html; http://genforum.genealogy.com/buell/messages/729.html; William T.H. Brooks papers, U.S. Army Heritage and Education Center, U.S. Army War College, Carlisle, Penn.

2. Peck, *Revised Roster*, 34; http://vermontcivilwar.org/index.php; Daniel F. Cooledge's compiled military service and government disability pension records; Cooledge Diary; U.S. Adjutant General's Office, *Correspondence Relating to the War with Spain and Conditions Growing Out of the Same, Including the Insurrection in the Philippine Islands and the China Relief Expedition, between the Adjutant-General of the Army and Military Commanders in the United States, Cuba, Porto Rico, China and the Philippines* (Washington: Government Printing Office, 1902), vol. 2, 1196; *St. Albans Daily Messenger*, October 3, 1900; General Alumni Society, *General Alumni Catalog, Medical Alumni, 1833–1907* (New York: Published by the General Alumni Society, 1908), 119; *Vermont (Ludlow) Tribune*, November 3, 1899; John N. Harris, *History of Ludlow Vermont* (Charlestown, N.H.: Mrs. Ina Harris Harding and Mr. Archie Frank Harding, Publishers, 1949), 108, 157, 158; *The Semi-Centennial Celebration of Black River Academy Ludlow, Vermont, August 25 and 26, 1885* (Ludlow, Vt.: Warner & Hyde, Steam Book and Job Printers, 1885), 21–22.

3. Peck, *Revised Roster*, 47; http://vermontcivilwar.org/get.php?input=2501; http://trees.ancestry.com/tree/60030596/person/42053085951; http://www.findagrave.com/cgi-bin/fg.cgi?page=gr&GSln=goodwin&GSfn=henry&GSmn=k.&GSbyrel=all&GSdy=1920&GSdyrel=in&GSst=6&GScntry=4&GSob=n&GRid=3711943&df=all&; James M.W. Yerrinton, *The Official Report of the Trial of Henry K. Goodwin for the Murder of Albert D. Swan in the Supreme Judicial Court of Massachusetts, Published by the Attorney General, Under Chapter 214 of Acts 1886* (Boston: Wright & Potter Printing Co., State Printers, 1887), 223–234; Harvey K. Goodwin's compiled military service record; Sarah J. Goodwin's veteran's widow's pension record; Letter, Harvey K. Goodwin to George Cowdery, August 11, 1861, Tunbridge, Vt., Historical Society; Information supplied by Euclid D. Farnham, Tunbridge, Vt.; *Boston (Mass.) Herald*, November 28, 1903; *Springfield (Mass.) Republican*, May 18, 1905; Henry K. Goodwin's compiled military service and government disability pension records.

4. Peck, *Revised Roster*, 52; http://vermontcivilwar.org/get.php?input=30047; Harlan P. Stoddard's compiled military service and government disability pension records; Matt Bushnell Jones, *History of the Town of Waitsfield, Vermont, 1782-1908* (Boston: George E. Littlefield, 1909), 19, 47, 474–475; U.S. Surgeon General's Office, *The Medical and Surgical History*, part II, vol. II, chapter 7, Sec. 2, 309; Robert W. Waitt, *Confederate Military Hospitals in Richmond* (Richmond, Va.: Richmond Civil War Centennial Committee, 1864), 11.

5. Peck, *Revised Roster*, 73, 80, 735; http://vermontcivilwar.org/get.php?input=606; George W. Bonett's compiled military service and government disability pension records; Nancy J. Bonett's veteran's widow's pension records; http://trees.ancestry.com/tree/17328413/person/28039718104; *St. Albans (Vt.) Daily Messenger*, January 22, 1908; William H. Jeffery, *Successful Vermonters; a modern gazetteer of Caledonia, Essex, and Orleans counties, containing an historical review of the several towns and a series of biographical sketches* (East Burke, Vt.: The Historical Publishing Company, 1904), 74, 75; *Caledonian (St. Johnsbury, Vt.)*, September 8, 1865.

6. Peck, *Revised Roster*, 74; email, Robin Van Mechelen to Paul G. Zeller, December 17, 2012; Letter, Robin Van Mechelen to Paul G. Zeller, January 1, 2013; email, Robin Van Mechelen to Paul G. Zeller, December 9, 2013; *Vermont Journal (Windsor, Vt.)*, June 1, 1855; John Carmody's compiled military service and government disability pension records; Windsor County, Vermont Court Records from Docket Book: Civil Case: Mary C. Carmody vs. John Carmody Docket Book May 1872; *New Hampshire Patriot and State Gazette (Concord, N.H.)*, December 31, 1885; http://www.findagrave.com/cgi-bin/fg.cgi?page=gr&GRid=113457026&ref=acom.

7. Peck, *Revised Roster*, 113, 588; http://www.vermontcivilwar.org/get.php?input=21619; James Laden's compiled military service and government disability pension records; http://www.findagrave.com/cgi-bin/fg.cgi?page=gr&GSln=Laden&GSfn=james&GSbyrel=all&GSdy=1919&GSdyrel=in&GSst=44&GScntry=4&GSob=n&GRid=24843321&df=all&; "South Dakota, State Census, 1915," index and images, *FamilySearch* (https://familysearch.org/pal:/MM9.1.1/MMH6-L46, accessed 08 Jul 2014), James E. Laden, South Dakota, United States; citing p. 143, State Historical Society, Pierre; FHL microfilm 2283560; 1917 South Dakota Census, http://interactive.ancestry.com/1059/M595_433-0299/4042931?backurl=http%3a%2f%2fsearch.ancestry.com%2fcgi-bin%2fsse.dll%3fgst%3d-6&ssrc=&backlabel=ReturnSearchResults.

8. Peck, *Revised Roster*, 118; George W. Gibson's compiled military service and government disability pension records; Elizabeth S. Gibson's veteran's widow's pension record; U.S. Surgeon General's office, *The Medical and Surgical History*, part 1, vol. 2, Chap. 2, sec. 2, 365; *Springfield (Mass.) Republican*, April 9, 1909; http://trees.ancestry.com/tree/34360143/person/19474271985; Edward O. Lord, ed., *History of the Ninth Regiment New Hampshire Volunteers in the War of the Rebellion* (Concord, N.H.: The Republican Press Association, 1895), 626–627, appendix 131; James L. Bowen, *History of the Thirty-Seventh Regiment Massachusetts. Volunteers in the Civil War of 1861–1865, with a comprehensive sketch of the doings of Massachusetts as a state, and of the principal campaigns of the war.* (Holyoke, Mass.: Clark W. Bryan & Company, Publishers, 1884), appendix IX; "Massachusetts, Deaths, 1841–1915," index and images, *FamilySearch* (https://familysearch.org/pal:/MM9.1.1/N4HB-G5G, accessed 02 Nov 2014), Elizabeth S Gibson, 28 Mar 1915; citing Tyringham, Massachusetts, 223, State Archives, Boston; FHL microfilm 2407887.

9. Peck, *Revised Roster*, 157; http://vermontcivilwar.org/get.php?input=9084; *St. Albans (Vt.) Daily Messenger*, November 12, 1900; John P. Bedell's compiled military service and government disability pension records; "Vermont,

Vital Records, 1760–1954," index and images, *FamilySearch* (https://familysearch.org/pal:/MM9.1.1/XFK5-D8C, accessed 02 Nov 2014), John P. Bedell, 28 Jul 1916, Death; citing State Capitol Building, Montpelier; FHL microfilm 1983310; *The Burlington Weekly Free Press*, August 3, 1916; http://www.findagrave.com/cgi-bin/fg.cgi?page=gr&GRid=114782291&ref=acom.

10. Peck, *Revised Roster*, 160, 361; Knight, *No Braver Deeds*, 31, 161, 194, 213; http://vermontcivilwar.org/get.php?input=13139; *The (Montpelier) Vermont Watchman and State Journal,* August 1, 1862; Henry A. Cummings' compiled military service and government disability pension records; "Vermont, Vital Records, 1760–2003," index and images, *FamilySearch* (https://familysearch.org/pal:/MM9.1.1/KFTB-TYD, accessed 10 Jun 2014), Mary Jane Cummings, Death, 14 Oct 1925, Bennington, Bennington, Vermont, United States; derived from Vermont birth, marriage, and death indexes and images, 1909–2008; http://vermontcivilwar.org/get.php?input=13143; Hiram P. Cummings' compiled military service record; Edmund M. Cummings's compiled military service record; Melissa J. Cumming's veteran's widow's pension record; "Vermont, Vital Records, 1760–1954," index and images, *FamilySearch* (https://familysearch.org/pal:/MM9.1.1/XFSM-62R, accessed 12 Jun 2014), Melissa Cummings, 30 May 1891, Death; citing State Capitol Building, Montpelier; FHL microfilm 540076; Caroline J. Cummings' veteran's widow's pension record; "Vermont, Vital Records, 1760–1954," index and images, *FamilySearch* (https://familysearch.org/pal:/MM9.1.1/XFJN-72H, accessed 10 Jun 2014), William Cummings and Caroline Johnson, 14 May 1861, Marriage; citing State Capitol Building, Montpelier; FHL microfilm 27522; "Vermont, Vital Records, 1760–1954," index and images, *FamilySearch* (https://familysearch.org/pal:/MM9.1.1/XFV2-SXR, accessed 10 Jun 2014), Wm Cummings and Caroline Johnson, 14 May 1861, Marriage; citing State Capitol Building, Montpelier; FHL microfilm 0027597; "Vermont, Vital Records, 1760–1954," index and images, *FamilySearch* (https://familysearch.org/pal:/MM9.1.1/XF3L-THQ, accessed 10 Jun 2014), Caroline Johnson Johnson, 26 Feb 1882, Death; citing State Capitol Building, Montpelier; FHL microfilm 540106; "Vermont, Vital Records, 1760–1954," index and images, *FamilySearch* (https://familysearch.org/pal:/MM9.1.1/XF8D-H9Z, accessed 12 Jun 2014), Amos Johnson and Caroline Johnson Cummings, 17 Sep 1874, Marriage; citing State Capitol Building, Montpelier; FHL microfilm 540106; *(Bennington) Vermont Gazette*, April 25, 1874; http://vermontcivilwar.org/get.php?input=13155; Silas A. Cummings' compiled military service record; http://vermontcivilwar.org/get.php?input=13160; *The Vermont (Montpelier) Watchman and State Journal,* August1, 1862; William H.H. Cummings compiled military service record.

11. Peck, *Revised Roster*, 157, 582; Ellery Bicknell Crane, *Historic Homes and Institutions and Genealogical and Personal Memoirs of Worcester County Massachusetts* (New York: The Lewis Publishing Co. 1907), 217; Jason O. French's compiled military service and government pension records; The Old Brigade Grand Army of the Republic Post 47, Johnson, Vt., Memorial Book; http://vermontcivilwar.org/index.php; U.S. Surgeon General's Office, *The Medical and Surgical History*, part 2, vol. 2, Chap. 6, sec. 3, 144; http://trees.ancestry.com/tree/412837/person/6014341748. Given in moderate doses tincture of the sesquichloride of iron acts as a tonic and astringent upon the alimentary canal, increasing appetite, promoting digestion and causing constipation of the bowels.

12. Peck, *Revised Roster*, 155, 174, http://vermontcivilwar.org/get.php?input=20752; Robert Johnson's compiled military service record; U.S. Surgeon General's office, *The Medical and Surgical History*, part 2, vol. 2, Chap. 9, sec. 4, 756; *The Vermont (Montpelier) Watchman and State Journal,* August 1, 1862; "New Hampshire, Death Records, 1654–1947," index and images, *FamilySearch* (https://familysearch.org/pal:/MM9.1.1/FS2X-VQ7, accessed 09 Jul 2014), Robert Johnson, 25 Mar 1891; citing Boscawen, Bureau Vital Records and Health Statistics, Concord; FHL microfilm 1001087; "United States Census, 1870," index and images, *FamilySearch* (https://familysearch.org/pal:/MM9.1.1/M6RW-X9X, accessed 16 Jul 2014), Robert Johnson, Vermont, United States; citing p. 36, family 268, NARA microfilm publication M593, FHL microfilm 000553119; "Vermont, Vital Records, 1760–1954," index and images, *FamilySearch* (https://familysearch.org/pal:/MM9.1.1/2VQC-VKZ, accessed 16 Jul 2014), Mary Ann Mcglynn, 20 Jun 1923, Death; citing State Capitol Building, Montpelier; FHL microfilm 002050384; Boatner, *The Civil War Dictionary*, 74–75, 172; Catton, *Reflections on the Civil War* (New York: Promontory Press, 1998), 56–58.

13. Peck, *Revised Roster*, 158; http://vermontcivilwar.org/get.php?input=22917; Edward H. Marcy's compiled military service record; Vilana Marcy's government dependent mother's pension record; Ephraim B. Marcy's compiled military service and government disability pension records; "Montana, Death Index, 1860–2007," index, *FamilySearch* (https://familysearch.org/pal:/MM9.1.1/VHC5-5RS, accessed 21 Jul 2014), Ephriam Marcy, 25 Sep 1916; citing "Montana Death Index, 1907–2007," Ancestrywww; "Vermont, Vital Records, 1760–1954," index and images, *FamilySearch* (https://familysearch.org/pal:/MM9.1.1/XFK3-CBX, accessed 21 Jul 2014), Ephraim Marcy and Abby Mason, 25 Aug 1860, Marriage; citing State Capitol Building, Montpelier; FHL microfilm 0027621; "Vermont, Vital Records, 1760–1954," index and images, *FamilySearch* (https://familysearch.org/pal:/MM9.1.1/XFXY-MSZ, accessed 21 Jul 2014), Abby M. Marcy, 04 Apr 1906, Death; citing State Capitol Building, Montpelier; FHL microfilm 540117; http://www.findagrave.com/cgi-bin/fg.cgi?page=gr&GSln=marcy&GSfn=abby&GSbyrel=all&GSdy=1906&GSdyrel=in&GSst=49&GScntry=4&GSob=n&GRid=102299520&df=all&; "United States Veterans Administration Pension Payment Cards, 1907–1933," index and images, *FamilySearch* (https://familysearch.org/pal:/MM9.1.1/2M2Z-G4W, accessed 22 Jul 2014), Ephraim B Marcy, 1907–1933; Ephraim B. Marcy's death certificate, Flathead County, Mont., vital records.

14. Peck, *Revised Roster*, 145; http://vermontcivilwar.org/get.php?input=5127; Lizzie B. Pierson, comp., *Pierson Genealogical Records* (Albany, N.Y.: Joel Munsell, Printer, 1878), 79–80; William P. Russell's compiled military service and government disability pension records; Lydia Russell's veteran's widow's pension record; "Vermont, Vital Records, 1760–1954," index and images, *FamilySearch* (https://familysearch.org/pal:/MM9.1.1/XFQX-B9G, accessed 22 Aug 2014), William P Russel, 04 Jun 1872, Death; citing State Capitol Building, Montpelier; FHL microfilm 540140; *St. Albans (Vt.) Messenger*, April 16, 1891; Hinckley and Ledoux, *They Went to War*, 195; Benedict, *Vermont in the Civil War*, 303.

15. Peck, *Revised Roster*, 169; http://vermontcivilwar.org/index.php; http://trees.ancestry.com/tree/44089974/person/26023582132; familysearch.org; http://trees.ancestry.com/tree/38555353/person/20058967375; "Vermont Vital Records, 1760–1954," database with images, *FamilySearch* (https://familysearch.org/ark:/61903/1:1:V89S-8ZC, 5 November 2017), Moses Stedman, 05 Apr 1857, Death; State Capitol Building, Montpelier; FHL microfilm 27,697; Jonathan Stedman's compiled military service record; Francis C. Stedman's compiled military service and government disability pension records; Henrietta Stedman's veteran's widow's pension record; "Vermont, Vital Records, 1760–1954," index and images, *FamilySearch*

(https://familysearch.org/pal:/MM9.1.1/2V7C-5Q7, accessed 9 December 2014), Henretta Angelia Tabor Stedman, 02 Jan 1936, Death; State Capitol Building, Montpelier; FHL microfilm 2,051,773; Irvin W. Stedman's compiled military service and government disability pension records; "Vermont Vital Records, 1760–1954," database with images, *FamilySearch* (https://familysearch.org/ark:/61903/1:1:2V7C-53B, 6 December 2014), Francis Cullen Stedman, 08 Oct 1917, Death; State Capitol Building, Montpelier; FHL microfilm 2,051,773 "Find a Grave Index," index, *FamilySearch* (https://familysearch.org/pal:/MM9.1.1/QVK5-BRVQ, accessed 9 December 2014), Miamma L Fuller Stedman, 1919; Burial, Orwell, Addison, Vermont, United States of America, Mountain View Cemetery; citing record ID 46616362; "United States Veterans Administration Pension Payment Cards, 1907–1933," index and images, *FamilySearch* (https://familysearch.org/pal:/MM9.1.1/QJD3-P1BX, accessed 9 December 2014), Irwin W Stedman, 1907–1933; "Vermont Vital Records, 1760–1954," database with images, *FamilySearch* (https://familysearch.org/ark:/61903/1:1:XF7Y-D7C, 3 November 2017), Jonathan Stedman, 22 Jul 1881, Death; State Capitol Building, Montpelier; FHL microfilm 540,148; "Vermont Vital Records, 1760–1954," database with images, *FamilySearch* (https://familysearch.org/ark:/61903/1:1:XF7Y-D7V, 3 November 2017), Mary Wisell Stedman, 06 Apr 1898, Death; State Capitol Building, Montpelier; FHL microfilm 540,148.

16. Peck, *Revised Roster*, 153; http://vermontcivilwar.org/get.php?input=30788; Noah C. Thompson's compiled military service and government disability pension records; David R. Thompson's compiled military service and government disability pension records; Zeller, *The Second Vermont*, 188–190; *St. Albans (Vt.) Daily Messenger*, April 17 and 21, 1871, December 21, 1871, July 21, 1876; *Caledonian (St. Johnsbury, Vt.)*, April 21, 1871; State of Vermont, *Journal of the House of Representatives of the State of Vermont, Biennial Session, 1878* (Rutland: Tuttle & Co., Official Printers and Stationers of the State of Vermont, 1879), 394; *Argus and Patriot (Montpelier, Vt.)*, August 16, 1876; "Wisconsin, Marriages, 1836–1930," index, *FamilySearch* (https://familysearch.org/pal:/MM9.1.1/XRGJ-VV9, accessed 02 Aug 2014), David Russel Thompson and Alma Jane Heath, 22 May 1886; citing reference cn 00289; FHL microfilm 1276058; "Wisconsin, Births and Christenings, 1826–1926," index, *FamilySearch* (https://familysearch.org/pal:/MM9.1.1/XR8Y-517, accessed 02 Aug 2014), Elma J. Heath in entry for Thompson, 12 Mar 1887; citing La Crosse, Wisconsin, reference 300 664; FHL microfilm 1302882.

17. Peck, *Revised Roster*, 153; http://vermontcivilwar.org/get.php?input=30788; ancestry.com; familysearch.org; fold3.com; Noah C. Thompson's compiled military service and government disability pension records; David R. Thompson's compiled military service and government disability pension records; Zeller, *Second Vermont*, 188–190; *St. Albans (Vt.) Daily Messenger*, April 17 and 21, 1871, December 21, 1871, July 21, 1876; *Caledonian (St. Johnsbury, Vt.)*, April 21, 1871; State of Vermont, *Journal of the House of Representatives of the State of Vermont, Biennial Session, 1878* (Rutland: Tuttle & Co., Official Printers and Stationers of the State of Vermont, 1879), p. 394; *Argus and Patriot (Montpelier, Vt.)*, August 16, 1876; "Wisconsin, Marriages, 1836–1930," index, *FamilySearch* (https://familysearch.org/pal:/MM9.1.1/XRGJ-VV9, accessed 02 Aug 2014), David Russel Thompson and Alma Jane Heath, 22 May 1886; citing reference cn 00289; FHL microfilm 1276058; "Wisconsin, Births and Christenings, 1826–1926," index, *FamilySearch* (https://familysearch.org/pal:/MM9.1.1/XR8Y-517, accessed 02 Aug 2014), Elma J. Heath in entry for Thompson, 12 Mar 1887; citing La Crosse, Wisconsin, reference 300 664; FHL microfilm 1302882.

18. Peck, *Revised Roster*, 23, 150, 152; http://www.vermontcivilwar.org/get.php?input=6602; Wilson D. Wright's compiled military service and government disability pension records; Benedict, *Vermont in the Civil War*, 17, 37–54; http://interactive.ancestry.com/5187/41547_B138961-00837/1168629?backurl=&ssrc=&backlabel=Return; http://www.findagrave.com/cgi-bin/fg.cgi?page=gr&GSln=wright&GSfn=wilson&GSmn=d.&GSbyrel=all&GSdy=1932&GSdyrel=in&GSst=6&GScntry=4&GSob=n&GRid=3766552&df=all&.

19. Peck, *Revised Roster*, 187; http://vermontcivilwar.org/index.php; *(St. Johnsbury, Vt.) Caledonian-Record* 22 April, 1914; familysearch.org; William H. Jeffrey, *Successful Vermonters; a Modern Gazetteer of Caledonia, Essex, and Orleans Counties, Containing an Historical Review of the Several Towns and a Series of Biographical Sketches* (East Burke, Vt.: The Historical Publishing Company, 1904), 333–335; Some of the Recollections of S.N. Eastman, M.D; Seth N. Eastman's compiled military service and government disability pension records; Groton Historical Society, *Mr. Glover's Groton, the Chronicle of Groton, Vermont 1789–1978* (Canaan, N.H: Phoenix Publishing, 1878), 212; "Vermont, Vital Records, 1760–1954," index and images, *FamilySearch* (https://familysearch.org/pal:/MM9.1.1/XF44-22G, accessed 20 December 2014), Evalona Eastman, 16 Jun 1903, Death; State Capitol Building, Montpelier; FHL microfilm 540,086; "Vermont, Vital Records, 1760–1954," index and images, *FamilySearch* (https://familysearch.org/pal:/MM9.1.1/VNRW-K9N, accessed 20 December 2014), Seth N Eastman, 13 Apr 1914, Death; State Capitol Building, Montpelier; FHL microfilm 1,991,507; *The (Montpelier) Vermont Watchman*, June 26, 1901.

20. Peck, *Revised Roster*, 212, http://www.vermontcivilwar.org/get.php?input=28384; 580; Works Progress Administration Vermont veterans' gravestone inscriptions card file; John Scott's compiled military service and government disability pension records; "Vermont, Vital Records, 1760–1954," index and images, *FamilySearch* (https://familysearch.org/pal:/MM9.1.1/XF43-9F2, accessed 16 Aug 2014), John Scott, 27 Jan 1904, Death; citing State Capitol Building, Montpelier; FHL microfilm 540142; *St. Albans (Vt.) Messenger*, November 6, 1900 and February 4, 1904; "Vermont, Probate Files, 1800–1921," index and images, *FamilySearch* (https://familysearch.org/pal:/MM9.1.1/N39J-SMK, accessed 17 Aug 2014), Lydia Scott, 1901; citing Chittenden County, volume Box 37 File 6231; FHL microfilm 4208253; "Vermont, Probate Files, 1800–1921," index and images, *FamilySearch* (https://familysearch.org/pal:/MM9.1.1/N39J-W6R, accessed 17 Aug 2014), John Sr. Scott, 1904; citing Chittenden County, volume Box 40 File 6810; FHL microfilm 4208423; http://vermontcivilwar.org/cem/virtual/getoscem.php?input=28385; Jonathan S. Scott's compiled military service record; "Illinois, Cook County Deaths, 1878–1922, 1959–1994," index, *FamilySearch* (https://familysearch.org/pal:/MM9.1.1/N76L-8TY, accessed 18 Aug 2014), Johnathan S. Scott, 1914; Illinois Deaths and Stillbirths, 1916–1947," index, *FamilySearch* (https://familysearch.org/pal:/MM9.1.1/N3HH-KX2, accessed 18 Aug 2014), Eliza Scott, 09 Aug 1930; citing Public Board of Health, Archives, Springfield; FHL microfilm 1892493; http://www.findagrave.com/cgi-bin/fg.cgi?page=gr&GSln=scott&GSfn=eliza&GSmn=a.&GSbyrel=all&GSdy=1930&GSdyrel=in&GSst=51&GScntry=4&GSob=n&GRid=66274183&df=all&.

Bibliography

Published Primary Sources

Adams, John G.B. *Reminiscences of the Nineteenth Massachusetts Regiment.* Boston: Wright and Potter Printing Company, 1899.

Adjutant General's Office. *Correspondence Relating to the War with Spain and Conditions Growing Out of the Same, Including the Insurrection in the Philippine Islands and the China Relief Expedition, Between the Adjutant-General of the Army and Military Commanders in the United States, Cuba, Porto Rico, China and the Philippines,* 2 vols. Washington: Government Printing Office, 1902.

Andrews, William H. *Footprints of a Regiment: A Recollection of the 1st Georgia Regulars 1861–1865, annotated and with an introduction by Richard M. McMurray.* Atlanta, Ga.: Longstreet Press, 1992.

Ayling, Augustus D. *Revised Roster of Soldiers and Sailors of New Hampshire in the War of the Rebellion.* Concord, N.H.: I.C. Evans, Public Printer, 1895.

Bidwell, Frederick D. *History of the Forty-Ninth New York Volunteers.* Albany, N.Y.: J.B. Lyon Company, Printers, 1916.

Bowen, James L. *History of the Thirty-Seventh Regiment Massachusetts. Volunteers in the Civil War of 1861–1865, with a comprehensive sketch of the doings of Massachusetts as a state, and of the principal campaigns of the war.* Holyoke, Mass. and New York City: Clark W. Bryan & Company, Publishers, 1884.

Castleman, Alfred L. *The Army of the Potomac. Behind the Scenes. A Diary of Unwritten History; from the Organization of the Army to the Close of the Campaign in Virginia, about the first day of January, 1863.* Milwaukee, Wis.: Strickland & Co., 1863.

Catalogue of the Officers and Students of the Brandon Seminary, Brandon, Vt., 1860. Brandon, Vt.: Printed at the Northern Visitor Office, 1860.

Daughters of the American Revolution. *Linage Book National Society of the Daughters of the American Revolution,* vol. 41. Harrisburg, Penn.: Telegraph Printing Company, 1915.

Department of the Army. Department of the Army Pamphlet No. 20–211, *The Personnel Replacement System in the United States Army.* U.S. Government Printing Office, Washington, D.C., August 1954.

English Combatant. *Battle-Fields of the South, from Bull Run to Fredericksburg: with Sketches of Confederate Commanders, and Gossip of the Camps,* reprint, Time-Life Books, Inc., 1984.

General Alumni Catalog, Medical Alumni, 1833–1907. New York: Published by the General Alumni Society, 1908.

Hewett, Janet B., Bryce A. Suderow, and Noah Andre Trudeau, eds. *Supplement to the Official Records of the Union and Confederate Armies.* 80 vols. Wilmington, N.C.: Broadfoot Publishing Company, 1998.

Hyde, Thomas W. *Following the Greek Cross or Memories of the Sixth Army Corps.* Columbia: University of South Carolina Press, 2005. First published 1894 by Houghton Mifflin.

Judd, David W. *The Story of the Thirty-Third N.Y.S. Vols.* Rochester, N.Y.: Benton and Andrews, 1864.

Little, Henry F.W. *The Seventh Regiment New Hampshire Volunteers in the War of the Rebellion.* Concord, N.H.: Ira C. Evans, Printer, 1896.

Lord, Edward O., ed. *History of the Ninth Regiment New Hampshire Volunteers in the War of the Rebellion.* Concord, N.H: The Republican Press Association, 1895.

Marks, James J. *The Peninsular Campaign in Virginia; or, Incidents and Scenes on the Battle-fields and in Richmond.* Philadelphia, Penn.: J.B. Lippincott & Co., 1864.

McClellan, George B. *McClellan's Own Story: The war for the Union, the soldiers who fought it, the civilians who directed it and his relations to it and to them.* 2 parts. New York: Charles L. Webster & Co., 1887.

McDaniel, J.J. *Diary of Battles, Marches and Incidents of the Seventh S.C. Regiment.* n.p., 1862.

Newell, Joseph K. *"Ours," Annals of the Tenth Regiment: Massachusetts Volunteers in the Rebellion.* Springfield, Mass.: C.A. Nichols & Co., 1875.

O'Brien, Thomas M., and Oliver Diefendorf. *General Orders of the War Department, Embracing the Years 1861, 1862 & 1863.* 2 vols. New York: Derby & Miller, No. 5 Spruce Street, 1864.

Peck, Theodore S. *Revised Roster of Vermont Volunteers and Lists of Vermonters who Served in the Army and Navy of the United States During the War of the Rebellion, 1861–66.* Montpelier, Vt.: Watchman Co., 1892.

Porter, John W.H. *A Record of Events in Norfolk County, Virginia, from April 19th, 1861, to May 10th, 1862, with a History of the Soldiers and Sailors of Norfolk County, Norfolk City and Portsmouth, who Served in the Confederate States Army or Navy.* Portsmouth, Va.: W.A. Fiske, Printer and Bookbinder, 1892.

Stevens, George T. *Three Years in the Sixth Corps,* 2nd ed. New York: D. Van Nostrand, Publisher, 1870.

Swineburne, John. *Reports on the Peninsula Campaign, Surgical Experience, & etc.* Albany, N.Y.: Steam Press of C. Van Benthuysen, 1863.

U.S. Government. *Official Register of Officers and Agents, Civil, Military, and Naval, in the Service of the United States on the Thirtieth September, 1867.* Washington: Government Printing Office, 1868.

U.S. Government. *Official Register of Officers and Agents, Civil, Military, and Naval, in the Service of the United States on the Thirtieth September, 1873.* Washington: Government Printing Office, 1874.

U.S. Government. *Official Register of Officers and Agents, Civil, Military, and Naval, in the Service of the United States on the Thirtieth September, 1874.* Washington: Government Printing Office, 1875.

U.S. Surgeon General's Office. *The Medical and Surgical History of the War of the Rebellion 1861-65.* 6 vols. Washington, D.C.: Government Printing office, 1870-1888.

U.S. War Department. *Revised Regulations for the Army of the United States, 1861.* Reprint. Harrisburg, Penn.: National Historical Society, 1980.

U.S. War Department. *War of the Rebellion: A Compilation of the Official Records of the Union and Confederate Armies.* 128 vols. Washington: Government Printing Office, 1902.

Vermont Adjutant and Inspector General. *Adjutant and Inspector General's Office of the State of Vermont, from October 1, 1863, to October 1, 1864.* Montpelier, Vt.: Walton Steam Press, 1864.

Vermont General Assembly. *The Acts and Resolves Passed by the General Assembly of the State of Vermont at the October Session, 1861.* Montpelier, Vt.: E.P. Walton, Printer, 1861.

Vermont General Assembly. *Roster of Vermont Men and Women in the Military and Naval Service of the United States and Allies in the World War 1917-1919.* Montpelier, Vt.: The Tuttle Company, Marble City Press, Rutland, Vt., 1927.

War Department. *Instructions and Forms to be Observed in Applying for Army Pensions Under the Act of July 14, 1862.* Washington: Government Printing Office, 1862.

War Department. *Revised Regulations for the Army of the United States, 1861.* Philadelphia: J.G.L. Brown, Printer, 1861; reprint, Harrisburg: National Historical Society, 1980.

Webb, Alexander S. *The Peninsula—McClellan's Campaign of 1862.* New York: Scribner's, 1881.

Yerrinton, James M.W. *The Official Report of the Trial of Henry K. Goodwin for the Murder of Albert D. Swan in the Supreme Judicial Court of Massachusetts, Published by the Attorney General, Under Chapter 214 of Acts 1886.* Boston: Wright & Potter Printing Co., State Printers, 1887.

Manuscripts

University of Vermont Bailey/Howe Library Special Collections, Burlington, Vt.

Bush, Napoleon. Civil War letter, miscellaneous family papers.
Fitch, Jabez. Ftich Family Papers. John R. Lewis to Samuel Sumner, Sr., dated July 1862. mss-976.
Hapgood, Charles M. Diary.
Leach, Chester K. Civil War letters, mss-717.
Montague, Hollis. Civil War letters.
Paige, Harlan P. Papers.
Parker, Moses A. Civil War letter, Parker Family Papers, mss-137.
Quimby, George W. Correspondence, mss-791.
Randall, George H. Papers, mss-548.
Wilder, Henry Harrison. Henry Harrison Wilder Papers.

Vermont Historical Society, Barre, Vt.

Bancroft, Smiley. Papers, 1840-1885. Ms 53.
Brown, Elijah S. Letters of. Misc file.
Cooledge, Daniel F. Civil War Diary 1862. Msc 197.
Dubois, Charles B. Memoir of his Civil War Experiences, June 1861-July 1864. CD-ROM 920 D852m. Original in University of Vermont Bailey/Howe Library Special Collections.
Eastman, S.N., M.D. 1907, Some of the Recollections of. XMSC 21:13.
Henry, William Writ. Family papers, 1846-1915. Doc 527-528.
Johnson family of Newbury, Vt. Papers, 1775-1886. Doc 574-575.
Savage, Lucius D. A Diary with Recollections of Prison and Hospital. 920 Sa92.
Towle, Ransom W., and Thomas N. Flanders. 1861-1865, Civil War correspondence of. Misc 246.
Veazey, Wheelock Graves. Papers, 1853-1939. Doc 99-100.

Other Sources

Adams, Jesse. Civil War letter, Cavendish Historical Society, Cavendish, Vt.
Adams, Jesse. Letter, Cavendish Historical Society, Cavendish, Vt.
Dean, Casper Honorus. Letter, Vermont in the Civil War, http://vermontcivilwar.org/index.php.
Goodwin, Harvey K. Letter to George Cowdery, August 11, 1861, Tunbridge Historical Society, Tunbridge, Vt.
Hammond, Francis D. Family information courtesy of Charles F. and Marion M. Walter.
Morey, Charles C. U.S. Army Heritage and Education Center, U.S. Army War College, Carlisle, Penn.
Partlow, Seth. Letter dated July 4, 1862. Chimbarazo Medical Museum, Richmond Battlefield Park, Richmond, Va.
Pratt, Esther Livingston to Ellen Maria Doty Schermerhorn. Letter dated February 13, 1862, in the possession of Joseph L. Broom.
Rand, Kirk. Civil War letters, Papers of Sallie Joy White, 1828-1936, Schlesinger Library, Radcliffe College, Cambridge, Mass.
Young, Frank R. Diary, U.S. Army Heritage and Education Center, U.S. Army War College, Carlisle, Penn.

Secondary Sources

Andrus, Michael J. *The Brooke, Fauquier, Loudon and Alexandria Artillery.* Lynchburg, Va.: H.E. Howard, 1990.
Atwater, Isaac. *History of the City of Minneapolis, Minnesota.* New York: Munsell & Co., 1893.
Bailyn, Bernard. *The Barbarous Years: The Peopling of*

British North America: The Conflict of Civilizations, 1600–1675. New York: Vintage Books, 2013.

Balzer, John E., ed. *Buck's Book: A View of the 3rd Vermont Infantry Regiment.* Bolingbrook, Ill.: Balzer & Associates, 1993.

Batchelder, Ira K. *Reunion Celebration Together with an Historical Sketch of Peru, Bennington County, Vermont.* Brattleboro, Vt.: Phoenix Job Print, E.L. Hildreth & Co., 1891.

Benedict, George G. *Vermont in the Civil War.* 2 vols. Burlington, Vt.: The Free Press Association, 1886 and 1888.

Beyer, W.F., and O.F. Keydel, eds. *Deeds of Valor: How America's Heroes Won the Medal of Honor,* 2 vols. Detroit, Mich.: The Perrien-Keydel Company, 1903.

Biographical Sketch Book. James M. Warner Post No. 4, Grand Army of the Republic, Morristown Historical Society, Morristown, Vt.

Blight, David W., ed. *When This Cruel War Is Over: The Civil War Letters of Charles Harvey Brewster.* Amherst: University of Massachusetts Press, 1992.

Boatner, Mark M. *The Civil War Dictionary.* New York: Vintage Civil War Library, 1991.

_____. *Military Customs and Traditions.* Westport, Conn.: Greenwood Press, 1956; repr., New York: D. McKay Co., 1976.

Brent, Joseph L. *Mobilizable Fortifications, and Their Controlling Influence in War.* Boston and New York: Houghton, Mifflin and Company, 1885.

Bryan, Charles F., Jr., and Nelson D. Lankford, eds. *Eye of the Storm: a Civil War Odyssey: Written and Illustrated by Robert Knox Sneden.* New York: Free Press, 2000.

Burton, Brian K. *Extraordinary Circumstances: The Seven Days Battles.* Bloomington: Indiana University Press, 2001.

Cabot, Mary R. *Annals of Brattleboro Vermont, 1681–1895.* 2 vols. Brattleboro, Vt.: Press of E.L. Hildreth & Co., 1922.

Carleton, Hiram. *Genealogical and Family History of the State of Vermont.* New York and Chicago: The Lewis Publishing Co., 1903.

Casdorph, Paul D. *Prince John Magruder: His Life and Campaigns.* New York: John Wiley & Sons, Inc., 1996.

Catton, Bruce. *The Army of the Potomac: Mr. Lincoln's Army.* Garden City, N.Y.: Doubleday & Company, Inc., 1952.

_____. *Reflections on the Civil War.* New York: Promontory Press, 1998.

Childs, Hamilton, comp. *Gazetteer of Washington County, Vt., 1783–1889.* Syracuse, N.Y.: The Syracuse Journal Company, Printers and Binders, 1889.

Coffin, Howard. *Full Duty: Vermonters in the Civil War.* Woodstock, Vt.: The Countryman Press, 1993.

Crane, Ellery Bicknell. *Historic Homes and Institutions and Genealogical and Personal Memoirs of Worcester County Massachusetts.* New York: The Lewis Publishing Co. 1907.

Crockett, Walter H., ed. *Vermonters: A Book of Biographies.* Brattleboro, Vt.: Stephen Daye Press, 1903.

Dameron, David J. *Benning's Brigade,* 2 vols. Westminster, Md.: Heritage Books, 2004–2005.

Devine, Shauna. *Learning from the Wounded: The Civil War and the Rise of American Medical Science.* Chapel Hill: University of North Carolina Press, 2014.

Dickert, David Augustus. *A History of Kershaw's Brigade.* Newberry, S.C: E.H. Aull, 1899.

Dodge, Prentiss C., comp. *Encyclopedia Vermont Biography.* Burlington, Vt.: Ullery Publishing Company, 1912.

Dowdey, Clifford. *The Seven Days: The Emergence of Robert E. Lee.* New York: The Fairfax Press, 1978.

Driver, Robert J. *1st Virginia Cavalry.* Lynchburg, Va.: H.E. Howard, 1991.

Duffy, John J., Samuel B. Hand, and Ralph H. Orth, eds. *The Vermont Encyclopedia.* Hanover, N.H.: University Press of New England, 2003.

Edwards, William B. *Civil War Guns.* Harrisburg, Penn.: The Stackpole Company, 1962.

Ellis, William A., ed. *Norwich University, 1819–1911; Her History, Her Graduates, Her Roll of Honor, Published by Major-General Grenville M. Dodge, Compiled and Edited by William Arba Ellis in Three Volumes.* Montpelier, Vt.: The Capitol City Press, 1911.

Faust, Drew Gilpin. *This Republic of Suffering: Death and the American Civil War.* New York: Fred A. Knopf, 2008.

Freeman, Douglas Southall. *R.E. Lee: A Biography,* 4 vols. New York and London: Charles Scribner's Sons, 1936.

Gaff, Alan D. *On Many a Bloody Field: Four Years in the Iron Brigade.* Bloomington: Indiana University Press, 1996.

Grant, Ulysses S. *Personal Memoirs of Ulysses S. Grant.* New York: Charles L. Webster & Company, 1886. Reprinted by Konecky and Konecky, Old Say Brook, Conn., 1992. Page references are to the 1992 edition.

Gregory, John. *Northfield's First Century: Centennial Proceedings and Historical Incidents of the Early Settlers of Northfield, Vt., with Biographical Sketches of Prominent Businessmen Who Have Been and Are Now Residents of the Town.* Argus and Patriot Book and Job Printing House, Montpelier, Vt., 1878.

Groton Historical Society. *Mr. Glover's Groton, the Chronicle of Groton, Vermont 1789–1978.* Canaan, N.H.: Phoenix Publishing, 1978.

Guernsey, Alfred H., and Henry M. Alden. *Harper's Pictorial History of the Civil War.* New York: The Fairfax Press, 1866.

Hagemann, James. *The Heritage of Virginia: The Story of Place Names in the Old Dominion.* West Chester, Pa.: Whitford Press, 1988.

Harris, John N. *History of Ludlow Vermont.* Charlestown, N.H.: Mrs. Ina Harris Harding and Mr. Archie Frank Harding, Publishers, 1949.

Harris, Malcolm Hart, comp. *Old New Kent County: Some Account of the Planters, Plantations and Places in New Kent County,* 2 vols. Baltimore, Md.: Clearfield, Co., 2006. First published in West Point, Va.: n. p., 1977.

Hastings, Earl C., and David Hastings. *A Pitiless Rain: The Battle of Williamsburg, 1862.* Shippensburg, Penn.: White Mane Publishing Company, 1997.

Heller, Charles E., and William A. Stofft. *America's First Battles, 1776–1965.* Lawrence: University Press of Kansas, 1986.

Hemenway, Abby Maria. *The Vermont Historical Gazetteer: A Magazine, Embracing a History of Each Town, Civil, Ecclesiastical, Biographical and Military.* 5 vols. Burlington, Vt.: Tuttle Co., 1923.

Hinckley, Erik S., and Tom Ledoux, comp. and ed. *They Went to War: A Biographical Register of the Green Mountain State in the Civil War.* Bloomington, Ind.: Trafford Publishing, 2010.

Jensen, Les. *32nd Virginia Infantry.* Lynchburg, Va.: H.E. Howard, 1990.

Johnson, Robert U., and Clarence C. Buel, eds. *Battles and Leaders of the Civil War. Being for the most part contributions by Union and Confederate officers.* 4 vols. New York: Century Co., 1887–1888.

Jones, Matt Bushnell. *History of the Town of Waitsfield, Vermont, 1782–1908.* Boston: George E. Littlefield, 1909.

Kennedy, Frances H., ed. *The Civil War Battlefield Guide.* Boston: Houghton Mifflin Company, 1990.

Keyes, Erasmus D. *Fifty Years Observation of Men and Events—Civil and Military.* New York: Charles Scribner's Sons, 1885.

Knight, Brian L. *No Braver Deeds: The Story of the Equinox Guards.* Manchester, Vt.: Friends of Hildene, Inc., 2004.

Lord, Francis A. *Civil War Collector's Encyclopedia.* New York: Castle Books, 1965.

Maharay, George S. *Vermont Hero: Major General Lewis A. Grant.* New York and London: iUniverse, Inc., 2006.

Manarin, Louis H. *Henrico County—Field of Honor,* 2 vols. Richmond, Va.: Printed by the Carter Printing Company, 2004.

Manarin, Louis H., and Charles H. Peple. *The History of Henrico County.* The County of Henrico, Virginia, 2011.

McKee, W. Reid, and M.E. Mason, Jr. *Civil War Projectiles II: Small Arms & Field Artillery.* n. p., 1975.

McWhitney, Grady, and Perry D. Jamieson. *Attack and Die: Civil War Military Tactics and the Southern Heritage.* Tuscaloosa: University of Alabama Press, 1982.

Melville, Dorothy Sutherland. *Tyler-Browns of Brattleboro.* Jericho, N.Y.: Exposition Press, Inc., 1973.

Miller, Henry W. *Railway Artillery; A Report on the Characteristics, Scope of Utility, etc., of Railway Artillery, in two vols.* Washington, D.C.: Government Printing Office, 1921–1922.

Peterson, Harold L., ed. *Encyclopedia of Firearms.* New York: E.P. Dutton and Company, Inc., 1964.

Pierson, Lizzie B., comp. *Pierson Genealogical Records.* Albany, N.Y.: Joel Munsell, Printer, 1878.

Poirier, Robert G. *They Could Not Have Done Better: Thomas O. Seaver and the 3rd Vermont Infantry in the War for the Union.* Newport, Vt.: Vermont Civil War Enterprises, 2005.

Pride, Mike, and Mark Travis. *My Brave Boys: To War with Colonel Cross and the Fighting Fifth.* Hanover, N.H.: University Press of New England, 2001.

Priest, John Michael, editor-in-chief. *One Surgeon's Private War: Doctor William Potter of the 57th New York.* Shippensburg, Penn.: White Mane Publishing Company, Inc., 1996.

Quarstein, John V. *The Battle of the Ironclads.* Charleston, S.C.: Arcadia Publishing, 2005.

_____. *Big Bethel: The First Battle.* Charleston, S.C.: The History Press, 2011.

_____. *Hampton and Newport News in the Civil War: War Comes to the Peninsula.* Lynchburg, Va.: H.E. Howard, Inc., 1998.

Rafuse, Ethan S. *McClellan's War: The Failure of Moderation in the Struggle for the Union.* Bloomington: Indiana University Press, 2005.

Rhodes, Robert H. *All for the Union: A Historical Record of the 2nd Rhode Island Volunteer Infantry in the War of the Great Rebellion as Told by the Diary of Elisha Hunt Rhodes.* New York: Orion Books, 1991.

Rosenblatt, Emil, and Ruth Rosenblatt, eds., *Hard Marching Every Day: The Civil War Letters of Private Wilbur Fisk, 1861–1865.* Lawrence: University Press of Kansas, 1992.

Schiller, Herbert M., ed. *Autobiography of Major General William F. Smith, 1861–1864.* Dayton, Ohio: Morningside House, Inc., 1990.

Sears, Stephen W. *To the Gates of Richmond: The Peninsula Campaign.* New York: Ticknor & Fields, 1992.

The Semi-Centennial Celebration of Black River Academy Ludlow, Vermont, August 25 and 26, 1885. Ludlow, Vt.: Warner & Hyde, Steam Book and Job Printers, 1885.

Slattery, Charles Lewis. *Felix Reville Brunot, 1820–1898, A Civilian in the War for the Union, President of the First Board of Indian Commissioners.* New York and London: Longmans, Green, Co., 1901.

Stevens, Hazzard. *The Life of Isaac Ingalls Stevens,* 2 vols. Boston: Houghton, Mifflin, 1900.

Titterson, Robert J. *Julian Scott: Artist of the Civil War and Native America.* Jefferson, N.C.: McFarland, 1997.

Tunnell, Ted, ed. *Carpetbagger from Vermont: The Autobiography of Marshall Harvey Twitchell.* Baton Rouge: Louisiana State University Press, 1989.

Tyler, D. Gardiner. *A History Pictorial Review of Charles City County, Virginia.* Expert Graphics, 1990.

Ullery, Jacob G., comp. *Men of Vermont: An Illustrated Biographical History of Vermonters and Sons of Vermont.* Brattleboro, Vt.: Transcript Publishing Company, 1894.

Waitt, Robert W. *Confederate Military Hospitals in Richmond.* Richmond, Va.: Richmond Civil War Centennial Committee, 1964.

Warner, Ezra J. *Generals in Blue: Lives of the Union Commanders.* Baton Rouge: Louisiana State University Press, 1988.

_____. *Generals in Grey: Lives of the Confederate Commanders.* Baton Rouge: Louisiana State University Press, 1959.

Welcher, Frank J. *The Union Army, 1861–1865: Organization and Operations, Volume 1: The Eastern Theater.* 2 vols. Bloomington: Indiana University Press, 1989.

Wert, Jeffery D. *General James Longstreet: The Confederacy's Most Controversial Soldier—A Biography.* New York: Simon & Shuster, 1994.

Wheeler, Richard. *Sword Over Richmond.* New York: Harper & Row, Publishers, 1986.

Wickman, Donald H., ed. *Letters to Vermont from her Civil War Soldier Correspondents to the Home Press.* 2 vols. Bennington, Vt.: Images from the Past, Inc., 1998.

Wiley, Bell Irwin. *The Life of Billy Yank: The Common Soldier of the Union.* Baton Rouge: Louisiana State University Press, 1992.

Wilkinson, Warren, and Steven E. Woodworth. *A Scythe of Fire: A Civil War Story of the Eighth Georgia Infantry Regiment.* New York: William Morrow, An Imprint of HarperCollins Publishers, 2002.

Wilstach, Paul. *Tidewater Virginia*. New York: Tudor Publishing Co., 1945.

Yerrinton, James M.W. *The Official Report of the Trial of Henry K. Goodwin for the Murder of Albert D. Swan in the Supreme Judicial Court of Massachusetts, Published by the Attorney General, Under Chapter 214 of Acts 1886*. Boston: Wright & Potter Printing Co., State Printers, 1887.

Young, Carlton. *Voices from the Attic: The Williamstown Boys in the Civil War*. Syracuse, Ind.: William James Morris, Inc., 2015.

Zeller, Paul G. *The Second Vermont Volunteer Infantry Regiment, 1861–1865*. Jefferson, N.C.: McFarland, 2002.

Periodicals

Carmichael, Peter S. "The Battle of Savage's Station." *Civil War*, Issue 51, June 1995.

Eisenberg, Albert C. "The 3rd Vermont has Won a Name': Corporal George Q. French's Account of the Battle of Lee's Mills, Virginia." *Vermont History*, Fall 1981, vol. 49, no. 4.

Goss, Warren Lee. "Recollections of a Private." *The Century, Illustrated Monthly Magazine*, vol. VIII, May 1885 to October 1885. New York: The Century Company, 1885.

Law, Evander M. "The Fight for Richmond in 1862." *The Southern Bivouac*, vol. VI, January 1887–May 1887.

MacDonald, George A., ed. "The Bloody Seven Days' Battles." *Vermont Quarterly: A Magazine of History*, vol. XV, no. 4 (October 1949).

Patchan, Scott C. "The Battle of Garnett's Farm." *Civil War*, Issue 51, June 1995.

Schneider, David H., "Lee's Armored Car," *Civil War Times*, vol. XLX, no. 1, February 2011.

Newspapers

Argus and Patriot (Montpelier, Vt.)
Boston (Mass.) *Herald*
Caledonian (St. Johnsbury, Vt.)
Caledonian-Record (St. Johnsbury, Vt.)
The Daily Dispatch (Richmond, Va.)
Daily (Chicago, Ill.) *Inter Ocean*
Fitchburg (Mass.) *Daily Sentinel*
Grand Forks (Minn.) *Herald*
Green Mountain Freeman (Montpelier, Vt.)
Kalamazoo (Mich.) *Gazette*
Lewiston (Penn.) *True Democrat*
Memphis (Tenn.) *Daily Appeal*
The Newport (Vt.) *Express and Standard*
Omaha (Neb.) *World Herald*
Philadelphia Inquirer
The Pottsville (Penn.) *Republican*
Providence (R.I.) *Evening Press*
Richmond (Va.) *Daily Whig*
Rutland (Vt.) *Daily Herald*
Rutland (Vt.) *Daily Herald and Globe*
St. Albans (Vt.) *Daily Messenger*
St. Johnsbury (Vt.) *Caledonian Record*
Sioux City (Iowa) *Journal*
Springfield (Mass.) *Daily News*
Springfield (Mass.) *Republican*
State (Columbia, S.C.)
Trenton (N.J.) *Evening Times*
Vermont Journal (Windsor, Vt.)
The Vermont (Montpelier) *Watchman and State Journal*
Watchman (Montpelier, Vt.)
Watertown (N.Y.) *Daily Times*

Index

Numbers in ***bold italics*** indicate pages with illustrations

Abbott, Dick 8
Abington, Conn. 138
Abington Cemetery, Abington, Conn. 138
Acme Iron Works 140
Adams, Jesse 8
Adams House 62
Addison, Vt. 96
Ager machine gun 69, 76
Aiken's Landing, Va. 89
Albany, N.Y. 17
Alexander's Bridge 62
Alexandria, Va. 105, 107, 123, 145, 151, 154, 165
Allen, Charles L. 155
Allen, Eliza 80
Allen, George E. 129
Anderson, George T. 56, 74
Andersonville, Ga. 138
Andrews, William H. 69
Annapolis, Md. 100, 135, 144, 152
Antibus, Hiram 14
Antioch Baptist Church 92
Arlington, Va. 12
Arlington, Vt. 89
Armington, Alonzo C. 15, 108
Army of Northern Virginia 81
Army of the Potomac 79, 80, 125, 127, 130, 131
Army of the Valley 59
Ashby, Turner 12
Ashland, Va. 60, 62
Atherson, Henry B. 39
Austin, Lusetta W. 161-162
Ayers, Dana C. 40
Ayres, Romeyn B. *42*, 116, 122

Backum, John 38
Bagley, William 106, 162
Bailey, Charles F. 39
Banks, Nathaniel P. 23
Barber, Brownson M. 94, ***95***
Barhamsville, Va. 46
Barksdale, William 68, 84, 90
Barnard, Benjamin S. 93
Barnes, Chauncey A. 161
Barnes, Emily M. (Dyer) 161
Barnum, John H. 159
Barry, James E. 82; 112
Barry, Matthew 12

Bartholomew, Eleazer Wells 61
Bass, Zacheus 155
Bath, N.Y. 5
Battles: Allen's Farm (Orchard Station/Peach Orchard) 80, 81-14; Antietam 131, 134; Big Bethel 4, 131, 160; Bull Run, first 137; Bull Run, second 131; Cedar Creek 131; Charles Town 131; Cold Harbor 131, 144, 148, 156, 163;Crampton's Gap 131; the Crater 139; Dam No. 1 ***31***-42, ***35***, 41, 141, 142; Eltham's Landing 49; Fair Oaks 55, 85, 120; Fisher's Hill 131; Ft. Stevens 131; Frayser's Farm 124, 131; Fredericksburg, first 131, 163; Fredericksburg, second, 131, 163; French's Field/King's School House 120; Funkstown 131; Gaines' Mill 59-60, 62-64, 86; Garnett's Hill 60-72, ***67***; Gettysburg 131, 139; Glendale 79, 80, 116, 123-124; Gouldin's Farm 72-77, ***75***, 143; Malvern Hill 124-125; Mechanicsville 62; Opequan 131; Petersburg 131, 144; Poplar Springs Church 144; Rappahannock Station 131; Reams' Station 131; Rich Mountain 11; Sailor's Creek 131; Savage's Station 90-110, ***92***, 123, 134, 138, 140, 145, 146, 147, 148, 149, 150, 152, 154, 156, 158, 160, 162, 164; Spotsylvania 131, 144, 163; White Oak Swamp ***118***, 120-124; the Wilderness 60, 131, 139, 133, 144, 163; Williamsburg 44-45, 131; Winchester 131, 140
Bayle, George K. 163
Beaver Dam Creek 4, 58, 62, 63
Bedell, Daniel C. 145
Bedell, Huldah (Carter) 145
Bedell, John P. 145, 146
Bedell, Mina "Minnie" (Conley) 146
Bedell, William H. 145
Belden, Phineas 96, 123
Belden, Shelden 96
Belle Isle, Va. 114, 144, 163
Bellevue Hospital Medical School 136

Bellows, Ruluf L. 40
Bellows Falls, Vt. 10, 141
Bennett, Leonard E. 37
Bennett, Willard K. 102
Benning, Henry L. 71
Bennington, Vt. 93, 123, 129, 142, 147, 149, 150, 151
Benson, Vt. 156, 123
Benton, Reuben C. 96, ***97***, 102, 148
Berkeley Plantation 80, 126, 127
Berkley, S.D. 143
Big Bethel, Va. 131
Bishop, Jeremiah 34
Bishop, Jerome 34
Bixby, Franklin 106
Black Hills 142
Black River Academy 134, 135, 136
Blunt, Asa P. ***21***, ***53***
Bonett, Fanny (Carr) 139
Bonett, George W. 108, 139, 140
Bonett, Luther 139
Bonett, Nancy Jane (Morris) 140
Bottom's Bridge, Va. 58, 80, 112, 115
Bradford, Nelson C. 129
Bradford, Vt. 10, 15
Brady, Peter 27
Brainard, Friend A. 98
Braintree, Vt. 104
Branch, Lawrence O'B. 60, 62
Brandon, Vt. 65, 94, 99
Brattleboro, Vt. 17, 20, 145, 149
Brentwood, N.H. 16
Briggs, Lucius 37
Brighton, Vt. 34, 37
Bristol, Vt. 158, 159
Britton, James H. 116, 123
Bromley's Station 84
Brook Turnpike 59
Brooke, John Mercer 81
Brooks, Almeria "Alma" B. (Drake) 133-134
Brooks, DeLarma 133
Brooks, John C.W. 133
Brooks, Lila (Harbaugh) 133
Brooks, Mary R. 133
Brooks, William D. 133
Brooks, William T.H. 16, ***17***, 28-30, 32, 33, 38, 44, ***51***, 68, 70, 79, 91, 92, 110, 115, 122, 133-134
Brown, Elijah S. 105, 110

187

Index

Brown, Ephraim 38
Brown, Joseph B. 92
Brown, Mable 143
Buck, Erastus 8, 37
buck and ball 106, 107, 140, 162
Bullard, Edgar 98
Burlington, Vt. 4, 5, 10, 79, 137, 139, 142, 156, 159, 164
Burns, William W. 68, 89, 90–92, 95,
Burnside, Ambrose 130, 134
Burnt Chimneys 30
Burnt Ordinary 46
Butler, Benjamin F. 138

Cabot, Vt. 15
Cambridge, Vt. 96, 148, 149
Cameron, Simon 153
Camp, William J. 71
Camp: Advance 12, 16; Baxter 6; Lyon 8, 20–21; Griffin 17, *18*, *19*, *20*, 22, 46, 53, 155, 162; Parole 100
Carlisle, Edwin M. 104
Carlisle, J. Howard 64
Carmody, John 123, 140–141
Carmody, Margaret (Leyden) 140
Carmody, Michael 140
Carmody, Thomas 140
Carpenter, Benjamin W. *52*, 122
Casey, Silas 58
Cavendish, Vt. 8, 39, 123, 143
Cedar Mountain, Va. 130
Centreville, Va. 154
Chain Bridge 8, 12, 17
Chandler, Charles M. *53*
Chandler, Edward A. 34
Chapin, William 136
Charles City Court House, Va. 131
Charles City Road 80, 81, 117, 123
Charleston, Vt. 8, 34, 36
Charlestown, Mass., State Prison 138
Charlestown, N.H. 141, 143
Chattanooga, Tenn. 134
Cheney, Watson 106
Chesapeake Bay 23, 131
Chester, Penn. 158
Chester, Vt. 9, 10
Chicago, Ill. 7, 136, 160, 165
Chickahominy River 49, 50, 54, 55, 56, 58, 59, 60, 62, 63, 64, 68, 71, 72, 73, 78, 80, 81, 84, 85, 131, 164
Chilton, Robert H. 80
Chimborazo Hill 82
Chinn Ridge, Va. 5
City Point, Va. 96, 135, 139, 146, 150, 152, 156, 158
Clair, Calvin 94
Clair, Joseph 94
Clark, James 70
Clark, John W. *53*
Clark, William H. 106
Clough, Isaac H. 37
Clough, John E. 106, *107*
Cobb, Howell 36, 57, 81, 84, 90
Cobleigh, Orville D. 127
coffee mill gun 69
Coggin's Point, Va. 130
Cohoke Station 84
Colburn, Mary (Hoyt) 15
Colburn, William H. 15

Colburn, Zerah 15
Cold Harbor, Va. 49, 131, 144, 148, 156
College Creek 26, 42
College of William and Mary 131
Comstock, Olney A. 99, **100**
Concord, Vt. 108
Connecticut units: 1st Connecticut Heavy Artillery 64
Convalescent Camp 123
Cooke, Charles M. 157
Cooledge, Daniel F. 58, 61, 93, 119, 134–136
Cooledge, Daniel W. 134
Cooledge, Leon D. 136
Cooledge, Lydia (Davison) 134
Cooledge, Viola A. (Marsh) 136
Corbin, David T. 107, **108**
Cornwall, Vt. 160
Courtney, Robert 72
Cowdery, George 137
Craftsbury, Vt. 98, 152, 153
Craftsbury, Branch Cemetery, Craftsbury, Vt. 153
Craftsbury Common Cemetery, Craftsbury, Vt. 152
Cross Keys, Va. 59
Cumberland, Md. 99, 149
Cumberland Landing, Va. 46
Cummings, Caroline J. (Johnson) 147
Cummings, Edmund M. 100, 147
Cummings, Edwin A. 125
Cummings, Henry A. 100, 146
Cummings, Hiram P. 100, 147
Cummings, Louisa (Gleason) 100, 146
Cummings, Mary Jane (Ellison) 146
Cummings, Melissa J. (Eaton) 147
Cummings, Peter 100, 146
Cummings, Silas A. 100, 147
Cummings, William E. 100, 147
Cummings, William H.H. 100, 147, 148
Cunningham, Frank 114
Currier, William H. 37
Custis, Daniel Parke 47
Custis, Martha (Dandridge) 47

Dakota Territory 142
Dam No. 1 30, **31**, 36, 38, 40, 41, **42**, 43, 142
Dana, Napoleon J.T. 89, 123
Daniels, William E. 114
Danville, Va. 140
Danville, Vt. 21, 60
Darbytown Road 80, 124
Darling, Jonathan R. 163
Darling, Sarah M. (Taisey) 163
Dartmouth College 17, 21, 53
Dartmouth Medical College 163
Davenport, David B. 39, 40
Davenport, Henry 40
Davidson, John W. 23, 28, 29, 31, 44, 58, 79, 91, 92, 94, 115
Davis, Alexander W. 104, 114
Davis, Carrie 12
Davis, Jefferson 41, 55
Davis, Wesley 36
Dean, Casper H. 73

Deep Creek, Va. 27
Denbigh, Va. 26
diarrhea 21, 95, 106, 114, 145, 146, 153, 155
Dibble, David J. 38
Dispatch Station 84
divorce 138, 141, 143, 144, 147, 159, 160, 161, 162
Dodge, Charles C. 105
Doncaster, England 150
Drake, James P. 133
Drake, Priscilla Holmes (Buell) 133
Draper, Jerome 129
Druon, Father Zeph 141
Drury's Bluff 83, 112
Dry Bridge 90
Duane's Bridge 62
Dubois, Charles B. 107, 115, 121, 128
Dudley, Charles P. 32, 33, 101, 103
Dudley Farm 79
Duxbury, Vt. 70, 104, 150

E. & T. Fairbanks Scale Co. 21, 140
Early, Jubal 44, 45
Eastman, Bernard S. 162, 164
Eastman, Cyrus D. 164
Eastman, Evalona (Darling) 163
Eastman, Harriett (Weed) 162
Eastman, Oscar D. 15
Eastman, Seth N. 106, 162–164
Eaton, John 147
Eaton, Susan 147
Eclectic Medical College of Pennsylvania 163
Edinburgh, Scotland 164
Elizabeth River 83
Elmer, James P. 96, **97**
Elmore, Vt. 145
Elmwood Cemetery, Granville, N.Y. 150
Elmwood plantation 56
Eltham's Landing, Va. 49
Evelynton Heights, Va. 127
Ewell, Benjamin S. 13, 26, 80, 120

Fair Oaks, Va. 55, 61, 80, 81, 83, 85, 120
Fair Oaks Station 56, 72, 80
Fairbanks, Erastus 4, 5, 6, 7, 9, 20, 21, 154
Fairfax, Vt. 106, 115
Fairfax County, Va. 18, 19, 20
Fall's Church, Va. 12, 13, 14
Farnham, Evelyn H., Jr. 14
field hospital, VI Corps, 2nd division 93, 95, 96, 98, 100, 101, 104, 105, 106, 107, 108, 109, 110, 111, 112, 117, 119, 120, 134, 135, 139, 146, 147, 148, 150, 152, 154, 156, 158, 160, 162, 164
Fish, Miner E. 96, **97**
Fish Hall Station 84
Fisk, Wilbur 37, 46, 50, 56, 63, 116
Fitchburg, Mass. 129
Flanders, George S. 123
Flanders, William 129
Fletcher, James 38
Florence Memorial Library 136
Fluker, William T. 60
Forestdale Cemetery, Holyoke, Mass. 144

Index

Forts: Davidson 58; Hamilton 133; Lincoln 63; Lookout 126; Magruder 44, 45; Monroe 4, 24, 25, 26, 39, 40, 86, 131, 135, 152, 154; Norfolk 82, 83; Sumter 4, 5, 127, 156
Fortune, Thomas H. 96
Foster, J. Frank 144
Fowler, John G. 15
Franklin, William B. 3, **49**, 50, 55, 58, 64, 66, 68, 72, 77, 79, 88, 90, 92, 110, 111, 112, 116, 122, 123, 124
Franklin, Vt. 106,
Fredericksburg, Va. 59, 131, 134, 163
French, Elizabeth "Lizzie" Miller (Potter) 149
French, George Q. 35
French, Jason O. 96–97, 148–149
French, Mark 148 148
French, Mary (Lyon) 148
French, Phillip S. 149
Front Royal, Va. 59
Fuller, William 33

Gaines, William 49
Gaines' House 49, **50**
Gaines' Mill 50
Galineaux, David 143
Gardiner, Anna E. 150
Garnett, James M. 56, 57, 61, 64, 68, 69, 73, 78
Garnett, James R. 56, 60, 64, 73
Garnett's Hill 56, 60, 63, 72
Garrow, John T. 30
Garrow Farm 30, 31, 38, 41; *see also* Burnt Chimneys; Garrow Chimneys; Merry Oaks; Three Chimneys
Garrow's field 30, 32
Genesee, N.Y. 147
Georgetown Heights, D.C. 8
Georgetown Heights reservoir 8
Georgia units: 1st Georgia Regulars 68, 69, 84; 2nd Georgia Infantry Regiment 68, 69, 70; 7th Georgia Infantry Regiment 71, 74, 76, 77; 8th Georgia Infantry Regiment 74, 76, 77; 9th Georgia Infantry Regiment 68; 10th Georgia Infantry Regiment 96; 15th Georgia Infantry Regiment 60, 70, 71, 74, 76; 16th Georgia Infantry Regiment 33, 36; 17th Georgia Infantry Regiment 68, 70, 71; 20th Georgia Infantry Regiment 71, 74, 76
Georgia, Vt. 5, 164, 165
Georgia Plains Cemetery, Georgia, Vt. 165
Getty, George W. 64
Gettysburg, Penn. 4
Gibson, Elizabeth S. (Parker) (Knight) 144
Gibson, Elvira E. (Basford) 144
Gibson, George W. 71, 143, 144
Gibson, Israel 143
Gibson, Sarah (Barry) 143
Glendale crossroads 123
Gloucester, Va. 25
Gloucester Point 26
Goddard, Elisha M. 40

Goodell, Jacob C. 15
Goodwin, Dolly (King) 137
Goodwin, Harvey K. 78, 79, 137, 138
Goodwin, Henry K. 138
Goodwin, James 137
Goodwin, Samuel M. 14
Goodwin, Sarah A. 137
Gordon, John B. 125
Gordonsville, Va. 25
Gorgas, Josiah 81
Gorman, Patrick 91
Gorman, Willis A. 68
Goshen County, N.Y. 94
Gouldin, Simon 78
Gouldin Farm 58, **65**, 78
Grand Army of the Republic 136, 149, 155
Grant, Elizabeth (Wyman) 10
Grant, James 10
Grant, Lewis A. 10, **11**, **19**, 51, 92, 94, 95, 103
Grant, Ulysses S. 5, 112, 144
Grapevine Bridge 55, 62, 79, 81, 84
Graves, Luther 39
Graves, Nathan 39
Great Warwick Road 27, 28, 43
Greenwood Cemetery, Bristol, Vt. 159
Griffin, Charles 12, 16, 17
Griffith, Richard 57, 68, 80, 81, 84, 90
Grimes, Franklin N. 38, 39
Groton, Vt. 8, 14, 163, 164
Gunnison, Eri S. 126

Hackney, Jesse M. 60
Hale, Oscar A. **66**
Half Sink, Va. 60
Half-way House 25, 27, 28
Halifax, Vt. 93
Halleck, Henry W. 129, 130
Hammond, Daniel F. 149
Hammond, Deborah (Hall) 140
Hammond, Ella Spencer 150
Hammond, Francis D. 41, 99, **100**, 150
Hammond, Francis Nahum 150
Hammond, Fred S. 149
Hammond, George W. 149
Hammond, Harriet Elizabeth (Chapin) 149
Hampton, Va. 4, 24, 39, 131, 135, 146, 160,
Hancock, Benjamin F. 14
Hancock, Winfield S. 18, **25**, 27, 28, 29, 30, 44, 45, 64, 68, 69, 70, 71, 72, 79, 91, 92, 115
Hanover, N.H. 53
Hapgood, Charles M. 30, 44,
Hardwick, Vt. 104
Harrington, Fernando C. 34
Harris, Henry L. 105
Harrison, Benjamin 80, 126
Harrison, William H. 126, 127
Harrison's Landing 80, 100, 102, 106, 108, 114, 123, 126, 127, 128, 129, 130, 131, 140, 142, 145, 147, 154
Hartford, Conn. 8
Harwood's Mill, Va. 27

Haxall's Landing, Va. 148, 154, 161, 165
Hayward, Henry R. 78, 79, 137
Hazzard, George W. 116, 122, 123
Heintzelman, Samuel P. 23, 30, 49, 55, 58, 61, 62, 72, 81, 85, 87, 89, 90, 124
Henahan, Martin 109
Henrico County, Va. 56, 78, 85, 112, 113, 120
Herring Creek, Va. 127, 129
Hill, Ambrose P. 60, 62, 63, 80, 124, 125, 130
Hill, Daniel H. 41, 60, 62, 80, 119, 122, 124, 125
Hill, Mandus W. 89
Hinkson, William 97, 148
Holmes, Hiram C. 36, 37
Holmes, Theophilus 80, 124
Holmes, Whitmore & Co. 141
Holt, Nelson K. 94
Holton, Edward A. 40
Holyoke, Mass. 144
Hon, David 147
Hood, John B. 64
Hooker, Joseph 43, 44, 45, 124
House, Thomas F. 8
Howard, Oliver O. 5
Howard County, Md. 12
Howard Dragoons 12
Hubble, Oliver 14
Huger, Benjamin 58, 59, 80, 81, 84, 123
Humphrey, John P. 69–70
Hunt, William 161
Hunter, Henry G. 129
Hunter, Truman H. 94
Huntington, Vt. 55
Huntsville, Ala. 134
Hutchinson, Alonzo 33–34
Hyde, Breed N. 6, **7**, 12, 16, 17, 32, 33, 34, 36, 37, 47, 107
Hyde, Caroline (Noyes) 6
Hyde, Russell B. 6
Hyde Park, Vt. 146

Indiana units: 7th Indiana Infantry Regiment 21; 19th Indiana Infantry Regiment 12–15
Invalid Corps: 40, 95, 101, 106, 126, 156; *see also* Veteran Reserve Corps
Invalid Corps units: Co. D, 9th Regiment 156; Co. F, 6th Regiment 126; Co. I, 1st Battalion 158; 171 Co., 2nd Battalion 159
Ireland, David 12

Jackson, Thomas J. "Stonewall" 29, 59, 119, 120, 122, 125, 142, 148, 154
James River 24, 25, 26, 27, 29, 43, 63, 72, 77, 79, 80, 83, 86, 93, 96, 98, 99, 101, 104, 106, 109, 112, 114, 115, 122, 123, 124, 125, 126, 128, 129, 130, 135, 145, 146, 150, 158, 161, 162, 163
Janes, Henry 15
Jenne, Benjamin R. 98, **99**
Jericho, Vt. 10,
Johnson, Amos 147

Index

Johnson, Mary Ann (McGlynn) 150, 151
Johnson, Robert 96, 150, 151, 152
Johnson, Vt. 35, 37, 38, 96, 148, 149
Johnston, Joseph E. 23, 24, 25, 41, 42, 55
Johnston, Willie 128
Jones, David R. 56, 68, 72, 73, 74, 81, 84, 90
Joplin, Mo. 160
Joyce, Charles H. *54*, 129,

Kalispell, Mont. 153
Kearny, Philip 44, 45, 89, 124
Keene, N.H. 144
Kemper, Delaware B. "Del" 91, 94, 95, 98
Kernstown, Va. 29
Kershaw, Joseph B. 58, 68, 81, 84, 90, 91
Kevill, Thomas 82, 83
Keyes, Erasmus D. 23, 27, 29, 30, *43*, 50, 55, 58, 77, 80, 85
Keyser, Hiram B. 161
Kimball, Frederick M. 66
Kimball Union Academy, Meriden, N.H. 53
Kingsbury, Newell A. 15
Knight, Andrew J. 144

Labor in Vain Creek 50
Labor in Vain Ravine 56, 64, 69, 74, 78
Labor in Vain Redoubt 64, 69, 71, 73
La Crosse, Wis. 160
Laden, Elizabeth "Eliza" (Schmidt) 142, 143
Laden, James (Kelly Leighton/Layton) 123, 142, 143
Laden, Lucy 142
Laden, Mary 142
Laffie, Andrew 65
Laffie, Mary 65
Lamar, Lucius M. 76, 77
Lamoile View Cemetery, Johnson, Vt. 149
Lancaster, N.H. 137
Land Merrimac 82
Langley, Va. 12, 17
Laurel Grove 85
Law, Evander 56, 58, 64
Lawrence, Mass. 138
Lawrenceburg, Ind. 21
Leach, Chester K. *45*, 127, 130
Lee, Robert E. 4, 41, 47, 55, 58, 59, 60, 62, 63, 64, 73, 74, 79, 80, 81, 82, 83, 84, 123, 124, 125, 130, 135, 140
Lee, Mrs. Robert E. 48
Lee, William Henry Fitzhugh "Rooney" 47, 59
Lee's Mill 3, 27, 28, 30, *31*, *42*, 43, 102
Leesburg, Va. 12
Leesburg Turnpike 12, 13
Levy, William M. 41
Lewinsville, Va. 12, 13, 14, 15, 16, 17
Lewis, John R. 102
Libby Prison 105, 135, 154, 160, 163

Lincoln, Abraham 4, 5, 9, 10, 23, 24, 26, 29, 30, 127, 160
Lincoln, Vt. 158
Lisbon, Ohio 16, 133
Littleton, N.H. 15
London, England 96, 150
Londonderry, Vt. 147
Long, Thomas 97, 148
Long Bridge Road 79, 117, 124, 125
Longstreet, James 41, 44, 60, 62, 63, 79, 80, 124, 125
Lord, Nathan, Jr. 20, *21*, 38, 40, *53*, 70
Lord, Nathan, Sr. 21
Louisiana units: 2nd Louisiana Infantry Regiment 30, 32, 36, 41; 5th Louisiana Infantry Regiment 96, 107, 108, 109, 140; 10th Louisiana Infantry Regiment 36, 96
Ludlow, Vt. 134, 135, 136
Lunenburg, Vt. 109

Maddox, John 107, 109, 110
Magruder, Edward J. 77
Magruder, Elizabeth (Bankhead) 26
Magruder, John B. "Prince John" 25, *26*, 27, 29, 41, 43, 56, 57, 59, 61, 64, 66, 68, 73, 74, 79. 80, 81, 84, 90, 91, 124, 125
Magruder, Thomas 26
Mahone, William 125
Maine units: 3rd Maine infantry Regiment 5; 4th Maine Infantry Regiment 5; 5th Maine Infantry Regiment 5, 72; 6th Maine Infantry Regiments 8, 64, 69, 72
Manassas, Va. 5, 17, 23, 24
Manassas Junction, Va. 23
Manchester, Vt. 32, 101, 102, 146, 147
Maple Hill Cemetery, Huntsville, Ala. 134
Marcy, Abby M. (Mason) 152, 153
Marcy, Edward 98, 152
Marcy, Ephraim 98, 148, 152, 153
Marcy, Marvin R. 152
Marcy, Vilana (Tallman) 152
Marion, Ind. 133
Marks, John J. 89
Martin, Guy C. 104
Martin, William Henry 54
Marvin, Squire A. 98
Massachusetts Institute of Technology 138
Massachusetts units: 2nd Massachusetts Heavy Artillery 138; 15th Massachusetts Infantry Regiment 87; 37th Massachusetts Infantry Regiment 144
McCall, George A. 62, 124
McClellan, George B. 1, 7, 9, 10, 11, 12, 16, 23, 24, 25, 26, 27, 28, 29, 30, 33, 42, 43, 44, 46, 49, 50, 55, 58, 59, 61, 62, 63, 66, 72, 77, 78, 79, 80, 81, 86, 87, 111, 112, 116, 122, 123, 124, 125, 126, 127, 129, 130, 131
McCluskey, John 60
McCormic, John 98

McCuin, Tom 110
McDowell, Irwin 5, 10, 23, 25, 29
McDowell, Va. 59
McGee, Ammon S. 98
McGhee House 62
McGlynn, Mary Ann (Tarpey) 150, 151
McGlynn, Phillip 150, 151, 152
McIntosh, William M. 70
McKinney, William 37
McLaws, Lafayette 56, 58, 81, 90
McLean, William 12
McMahon, Martin T. 1
Meader, Charles C. II 15
Meadow Bridges 60, 62
Meadow Station 84
Meagher, Thomas F. 87
Mechanicsville, Va. 60, 62
Mechanicsville Bridge 60
Mechanicsville Turnpike 62
Medal of Honor 39, 128
Menard, Louis 143
Meredith, Solomon 12, 14
USS *Merrimac* 81
Merry Oaks 30
Meserve, Amos H. 15
Middle Granville, N.Y. 150
Miles, Chauncey 8
Milton, Vt. 165
Milwaukee, Wis. 160
Minnesota units: 1st Minnesota Infantry Regiment 91
Minor, George 82
Mission, S.D. 143
Mississippi units: 13th Mississippi Infantry Regiment 68, 84
Molecular Telephone Company 138
Monkton, Vt. 73
Montana Soldiers' Home 153
Montgomery, William R. 135
Montgomery, Vt. 65
Montpelier, Vt. 16, 20, 33, 40, 95, 130, 134, 139, 145, 159
Montpelier Seminary 164
Moore, Orville E. 106, 107
Morell, George W. 64
Morrisey, Thomas 93
Morristown, Vt. 38
Morrisville, Vt. 146
Mott, Thaddeus P. 16, 31, 32, 34, 116, 120, 122
Mt. Pleasant Cemetery, Lodi, Wis. 165
Mountain View Cemetery, Orwell, Vt. 157, 158
Munford, Thomas T. 122
Munson's Hill, Va. 12, 13
Murray, James R. 104
Murray, Richard 110

Naglee, Henry M. 115, 116
National Cemeteries: Hampton 39; Los Angeles 138, 162; Loudon Park 148; Seven Pines 99, 120, 147; Yorktown 38
National Military Asylum, Washington, D.C. 16
Nelson, Thomas, Jr. 108
New Bridge 50, 58, 60, 62, 80
New Bridge Road 56
New Hampshire Soldiers' Home 141

Index

New Hampshire units: 1st New Hampshire Infantry 53; Regiment; 9th New Hampshire Infantry Regiment 144
New Jersey units: 2nd New Jersey Infantry Regiment 69
New Kent Court House, Va. 46
New Orleans, La. 13, 109, 110
New Vienna Road 12
New York City 94, 95; 150
New York units: 1st New York Light Artillery 116; 3rd New York Artillery 16, 31, 116; 5th New York Cavalry Regiment; 20th New York Infantry Regiment 94, 120, 121; 33rd Infantry Regiment 9, 73, 74; 43rd New York Infantry Regiment 64, 68, 70, 71; 57th New York Infantry Regiment 110; 65th New York (also known as the 1st Regiment U.S. Chasseurs) 12, 14; 77th New York Infantry Regiment 43, 73, 74; 79th New York Infantry Regiment 12, 14; 82nd New York Infantry Regiment 92; 88th New York Infantry Regiment 92
Newbury, Vt. 14, 15, 107, 162
Newport News, Va. 24, 25, 26, 130, 142, 160
Newport News Point 24, 25
Nicholson, Ira A. 94, 95
Niles, Jason D. 36
Niles, Stephen B. 36
Nine Mile Road 56, 57, 61, 64, 68, 80
Norfolk, Va. 82, 83
Norfolk United Artillery 82, 83
Norfolk United Fire Company 82
North Carolina units: 15th North Carolina Infantry Regiment 31, 33, 36
Norwich, Vt. 15
Norwich University 10
Noyes, Edwin M. 14, 15, 32, *33*, *51*

Old Tavern 61, 63, 64
Old Village Cemetery, Groton, Vt. 164
Orchard Station 84, 90, 110,
Orwell, Vt. 156, 157

Paddleford, Francis "Frank" C. 73–74
Page, Charles H. 37
Paige, Harlan P. *70*, 71
Pamunkey River 46, 49, 59, 112
Parker, George H. 65
Parker, Moses A. 15, 108–109
Parmalee, Moses P. 9
Parsons, Abel K. *51*
Patch, Abial H. 104
Patrick Station, Va. 151
Pawlet, Vt. 99, 102, 149
Peach Orchard 84, 85,
Peck, William H.H. *101*, 102
Pegram Farm 144
Pellett, Francis B. 137–138
Pennsylvania units: 49th Pennsylvania Infantry Regiment 64, 69, 72, 73, 74; 63rd Pennsylvania Infantry Regiment 89; 72nd Pennsylvania Infantry Regiment 91; 106th Pennsylvania Infantry Regiment 91
Peru, Vt. 93, 147
Petersburg, Va. 7, 82, 112, 129, 130, 131, 139, 140, 144
Petersham, Mass. 144
Pettit, Rufus D. 116
Phelphs, Edward E. *51*
Phelps, John W. 4
Philadelphia, Penn. 93, 109, 126, 127, 131, 135, 139, 145, 150, 158
Philippine Islands 136
Phillips (Exeter) Academy, Exeter, N.H. 17
Pingree, Samuel E. 34, *36*, 37, 38
Pittsburg, N.H. 38
Pleasant View Cemetery, Ludlow, Vt. 136
Pleasant View Cemetery, Morrisville, Vt. 146
Plumley, George K. 163
Plymouth, Vt. 93, 104, 134, 136, 138
Plympton, Salem M. 32
Poe, Orlando M. 12, 14
Point Lookout, Md. 109, 125,
Pomfret, Conn. 138
Pomfret, Vt. 34
Pope, John 130, 131
Poquoson River 27
Port Royal, Va. 26
Porter, Fitz-John 25, 46, 49, 55, 58, 59, 60, 61, 62, 63, 64, 68, 77, 123, 124, 125
Portsmouth Grove, R.I. 145
Portsmouth navy yard 82
Potomac River 9, 12, 17, 23, 131, 151
Potter, William W. 110, 119
Price, Mrs. Charles L. 56
Priest, Daniel Mahlon 93
Prince Street Military Prison, Alexandria, Va. 151
Providence Forge, Va. 59

Queen's Creek 26, 43
Quimby, George W. 114

railroad battery 81, *82*, *83*, 112
Railroads: Baltimore & Ohio 11; Illinois Central 7, 11; Orange & Alexandria 23; Ohio & Mississippi 11; Richmond & York River 23, 49, 56, 57, 58, 59, 60, 72, 80, 81, 82, 83; Virginia Central 62
Ramsey, John W. 107, *108*
Rand, Kirk 47, 54, 120
Randall, Francis V. 106
Randall, George H. 61
Rappahannock River 23, 24
Read, Thomas *51*
Revolutionary War 26, 25
Reynolds, Edwin F. 39
Reynolds, Orlando B. 54
Richardson, Israel B. 5, 30, 68, 81, 89, 92, 115, 116, 122
Richmond, Va. 23, 24, 38, 42, 43, 45, 49, 55, 56, 60, 61, 62, 78, 81, 82, 83, 84, 85, 89, 94, 98, 99, 105, 112, 113, 114, 119, 129, 130, 131, 135, 137, 139, 142, 142, 144, 146, 147, 148, 150, 152, 154, 156, 158, 160, 161, 163, 164, 165
Ring, John A. 158, 159
Ripley, Roswell S. 125
River Dan 140
River Road 79,
Robertson, J. Murray 134
Robinson, Amos H. 15
Rocketts 82
Rockingham, Vt. 141
Rodes, Robert E. 125
Roe, John 38
Rogers, Frederick C. 71
Rogers, John 110
Romankoke Station 84
Rood, Vernon D. 106
Rose Bud River 142
Rosser, Thomas L. 13, 15, 16
Rowell, Richard H. 37
Ruffin, Edmund 127
Russell, Isaac N. 153
Russell, Lydia (Bass) 153, 154, 155
Russell, Martha (Pierson) 153
Russell, William P. 2, 96, 103, 110, *111*, 153, 154, 155, 160
Ryegate, Vt. 151, 162

St. Albans, Vt. 7, 96, 144
Saint Catherine's Cemetery, Charlestown, N.H. 141
St. Clair, Mich. 5
St. Johnsbury, Vt. 3, 6, 8, 21, 128, 137139, 140
St. Paul, Minn. 161, 162
Sampson, Merrill T. 94
Sanders, Rosson O. 109
Sandston, Va. 99, 120, 147
Santa Cruz, Philippine Islands 136
Savage, George M. 84, 85, 86, 112; 113
Savage, Lucius D. 117, 119
Savage, Mary 112
Savage's Station 60, 74, 78, 84, 86, *87*, 88, 89, 90, 104, 112, 114, 115, 116, 120, 135, 136, 147, 154, 163
Savage's Station Hospital 60, 74, 79, 80, 84, *86*, *87*, 89, 90, 105, 113, 114, 119, 123, 135, 143145, 146, 148, 150, 152, 154, 156, 158, 160, 164
Sawin, William J. 73, 110, *111*, 154
Scott, Eliza 165
Scott, John 105, 164, 165
Scott, Jonathan S. 165
Scott, Julian A. 38
Scott, Lydia J. (Gabree) 164
Scott, William 8, 9, 38
Scott, Winfield 11
Seagar, Charles W. 99–100
Sears, Williams H. 93
Seaver, Thomas O. 8, 33, 61
Sedgwick, John 3, 4, 30, 81, 89, 90, 123, 124
Semmes, Paul J. 58, 90, 91, 96, 106, 107, 109
Seven Days 1, 62
Shaftsbury, Vt. 129
Shaler, Alexander 12
Shattuck, Samuel A. 65–66
Shaw, Henry C. 152
Shenandoah Valley 23, 29, 59, 130
Shields, John 29

Ship Point, Va. 24
Shonio, George A. 70
Shoreham, Vt. 94
Slatersville, Va. 46
Slocum, Henry W. 64, 68, 77, 79, 123, 127
Smalley, David A. 10
Smalley, Henry A. 10, *11*, 27, 32, 51, 92
Smalley, Laura (Barlow) 10
Smith, Emery L. *111*, 112
Smith, Gustavus W. 41, 55
Smith, William F. *7*, 8, 9, 12, 16,, 17, 23, 24, 25, 27, 28, 29, 30, 31, 32, 33, 38, 41, 43, 44, 45, 46, 47, 49, 50, 55, 58, 59, 61, 62, 63, 64, 68, 72, 73, 74, 77, 78, 79, 80, 87, 88, 89, 90, 91, 92, 94, 110, 111, 112, 114, 115, 116, 120, 121, 122, 123, 124, 125, 126, 127, 131, 141
Smoot's Hill, Va. 37
South Carolina units: 2nd South Carolina Infantry Regiment 90; 3rd South Carolina Infantry Regiment 90; 7th South Carolina Infantry Regiment 68, 69, 90, 94, 95, 96; 8th South Carolina Infantry Regiment 68, 69, 90, 95, 96
South Granville, N.Y. 149–150
South Hero, Vt. 165
Spaulding, Charles C. 32
Spotted Tail Agency 142
Springfield, Vt. 17, 36, 123, 141
Stannard, George J. 5, *6*, 12, *52*, 54
Stannard, Rebecca (Pattee) 5
Stannard, Samuel 5
Starksboro, Vt. 160
Stearns, Leonard A. 71
Stedman, Cora A. 157
Stedman, Deborah (Jones) 156
Stedman, Earl F. 157
Stedman, Elvira (Skeels) 157
Stedman, Eva A. 157
Stedman, Francis C. 100–101, 155, 156, 157
Stedman, Henrietta "Etta" A. (Tabor) 157
Stedman, Ida M. 156
Stedman, Irwin 100–101, 155, 157, 158
Stedman, Jonathan 155, 157
Stedman, Mary L. (Wisewell) 156
Stedman, Mary O. 157
Stedman, Mary S. 157
Stedman, Miamma L. (Fuller) 157, 158
Stedman, Moses 156
Stedman, Moses A. 157
Stevens, Isaac I. 12, 13, 16
Stevens, Walter H. 82
Stiles, Henry 102
Stoddard, Carrie (Spaulding) 139
Stoddard, Electa J. (Sabins) 138, 139
Stoddard, Harlan P. 105–106, 138, 139
Stoddard, Horace B. 139
Stoddard, Ida S. 139
Stoddard, Lathrop T. 139
Stoddard, Laura E. (Sterling) (Prosser) 139
Stoddard, Mary (Porter) 138

Stoddard, Thompaon W. 139
Stoddard, William H. 139
Stoddard, William T. 138
Stone, Edward P. *53*
Stone, Miles K. 108
Stone, Silas H. 60
Stoneman, George 33, 50
Stoughton, Edwin H. 9, *10*, 31, 32, 38, *52*, 71
Stoughton, Henry E. 9, *52*
Stoughton, Laura Elmira (Clark) 9
Stuart, James Ewell Brown "Jeb" 13, 58, 59, 60, 81, 86, 127
Sully, Alfred 89, 123
Summit Station 84
Sumner, Edwin V. 23, *43*, 44, 55, 58, 61, 62, 68, 72, 79, 80, 81, 84, 87, 88, 89, 90, 91, 111, 112, 123
Sumner, Samuel, Jr. 102, *103*
Sumner's Lower bridge 79
sutler 30, 61, 143
Swan, Albert D. 138
Swanton, Vt. 104, 149
Sweet Hall Station 84
Sykes, George 25, 49
syphilis 37

Tarpey, John 150
Tarpey, Mary (Cole) 150
Terrill, John 813
Thayer, Samuel W. 139, 154
Thetford, Vt. 10
Thin Elk 143
Thompson, Alden 158
Thompson, Alma Jane (Heath) 160
Thompson, David R. 158, 159, 160
Thompson, Noah C. 158, 159
Thompson, Matilda (Heath) 158
Thompson, Victoria L. (Orcutt) 158, 159
Three Chimneys 30
Thurston, Quincy F. 55–56
Tilley, John 60–61
Tilton, N.H. 141
Toano, Va. 46
Toombs, Robert 56, 68, 69, 70, 71, 74, 76
Topsham, Vt. 106, 162
torpedo 43
Towers, John R. 77
Townsend, Vt. 146
Trent, Peterfield 78, 79, 88
Trent House 78, 79, 88
Trinity Cemetery, Mission, S.D. 143
Tripler, Charles S. 21, 86
Troy, N.Y. 70
Tunstall's Station, Va. 49, 59, 84
Turkey Bend 124
Turkey Creek 124
Turkey Hill 62
Turner, Charles 37
Tuttle, Lyman N. *53*
Tuttle, Oscar L. *53*, 71
Twiggs, David E. 133
Twitchell, Marshal H. 71
Tyler, John S. *73*, 74, 122
Tyler House 50
Tyringham, Mass. 144

United Fire Company 82
United States Army Corps: I 62; II 69, 72, 79, 80, 81, 84, 88, 89, 112, 115; III 72, 81, 85, 89, 90; IV 77, 80, 84, 85, 88, 115; V 62, 77,123; VI 68, 72, 74, 117, 119, 123, 127, 131, 134, 140, 141, 146
United States Army General Hospitals: Baptist Institute 139; Baxter 139, 142, 156, 159; Broad and Cherry St. 93; Brooklyn College 95; Camden Street 142, 148; Camp Parole 100, 148, 152; Carver 37; Chesapeake 146; Convalescent Camp, 123, 145; Fairfax Seminary 14; Fort Monroe 39, 152; Governor Smith 145, 149; Hammond 100, 109, 126, 156; Harwood 39; Long Island College 104; Lovell 145; McKim's Mansion 143; Philadelphia Episcopal 127; St. John's College 144; Satterlee 109, 126, 135, 150; South Street 145; West's Buildings 144
United States Coast Survey 12
United States Military Academy 5, 6, 7, 9, 10, 16, 26, 49; *see also* West Point
United States National Cemeteries: Hampton 39; Los Angeles 23, 162; Loudon Park 148; Seven Pines 99, 120; Yorktown 38
United States Navy 25
United States Pension Bureau 136, 143, 145, 150, 151, 153, 155, 162, 164
United States Topographical Engineers 7, 12, 49
United States units: Griffin's Light Artillery 12, 16; 1st U.S. Artillery 11; 4th U.S. Infantry Regiment 9; 5th U.S. Artillery 12; 5th U.S. Cavalry Regiment 12; 5th U.S. Infantry Regiment 12; 6th U.S. Infantry Regiment 9; 13th U.S. Infantry Regiment 142; 22nd U.S. Infantry Regiment 142; 37th U.S. Volunteer Infantry Regiment 136; Berdan's Sharpshooters 40, 64, 69, 71
University of New York 136
University of Vermont 136
Upton, Emory 159
Urbanna, Va. 23, 24

Veazey, Annie (Stephens) 16, *17*, 47, 51, 54, 107, 126
Veazey, Jonathan 16
Veazey, Julia (Beard) 16
Veazey, Wheelock G. 16, 17, 47, 51, 54, 107, 126
Vergennes, Vt. 32
Vermont State Hospital 139
Vermont units: 1st Vermont Infantry Regiment 4, 6, 10, 160; 2nd Vermont Infantry Regiment 5–6, 8, 12, 13, 15, *18*, 22, 30, 33, 37, 45, 46, 47, *52*, 54, 55, 61, 63, 65, 7378, 79, 92, 93, 102, 105–107, 110, 111, 116, 117, 119, 120, 122, 126, 127, 129, 134, 137, 138, 139, 154; 3rd Vermont Infantry Regiment 6, 7, 8, 9, 12, 13, 14–15, 16, 17, *18*,

20, 21, 22, 31, 32, 33–38, 47, 51, 61, 92, 107–110, 115, 121, 126, 128, 139–140, 141; 3rd Vermont Light Artillery 165; 4th Vermont Infantry Regiment 9. 10, *19*, 20, 21, 31, 32, 33, 38, 39, 44, 53, 58, 60, 61, 68, 70, 71, 72, 92, 110, 114, 123, 125, 127, 127, 142, 143; 5th Vermont Infantry Regiment 10, 17, *19*, 20, 21, 22, 27, 28, 32, 41, 42, 51, 54, 61, 65, 70, 88, 92, 94, 95, 96, 98, 101, 102, 104, 110, 114, 119, 123, 145, 146, 147, 148, 149, 150, 151, 152, 153, 154, 155, 156, 158, 159, 160; 6th Vermont Infantry Regiment 3, 21, *20*, 21, 38, 39, 40, *53*, 55, 66, 71, 72, 73, 92, 104, 105, 107, 110, 111, 114, 123, 130, 139, 162, 164; 9th Vermont Infantry Regiment 9147; 13th Virginia Infantry Regiment 139; 16th Vermont Infantry Regiment 17; 17th Vermont Infantry Regiment 139, 142, 148; 165
Veteran Reserve Corps 156, 149; *see also* Invalid Reserve Corps
Veteran Reserve Corps units: 171 Co., 2nd Battalion 156
Vienna Road 12
CSS *Virginia* 26, 81
Virginia Peninsula 24, 26
Virginia units: Alexandria (Va.) Light Artillery 91; 1st Virginia Cavalry Regiment 12, 13; 2nd Virginia Cavalry Regiment 122; 9th Virginia Cavalry Regiment 47, 59; 13th Virginia Infantry Regiment 13; 32nd Virginia Infantry Regiment 30; 41st Virginia Infantry Regiment 83
Voodry, Josephus W. 109

Waggone, Eldora L. 138
Waitsfield, Vt. 138, 139, 153

Waitsfield Village Cemetery, Waitsfield, Vt. 139
Walbridge, James H. 92, *93*, 94, 110
Warren, Vt. 70
Warrenton, Va. 141
Warwick County, Va. 26
Warwick Court House 28, 29
Warwick Line 26, 27, 29, 42
Warwick River 27, 28, 29, 30, 31, 38, 41, 43
Washington, George 47, 48
Waterford, Vt. 108, 127, 139
Water's Creek 27
Waterville, Vt. 36
Watt House 62
Welch, Jim 8
Wells River, Vt. 107
West, Preston C.F. 12
West Cemetery, Middlebury, Vt. 155
West Point 7, 11, 133; *see also* United States Military Academy
West Point, Va. 23, 49, 84,
West Point Station 84
West Rutland, Vt. 157
Western Run 124, 125
Westminster, Mass. 37
Westover Church 127, *128*
Wheeler, John 127
Whitcomb, Emerson E. 36
White, Henry 40
White House 46, *48*, 49, *76*, 77, 89, 112
White House Landing *47*, 49, 58, 59, 63, 72, 77, 81, 86, 87, *88*
White House Station 84
White Oak Swamp 58, 61, 77, 80, 89, 90, 91, 101, 104, 111, 112, 114, 116, *117*, 119, 120, 121, 122, 141146
White Oak Swamp Bridge 79, 111, 115, 116, 120, 122, 123, 124, 142
White Oak Swamp Road 79, 80
Whiting, Henry 5, *6*, 7, *52*, 92, 105, 131

Whitwell, Charles 53, 54
Whitwell, Elizabeth 53
Whitwell, Francis 53
Wilder, Henry H. 98, *99*
Wilkins, John R. 102
Williamsburg, Va. 25, 26, 43, 45, 46, 49, 131
Williamsburg Road 62, 79, 80, 81, 82, 84, 88, 89, 90, 91, 92, 95, 101, 114, 116, 119, 120
Williamstown, Vt. 106
Willis Church Road 79, 117, 124, 125
Winchester, Va. 59
Winhall, Vt. 1065, 147
Wisconsin Soldiers' Home 160
Wisconsin units: 5th Wisconsin Infantry Regiment 64, 68, 72
Wood, George E. 104
Wood, S.D. 143
Woodbury, Vt. 145
Woodbury's Bridge 62
Woodlawn Cemetery, Penacook, N.H. 150
Wool, John E. 26
Worcester, Vt. 97, 148
Wormley's Creek 30
Worthen, Betsey 10
Worthen, Henry N. 10, *52*
Worthen, Thomas 10
Wright, Ambrose R. 125
Wright, Amos A. 114, *115*
Wright, Emily Mary (Dyer) 161, 162
Wright, Helen 161
Wright, Horatio G. 3
Wright, Maria (Smith) 160
Wright, Reuben R. 160
Wright, Wilson Daniel 160, 161, 162
Wynne's Mill 27, 30

York County, Va. 24
Yorktown, Va. 25, 26, 27, 29, 30, 38, 40, 42, 43, 131
Young's Mill 27, *28*, 29

www.ingramcontent.com/pod-product-compliance
Lightning Source LLC
Chambersburg PA
CBHW081558300426
44116CB00015B/2930